Tommy the Cork

**Washington's Ultimate Insider
from Roosevelt to Reagan**

David McKean

26013

STEERFORTH PRESS
SOUTH ROYALTON, VERMONT

In memory of my parents

Library of Congress Cataloging-in-Publication Data

McKean, David.
  Tommy the Cork : Washington's ultimate insider from Roosevelt to
Reagan / David McKean. — 1st ed.
      p. cm.
  Includes bibliographical references (p.) and index.
  ISBN 1-58642-068-2 (alk. paper)
  1. Corcoran, Thomas G. 2. Political consultants — United
States — Biography. 3. United States — Politics and
government — 1933–1953. 4. United States — Politics and
government — 1945–1989. I. Title.
E748.C863 M38 2004
324'.092—dc22

                              2003023987

FIRST EDITION

CONTENTS

ACKNOWLEDGMENTS

While this is the first full-length biography of Thomas G. Corcoran, he makes a cameo appearance, sometimes assuming a starring role, in hundreds of books dealing with American politics in the twentieth century. During the New Deal Corcoran sometimes dominated newspaper coverage. And there are thousands of pages of FBI transcripts that provide a detailed portrait of him working as a lobbyist during the time he was wiretapped.

Beyond the books, articles, magazines, newspapers, and transcripts, this book is based largely on an extensive collection of Corcoran's personal and legal papers held in the Library of Congress, as well as interviews with numerous individuals who knew him and worked with him — and a few who even served with him in government more than sixty years ago.

This was not an easy book to publish — Corcoran was of another generation, and while he was one of the most colorful political figures of the twentieth century, he operated largely behind the scenes and is therefore not a household name. I'm enormously grateful to Tom Powers and Chip Fleischer at Steerforth Press for seeing the merit and importance in publishing this biography.

I am also deeply appreciative of the many friends and colleagues who read drafts and provided helpful advice along the way: Cliff Sloan, Jon Alter, Phil Johnston, Vern Newton, Doug Brinkley, and Don Ritchie. Laura Jorstad and Robin Dutcher at Steerforth did a splendid job editing the manuscript. I would also like to thank Charles Kaye, Peter Truell, John Culver, and Lincoln Cleveland for their assistance.

I offer special thanks to the following people who were extremely generous: Jim Rowe, who first suggested I write a biography of Tommy Corcoran; Larry Gurwin, a fine journalist, editor, and invesitgator, who offered numerous insights along the way; John Zentay, who patiently read and edited an early draft and who constantly sent me helpful articles and information; my brother John McKean, who helped identify some of the critical themes in the book; Jamie Hunter, who served briefly but ably as my research assistant; Michael Janeway, whose comments were incredibly helpful; my wife, Kathleen Kaye-McKean, who showed extraordinary patience and offered constant encouragement during the six years of research and writing; John Lane, who was devoted to Corcoran and spent hours talking to me about him; Tim Corcoran, who likewise was extremely generous with his time and shared many stories about his father; and, finally, my cousin Rowland Evans Jr., who for many years was a wonderful mentor and friend to me. Rowly died on March 23, 2001. He loved Washington and the never-ending debate of great issues, but he also loved, and helped me understand, that the story behind the story was often the most interesting.

An Irish Ballad

It was one of the hottest nights of the summer — the kind of night in the nation's capital when even the incessant buzzing sound of the cicadas seems to be muffled by a sweltering heat. Harry McPherson, former special counsel to Lyndon Johnson and now one the city's most prominent attorneys, was returning by car from a dinner party just after midnight. He was feeling a little numb from the heat and from the red wine and all the talk of how the presidency of Jimmy Carter seemed to be adrift. McPherson slowed to a stop as the light turned red at Woodley Road in the tony Cleveland Park area of northwest Washington. He sat quietly behind the steering wheel in his air-conditioned car. The streets were deserted, and the shadows from the large, green, leafy maple trees were still. Washington was not like New York: People went to bed. All of sudden he heard what he later described as a "faint tenor." McPherson rolled down his window, looked up the street, and saw Tommy Corcoran. He was walking by himself, singing an Irish ballad "with a kind of wonderful, romantic lightness."

McPherson had not known Corcoran well even though they had both been close to Lyndon Johnson. Tommy was much older. He had helped get Johnson started in Washington, and when he wanted to speak to the Texan he didn't go through staff. But McPherson knew the stories about Corcoran's lobbying that were legend in Washington. He was "smart as the blazes, but a little on the edge," McPherson later recalled. He also knew Corcoran had been one of the leaders of the Roosevelt brain trust and that he and Ben Cohen had drafted some of the most important legislation of the New Deal: laws that regulated the operations of the stock market and the utility companies and set standards for housing and labor practices.

Funny, McPherson thought to himself, not long ago he had seen Ben Cohen out walking his small dog, a terrier named Mr. Dibbs, in Dupont Circle at around one in the morning. McPherson knew that Corcoran and Cohen had had a reputation for working all hours of the night. As the light turned green on Thirty-fourth Street, McPherson chuckled to himself: These two old men still couldn't go to bed early.

◆　◆　◆

Tommy Corcoran was at one time considered one of the most influential men in the country. He was as colorful and fascinating a political figure as Washington has ever produced. An ebullient and captivating personality, Corcoran wielded substantial power, initially from within government and later from outside. He never held a position of great stature, but nevertheless he played a major part in some of the most significant events in the nation's political history during the twentieth century. The story of his life as a Washington personality and power broker illuminates how the exercise of power changed in the years from Roosevelt to Reagan.

As a young Harvard-trained lawyer, Corcoran first learned about power at the knee of one of the most revered jurists in American history: Oliver Wendell Holmes. After a year of clerking for the great lawyer on the Supreme Court, Corcoran came away with a sense not only of the majesty of the law but also of its imperfections. He learned that the law did not assure equal justice, and he recognized how it could be used as a tool of enormous power.

He next witnessed how power was used — and abused — on Wall Street, where he spent five years working for one of New York's most prestigious firms. After becoming something of an expert in corporate transactions, he left New York for the hurly-burly of political life in Washington, where he became one of the most significant forces in the New Deal.

The New Deal, a phrase coined by Governor Franklin Delano Roosevelt at the 1932 Democratic National Convention, became the label for the campaign of economic and social reform that President Roosevelt led from 1933 to 1940. During the Great Depression, whose beginning most historians peg to the stock market crash of 1929, the nation suffered 25 percent unemployment, falling tax revenues, and a crisis of confidence in the financial markets. Roosevelt used a panoply of economic programs to provide not only economic relief but also a reorientation of American society that he once described as "an assurance of a rounded, permanent national life."

During the early years of the New Deal, Corcoran occupied a legal job at the Reconstruction Finance Corporation, a sprawling government agency with great influence over many parts of the national economy. From his perch as a midlevel bureaucrat, Corcoran managed to ingratiate himself with the president of the United States, becoming a speechwriter, political adviser, and friend to Roosevelt. Corcoran also teamed up with

Benjamin Cohen, a man diametrically opposed to him in background and temperament, to write laws that, in the words of New Deal historian Jordan Schwarz, would "stand the test of constitutional challenge and of history."

In many respects Corcoran in the 1930s anticipated President Kennedy's call to public service in the 1960s. Corcoran was never elected to anything and did not have Kennedy's bully pulpit to attract the best and the brightest; nevertheless he built an organization of hundreds of lawyers in Washington that projected an alternative to the party hacks who had occupied both the Democratic National Committee and the civil service. Attracted by Corcoran's optimism, energy, and pragmatism, some of the best minds in the country came to Washington to join him in the government. He moved his men around like chess pieces on a board, creating an unparalleled network throughout the government.

During the Great Depression, Corcoran witnessed major lobbying campaigns by big business as Wall Street bristled at any attempt at regulation and used campaign contributions in tandem with massive public relations campaigns to affect the outcome of legislation. Because he had worked on Wall Street himself, Corcoran became a one-man fortress in defense of the government's attempts at controlling the excesses of industry.

Corcoran left government at the beginning of the Second World War to start a family and to make more money. As a lawyer in private practice he witnessed profound changes in the nation's capital and participated in the rise of modern lobbying. The term *lobbying* came originally from England, where in the mid–seventeenth century citizens had waited in an anteroom, or lobby, off the great hall of Parliament to voice their grievances to their representatives in the House of Commons. In America lobbying dates back to the nineteenth century, when colorful figures such as Sam Ward were renowned for swaying movers and shakers in Washington with fine food, expensive wine, and abundant charm. The rise of big business in the twentieth century meant that corporations increasingly expended resources to influence politicians. But knowing who to talk to and how to get things done was not as easy as it once had been.

Washington, a sleepy southern town, was rapidly evolving into an economic epicenter. The government, which had financed a massive public works campaign during the New Deal, now partnered with private industry to mobilize the country for war. As the importance of the federal government grew, so did the attendant maze of federal bureaucracy — one that Corcoran understood perhaps better than anyone else of his generation and one in which he had extraordinary contacts, due in large part to the elaborate network he had created and continued to cultivate. When Corcoran was not trolling the halls of the U.S. Capitol, he was in his office furiously working the phones with cabinet secretaries, White House officials, senators, and congressmen.

Indeed, Corcoran embraced his work in the private sector with the same zeal he brought to public service. He devoted himself to influencing governmental decisions affecting his clients. Despite his strong identification with the Roosevelt administration, the vast majority of his lobbying seems to have been ideologically neutral. He viewed himself as accountable only to his clients — and sometimes the clients were the same companies or individuals he had scorned when he worked in the government. Corcoran knew how to get the job done.

While he continued to be driven by the pragmatism that had characterized his years in public service, there is no doubt that Corcoran also became more conservative in his political views. After the Second World War he viewed government less as a vehicle for influencing social policy and improving people's lives, and more as a bulwark against communism — the destruction of which he embraced through many of his corporate clients. He also became a family man and, emulating the Kennedys, worked to ensure that his children would have every advantage.

Yet Corcoran's legacy ultimately would be a mixed one, due in large part to his professional ethics. Because he sought to attain a favorable outcome for his clients by any means necessary, Corcoran sometimes skirted the edge of propriety, and occasionally stepped over it. He used bluff and bluster; he cajoled and charmed; he traded and promised. Along the way he was investigated by both houses of Congress, the Federal Bureau of Investigation, and the District of Columbia Bar.

Corcoran is important because of the significant role he played in the New Deal and his years as one of Washington's foremost lobbyists, but he is also an intriguing figure because his personality played such a role in his success. Professionally, Corcoran blazed a trail that many other well-educated young people who came to Washington would ultimately follow: He was a government lawyer who became a lobbyist. But he possessed a personality, charisma, and energy that gave him extraordinary power not usually associated with such anonymous professions. As the historian Kenneth Davis has written, "He had a rare ability to spread around him the energy of his excitement of his dramatic view of the world as a war of opposites — light versus dark, good versus evil, truth versus falsehood — with each warring element multitudinously personalized."

Corcoran's contradictions were sometimes masked by his effervescent personality. He had a wonderful sense of humor and loved to entertain anyone who would listen. He also possessed a deep reservoir of kindness that stood in sharp contrast to his competitors at the top of Washington's ruthless legal practice. Many of those who knew him well described him as the most generous man they had ever met.

He could be overly demanding, even unrelenting, with his own family, although he held everyone to high standards. One story from the 1970s is particularly illustrative. Corcoran and his younger law partner Robert Perry had dropped in on the ambassador to Guatemala at his residence one summer morning. As the two lawyers waited, Corcoran spied a piano in the corner of the drawing room. He went over, sat down, and played a classical piece with such dexterity and ease that Perry was in awe. After Corcoran finished, Perry said to him, "Tommy, that was beautiful, just beautiful. God, I wish I could do that." Corcoran, who was somewhat smaller, looked up at him, clearly irritated. Perry had been something of a protégé of his, but now Corcoran poked his finger in Perry's chest and said, "No you don't. Because, if you really wanted to, you would do it!" For Tommy Corcoran, life was all about grabbing the brass ring.

PART ONE

The Early Years

1

Most Likely to Succeed

As a young boy Tommy Corcoran thought he might want to be a teacher, a writer, or perhaps an actor or musician. Growing up in Pawtucket, Rhode Island, at the turn of the twentieth century, Corcoran saw nothing but opportunity before him. He was not rich; he later described his parents as "lace curtain" Irish, middle-class, second-generation Americans. But his parents were also driven. Corcoran wrote that "inspired by a father who never knew fatigue and an ambitious mother, I grew up knowing I must succeed. . . ."

Young Tommy had brains, determination, and extraordinary energy. He seemed to be able to accomplish whatever he set his mind to. Part of his ability stemmed from his temerity. In Tommy's childhood his father, Patrick, liked to tease him and his two younger brothers, David and Howard, about the "ghosts" in the attic of their house. The attic was a dark and musty space, punctuated by gables and crowded with old furniture and steamer trunks that his maternal grandfather had taken on voyages around the world. David taunted his older brother by declaring that Tommy would never dare to set foot in such a spooky place. Nevertheless, one day Tommy picked up the pillow and blanket off his bed and proclaimed that his was "going to live in the attic." And for a short time, he did.

Tommy's paternal grandparents, Patrick and Bridgette, immigrated to the United States from "somewhere in the interior" of Ireland, probably Tipperary or Roscommon. They settled in New York, where Tommy's father, Thomas Patrick Corcoran, was born. When the boy was only two, Patrick died in a fall from scaffolding at a construction site. Bridgette struggled in the city for the next decade; then, in 1873, she and her twelve-year-old son followed friends to Pawtucket, where there were jobs in the mills.

Bridgette Corcoran worked six days a week, "for pennies," according to her grandson.

◆ ◆ ◆

On his mother's side, Tommy's ancestors were a "clan of fishermen and sailors from Kinsale" who had made their way from Ireland to Canada and ultimately settled in pre–Revolutionary War New England. Tommy's maternal grandfather, David O'Keefe, had been born in Canada but moved to Taunton, Massachusetts, as a young boy. At age eleven he was working in a paint store for twenty-five cents a day. Five years later David O'Keefe became an apprentice seaman, and at nineteen he received his captain's certificate from the prestigious Nautical Board of Massachusetts. Shortly thereafter, in 1849, O'Keefe joined the rush for gold in California, "following the diggings" up to Montana. He never struck it rich. Eventually he wandered back to San Francisco, where he signed on as first mate on a full rigger sailing to Australia, New Zealand, and China. On the voyage, the captain died; O'Keefe was promoted to captain on the spot. Family legend had it that before he returned home, the ship stopped in the Sandwich Islands, where O'Keefe danced with Lulla-fallani, the last queen of the islands.

Upon returning to Massachusetts, Captain O'Keefe settled in the small town of Taunton, just across the border from Rhode Island, and turned his attention to business. He built and operated a fleet of ships — large fore-and-aft schooners that were more economical than the pre–Civil War steamships. O'Keefe started a shipping business and moved cargo up and down the East Coast, making a small fortune in the process. He also settled down to marriage and raised three sons and a daughter, Mary. As Tommy would later describe the family, "They were as self-consciously close to broadcloth aristocracy as Irish Catholic stock ever got in old New England."

By 1896 Mary O'Keefe (known as Josephine), tall and not particularly comely, had fallen in love with Thomas Patrick Corcoran, known as Patrick. Although at five foot two he was noticeably shorter, she thought he was handsome and admired his ambition. Indeed, Corcoran had graduated from Brown University, a small but distinguished Baptist college, and gone on to receive his law degree from Boston University. He had helped defray the costs of his college education by selling newspapers on the trolley that he rode daily between Pawtucket and Providence. While in law school in Boston, he had simultaneously operated a newsdealer's store in Pawtucket. Patrick stood out from the other young Irishmen she knew in another way: He didn't drink alcohol.

For his part, Patrick admired Josephine's intelligence and, as Tommy would write many years later, the fact that she "played the piano as nimbly as a swallow flies." Moreover, Mary's family, although Republican, were clearly in a higher economic and social stratum than his own. They were married later that year and bought a two-story row house on Randall Street in Pawtucket.

At the time Pawtucket was one of the most important manufacturing centers in the country. The city had experienced rapid growth in the late eighteenth century when Moses Brown, who had made his fortune in shipping, decided to invest in a machine that would manufacture thread. He opened his first mill at the edge of the Narragansett Bay, just across the river from Fall River, Massachusetts: *Pawtucket* was Native American for "by the river." When James Madison wore a woolen suit that had been manufactured in Pawtucket to his inauguration in 1800, the town was on the map. Over the next several decades thousands of Irish, English, Scottish, and French Canadian immigrants settled in Pawtucket as dozens of textile mills were opened. Patrick and Josephine had three children in quick succession: Tommy, David, and Howard. With the bills mounting, Patrick had hung out a shingle and established a general commercial legal business. As his practice grew and his circle of friends widened, he became increasingly interested in civic affairs and local politics. In 1899 he was elected a member of the Pawtucket School Committee, where he teamed up with former Brown classmate and later neighbor Alexander Meiklejon, who would one day become the president of Amherst College. The two of them set about reorganizing the Pawtucket public school system. Three years later Corcoran was elected to the state legislature.

As a reform politician, he fought at various times against his own party, the Democrats, as well as Republicans and even his own bishop. In his devotion to the needs of schools and schoolteachers, he was willing to take on anybody and anything, and on one occasion horrified his other clients by acting as counsel to what he considered underpaid teachers in the state's first schoolteachers' strike.

Notwithstanding his controversial political stands, Patrick established a law practice that included some of the region's largest and most important businesses. Clients included the Pawtucket Institute for Savings and the Blackstone Valley Gas and Electric Company. With a steady and rising income, Patrick and Mary decided to buy a single-family home on Sanford Street in one of Pawtucket's middle-class neighborhoods.

Corcoran had developed a reputation as a fine lawyer, but he also had a knack for politics. He could play the violin and carry a tune. People enjoyed his company and respected his intellect. He founded the local Rotary Club. In 1906 he declared his candidacy for mayor of Pawtucket.

Patrick Corcoran was following the path of many American Irish in the first two decades of the twentieth century — using politics as a means to social and economic advancement. Unlike other immigrant groups, the Irish had advantages in the political arena: They spoke English and had inherited a centuries-old political history in their struggles with the English.

The 1906 campaign for mayor of Pawtucket was a classic local election in which both sides mobilized their foot soldiers. Patrick's opponent organized "blood-quickening parades" in which, as young Tommy vividly remembered, "Bands of men marched around out block shouting their champion's slogan and waving flaming torches." The Democratic City Committee published a pamphlet accusing the city council of "manipulating the personal property lists through tax assessments" and supported Corcoran as someone "who will scrutinize these acts by publicly preventing the consummation of these nefarious acts." The committee described him as "a young man of ability, integrity, industry and backbone." The problem was, Patrick may not have been Irish enough.

Although he received the endorsement of the Democratic establishment, Corcoran lost, attributable in Tommy's view to his father's "famous abstinence" and no small measure of electoral chicanery: "In those days ballot boxes were stuffed more generously than Christmas turkeys." Two years later he made another run for public office, attorney general of Rhode Island. He lost again and returned to his law practice for good.

Tommy was born on December 29, two days before the first year of the twentieth century. His birth was quickly followed by those of his brothers. As children the three boys were inseparable, although Tommy was clearly the leader. Mary Corcoran often dressed her little boys in matching clothes and forced them to wear bows in their hair or sailor hats. During the evenings Patrick, who shared his wife's musical interests, played the violin while Mary accompanied him on the piano and the children gathered around to sing Irish ballads and sea chanties.

On weekends the family often visited his mother's parents in Taunton, where the O'Keefes had a large house that faced "Jim Goose's" pond. Tommy also spent many of his early summers in Massachusetts floating a raft on the pond, exploring the veritable jungle that grew on Captain Church's undeveloped lots, and, as dusk fell, waiting "for the horse drawn ice cream cart to come down the elm shaded street."

In Pawtucket the Corcoran family lived across the street from a parochial school, but the children all went to public school. Tommy did well in school, played football and baseball vigorously, and generally enjoyed himself with his two younger brothers. By the time he reached high school, he was a prize scholar and debate champion, and had the lead role in *Charley's Aunt.* He later recalled that after being "nominated by a little Jewish kid," he "won the presidency of the senior class."

By 1918 he had followed his father's footsteps to Brown University. As Tommy settled into the life of a freshman in a college of a thousand students, a million American soldiers had arrived in France: The great Allied counteroffensive was under way. By the end of his first semester, the Allies had triumphed and President Wilson announced that he would attend the European peace conference. Reflecting the optimism of the era, Tommy Corcoran approached college with a vision of the American renaissance.

Although he majored in English, Corcoran studied modern languages and immersed himself in the classics. He was as adept at the social sciences as at natural science, and by his junior year he was Phi Beta Kappa. He was also the class vice president and president of the debating team. He later recalled that "the debate training I received under [Professor] George Hurley" was "the most precious thing I took away from college." Corcoran believed he learned "an ability to use language as a utilitarian tool."

During summers in college Tommy headed for the White Mountains of New Hampshire, where he worked as a hutboy with the Appalachian Mountain Club. He cleared trails, guided hikers, and helped build a camp on Mount Washington. Hauling supplies on his back up and down the mountain made him "strong as an ox."

His physical strength made him a fine athlete in college. Two years before his arrival, the Brown football team had played in the Rose Bowl; it remained a national powerhouse. With his short, sturdy build and fierce determination, Corcoran starred as a running back.

Corcoran was also a fine musician and an accomplished actor. Like his father, he learned to play the piano and later the accordion. He could play by ear, popular tunes as well as classical compositions. The university's theatrical company, Sock and Buskin, produced a full season of plays, and Corcoran starred in many of the productions in roles ranging from "humble parsons to silky counts." He reportedly knew Gilbert and Sullivan "from A to Z."

Tommy's father, Patrick, had founded the first Catholic college fraternity at Brown, but Tommy decided not to join because, he later explained, "anti-Catholic prejudice had subsided enough on campus so that Catholics didn't advertise their differences." Although enormously popular, he rarely socialized with women: "Mother had given me an abiding discomfort about women." Mary believed that her son was destined for great things and that he should not marry too young.

By the time he graduated from college, Tommy Corcoran had become a campus legend. His senior yearbook stated that "There are few activities he has not had a liberal share in and very, very few men who do not know him." Corcoran was famed for his deft sense of humor and his ability to keep an audience laughing. But beneath the jovial exterior, he was fiercely competitive and often stayed up all night to study for an exam.

As the senior class assembled at the First Baptist meetinghouse for commencement in 1921, Tommy Corcoran was its valedictorian. Thinking perhaps he might someday become an academic, Corcoran stayed on for another year at Brown and earned a master's degree in the classics.

During his last year at Brown, Corcoran decided again to follow his father's career path and applied to Harvard Law School. He was admitted to a class that included future Illinois governor and two-time presidential candidate Adlai Stevenson. Brown had provided him with access to the liberal arts; at Harvard Law he found himself surrounded by some of the greatest minds in the country, including Professors Roscoe Pound, a future dean of the law school, and Felix Frankfurter.

During his first year Corcoran's grades were among the highest in his class. He was clearly a candidate for one of the editor positions on the *Harvard Law Review;* they were handed out on the basis of not only grades, but also balloting by the current board. A year ahead of Corcoran was a brilliant, young student named James M. Landis, the son of Presbyterian missionaries and a graduate of Princeton. Landis's own grades topped the first-year class; he was the case editor for the *Review*. According to Corcoran, Landis became his "benefactor" on the *Law Review* and permitted him "to serve as the first Irishman on the editorial board" as note editor.

During his third year of law school, Corcoran's academic excellence caught the eye of Professor Frankfurter, who subsequently became his most important mentor. Frankfurter not only recognized Corcoran's intelligence, but also had extraordinary insight into his character: "He is struggling very hard with the burden of inferiority imposed on him because of his Irish Catholicism by his experiences at Brown, in Providence and in Boston." Corcoran persevered and at the end of his third year won the coveted Sears Prize for academic excellence, which came with a four-hundred-dollar grant.

Unclear as to what he wanted to do and inspired by Frankfurter, Corcoran considered teaching law. After receiving his degree cum laude, he stayed on for an additional year of graduate study and obtained his SJD, doctor of science of jurisprudence. Harvard Law School was at that time developing a new cadre of scholars to succeed a faculty of men who were brilliant, but also aging. Corcoran and eight more of the brightest young graduates were selected to be part of this new faculty as teaching fellows. Corcoran was assigned to Felix Frankfurter because he was interested in utilities and Frankfurter taught certain courses in administrative law.

At Frankfurter's urging, Corcoran wrote an article for the *Law Review* titled "Petty Offenses and Constitutional Guarantee by Jury." He later described how he had gone "to New York to find out why the DA's office wasn't working with the Prohibition law," and wrote, "I found out why. Everyone was asking for a grand jury and there wasn't enough money in the world to give them all a grand jury. So anybody who violated the prohibition law could get off for $5.00 if he pleaded guilty to anything at all." It was possible, in other words, to game the system.

Corcoran enjoyed the teaching but barely made enough money to pay his rent. To subsidize the meager funds his parents provided him, during his last few years at Harvard he had tutored fellow students (for two dollars per class each) on how to pass exams in some of the tougher courses. With his degree in hand, he now decided to enter private practice and make some real money.

Professor Frankfurter had contacts at most of the best firms in the country. He recommended Corcoran to Joseph Cotton, one of the top lawyers on Wall Street and the managing partner at Cotton and Franklin. Cotton interviewed Corcoran and made him an offer on the spot. Like Corcoran, Cotton was from Rhode Island, although he'd grown up in the rarefied world of Newport. Cotton knew that Corcoran was brilliant, but he also sensed that the young Irish Catholic from hardscrabble Pawtucket was hungry for success.

By the second decade of the twentieth century, U.S. Supreme Court justice Oliver Wendell Holmes had established himself as a legendary legal thinker and one of the most influential Supreme Court justices in American history. Born into a Boston Brahmin family, Holmes had served in the Union infantry during the Civil War, where he was wounded three times. After the war he joined the faculty of Harvard Law School and befriended the likes of William and Henry James. At the age of forty-two Holmes wrote his most famous treatise, *The Common Law,* a theory of law that quickly became one of the best-known contributions to American legal scholarship. The next year Holmes was appointed to the Massachusetts Supreme Court by Governor John Davis Long. Twenty years later, in 1902, Holmes was appointed to the U.S. Supreme Court by President Theodore Roosevelt. For the next thirty years he was to exert an unrivaled influence over the legal profession through his many famous dissents on the Court.

Corcoran's plans to enter private practice with Cotton and Franklin were sidetracked in 1926 when he received a letter from Justice Holmes. Corcoran was startled to read that he had been accepted as the legal clerk for the justice, a great honor. What surprised Corcoran the most was that he was even under consideration: He had never interviewed or applied for a clerkship. Holmes had entrusted to Professor Felix Frankfurter the task of recommending to him the brightest and most capable students, and Frankfurter had singled out Corcoran after the young scholar's *Harvard Law Review* article.

Before Corcoran accepted, he traveled to New York to ask Cotton if he could defer the offer to join the law firm for a year. "Of course," Cotton replied. "A year of the burnish of Washington cannot but help an Irishman from Pawtucket."

In the fall of 1926 Corcoran arrived in Washington, DC, renting a small garret on Eighteenth Street for four dollars a month. During the first two decades of the twentieth century, the nation's capital was a sleepy southern town. Jim Crow laws segregating the races were strictly enforced, and the white population all but deserted the city during the humid summers. Although the Capitol had been finished a century earlier, there were only a handful of other government buildings. Still, like the rest of the country, the city was enjoying a period of prosperity marked by economic growth and physical expansion. On Connecticut Avenue the grand Mayflower Hotel was being built, and just down the street, near the Department of the Treasury, the smaller but equally elegant Hotel Washington was rising. For a young man from Pawtucket, Rhode Island, it was an exhilarating time to be in the nation's capital.

2

A Wonderful Education

As he approached the front door of the four-story manse at 1710
I Street, Corcoran brushed down the lapels of his new blue suit one
last time. He climbed the steps and rang the doorbell. As Corcoran later
recalled in his unpublished memoirs, a young woman, the maid, opened
the door and said in a cheerful Irish brogue, "Can I help you?"

"I'm Thomas Corcoran and I am here to see Justice Holmes. I believe
he is expecting me."

Corcoran was shown into the hallway. A few minutes later double
doors opened and an elegantly dressed, white-haired lady greeted him.
Fanny Holmes, née Fanny Bowditch Dixon, was eighty years old and,
though only five feet tall, carried herself in a regal manner. She smiled
slightly. "Mr. Corcoran, you are going to see the Justice, but I want to talk
to you first." She continued, "You are from Boston, and you are an
Irishman. We know all about you. What do you know about us?"

Corcoran returned her smile. "Why Mrs. Holmes, I've heard all there is
to say about the Justice. I'm excited, very excited."

"Well," Mrs. Holmes said, "that's important. I just want you to know.
Do you know what a Unitarian is?"

Corcoran hadn't expected to be interrogated by the justice's wife, but
he didn't flinch. "Oh, yes," he replied. "I think I know what a Unitarian
is. A Unitarian is a kind of refined Congregationalist."

Mrs. Holmes eyed the young, sturdy man before her. "Well," she said,
"that will do if you want to put it that way, but if you want to put it very
simply, a Unitarian in Boston is the least you could be. We were
Unitarians." With that, she showed Corcoran the elevator with its sliding
wrought-iron door. The two of them then ascended to a second floor of
the house. They first walked through one room that was lined with book-
cases around the four walls — this room, explained Mrs. Holmes, was
where Corcoran would conduct his research. Double doors opened into
the justice's study, which featured a big flat-topped desk that had
belonged to Holmes's grandfather; next to it was a big leather chair with

an adjustable footrest. The desk faced a large window overlooking the garden. On the other side of the room was a standing desk where the justice often worked and where he now stood. "Mr. Corcoran, I am pleased to meet you." He spoke with a Boston accent — distinctly Boston Brahmin.

When Tommy Corcoran first met Oliver Wendell Holmes, the justice was eighty-five years old. He had a long, bushy white mustache, thick, white eyebrows, and blue-gray eyes that locked his visitor in a penetrating stare. When he worked he often smoked Cuban cigars purchased from the luxury importer S. S. Pierce. He was slightly stooped but still thin and fit from his daily walks.

For the next twelve months, beginning in the fall of 1926, Corcoran clerked for the justice. They developed an extremely close relationship that continued until Holmes's death in March 1935. Years later, Washington journalist Joseph Alsop wrote that "Holmes became Corcoran's substitute for a personal God, and Corcoran, by his irrepressible gayety, by the very warmth of his affection, endeared himself to Holmes as few others had succeeded in doing."

Corcoran quickly adapted to Holmes's daily routine as well as to his idiosyncracies. The present-day Supreme Court building had not yet been built; the Court convened in small chambers on a lower level of the U.S. Capitol. Holmes, however, did not use an office in the cramped Capitol, preferring his study with its private library. Every morning when Corcoran arrived at I Street, he and the justice would immediately begin to review cases. Holmes did not allow newspapers in the house. He used to tell his clerks that "if anything important happens, my friends will tell me." Nor did he allow a typewriter; everything had to be written out in longhand. After he had finished with the notes for a case, Holmes burned them in his fireplace.

Corcoran was responsible for entering the cases in the docket, but his most important responsibility was to study the petitions for writs of certiorari, or requests for review of lower-court decisions. The Supreme Court does not to hear a case unless it raises an important constitutional issue, decisions of different circuit courts of appeal conflict, or the case is otherwise a matter of very great general importance. In considering the petitions, Holmes counted on Corcoran's good judgment and knowledge of legal precedent.

Holmes and Corcoran reviewed the petitions each morning, with Corcoran standing by the judge's flat-topped desk with half a dozen or so briefs stacked beside him. Then they would together review the cases, Corcoran reciting the facts and Holmes writing them down in his small, distinctive script on unlined white paper. Corcoran would sum up the arguments and make a recommendation. Holmes would often challenge his clerk's reasoning and, once he was satisfied that they had thoroughly discussed the case, would make a decision.

However, Holmes rarely discussed major cases with his clerks. Corcoran's role in the most important cases was simply to retrieve the requisite opinions for the justice, not to summarize them. The justice often told Corcoran, "See if you can find the Massachusetts Reports by my favorite author" — always referring to himself. He would add with a smile, "Why not? I have a right to suit myself. If I don't like it, I change it. So naturally, I like the way I write it."

When the Court was hearing a case, Holmes would dress in his black frock coat, the traditional dress of the Court, and be driven to Capitol Hill, leaving Corcoran behind to conduct his research. In the afternoon Holmes would return and make notes from what he had heard in the morning. Then he and Corcoran would go for a walk. During these walks Holmes would talk about any number of subjects: philosophy, religion, war.

Once, on one of their strolls, the justice asked Corcoran, "You've read the New Testament, of course. Have you read the Old Testament?" When Corcoran admitted to only a passing acquaintance, Holmes assigned him three chapters to read that night. Corcoran remembered, "The next day when we walked we went over it." Holmes was not overtly prejudiced against Catholics, but, according to Alger Hiss, who had preceded Corcoran as Holmes's clerk (and who would be accused during the 1950s of spying for the Soviet Union and convicted of perjury), the justice "grew up at a time when intellectuals, particularly free thinking individuals, found the conformity of the Catholic Church, especially in Europe, a horror." Hiss remembered that when they once drove to a monastery, Holmes got out of the car, walked through the rose garden, and said, "Isn't it astonishing that people who have such benighted ideas can appreciate such beauty as these roses?" But Holmes never showed any disdain for Catholicism that Corcoran noticed. On the contrary, the justice seemed both intrigued and impressed by how Corcoran balanced his religion with his adventurist spirit. Corcoran recalled, "I was the first Irish Catholic law clerk he had. He wondered how the hell a practicing Irish Catholic from Boston could have gone to a place called Brown University, where the President was a Baptist minister, and then to agnostic Harvard Law School. He was very interested in what went on in my mind."

Holmes could also reveal what Corcoran called a "lovely sense of humor" during these walks. On one occasion they were walking along Pennsylvania Avenue when a curvaceous young blonde walked past them. Holmes watched her carefully until she turned the corner at Fifteenth Street; then he turned wistfully to Corcoran: "Ah, to be eighty again." Sometimes Holmes's humor was laced with a patronizing view of the world. For instance, he and Corcoran often strolled past the Civil Service Building and watched the employees leaving their jobs. According to Corcoran, Holmes used to say, "You know, little boy, do you think the Lord God intended every one of those civil servants should be fertilized?"

During the year that he clerked for Holmes, Corcoran did not have a personal life beyond his work. As he put it, "My fare was completely intellectual." Every evening he returned to his small apartment and devoured books that Holmes had recommended to him. Besides the Old Testament, he read Montaigne and Burke and Lord Acton. According to Corcoran, "I had a wonderful education."

Holmes once described Corcoran as "quite noisy, quite adequate and quite noisy," but he grew very fond of the young Irishman. Corcoran became more than a legal clerk to Justice Holmes: He served as the older man's companion and caregiver. In the late afternoons Corcoran often read out loud to the justice, who sat slouched in his large leather chair, hands folded, listening. "I'd be reading to him and the lights would be down. All of a sudden we'd be talking about the Norman knights. Ye gods! He was still in the Civil War!" After they finished a book, the justice would carefully record the title in a black notebook. By the time of his death in 1935, Holmes had read more than thirty-five hundred books and had written down the title of each in his neat script. He had asked that the volume be destroyed on his death, but Corcoran, recognizing its historical value, had smuggled it out of the house and given it to the Harvard Law School Library.

◆   ◆   ◆

Corcoran also handled the justice's finances, which consisted principally of balancing his checkbook, a task that consumed an inordinate amount of time. As Corcoran described it, "We'd go over it and we'd go over and we'd go over it." Holmes was incredibly parsimonious. On one occasion when Corcoran had purchased a package of LifeSavers at the drugstore, Holmes admonished his young assistant that he had just "paid out the interest on $1.00 for a year." On another occasion, Mrs. Holmes told her husband to take Corcoran with him to a lecture that he was attending. Holmes refused, because it cost five dollars. The next day Corcoran overheard the justice tell his wife, "It wasn't worth $5.00. I'm glad I didn't take the boy." Corcoran passed off Holmes's frugality as being "like all Yankees."

One of the great benefits of working for Holmes was the opportunity to meet the luminaries, intellectuals, and high government officials who frequently called on him. Corcoran became acquainted with the other members of the Court, particularly Justice Louis D. Brandeis and Chief Justice Charles Evans Hughes. On March 3, 1926, Corcoran and Holmes were enjoying a lunch celebrating the justice's eighty-fifth birthday. They had just uncorked a magnum of champagne sent by the British ambassador when Chief Justice Hughes stopped by to wish Holmes a happy birthday. As they sat around the table, Holmes said to Hughes, "Mr. Chief Justice, gaze on me with awe. Before you stands a vessel of that not-yet-forgotten champagne."

In the summer of 1927, with the Court in recess, Corcoran accompanied Holmes to his home in Beverly Farms, Massachusetts, along Boston's North Shore. The house, which had belonged to his father, was a sprawling, comfortable Victorian overlooking the ocean. Life in Beverly was generally quiet and restful, but in 1927 the entire nation, and especially Boston, was gripped by the politically charged case of Sacco and Vanzetti.

Nicola Sacco and Bartolomeo Vanzetti were Italian immigrants and self-described anarchists. On May 5, 1927, they were arrested and charged with the murder of a postal worker in South Braintree, Massachusetts. Their trial became a political showcase for the growing jingoism and anti-communist feelings sweeping the nation. Despite the circumstantial evidence presented by the prosecution, Sacco and Vanzetti were found guilty of murder and sentenced to die.

As they awaited their execution date on August 23, riots broke out across

Boston. Demonstrators thronged to the Boston Common to protest. The Boston police, armed with riot guns, were put on twenty-four-hour emergency duty, and extra guards were posted at government buildings.

While the execution date drew ever closer, the defendants' legal team tried to persuade the U.S. Supreme Court to review the case. Since the Court had adjourned for the summer, the only recourse was through individual justices, and because Holmes was in charge of the New England circuit, he was drawn into the controversy. The defendants' legal team held out hope that Holmes would come to their rescue. He had condemned the lynching of blacks in a famous case known as *Moore v. Dempsey* four years earlier, and it was well known that Holmes's protégé at Harvard Law School, Felix Frankfurter, adamantly opposed the execution of the two men.

In the early evening of August 10, chief counsel for the defense Arthur Dehon Hill (who was a close friend of Frankfurter's), his co-counsels, and several reporters descended on Holmes at his home in Beverly Farms. The throng of lawyers and reporters aroused, Corcoran later recalled, "the apprehension of friendly neighbors." Holmes invited the legal team into his house while the press waited outside. Hill implored him to issue a writ of habeas corpus, which would have required a review of the evidence. The lawyers argued for more than two hours while Holmes listened attentively. Although he was sympathetic to their pleadings, he nevertheless refused.

As the lawyers filed out of the house, the police arrived and a guard was posted on the front steps. Inside the house, Holmes stood gazing out over the moonlit ocean. Corcoran, visibly upset by the meeting, asked, "But has justice been done, Sir?"

Holmes turned and stared at his clerk. "Don't be foolish, boy. We practice law, not 'justice.' There is no such thing as objective 'justice,' which is a subjective matter. A man might feel justified in stealing a loaf of bread to fill his belly; the baker might feel it most justified for the thief's hand to be chopped off, as in Victor Hugo's *Les Misérables*. The image of justice changes with the beholder's viewpoint, prejudice or social affiliation. But for society to function, the set of rules agreed on by the body politic must be observed — the law must be carried out." For Corcoran, the moral relativism of the legal system was forever imprinted in his brain.

PART TWO

The New Deal Years

3

The Coming of the New Deal

During the year he worked for Justice Holmes, Corcoran had lived a spartan life yet was still unable to save money on his meager salary of four thousand dollars a year. When the clerkship ended in the fall of 1927, then, he decided "to make a million dollars." Corcoran had not grown up poor, but neither had he enjoyed wealth. His year in the nation's capital with Justice Holmes had exposed him to a class of American society that he had previously only imagined. With a four-story Washington town house, a summer home along the Massachusetts "gold coast," and Irish servants, Holmes could dedicate himself to public service and still live very comfortably.

Corcoran was undoubtedly motivated by the challenge to become financially successful, but he also wanted to test his mettle. Nowhere was the excitement greater and the competition fiercer than in New York City. Corcoran, now twenty-seven years old, feared that he "was getting started late," but he had a job waiting for him at Cotton and Franklin. The firm was small but highly regarded primarily because, as Corcoran later noted, "These men had large minds."

Cotton and Franklin had been founded by William McAdoo shortly after World War I. A decade earlier McAdoo had married President Woodrow Wilson's daughter in a White House ceremony, and following this entrée to the highest circles of Washington officialdom went on to an illustrious career in government. He was appointed the first chairman of the Federal Reserve Board and, during the war, served in his father-in-law's cabinet as secretary of the Treasury. After Wilson died, McAdoo inherited the leadership of the Democratic Party. He served one term as U.S. senator from California and was a candidate for president of the United States on three occasions. By 1927, the year Corcoran joined the law firm, McAdoo was chairman of the giant chemical concern Allied Chemical & Dye; Cotton and Franklin was run by George Franklin, a Republican, and Joseph Cotton, a Democrat.

Joseph Potter Cotton, the managing partner, was known as one of the most brilliant practitioners of his generation. A descendant of John Cotton, the Puritan minister, he had been class poet at Harvard College, first in his class at Harvard Law School, and assistant to Herbert Hoover, the director of the American Relief Committee, during World War I. Although a brilliant lawyer, Cotton looked and acted like an eccentric, blue-blooded professor. He was bald, smoked a corncob pipe, and wore rumpled suits. The firm's unadorned decor reflected his relaxed style. Corcoran once accompanied Cotton to the offices of the powerhouse law firm of Sullivan and Cromwell after they had been refurbished by the famous interior decorator Dorothy Draper. Corcoran was amazed at how she "could make a law office look like an empire."

What most impressed Corcoran was how Cotton combined distinct intellectual curiosity with keen business acumen. Corcoran admired the way Cotton "taught us to make money in the law. It wasn't just a matter of earning high fees, but of being permitted by the investment bankers to invest in the stocks that they reserved for themselves before offering a public issue." Looking back on his early career, Corcoran remarked many years later that Cotton "tackled pioneering problems of corporate law." For example, "When an impossible case appeared on the horizon, he saw to it that it solicited him, like the Chrysler-Dodge merger which several firms tried to push through the Justice Department. They failed; Cotton was given the case and he succeeded."

Corcoran not only admired Cotton but was also attracted to his daughter, Isabel, and began to date her. Almost exactly his age, she was a willowy blonde with a sophisticated air. They became engaged, but while Corcoran was making a significant amount of money, he didn't feel financially secure enough to undertake marriage. As the engagement wore on, Ms. Cotton, according to Corcoran, "decided I was too busy to pay the attention to her that an aristocratic girl deserved and she married another man."

Corcoran was indeed constantly working. As an associate at the firm, he specialized in corporate law, acquiring expertise in stock offerings, mergers, and acquisitions. He learned the intricacies of the business: how issues were underwritten, how to write a prospectus, and how to read the small print in a holding company's annual report.

As he had throughout his life, he impressed his colleagues with his extraordinary work ethic. An apocryphal story had it that Corcoran wore a green eyeshade on occasion, not to protect his vision, which was fine, but rather to focus his concentration even more firmly on his work. Indeed, Corcoran often worked in his offices until the early-morning hours, sometimes curling up on the floor in a Hudson's Bay blanket for a few hours of sleep. On one occasion a cleaning lady stumbled over him and, fearing someone had died, ran to sound the building alarm.

He was not, however, chained to his desk. Forever meeting with someone, Corcoran developed an unparalleled network of contacts in the financial markets and banking industry.

Professor Frankfurter had asked Cotton to help him find jobs for some of his best students. Cotton passed this responsibility on to Corcoran, and the young lawyer became something of a placement bureau for Harvard Law graduates, as well as graduates from other top law schools, in New York City. But, as Joseph Lash pointed out in his book *Dealers and Dreamers,* Corcoran "always had difficulties with placing . . . the Jewish boys." It was not for lack of trying. According to Lash, Corcoran wanted to please Frankfurter, notwithstanding that "among the prejudices he brought with him from Pawtucket and his Irish background was a depreciatory sense of Jews as 'kikes.'"

Corcoran carried around a black notebook in which he wrote down an applicant's name, his law school, and the positions for which he was most qualified. As one colleague noted, "he brought the fervor of a missionary and a phenomenal knack of putting the right man in the right job."

Even when away from the office, he was constantly engaged in some activity. On weekends he often let off steam by getting out of the city and taking long hikes in the Catskill Mountains. Although Catholic, Corcoran did not attend church regularly and instead preferred to rise early on Sunday mornings and knock on the doors of the apartments of some of his fellow associates. Together they would board the West Shore Railroad and head up to the Catskills. Once in the country, Corcoran led the young lawyers up and down wooded trails until dusk. Indeed, Corcoran was noted for his irrepressible spirit. When a member of the firm announced that he was moving to Hawaii, Corcoran organized a farewell party. He staged a skit that he had written, composed a rhyming verse, and outfitted the all-male chorus in hula skirts.

Corcoran also dabbled in local politics and supported reform of Tammany Hall. He also undoubtedly closely followed the presidential campaign of Al Smith, the Democratic governor of New York who in 1928 became the first Catholic to win the nomination of a major political party. Although Smith ran a spirited campaign against the Republican candidate, Herbert Hoover, he encountered widespread religious bigotry and lost overwhelmingly.

To save money, Corcoran lived at the St. George Hotel in Brooklyn. Early every morning he would walk across the Brooklyn Bridge to Manhattan, where skyscrapers seemed to be rising on every block. Each week he marveled as the Cities Services Building and Chrysler Building, then under construction, added floor upon floor, competing for the honor of tallest building in the city, and was amused when Chrysler won by erecting a steel spire.

In his first two years at the firm Corcoran made a good salary and, with sound investment and his frugal lifestyle, accumulated nearly a quarter million dollars. This was the equivalent of several million dollars today and a significant amount of money for someone under thirty years of age at the time. He seemed captivated by playing the market, and he was even investing for his family members. He wrote his mother about "the fifty warrants for Fourth National that I sent you for Howie." Howard was in law school at the time; Tommy was paying half his tuition. Tommy's other brother, David, was a businessman in Tokyo. In one letter Tommy informed David, "The market's going up and things are a lot better. . . . We'll be rich yet."

But when the stock market crashed in 1929, Corcoran lost most of his money. He wrote one friend, "I've lost a stock market fortune in box car figures and as a sheer matter of pride I'm going to make it back before anything else." Although Corcoran wanted to make a lot of money, he didn't particularly care about material possessions, and with no wife or family he was able to shrug off the crash. He later recalled that "Wall Street had had many a 'panic' before, and we all believed the 'temporary condition' would reverse itself." But Corcoran was no longer engaged by his work and confided to his mother, "If I had a million dollars, I would go."

Events in 1929 affected Corcoran in other important ways. In the spring Fanny Holmes, the justice's wife, had been recovering from the flu when she took a bad fall in the bathroom and fractured her hip. At eighty-eight she no longer had the ability to heal quickly and was in great pain. On the last day of April she died in her sleep. Some weeks later

Corcoran took the train from New York to Washington to visit Holmes. On entering the second-floor study at I Street he found the old justice sitting at his desk playing solitaire. For Corcoran, "It had a certain symbolic significance." He expressed his sorrow and told his mentor how good his wife had been to him during his year as a clerk. Holmes held out a card, looked at his young friend, and said, "She made life poetry for me. She was very lovely."

Around the same time, Joseph Cotton was tapped by President Hoover to be undersecretary of state. Cotton asked Corcoran to come and work for him, but the young lawyer did not feel financially secure enough to return to government. Corcoran had other opportunities in Washington. John Lord O'Brien, a distinguished attorney from Buffalo and later one of the founders of the Washington firm of Covington and Burling, had worked with Corcoran on Wall Street and been impressed by his energy and brilliance. When O'Brien was appointed the assistant attorney general, he too asked Corcoran to work for him, but the young lawyer again declined.

By 1932 Corcoran had managed to save enough money to consider leaving New York. Moreover, the depression had reduced the volume of his work at Cotton and Franklin, and the firm slashed his salary. This angered not only Tommy but his father as well, who complained to him that the firm "foolishly cut your salary after all you had done for them. . . ." Corcoran discussed his woes with Professor Frankfurter, who called Wall Street firms such as Cotton and Franklin "legal bondage" and encouraged his former student to consider government service. With the depression continuing, Corcoran also remembered some advice Justice Holmes had given to him: "You can't just sit outside and do nothing but criticize. You've got to be in the arena where you're working with the actual problems of government."

The opportunity came when Eugene Meyer, chairman of the Federal Reserve Board, invited George Franklin, senior partner of Cotton and Franklin, to join the newly established Reconstruction Finance Corporation as its general counsel. The RFC, which Meyer also headed, had been established on January 22 to provide loans for banks, railroads, insurance companies, and even agricultural cooperatives. It was viewed as a vehicle to jump-start the economy. Under Charles G. Dawes, vice president under Calvin Coolidge, the RFC loaned $1.2 billion in its first six months.

Walter Lippmann, the social and political commentator, once observed that in a sense the New Deal started not with election of Roosevelt, but with the RFC, which had been established by Hoover.

Franklin was ready to accept the post when Joseph Cotton was suddenly killed in an automobile accident in Baltimore. Franklin decided not to leave the firm and recommended Corcoran instead. Even though he was a Democrat, Corcoran had a favorable impression of President Hoover and strongly supported the notion of using a government agency like the RFC to make loans to businesses in order to stimulate the national economy. On the advice of his former professor Felix Frankfurter, Corcoran had read the economic theories of Harold Laski and John Maynard Keynes and strongly believed in the effectiveness of public works. Although the general counsel position was given to Martin Bogue, a former corporate lawyer from New York, Corcoran accepted a job as one of his assistants.

Corcoran returned to a city that was far different from the one he had left only four years before. In 1927 the nation's capital was in the midst of a building boom, but in 1931 even the District of Columbia was experiencing hard times. On the outskirts of the city, dozens of "Hoovervilles" — ramshackle shelters — were thrown together as the unemployed descended on the capital. Each day hundreds of protesters, mostly the homeless, gathered in front of the White House or on the Capitol grounds to demand that the government take action. Those vacant lots not filled with shanties were converted to vegetable gardens to help feed the poor who couldn't afford the thirty-five cents it cost for a pound of chicken.

Corcoran and several other young attorneys, including a colleague at the RFC, Edward Foley Jr., rented a small house on Thirty-fifth Place in Georgetown. Foley, like Corcoran, was Irish Catholic. Originally from Syracuse, New York, his father had been a prominent Republican. After graduating from Fordham Law School, Foley had come to Washington to join the Hoover administration. He and Corcoran became close friends.

Corcoran also resumed his regular visits to Justice Holmes, who was now ninety-one years old. The young lawyer would come by in the evenings and the justice's Irish cook would make them dinner. After dining they would adjourn to the study and Corcoran would read to Holmes. As Corcoran recalled, "My first year was just an introduction to the wonder of him."

While Corcoran enjoyed being back in the city, making new friends and seeing Holmes, for the first time in his professional career he was bored. He specialized in reviewing loans for municipal power plants. Even more distressing than his particular job was that he found himself working in a bureaucracy that seemed unable and unwilling to respond to the very needs that it had been created to address.

By July the economic depression had worsened considerably. Congress responded by passing the Relief and Construction Act, enabling the RFC to provide loans for local public works and to lend money to states for relief programs. The borrowing power of the RFC shot up to $3.3 billion. However, the agency had only a minor economic impact and was bogged down in bureaucratic red tape. Banks feared the onus of an RFC loan after Speaker John Nance Garner of Texas and Senator James Byrnes of South Carolina both insisted that RFC loans be publicized. States refused to apply for the three hundred million dollars available to them because they were first required to acknowledge virtual bankruptcy. By October 1, 1932, the RFC had made only thirty-five million in loans to states and public relief agencies. The RFC also had the ability to make agricultural loans, but here too, the agency had little impact on commodity prices.

In the summer of 1932 a discouraged Corcoran wrote to Frankfurter, "Very little stuff of half decent economic feasibility has come in from private enterprise." Corcoran also complained that even when banks sought loans, the RFC acted with agonizing slowness. Strong applications by state and local governments for public works were often greeted with unfounded skepticism by conservative political appointees, who simply believed that the federal government should not be competing with private enterprise. Corcoran blamed President Hoover for the economic paralysis. He was predisposed to dislike Hoover anyway, because the president had failed to offer Justice Holmes the chief justice position in 1930 when William Howard Taft stepped down. Holmes was ninety years old at the time and would not have accepted the post — which in Corcoran's mind was all the more reason it should have been offered to him. Corcoran wrote his brother David that Hoover "has been afraid to lead on anything."

Corcoran's disillusionment gave way to cautious optimism in the fall when Franklin Roosevelt defeated President Hoover in a landslide victory. FDR garnered almost twenty-three million of the nearly thirty-nine million votes cast, and nearly 90 percent of the electoral college. Corcoran had not been particularly impressed with FDR when he was governor of New York. But Justice Holmes told his young friend, "Even though Roosevelt may not have the intellect, he has the temperament." Holmes, according to Corcoran, believed that this was exactly what the country needed, and given that Holmes was a Republican, Corcoran decided to reserve judgment. Moreover, Felix Frankfurter fervently supported Roosevelt. Since his salary had risen to nine thousand dollars, Corcoran decided that he could afford to stay in Washington and remain in government a little while longer.

President Roosevelt first met Professor Felix Frankfurter during World War I, when Roosevelt was the assistant secretary of the navy and Frankfurter the head of the War Labor Policy Board. Roosevelt was impressed by Frankfurter's intelligence, and the two men developed a friendship. As governor of New York, Roosevelt frequently called on Frankfurter, who was by this time a professor of law at Harvard, for advice on public utility regulation in the Empire State. "Felix has more ideas per minute than any man of my acquaintance," Roosevelt observed on one occasion.

By the time of FDR's inauguration on March 4, 1933, the economy was in desperate shape. More than five thousand banks had suspended operations at some point during the previous two years. Twenty-four states had declared bank holidays. In order to prevent runs on banks, almost every bank in the nation had closed or restricted its operations. On the first day that the new Congress met after the inauguration, both chambers overwhelmingly passed the Emergency Banking Relief Act granting the new president unprecedented power to take emergency actions with regard to the nation's banking system. Corcoran, not wanting to lose his personal savings a second time, decided to take "one half out of the bank and leave one half in."

Not only were banks failing, but the financial markets were near collapse as well. In February 1933 the Senate Banking Committee had commenced hearings into the improprieties and manipulations on Wall Street. The committee's chief counsel, Ferdinand Pecora — later a close friend of Corcoran's — interrogated a parade of Wall Street bankers and brokers who admitted to unethical and sometimes illegal market practices.

In the wake of these hearings President Roosevelt asked Frankfurter to assemble the best possible legal team to review the nation's securities laws.

Frankfurter immediately called Tommy Corcoran. Next, Frankfurter enlisted the help of a cerebral young lawyer named Benjamin Cohen.

Whether he knew it or not, Frankfurter had paired two lawyers who became perhaps the best legal team in the annals of American government. Indeed, one reporter noted, Corcoran and Cohen together wielded "more influence at the White House and throughout the White House, and are more of a force through the entire reaches of the government than any pair of statesmen in Washington."

4

Battling Wall Street

In early March 1933, on the occasion of Oliver Wendell Holmes's ninety-second birthday, Corcoran helped organize a small luncheon party at the justice's home on I Street. Felix Frankfurter was there, as was Donald Hiss, Holmes's secretary and the younger brother of Alger Hiss. Unbeknownst to the justice or the other guests, Frankfurter had also invited the newly inaugurated president, Franklin Roosevelt. At around noon the president arrived in large black sedan accompanied by his son James and his wife, Eleanor. The president was helped up the stairs to Holmes's house. Even though he was confined to a wheelchair, Roosevelt had enormous presence. For one thing, he was exceedingly handsome, with a strong square jaw, flashing blue eyes, and a broad smile. He wore a pince nez and a gray wool cape that gave him a distinctly aristocratic air. After greeting the justice, he extended his hand to Tommy Corcoran. Corcoran, only thirty-three years old, an obscure government attorney, had just met the man who would change his life.

The country was still under Prohibition, but Donald Hiss had managed to secure a magnum of champagne from a bootlegger. Hiss, however, told Holmes that the British ambassador had sent the champagne — as the ambassador had done when Corcoran was secretary. Holmes called champagne "fizzle water," but he enjoyed it and had long since finished the last bottle in his wine cellar. He drank three or four glasses and cheerfully told the fifty-one-year-old Frankfurter, "Young fellow, I don't want you to misunderstand things; I do not deal with bootleggers, but I am open to corruption."

Prohibition would be repealed at the end of the year, an act that seemed to give the economy a brief stimulus. But the underlying fundamentals of the economy continued to be extremely weak. The Federal Trade Commission, which monitored the financial markets, reported that major industries were no longer registering new securities. In Congress, the House Commerce Committee issued a report stating that "during the postwar decade, some fifty billion of new securities were floated in the United States. Fully half . . . have proved to be worthless." Americans had lost faith in the financial markets; speculation and corruption seemed endemic and irreversible.

Part of the problem was the absence of uniform national legislation regulating the securities business in the United States. Both the underwriting and the trading of stocks were regulated on a state-by-state basis. In order to float a new issue nationally, forty-eight different state securities commissions needed to grant approval. No single enforcement agency monitored the trading of stocks, and the system was rife with manipulation.

Upon taking office in 1933, FDR outlined an extraordinarily ambitious program for his first one hundred days. Congress passed numerous recovery measures, including the Federal Emergency Relief Act, the National Employment System Act, the National Industrial Recovery Act, the Agricultural Adjustment Act, and the Economy Act. Congress also created the Civilian Conservation Corps, the Tennessee Valley Authority, and the Federal Deposit Insurance Corporation. The power and reach of government were vastly expanded.

The president had announced that securities and exchange legislation also would be among the "ten" must items of his first hundred days. Roosevelt appointed Samuel Untermeyer, an aging lawyer who had been the counsel for the 1912 Pujo "Money Trust" hearings, to draft the law. When Untermeyer proposed nothing more than the supervision of stocks and bonds by the post office, FDR turned to the author of the 1932 Democratic plank on securities reform, Huston Thompson, a former FTC commissioner. But Sam Rayburn of Texas, the chairman of the powerful House Commerce Committee, was not impressed by Thompson's efforts and advised the president to find someone else and to begin yet again.

In the Senate, meanwhile, hearings before the Senate Banking Committee were attracting national attention. In November 1932 Senator Duncan Fletcher of Florida had asked New York lawyer Ferdinand Pecora to take over the investigation into the banking industry and stock market — which despite months of hearings had produced few revelations. Pecora called his first witness, National City Bank chairman Charles Mitchell, on February 21. In the grand caucus room, one of the largest assembly rooms in the Senate and noted for its Corinthian columns, Pecora forced Mitchell to admit that not only had he paid no

income taxes in 1929, but the bank had engaged in illegal transactions
with another investment firm as well. Six days later Mitchell resigned.

In subsequent hearings Pecora exposed further corruption on Wall
Street. The newspaper coverage was intense and provoked national indig-
nation. On Capitol Hill, Senator Burton K. Wheeler of Montana reflected
the public sentiment when he said, "The best way to restore confidence in
the banks would be to take the crooked bank presidents out of the banks
and treat them the same way we treated Al Capone when he failed to pay
income tax."

But Wall Street refused to be steamrollered and countered with a
relentless and effective lobbying campaign in Congress. For a brief time
it appeared as though the securities legislation in the Senate might fail.
Roosevelt was concerned, fearing that if his administration was handed
such a significant defeat, he would be viewed as ineffective — and, far
worse, that the depression might deepen. The president telephoned Felix
Frankfurter in Cambridge, asking him to come to Washington with a
team of lawyers capable of overhauling the nation's securities laws.

Early on the morning of Friday, April 7, 1933, Professor Frankfurter,
accompanied by Ben Cohen and James Landis, arrived at Union Station
aboard the *Federal Express*. They were met by Corcoran on the platform.
Since Corcoran was the only one among them who actually lived and
worked in Washington, they initially convened in his small office at the
RFC. After Frankfurter laid out the broad parameters of a legislative
strategy, they rented a suite at the Carleton Hotel where the three young
lawyers could work without interruption. The professor left to spend the
weekend at the White House.

Corcoran and Landis had been friends at law school. Neither of them
knew the shy Cohen, who was tall, lanky, and six years their senior. For
the next forty-eight hours the three men worked closely together, drafting legislation to regulate the American securities industry. Landis,
Harvard's first professor of litigation, had the best understanding of how
the markets worked, although Corcoran, with his years on Wall Street,
also had important experience. Cohen was the legal technician — a brilliant draftsman. He had spent several years in London working for a
Zionist organization and was familiar with the disclosure provisions of
the British Companies Act, which would be the model for their draft.
Although Corcoran's political experience had been limited, he *had*

worked in Washington, and of the three lawyers he knew the most about Congress and what might pass.

To help with the typing, Corcoran asked the RFC to send over a young secretary named Peggy Dowd. Dowd, later described by her cousin, *New York Times* columnist Maureen Dowd, as a "dimpled, green-eyed, Grace Kelly type," was only twenty-two years old. She had met Corcoran a few weeks earlier when she had been sent to his office by the chief of the secretarial pool. "You're Irish. Maybe you can handle him," she was told. Indeed, during their first encounter Corcoran sat behind his desk chomping on a cigar and barking orders when Peggy interrupted him and said coolly, "Take the cigar out of your mouth or I won't take dictation from you." Corcoran, looking stunned but amused, obliged.

The three lawyers and their secretary worked through the weekend, drinking coffee, taking catnaps, and occasionally going out for a quick meal. On one occasion they entered an elevator to be greeted by the fierce stare of J. P. Morgan Jr., who had rented a suite of rooms above them to plot a counterstrategy. They silently rode the elevator together.

When Frankfurter returned Sunday night to review their work, he found a bill that was much more restrictive — and therefore hostile to Wall Street — than he had anticipated. But after conferring with his three young protégés, whom he now referred to as "the three musketeers," he agreed to defend it before Rayburn's House Commerce Committee the next month, on May 3.

A diminutive figure at the long oak table in the commerce committee hearing room, Frankfurter explained point by point why it was necessary to provide the public with adequate information about the issuance of new securities. He proclaimed a need to make the administration of the law "almost a matter of mechanical and compulsory routine." Only then would the public be adequately protected.

Frankfurter's presentation was persuasive. By 5 P.M. the committee had agreed in principle to the legislation, although several sections would have to be reworked. Frankfurter immediately returned to Cambridge to pack his suitcases. The professor had been granted a sabbatical from Harvard and had accepted a position at Oxford University. He sailed for England only a few weeks after his testimony before the commerce committee. Chairman Rayburn asked Corcoran, Cohen, and Landis to continue the drafting process. Landis and Cohen set up shop in the musty basement office of the House Legislative Counsel, and at night worked in their seventh-floor hotel room. Tommy Corcoran, who was still working at the RFC, joined them in the evenings and, as he remembered it, "drank coffee laced with sugar and memorized the ceiling patterns." He also tried to mediate between Landis and Cohen, both former clerks to Justice Brandeis, who were not getting along. Although shy, Cohen refused to be bullied by the more arrogant Landis and refused to make the changes Landis suggested. Cohen wrote to Frankfurter, "Things were a little trying for a while, but I guess we will pull through all right. Tom is a prince and someday will be a king."

With Frankfurter in England, Corcoran and Cohen regularly sought advice from one of the professor's mentors, Justice Louis Brandeis. In 1933 the justice was seventy-seven years old and had been on the Supreme Court since being appointed by President Wilson in 1916. Although in his youth he had been a Republican, by the second decade of the twentieth century he was a prominent legal and political activist well known for his distrust of the concentration of power in either business or government. In 1913 he published a series of articles in *Harper's Magazine,* later published as a collection in a book titled *Other People's Money,* in which he argued that corporate consolidation posed an ominous threat to individualism and ultimately to democracy.

Corcoran regularly wrote to Frankfurter at Oxford, keeping him abreast of his meetings with Brandeis, whom he had nicknamed Isaiah after the prophet. In one letter Corcoran told Frankfurter, "Long talk with Isaiah sticking. Don't worry." And on another occasion, as the bill neared a vote on the floor of the House, Corcoran reassured Frankfurter, "Even if you haven't anything but cables, you can always be comfortable that I always take advice — and that I haven't moved an inch in a general course without going to L. D. B." Brandeis was also keeping Frankfurter informed: "Tom Cochrane [sic] is doing grand service, and everyone loves him — quite naturally."

Corcoran and Cohen were also consulting on a daily basis with the chairman of the House Commerce Committee, Sam Rayburn of Texas. Rayburn, short, stocky, bald, and charismatic, quickly recognized the dazzling brilliance of the two young lawyers. Rayburn recalled that "I always told them what I wanted and by God, they'd give you what you wanted."

He also recognized how well the pair complemented each other's talents: "Taken together, those two fellows made the most brilliant man I ever saw."

The drafting process continued well into the summer. Wall Street interests demanded additional hearings, and coteries of corporate lawyers, led by John Foster Dulles — later President Eisenhower's secretary of state — came to Washington to object to what they perceived as the heavy-handed regulation being proposed by the administration. Corcoran would later remember Dulles as nothing more than a "grudge-bearing aristocrat" who refused to compromise. In fact, the legislation, modeled on the British system of securities regulation, was relatively modest in scope. While the bill curbed some speculative excesses, its primary thrust was to provide self-regulation through the disclosure of all material elements in the registration of a security.

After numerous hearings and nearly four weeks of deliberation by the Congress, the bill to regulate the securities industry was reported out of committee and called up for debate on the floor of the House of Representatives. With Cohen sitting by his side and Corcoran in the gallery, Chairman Rayburn gripped the lectern and presided over six hours of debate. Rayburn successfully fended off any amendments that might have jeopardized passage of the bill, and it won unanimous approval.

After his spring in Washington spearheading the drafting of this legislation, Cohen returned to New York. A few weeks later Edward Foley Jr., Corcoran's roommate, called Frankfurter to ask him to suggest a good man to head the legal staff at the Public Works Administration. Foley had gotten his job at the PWA on Corcoran's recommendation, and while he was an excellent lawyer, he was also extremely young. Frankfurter promptly responded to Foley, "I have just the man for you. He knows more about public works than anyone I know. His name is Ben Cohen." Foley had met Cohen a few times in Corcoran's presence, but he didn't really know him. So he asked Corcoran, "Who on earth is this man of Frankfurter's?"

Corcoran smiled. "I'll get him for you."

5

The Little Red Schoolhouse

In drafting the Securities Exchange Act, Tommy Corcoran, Ben Cohen, and James Landis had worked extremely closely with one another, sometimes creating an uneasy tension, but often resulting in a creative and exciting process. Corcoran's respect for Landis's intelligence was reinforced, though he had questions about the man's commitment to real reform. Corcoran felt Landis was "an easily flattered man" whom the president could buy off "with a rosy glow of false optimism." Landis drifted away from his partnership with the two men, at least in part because he was married and Corcoran and Cohen were bachelors. Landis sent for his wife and daughters in Massachusetts to come to Washington. After Cohen returned to Washington, he and Corcoran quickly became extremely close friends even though they were truly an odd couple.

Ben Cohen was the son of a prosperous scrap iron dealer from Muncie, Indiana. Six years older than Corcoran, he had graduated with a degree in economics from the University of Chicago, where Professor Harold G. Moulton called him "the most brilliant student I ever taught." Cohen also received a law degree from the University of Chicago and then went to Harvard for postgraduate legal studies, where, like Corcoran, he caught the eye of Felix Frankfurter.

After Harvard, Cohen clerked for a circuit court judge and then, on the recommendation of Frankfurter, for Supreme Court justice Louis Brandeis. After his clerkship, while he was in London working for a Zionist organization, he became involved in the only romantic relationship of his life. After the romance ended, Cohen returned to the United States. He entered private practice and made a small fortune on Wall Street investing in the stock of the Chrysler automobile company. On the recommendation of Justice Frankfurter, Cohen decided to try public service and, with Corcoran's help, landed a job as the associate general counsel to the Public Works Administration, where, like Corcoran, he ultimately exercised significantly greater power and influence than was suggested by his inconspicuous title.

Cohen was shy and bookish, and though he had worked on Wall Street, he had the air of a professor with his unkempt hair, baggy suits, and wire-rimmed glasses. Corcoran was ebullient, energetic, and emotional, but he found in Cohen an intellectual soul mate. Recognizing that his friend had no ability to promote himself, Corcoran sang the praises of Cohen to anyone who would listen.

As bachelors, Corcoran and Cohen enjoyed a much different lifestyle from Landis's. With no family and with few diversions, they entertained themselves in the evenings by gathering friends from other parts of the government for dinner and an evening of debate about the issues of the day. Corcoran drank sparingly, but he could often be found after work at Martin's Bar on Wisconsin Avenue regaling his colleagues with stories.

On weekends Corcoran liked to host dinners, but his house on Thirty-fifth Place was proving too small for entertaining. Ben Cohen had a small apartment and since he spent virtually all of his free time with Corcoran anyway, Peggy Dowd, the young secretary from the RFC who was increasingly serving as Corcoran's private assistant, suggested that the two young lawyers rent a house together. Corcoran located a redbrick house in Georgetown, which soon came to be known as the "Little Red Schoolhouse" — a reference to both tenants' intellectualism and perceived radicalism.

Several other young lawyers whom Corcoran had known in New York and then recruited for the RFC were invited to join them as housemates, including Tom's youngest brother, Howard; Dick Guggenheim, a Republican, graduate of Harvard Law School, and scion of the San Francisco shipping family; Ed Burke, later the chief counsel of the Securities and Exchange Commission; Stuart Guthrie, the oldest of the group and a former Teddy Roosevelt supporter; Merritt M. Willis, a Philadelphian and graduate of Harvard Law School; and Frank Watson, also a Harvard Law School graduate. No particular political orthodoxy bound together the occupants of the Little Red Schoolhouse. As Frank Watson recalled, "We arrived with no particular theories about remaking the world. I never heard Tom mention anything of that kind. He was in Washington to straighten out a mess, and as soon as the mess was straightened out, he was going to leave. And so were all the rest of us." With that objective in mind, Corcoran urged his roommates and friends to "take fire from one another."

The house at 3238 R Street had been used by Ulysses S. Grant as his summer White House during his terms as president. It was a very old, large, three-story, Italianate building. The walls needed to be painted, and the hardwood floors sanded. Watson remembered that the house was poorly insulated and its heating system was terribly inefficient: "The coal came in there by the ton, and it didn't seem to last a week to the truckload."

The young men living at R Street took turns managing the finances of the house. Corcoran set the salaries at the RFC for the lawyers in the counsel's office and no one made more than ten thousand dollars a year, but because there were so many of them sharing costs, the rent was relatively cheap for even the most modest wage earner. Still, they always seemed to exceed the monthly assessment. They hired a housekeeper and a gardener, but, according to Watson, "The costs ran out of sight because Tom would bring in three or four guests any night, without saying a word, and then other nights there would not be anybody but the cook would have made a big dinner because nobody would have reported that he would be out." Watson concluded, "It was a very poorly managed affair."

Those evenings when all the roommates were actually home were festive occasions. Tommy provided the entertainment, taking a turn on the accordion — which he had only recently taught himself to play — or the piano, which he had been playing since childhood. Indeed, Corcoran's musical talent would prove to be extremely useful in Washington as a means for disarming his enemies and charming his friends. Watson recalled that "Tom was the leader of the group. [H]e wanted everybody to be happy. . . . He kept his eye on everybody. He was an all-engrossing personality."

One evening Corcoran invited to dinner Carlisle Bolton-Smith, a Memphis-born lawyer. Corcoran had enticed Bolton-Smith to leave the prestigious law firm of Cravath, Swaine and Moore in New York for a job at the Department of Agriculture. About 9 P.M. the telephone rang and Corcoran answered. "It was Hobby Hobson. He and Tommy chatted for a minute," Bolton-Smith recalled many years later. "Then Tommy said, 'Why don't you come over here and bring your piano!' " Hobson was a fine classical pianist, and about an hour later he showed up, followed by four men carrying his piano. They placed it adjacent to Corcoran's piano in the living room and the two of them played together into the early hours of the morning.

The activity at the Georgetown house was so constant and frenetic that Corcoran and Cohen also rented an apartment at 1610 K Street where they could go to work in the evenings. The two young lawyers would often work for forty-eight hours straight. After a marathon drafting session, Cohen would unwind by going to the movies, where typically he would watch the opening credits and then fall fast asleep. Joe Rauh, a fellow New Dealer, remembered how Cohen would "talk about how he loved movies, but I don't think he ever saw any."

Tommy didn't have any close female friends during this period. Indeed, one young New Dealer, Cornelia Wickenden, claimed that "Tom was anti-female." Corcoran placed men all over the government, but according to Wickenden, he never recommended "a woman above the rank of secretary." Tommy's views on women were derived from a number of sources. He had grown up in a very Catholic household and tended to have conservative social mores. He didn't believe, for instance, that boys and girls should be educated together: "It bothers me somehow to have the breeds of cat mix." Moreover, his mother had warned him not to trust women, and his brief infatuation with Isabel Cotton seems to have validated that view. And finally, there just weren't very many women in government or the overall workforce.

When Tommy wanted to relax, he often dropped by Justice Holmes's town house to read to him. The old jurist still had a vibrant intellect and a biting wit, and Corcoran thoroughly enjoyed his company. Besides the Hiss brothers, Corcoran made the acquaintance of other of Holmes's law clerks, including Mark DeWolfe Howe and H. Chapman Rose. But it was Holmes's clerk during the 1934–1935 session with whom Corcoran became particularly friendly.

James H. Rowe grew up in Butte, Montana. After graduating from the University of Montana, he attended Harvard Law School where, like so many of the most capable students, he became a protégé of Professor Frankfurter. Frankfurter encouraged him to work in Washington after law school. He spent two years as an attorney at the National Emergency Council. Frankfurter then arranged for him a clerkship with Holmes. At six foot two, Rowe towered over the smaller and more sturdy Corcoran. Even though Rowe was nine years younger, the two men became close friends. Corcoran was attracted to Rowe's easy manner, self-deprecating wit, and strategic mind, and Rowe, somewhat in awe of Corcoran's energy, was delighted by his humor and optimism. It was a friendship that would last for nearly half a century.

By the fall of 1934 Corcoran had moved over to the Treasury Department to be assistant to Undersecretary Dean Acheson, who at forty years old was considered one of the rising young stars of a young administration. Acheson gave Corcoran two jobs: working with the RFC on the fragile bank situation and supervising the Coast Guard.

The Coast Guard was a small, antiquated agency with the dual missions of search and rescue, and enforcing tariffs. Because of Prohibition, the Coast Guard had been particularly involved in patrolling the country's ports and coasts to catch bootleggers. While Rear Admiral Harry Hamlet had requisitioned numerous old World War I destroyers to carry out its mission, the service was in need of modern vessels and new leadership. Although the Coast Guard had drawn up specifications for new vessels, Corcoran worked with the Navy Department to design more modern, versatile ones. Corcoran managed to obtain thirty thousand dollars — at the time a significant amount of money — from the Public Works Administration to build them, and then had them loaned by the navy to the Coast Guard.

Within months of Corcoran's move to Treasury, the secretary, William H. Woodin, became incapacitated by throat cancer and Dean Acheson was given the title of acting secretary. Corcoran enjoyed working with Acheson and enthusiastically informed Frankfurter that "Dean's relations with me are very confidential and of the best," although he noted somewhat impishly that Acheson "gives me the impression . . . that he doesn't understand and is a little afraid of my extracurricular activities 'running the rest of the government.'"

The president and the acting secretary did not enjoy such a close relationship. President Roosevelt was concerned that banks continued to resist lending and that, to stimulate the economy, he needed to raise commodity prices — necessitating, he believed, that he raise the price of gold. Roosevelt thereupon urged the Treasury Department to buy gold until the price rose. Acheson opposed the idea on the grounds that the Treasury Department did not have the legal authority to buy gold at a price higher than the current statutory limit. However, Roosevelt concluded, "I say it is legal," and the discussion ended. Acheson, outraged by what he perceived as the president's heavy-handed meddling, resigned. Corcoran, loyal to Acheson, felt the acting secretary had been treated "very cheaply and crudely." It was his first exposure to Roosevelt's sometimes rough handling of staff.

In the wake of Acheson's dispute with the White House, Corcoran wrote Frankfurter that he felt he should begin to consider other possible positions in the administration, although he despaired of finding anything that would suit him as well as the Treasury job: "My relations with Dean were ideal: My job didn't interfere with my work; he asked no questions about my running around town." Professor Frankfurter agreed to help and in late September typed a note to Missy LeHand, the president's personal secretary. "Dear Miss LeHand," Frankfurter wrote, "I venture to give this note to a very dear friend of mine, Thomas G. Corcoran. . . . He is a most valuable public servant and one of the most indefatigable workers for the success of this administration. From time to time he may come to you about matters, and I commend him to you warmly. He is a person of entire dependability."

Besides being the president's secretary, LeHand performed many of the functions of a modern-day chief of staff, acting as a gatekeeper and making sure that various tasks assigned by the president were followed through with. She was Catholic, unswervingly loyal to her boss — and, as it happened, very pretty. Although it is not clear when she first met Tommy Corcoran, she was immediately charmed by him. One evening shortly after Tommy and Missy had become acquainted, the president had a small dinner party. Roosevelt often enjoyed watching a movie after dinner, but for some reason there was no entertainment this particular evening. As Joe Alsop later described it, LeHand suggested Corcoran and he "was summoned, and played [the piano] before the President, with his fair and goodly countenance."

By mid-December Corcoran's position at the Treasury Department had become untenable, and he expressed his unhappiness in a letter to Frankfurter: "I can stay in the Treasury indefinitely: nobody will fire me. But I'm terribly under suspicion as Dean's right hand; and there's transferred to me a lot of the defensive feeling. . . ." Corcoran decided to return to his old job at the RFC. "I don't think I'll make a mistake. It's my temporary strategic retreat."

The RFC was now headed by a Roosevelt loyalist, Jesse Jones, a sixty-year-old Texan known as a political operator who could get things done. Jones was a large, square-jawed man with a white mane of hair. One colleague later wrote, "Jones loved power, thought big and had his way." Corcoran also had a new boss in the general counsel's office, Stanley Reed. Reed had been practicing law in Kentucky on behalf of tobacco companies when President Hoover appointed him general counsel to the Federal Farm Bureau in 1929. He was a skilled lawyer and soon had Corcoran's respect, as well as his friendship. Reed also gave Corcoran enormous leeway in his job by unofficially designating him a sort of chief of staff without portfolio, with duties that varied from bank reorganizations, to oversight of the Coast Guard, to financing the Electric Home and Farm Authority and other aspects of public hydraulic power.

Corcoran recruited numerous young lawyers, mostly Harvard law graduates, to come work at the RFC. As one of the recruits, Thomas Emerson, recalled, "Frankfurter sent me to Corcoran, which was the classic way to get a job in the New Deal." During the years with the RFC, Corcoran recruited some three to four hundred lawyers in a variety of agencies and departments. He gave great attention to placing lawyers he felt might "take fire from one another" in the same department. The press began to refer to the "Corcoran gallery of lawyers," as distinguished from the Corcoran Gallery of Art. New Deal historian Jordan Swartz has written that Corcoran "spearheaded a cultural revolution" by introducing the best and brightest young Catholic and Jewish lawyers into what had heretofore been a strictly WASP enclave.

As quickly as he hired bright young attorneys, he put them to work. Charles F. Wyzanski Jr. was only twenty-six and a recent graduate of Harvard Law School when Corcoran found him a position in the Department of Labor. On his first day of work, Secretary of Labor Frances Perkins asked him to accompany her to a conference at the White House on public works. When Perkins introduced the young lawyer to the president, Wyzanski grew nervous and blurted out that he had actually voted for Herbert Hoover. Roosevelt smiled and replied, "I don't care" — but then, as if to tweak the young man for his poor judgment, demanded for the next day the draft of a bill on the ideas encompassed by the conference. Wyzanski returned to his office in a panic and called Corcoran, who told him not to worry, gave him some guidelines, and suggested some ideas. Wyzanski worked through the night; a bill was on the president's desk when he arrived for work in the morning.

Another young lawyer, Frank Watson, remembered that he was working in a Boston law office when he received a call from Corcoran. Within a very short time Watson had moved to Washington and was working at the RFC on multimillion-dollar bank transactions. As he later explained, "Without any particular title of authority, Tom just ran things. He assigned work, and gave us a little background on each bank we were working on." For Watson, "it was a very heady experience."

Corcoran continued to make regular reports to Professor Frankfurter on the progress of all the Harvard Law graduates as well as on the new administration in general. For his part, Frankfurter continued to promote his young protégé to anyone in the administration who would listen, including Raymond Moley, the president's most important adviser and de facto chief of staff, and even to the president himself. After he returned from Oxford in June 1934, Frankfurter resumed his visits to Washington, often traveling to the capital two or three times a month. According to Joe Rauh, another of Frankfurter's protégés, the professor "would see Roosevelt, and then he would see Tom."

6

Frankfurter's Hotdogs

As 1933 came to a close it was becoming apparent that the first securities bill, which had emphasized self-regulation through such means as disclosure — making public the finances of a corporation as well as its principal investors — was inadequate to restore confidence in the markets and prevent another financial collapse. The markets had stabilized, and there had even been a brief bull market during the first part of the year, but it had been stymied by a rash of short selling when market manipulators such as the financier Joseph P. Kennedy bet against a sustained recovery.

Public confidence in the nation's financial system remained low. A few days after Christmas, President Roosevelt summoned his principal economic adviser, former assistant secretary of state Raymond Moley, and told him to find someone to prepare a new bill that would provide an adequate oversight mechanism for the securities laws on the books.

Before joining Roosevelt in the White House, Moley had been a professor of public law at Columbia University. He was considered the leader of the Roosevelt "brain trust," the collection of young reformers who provided the intellectual underpinning for the early New Deal. Moley, who had only recently left government to assume the editorship of *Today* magazine, actually considered himself a conservative, and he "somewhat reluctantly . . . called in Tom Corcoran and Ben Cohen," whom he recognized had done an able job on the securities legislation earlier in the year. Moley told the president that "they would require watching, or their exuberance would get out of hand." Despite his reservations about their liberal philosophy, which he primarily ascribed to their relationship with Felix Frankfurter, he was nevertheless impressed with their energy.

The president accepted Moley's recommendation, and Corcoran and Cohen were again enlisted to draft legislation on behalf of the White House. They worked at a frenetic pace. Corcoran turned once more to Peggy Dowd, the young secretary at the RFC who had helped him prepare the 1933 Securities Act. Dowd, svelte and strawberry blond, had been secretary to Corcoran's R Street housemate and RFC colleague Frank Watson. Watson described her as "a brilliant individual and a beautiful girl." According to Watson, "She could type so fast you could hardly see the keys move, and at the same time carry on a conversation or ask a question." Corcoran was impressed by her competence, but increasingly he also enjoyed flirting with her. With Dowd typing and retyping numerous drafts, Corcoran and Cohen completed the basic bill in just days, although they continued to revise its language for weeks. On February 9 President Roosevelt sent legislation to Capitol Hill recommending exchange and regulatory legislation to protect investors, safeguard values, and eliminate "as far as it may be possible . . . unwise and destructive speculation." The fifty-page, highly technical bill had many purposes, including the regulation of corporate practices, foreign exchange, and the securities markets. It was referred to the House Commerce Committee, headed by Corcoran's friend Sam Rayburn, and to the Senate Banking Committee chaired by elderly Duncan U. Fletcher, a Florida Democrat.

Opposition to the bill from the Wall Street investment houses was immediate and unrestrained. According to Rayburn, Wall Street cobbled together "the most powerful lobby ever organized against any bill which ever came up in Congress." Richard Whitney, president of the New York Stock Exchange and a classmate of Roosevelt's at both Groton and Harvard, actually rented a mansion in Georgetown, nicknamed the Wall Street embassy, in order to direct the lobbying effort personally.

Whitney found important allies in the financial press. The *Wall Street Journal* described the bill as part of a disturbing trend toward "social control." *Business Week* charged that the bill was "ruthless" and "clumsy." The same magazine also claimed that those attempting to regulate the "delicate machinery" of the financial markets were doing so with "all the finesse of a Russian peasant." Even Corcoran's old boss at the Federal Reserve, Eugene Meyer, now the publisher of the *Washington Post*, claimed that the bill presaged "a State Control of Industry." Meyer pointedly criticized "the young intellectuals who are apparently directing the policy of this administration for their inexperience, their experimentation and their self-righteousness."

Corcoran was stung. Ben Cohen wrote to Frankfurter that Tommy had been "dreadfully alone in the battle," and that "he is a very tender and sensitive soul, much more so than his usual cheerful self would lead one to believe." Corcoran may have taken some solace from a letter he received in July from a Wall Street lawyer friend, Stuart Hedden. "They certainly do think around this town [New York City] that you are a pretty terrible fellow," Hedden wrote, "but as you know, you have many staunch defenders."

On Capitol Hill, Sam Rayburn worried as hostility both to Corcoran and to the bill intensified. Not only were Wall Street and the financial press opposed to the legislation, but some in the administration, including the top officials at the Department of the Treasury, the Federal Reserve, and the National Recovery Administration, were hoping it would fail. General Hugh Johnson, known as "Iron Pants," was in charge of the NRA, which issued codes governing American industry and the economy. Johnson had established a committee in the administration, the Capital Goods Committee, to suggest ways to revive the American economy, and, working with counsel to the New York Stock Exchange, he recommended that the legislation be defeated.

Corcoran may have felt alone and on the defensive, but he knew he had the support of the president and he began to fight back. He sifted through his network of contacts to find allies who might help. He knew a lawyer at the NRA, Milton Katz, whom he had originally hired at the RFC. One day Corcoran asked Katz to come to Chairman Rayburn's office. Katz arrived to find Rayburn, Cohen, and Corcoran all present. Explaining that Johnson, Katz's boss at the NRA, and the New York Stock Exchange were collaborating, Corcoran got right to the point: "Milt, now we've just got to lick these people. This is crucial, and we want you to work with us on it. You're in a strategic position and you can find out exactly what they are up to."

Katz, who recalled the scene many years later, remembered feeling confused by Corcoran's comments. "You mean you want me to resign and work for you?"

"Hell, no," Corcoran snapped back. "You're no use to us here. You're of use to us precisely because you're there."

Katz, now recognizing that Corcoran wanted him to act as a mole, recoiled. "I don't know, but it is my impression that as a lawyer, I have some responsibility to my clients."

"Where did you get all that nonsense?" Corcoran yelled. "You do what you're told."

But Katz demurred and eventually he left Rayburn's office, as he put it, "disgraced."

Working with Rayburn, Corcoran devised a plan to weaken the opposition. Several respected moderates among the brokerage and investment houses understood that some government oversight and enforcement was both needed and inevitable. Prominent investment bankers such as Robert Lovett of Brown Brothers, Harriman, and James V. Forrestal of Dillon, Read were offered the opportunity not only to testify but also to work with Corcoran and Cohen on redrafting certain portions of the bill.

Corcoran and Cohen negotiated with officials at the Treasury and the Federal Reserve as well. They agreed to give the Federal Reserve the power to provide more elasticity to the nation's money supply by lowering and raising margin requirements. They also reduced the bill's liability provisions. Raymond Moley, Roosevelt's top adviser at the time, wrote Felix Frankfurter that Corcoran and Cohen had done "a magnificent job." Moley praised the young lawyers for having been "tactful and skillful in handling the obvious necessity of yielding certain important aspects in the interests of holding to the essentials."

As hearings on the legislation neared, Rayburn, who had come to admire both Corcoran and Cohen greatly, decided that Corcoran could defend the bill better than anyone else in the administration, and so he asked him to testify. On March 9, 1934, Tommy Corcoran, thirty-four years old, sat alone at the long oak table in the commerce committee room. As members from the House of Representatives on the dais peppered him with questions, he proved himself not only knowledgeable about the securities industry, but an able debater as well. He confidently answered detailed questions from the general counsel of the New York Stock Exchange. And when congressmen attempted to challenge his bona fides, he successfully parried their attacks: When Republican John Cooper of Ohio asked Corcoran why he was there, if he was officially representing the RFC, and if he had been authorized to draft the securities and exchange bill, Corcoran blithely replied that his activities were "something extracurricular."

Although Corcoran had met Roosevelt on more than one occasion, his appearance before the Rayburn committee captured the president's attention. FDR telephoned the young lawyer and congratulated him on a stellar performance: "By God, you're the first man I've had who could handle himself on the Hill."

But the fighting was not over. Debate opened on the floor of the House of Representatives, with the chairman of the committee, Sam Rayburn, leading off. Rayburn eloquently described the substance of the legislation and then inveighed against the New York Stock Exchange for waging such an intense, hostile, and protracted propaganda campaign against the bill.

The Republicans ignored Rayburn's charges. Leading the Republican attack was Harold McGugin of Kansas, who took the floor and complained that "It is not the Fletcher-Rayburn bill, it is the Corcoran-Cohen bill." According to McGugin, "These gentlemen are a couple of self-styled intellectuals, a couple of Felix Frankfurter's protégés, a couple of men who do not and could not obtain the support of any congressional constituency in the United States, yet they can write the bill, sit in the galleries and watch Congress move while they crack the whip."

Following McGugin, Republican Fred Britten of Illinois took direct aim at Corcoran and Cohen, labeling them "Frankfurter's hotdogs," and "the scarlet fever boys down in the little red house in Georgetown." Britten amplified his red-scare message by charging that Corcoran and Cohen hoped to "Russianize everything under the unqualified and unprepared Federal Trade Commission."

After Britten's venomous attack, Sam Rayburn jumped to his feet and addressed his colleagues, speaking slowly in his Texas accent. "I thought we had had enough of this little red house stuff — and it is stuff." Rayburn said it was unfair to enlist the services of Corcoran and Cohen, whom no one disputed as experts in the field, and then to characterize them "as being somebody from Russia or being tainted with socialism or communism." They were, he went on, "two of the ablest young men it has been my privilege to know."

Despite the bitter tone of the debate, the House passed the bill 280 to 84. In the end the congressmen had voted with their constituents, who were clearly demanding that the financial markets be brought under government supervision. On June 6 the president, with Corcoran, Cohen, Rayburn, Fletcher, and Pecora standing behind him, signed the legisla-

tion establishing the Securities and Exchange Commission. Author Ron
Chernow later observed what Tommy Corcoran undoubtedly felt at the
time: "The money changers had been chased from the temple by the Irish,
the Italians, and the Jews — the groups excluded from Wasp Wall Street
during the 1920's."

Even before the ink was dry on the president's signature, Corcoran
began pressing for the appointment of his colleague Ben Cohen to the
five-person commission that would control the new agency. Cohen was
too modest to push his own name forward, but Corcoran had no such
reservations. He succeeded in convincing Moley, who told Roosevelt that
Cohen was "as able as Landis and more experienced." But FDR demurred,
fearing an anti-Semitic backlash. From England, Frankfurter wrote to
Corcoran a dispirited letter: "I don't have to tell you that the leading
Jewish bankers and the leading Jewish Wall Street lawyers feel about Ben
Cohen's influence and the myths of my own influence in the administration precisely as their non-Jewish colleagues in finance and at the bar."
Not wishing to place the president in an awkward position, Cohen
removed himself from consideration.

In late June Roosevelt asked one of the richest men in the country,
Joseph P. Kennedy, to be chairman of the Securities and Exchange
Commission. Kennedy had raised substantial funds for Roosevelt in 1932
and had lobbied many of his business associates to support the
Democratic nominee. In return, Kennedy hoped to be appointed secretary of the Treasury. When Roosevelt offered only the chairmanship of a
new commission, many felt that Kennedy would turn it down, but to
everyone's surprise and to Corcoran's horror, he accepted. Reflecting on
the choice of Kennedy years later, Corcoran observed that "Roosevelt
didn't want strong men in the cabinet," yet "Joe had the sense to recognize the opportunity" and understood that "there was stature with the
SEC." Corcoran feared that Kennedy would be in the pocket of Wall
Street, but he didn't personally lobby against the man, telling Moley,
"We've got four of the five [commissioners] anyway. Four are for us and
one is for business." Other liberal insiders were equally distressed.
Secretary of the Interior Harold Ickes referred in his diary to Kennedy as
"a stock market plunger."

After securing office space in the Interstate Commerce Building on
Pennsylvania Avenue, Kennedy set about winning over his critics. Less

than a week after being nominated, he met with Corcoran and Cohen to seek their advice on a variety of subjects related to the commission. He asked them point-blank, "Why do you fellows hate me?" He assured them that he was not predisposed to Wall Street, that he knew there were others with more knowledge of the law than he had, and that he would build a first-rate staff. Corcoran, still smarting from Roosevelt's decision not to nominate Cohen as a commissioner, now urged Kennedy to appoint his friend as the commission's chief counsel. But Kennedy instead chose John Burns, a Boston judge and an old friend who, ironically, had been a classmate of Corcoran's at Harvard Law School. Corcoran remained skeptical of Kennedy, but eventually acknowledged that "Joe picked good men to put in, and he won people over. . . ." Eventually, Kennedy would even win over Corcoran.

7

Battling Big Business

The midterm election of 1934 greatly strengthened the hand of President Roosevelt. Democrats added to their majorities in both the House of Representatives and the Senate, where they now held nearly two-thirds of the seats. Roosevelt viewed the election as a strong endorsement for the New Deal policies that he had set forth two years earlier. In his State of the Union address to the Congress in 1935, the president talked of building a democracy that was free of "the appetite of great wealth and power" epitomized by the nation's economic conglomerates. Roosevelt was set to take on the concentration of power in the public utilities industry. There was only one thing in his way: his vice president, John Nance Garner.

A few weeks after the speech, Roosevelt sent thirty-four-year-old Tommy Corcoran to talk with Vice President Garner about the proposed public utility holding company bill that the president supported. Garner, who was from Texas, had been the Speaker of the House of Representatives when he was chosen as Roosevelt's running mate to provide regional balance and congressional support for the Democratic ticket in 1932. After the election Roosevelt virtually ignored his vice president, causing Garner to ultimately characterize the vice presidency as "not worth a pitcher of warm spit." But in this particular instance Roosevelt knew that if Garner, a former banker and businessman, opposed the legislation, its chances for passage would be severely diminished.

As vice president, Garner spent much of his time at the Capitol presiding over the Senate. He kept a small office adjacent to the old Supreme Court chamber in the Capitol that many senators affectionately referred to as the "doghouse." Garner would invite senators to the doghouse for drinks. With a highball in one hand and a cigar in the other, the vice president occasionally traded votes and plotted strategy, but mostly he regaled his guests with stories.

Corcoran was back working at the RFC, but the president increasingly called on him to perform duties for the White House. Roosevelt sent

Corcoran to meet with the vice president in order to "head him off" in his opposition to the holding company bill.

When Corcoran arrived at his office in the Capitol, Garner — overweight and florid — was sitting behind his desk. "Have you had a drink?" Garner asked.

"No," replied Corcoran, who never drank when he was conducting business and drank only sparingly in social settings.

Garner got up to fetch the whiskey bottle, but Corcoran demurred. The vice president looked slyly at Corcoran. "When I am going to have an intellectual discussion, I make it a rule never to talk to a man until he has a drink, if I have one." The vice president poured out a large tumbler of whiskey and handed it to the young White House aide. Corcoran had never met Garner before and he figured he should make a good impression, so he accepted the drink. As Corcoran remembered it, "[T]he message never got delivered, and I was stiff when I got back to the White House and reported to Frankie."

Roosevelt, however, didn't give up that easily. A few days later FDR sent Frankfurter to talk with Garner, calculating that perhaps the vice president would respond better to someone with a little more gravitas than his young emissary. But according to Corcoran, when Frankfurter returned from his visit with Garner, "He wasn't just stiff, he couldn't stand up. He couldn't even remember what Garner said, or what he said." In the end, however, Garner agreed with the president, claiming that the holding companies "have brought it upon themselves," and "cannot be permitted to go on as they were."

The public utility holding company bill was the result of investigations by the Federal Trade Commission and the House Commerce Committee in 1934. Both investigations had independently discovered that the nation's public utility holding companies were the financial empires of a very few businessmen. Three holding companies controlled nearly half the electricity generated in the United States.

Investigators also discovered that several public utility holding companies had engaged in shady accounting practices. By loading their capital accounts with arbitrary or imaginary amounts, the electric utility owners established a basis for excessive rates. The companies also racked up excessive debt-to-equity ratios by selling bonds that devalued shareholder equity. In one instance, Samuel Insull's Midwest Utilities Company collapsed and he fled to Europe to avoid prosecution, leaving thousands of investors with millions of dollars in worthless stock certificates.

The president asked Corcoran and Cohen to draft legislation regulating the distribution of electric current in interstate commerce. Working furiously, the two young lawyers produced a comprehensive bill that included a section later known as the "death sentence" provision: Any holding company would be dissolved within five years unless the Federal Power Commission certified that its "continuance was necessary for the operation of an economic unit in contiguous states, and in such cases, the remaining holding company would be limited to a single tier." Corcoran and Cohen had drafted the language because Roosevelt believed that it was a political imperative. Privately, however, they were not comfortable with so draconian an approach. Cohen wrote to a friend, "Tom and I will be branded as dangerous radicals, although we were in fact, the only real conservatives."

On February 6, 1935, Sam Rayburn on the House side and Montana's Burton K. Wheeler on the Senate side introduced the legislation. Rayburn had chastised the New York Stock Exchange for its 1934 lobbying campaign against the Securities Exchange Act, but that effort paled in comparison to the one mounted now by the utility companies.

The utilities set up operations in the Mayflower Hotel, including dozens of lawyers and lobbyists along with company executives such as Roosevelt's future opponent Wendell Willkie, at that time the head of Commonwealth and Southern. The utilities used every tactic at their disposal, ranging from disinformation to intimidation. A whispering campaign began that the president was suffering from mental instability. The companies organized a massive letter-writing campaign as well, although the letters and telegrams turned out to be from nonexistent constituents. Congressmen were bluntly told that if they did not vote against the public utilities bill, their opponents in the next election would be provided with enough funds to ensure victory. A friend of Rayburn's wrote that as the congressman prepared for the debate, he became incensed by the lobbyists' heavy-handed tactics: "He hates them with a venomous hatred." The president was greatly alarmed, calling the utility lobby "the most powerful, dangerous lobby that has been created by any organization in this country."

As the two sides girded for battle, Corcoran suffered a great personal loss. Oliver Wendell Holmes caught a cold just as friends and former clerks were planning his ninety-fourth birthday. On March 5, 1935, three days before the celebration, the justice began to have trouble breathing. The old man reluctantly accepted medical assistance, and an oxygen tent was set up in his bedroom. Even though his health was deteriorating, Holmes never lost his wry sense of humor. When one of his former clerks, Jim Rowe, saluted him and gently said, "Every soldier to his tent," the justice thumbed his nose at him in mock contempt. Corcoran came over to the house after work on the evening of March 6. At two-fifteen the next morning Justice Holmes died with Tommy Corcoran at his bedside. Felix Frankfurter would later tell Franklin Roosevelt that "of all his secretaries, Tom was the dearest to him."

By April the utilities seemed to be swaying public opinion. Their protests of being victimized by an overbearing government led the humorist Will Rogers to crack, "A holding company is something where you hand an accomplice the goods while the policeman searches you." Senator Wheeler remarked that "there has been more lying propaganda about this bill, and on a larger scale, than any other bill I have ever seen." After conferring with Corcoran and Cohen, Wheeler decided that the only way to expose the lies was to hold public hearings.

Burton Wheeler, elected to the Senate from Montana in 1922, was originally from Hudson, Massachusetts, not far from Taunton where Tommy's grandfather David O'Keefe had lived. After attending the University of Michigan Law School, Wheeler had practiced law in Butte, Montana, and then run successfully for the state's House of Representatives and district attorney. In the U.S. Senate his role as the Senate prosecutor in the Teapot Dome scandals during the Harding administration earned him a spot alongside Robert La Follette on the National Progressive Party ticket in 1924. Wheeler was a legendary figure in Washington, highly capable and fiercely independent. He and Corcoran hit it off immediately.

Although outnumbered by hordes of corporate lobbyists, Corcoran worked the halls of Congress tirelessly: questioning government witnesses, ghost-writing letters to colleagues and constituents on behalf of congressmen supportive of the legislation. After convincing Senator

Wheeler to schedule hearings, Corcoran and Cohen met with the senator on several occasions at his Virginia home to coach him on the intricacies of the legislation. As he had during the hearings on the stock exchange bill, Corcoran testified before Wheeler's committee. Senator Hastings, Republican of Delaware, asked Corcoran if the purpose of the bill "was to get rid of the concentration of wealth."

"No," replied Corcoran, "it is not the concentration of wealth. It is the concentration of power over other people's money."

On May 29, 1935, the Senate was ready to vote. The showdown came before final passage on an amendment offered by Senator William Dieterich, Democrat of Illinois, to delete the death sentence provision. Corcoran knew that Dieterich's amendment would eviscerate the bill and that several Democratic senators, including Alva Adams of Colorado, were "swing" votes. Although he had no authority to do so, Corcoran conveyed to Adams that he would see to it that the mining office of the SEC would be located in Denver. Adams, who had been lobbying the SEC for the office, voted with the president and brought along a sufficient number of his colleagues so that the Dieterich amendment was defeated by one vote.

In the House of Representatives, commerce committee hearings continued for six weeks, with witness after witness. The hearings often lapsed into bitter exchanges between members themselves, and the questioning of witnesses was frequently laced with acerbic rhetoric. By June the committee was ready to vote, but Rayburn knew that it would not report out the bill unless the death sentence provision aimed at holding companies was removed. He reluctantly capitulated, hoping that by the time the bill reached conference between the House and the Senate, the provision could be reinserted. First, of course, the House had to pass the bill.

The final debate began on June 27, the hottest day of the year to date. With a temperature exceeding ninety degrees inside the House chamber, the only relief on the floor was offered by strategically placed electric fans. Leading House forces opposed to the bill was George Huddleston of Alabama, a short, red-haired orator from Birmingham. Huddleston stood and drawled, "This bill is a mystic maze." Referring to Corcoran and Cohen, he claimed the bill had been written by two bright young men brought down from New York to teach Congress how to shoot. He continued, "I pay them tribute for the exceeding skill they have shown in weaving in and weaving out, piling words upon words, phrase upon phrase, clause upon clause, until a Philadelphia lawyer would get down on his knees and pray to be delivered from the task of interpretation." His remarks were greeted first by laughter and then by applause.

Rayburn strode to the podium in the well of the House chamber. His bald head glistening, he raised his hand, pointed in the direction of Huddleston, and directly responded to the Alabamian's charge that the bill was too complicated: "If you ever have to handle a bill like the Securities bill of 1933, the Stock Exchange Act of 1934, or the Holding Company Bill of 1935, you will want all the expert advice and help you can get. I met Mr. Corcoran in the latter part of 1933 or 1934. He impressed me. If ever he made a move that was important without coming to me first and asking my consent or what I thought about it, I do not remember it."

After the debate in Congress that day, Corcoran went to the White House to report to the president. Roosevelt received Corcoran in his private quarters. After discussing the day's events, he asked him to accompany him to dinner at Joe Kennedy's rented mansion, known as Marwood, fourteen miles northwest of Washington on the banks of the Potomac River in Maryland. Besides Corcoran, Roosevelt's secretary, Missy LeHand, her assistant, Grace Tully, and the counsel to the SEC, John Burns, piled into two large black sedans and accompanied the president.

As it happened, Arthur Krock, the *New York Times* bureau chief, was staying at Kennedy's house that weekend. Kennedy had informed Krock only a few hours earlier that the president was coming over, and, knowing of FDR's dislike for him, Kennedy had asked the newspaperman to stay out of sight. As the cars pulled up to the front door, Krock fled up the stairs, but became, as he recalled, "an involuntary eavesdropper." In recounting the arrival of the president, Krock later noted the presence of Tommy Corcoran, whom he described as "chief drafter of the utilities holding company bill, which is to be voted on in Congress, today and tomorrow."

Kennedy offered the president and his other guests mint juleps (Corcoran declined). Krock later reported that "the President's laughter soon rang out all over." After dinner, Kennedy and his guests watched a movie, a legal thriller titled *Ginger* starring Jane Withers. There was more drinking, and at one point the guests began to respectfully mimic the president's Yankee pronunciation of *boat* by saying *bhutt*. Krock wrote that whenever Roosevelt said "boat" or "float," Missy LeHand, to the amusement of everyone, would say "bhutt" or "flutt."

Then, Krock recorded, "Mr. Corcoran took out his accordion and the real merriment began. The President joined in all the songs, in a rather nice tenor-baritone. . . ." Corcoran played "Tom Tooland," a ballad about a young Irishman who succeeds in politics. The president laughingly reminisced that after the 1932 convention, "we needed some campaign songs," and "the only thing we could come up with was 'the old GOP ain't what it used to be.'" Corcoran immediately began to play the song, but he changed the words to "Old George Huddleston, he ain't what he used to be." When he finished playing, Corcoran said, "I've never been drunk in my life, but if this [death sentence] amendment goes through tomorrow, I'm going to get stinking." The president tilted his head back and roared with laughter.

Around midnight, with the party still in progress, Krock fell asleep, pondering, as he put it, "the paradoxes of men who occupy the highest office in the land."

On July 1, as the House prepared to vote on the holding company bill, Ralph Owen Brewster, Republican congressman of Maine, strode to the well of the House chamber and asked to be recognized. He proceeded to denounce Tom Corcoran, whom he claimed had stopped him in Statuary Hall, the hallway off the House chamber lined with statutes of former congressmen, and threatened to stop construction on the Passamaquoddy Dam in his district unless Brewster voted for the death sentence amendment. After Corcoran fervently denied the allegations, Brewster called him a liar, to which Corcoran hotly replied, "We'll see who's the liar." The House immediately ordered the rules committee to investigate the matter.

Investigators from the House Rules Committee worked to piece the story together. The Public Works Administration had already allocated funds for the Passamaquoddy Dam, and Vice President Garner was slated to break ground on July 4 by igniting the first dynamite blast. Indeed, the project required state approval. Its future was therefore largely out of the hands of the federal government and seemingly beyond the control of Tommy Corcoran.

While the facts seemed to be on his side, Corcoran, only thirty-five years old, was nervous. He retained as counsel Ferdinand Pecora, former Senate banking counsel and now a New York State Supreme Court justice. Testifying before the rules committee a few days later, Pecora at his side, Corcoran acknowledged speaking to Brewster in Statuary Hall about both the dam project and the impending vote, but, he told the committee, he only warned Brewster that his credibility with the administration was finished if he went back on his promise to protect the death sentence provision. Corcoran fervently denied that he had either explicitly or implicitly linked Brewster's vote on the holding company bill to the dam project. When he concluded his testimony, Pecora patted him on the back and later cheerfully told members of the press, "It was marvelous."

Corcoran's version of events was bolstered by a witness to the conversation, Ernest Gruening, the administration's chief policy maker for Puerto Rico and an old friend of both Brewster's and Corcoran's. Gruening claimed that Corcoran had never threatened Congressman Brewster. Other witnesses before the committee included eight congressmen, among them Brewster's two colleagues from Maine, who testified that they believed Brewster had supported the death sentence provision and were surprised that he had voted against it. The clear implication was that Brewster had changed his vote under pressure from lobbyists and that he — as historian Arthur Schlesinger later conjectured — "might well have made his subsequent charges to cover an otherwise inexplicable retreat."

Time magazine described Corcoran's testimony before the rules committee as delivered "with cold, lucid driving fury." *Time* asserted that Corcoran "tore Ralph Brewster's tale to shameful shreds." The *New York Times*, which had originally editorialized that Corcoran's alleged activity had been "in a strict and moral sense . . . a corrupt way of trying to win favor and gain support," now concluded simply that "Hot weather makes hot words."

In addition to his testimony before the rules committee, Corcoran was asked by President Roosevelt to provide him with "a complete statement of all your dealings" with Brewster. Working through the night, Corcoran prepared an eight-page, single-spaced response with a cover letter that said in part, "I do feel that I may have convinced the Committee this morning that, however few effective guns I carry, I'm a man o' war flying one flag — and that Mr. Brewster is just a shady privateer with forged letters of marriage from both sides!" Roosevelt read Corcoran's defense of his actions and sent him a succinct reply: "Dear Tom, Stout Fellow!"

Meanwhile, the public utilities bill was in conference between the House and the Senate. Although Corcoran and Cohen were barred from participation in the conference committee negotiations, they continued to play an important role behind the scenes, huddling every evening with the Democrats to strategize for the next day. At one point in late August, Republican congressman John G. Cooper of Ohio complained that "Messrs. Corcoran and Cohen, the authors of the original decree to eliminate holding companies, have rewritten that decree in new language, but the sentence of death remains. Do you think that anyone will be deceived by this different shroud of language in which death has been newly wrapped?"

The bill that finally emerged from conference fell far short of that initially imagined by Roosevelt and Rayburn, but it did contain a modified death sentence provision that compelled holding companies to reorganize under SEC oversight. It required, for example, that companies register with the SEC, furnish it with detailed financial information, and seek its approval before undertaking any number of financial transactions, including payment of dividends, issuance of securities, or plans for reorganization. Still, the battle was not completely over: Power companies across the country operated on the premise that the act was unconstitutional and therefore unenforceable. They filed numerous lawsuits challenging the recently passed legislation, and by the summer of 1935 the federal courts were ready to hear a challenge brought by one of the biggest groups in the country controlling the electric utility industry, the Electric Bond and Share Company.

The attorney general, Homer Cummings, with the president's approval, sought the assistance of Corcoran and Cohen litigating the constitutionality of the Public Utilities Holding Company Act. Corcoran also suggested that the Justice Department assign two additional lawyers to help them: James Lawrence Fly, who had been a classmate of his at Harvard Law School, and Robert Jackson, a lawyer at the Treasury Department, who had been very involved in the early executive maneuvering over the Holding Company Act. Corcoran liked Jackson who, like him, was Catholic and a reformer. The previous year Jackson had gained

acclaim for his successful prosecution of Andrew Mellon, former secretary of the Treasury, for tax evasion. A skilled courtroom lawyer, Jackson
would go on to be appointed solicitor general, attorney general, chief
prosecutor at Nuremberg, and associate justice of the Supreme Court.

Corcoran, Cohen, and Jackson set up shop at the RFC and spent hours
going over precedents to uphold the constitutionality of the law. Working
feverishly, they completed the government's draft at about 3:30 A.M. on
the eve of opening arguments. The document was then entrusted to one
of Corcoran's assistants, who drove it to the airport for the 4 A.M. flight
to New York so that the case could be filed in U.S. District Court later
that morning. Bleary-eyed and exhausted, Corcoran, Cohen, and Jackson
stumbled out of the RFC to an all-night restaurant across the street,
where they celebrated with scrambled eggs and hot coffee.

In the ensuing weeks, government lawyers battled the lawyers for the
Electric Bond and Share Company. Eventually the case made it all the way
to the Supreme Court. Corcoran sat in the packed courtroom, a few rows
in front of President Theodore Roosevelt's daughter, Alice Roosevelt
Longworth, as Ben Cohen nervously presented the government's case in
a trembling voice. Notwithstanding the polished and forceful presentation of the utility lawyers, Cohen prevailed: The constitutionality of the
Holding Company Act was upheld.

The Corcoran-Brewster debacle resulted in separate House and Senate
investigations of the lobbyists. Although the House investigation was
marred from the beginning, the Senate investigation, headed by Hugo
Black, found that the power lobby had engaged in an unparalleled effort
to influence the legislative process. Corcoran had taken on one of the
most powerful lobbies in the history of Washington and persevered. The
Holding Company Act that he helped win passage of ultimately proved
an effective means of breaking up the big conglomerates.

In the summer of 1935 Corcoran wrote to a friend, "Storms make a
sailor — if he survives them." During the three years that he had worked
in the New Deal, Corcoran had navigated successfully through many
storms. He had proven himself not only loyal to the man he referred to as
the "Skipper," President Roosevelt, but also an effective operator. He was
rapidly becoming one of the most influential men in Washington.

8

Apex of Power

A president reveals something of himself by the men and women he chooses to surround him. Throughout American history, presidents have chosen top assistants who have very different skill sets, but most of the behind-the-scenes "confidence men" have shared some common traits. They have traditionally sought anonymity, allowing their boss to gain the credit for success — and in the event of failure they have been willing to serve as the lightning rod.

In the nineteenth century, presidential aides were usually relatives or close friends who tended to perform clerical duties, such as correspondence. The volume of work was enormous; in 1825 outgoing president James Madison lodged a complaint with Congress about the lack of adequate staff support. President Lincoln had only two staff assistants: John Hay and John Nicolay. By 1881 President James Garfield, after completing his term as president, concluded that the chief executive's top aide ought to be held in higher esteem than the secretary of state. By the time Franklin Roosevelt was elected and Tommy Corcoran came to Washington, Congress had increased White House staff to four in addition to the clerical workers. Over the next five decades Corcoran would watch the White House staff balloon to more than six hundred.

Franklin Roosevelt never actually had a chief of staff, although several individuals filled the role of chief political strategist. Louis Howe came to the White House from the New York governor's office, where he had worked for Roosevelt. Raymond Moley served the president from his perch as an assistant secretary of state. Tommy Corcoran never left the RFC, and Harry Hopkins — perhaps Roosevelt's most trusted aide during his entire presidency — was secretary of commerce.

By the twentieth century presidential aides had accrued enormous influence — sometimes attaining in a few years more power than elected officials who'd spent a lifetime in Congress. In many ways the presidency of Franklin Roosevelt marked a watershed in the importance of presidential staff. Tommy Corcoran was one of the first behind-the-scenes staffers to be publicly recognized for his influence over both policy and political matters.

All the publicity that Tommy Corcoran had garnered from his dispute with Congressman Brewster ended any remaining vestige of anonymity he may have coveted. Thirty-five years old, he had been spotted by many in the press as an up-and-coming whiz kid in the administration. Writing in the *New York Times Magazine,* Delbert Clark called him "a symbol of how Mr. Roosevelt operates" and referred to him as a "full-fledged brain truster." Also in the *Times,* columnist Arthur Krock, who had eaves-dropped on Corcoran at Joe Kennedy's house several months earlier, wrote that he was "an able, brilliant young Harvard man, who thinks closely along the same lines as another Harvard man," the president of the United States.

Part of Corcoran's growing stature with the press was his ability to cultivate reporters. According to Joseph Alsop, who was a young journalist at the time and writing a column with Robert Kintner, their connection to Corcoran "was one of the keys to the early success of our column." Alsop would later explain that most journalists "stuck to the power centers like the Senate and White House and more or less ignored the kind of legislative policy that Corcoran and Cohen were constructing."

But just as he seemed to be hitting stride in his career, he was again faced with a great personal loss. Tommy's mother succumbed to uremia on October 6, 1935, at the age of sixty-one. Mary O'Keefe had instilled a burning ambition in all her sons, and she had been enormously proud of Tommy's accomplishments. During Tommy's clerkship with Justice Holmes, she had written to Fanny Holmes, expressing her great joy that ". . . my boy should have the friendship and teaching of you and Mr. Holmes." She called his experience "one of the happiest things in my life." Tommy would later write that his mother "had a raven's memory and an eagle's will."

A little more than a month after his mother's death, Secretary of the Interior Harold Ickes scribbled in his diary, "Recently Louis Howe has been put out of business by his illness, Corcoran has been called in to help out in the White House offices, and the liberals are certainly hoping that he will become a permanent fixture there because he is not only a liberal, he is a very able lawyer with general all-round ability and, I believe, a keen political sense."

Howe, a former newspaperman, had been Roosevelt's most trusted political adviser for more than twenty years. Since 1910, the year Roosevelt was elected to the New York State Senate, Howe had navigated his political career, from his campaign for the vice presidency in 1920 to governorship of New York and then to the presidency: Howe, more than anyone else apart from the president's wife, Eleanor, had sustained Roosevelt's optimism, energy, and determination. By 1936 Howe was gravely ill and steadily faded from center stage at the White House until his death on April 18 of pneumonia. Tommy Corcoran replaced Howe in many ways, as he became both a trusted adviser and personal companion to the president.

Corcoran also benefited from the falling-out between the president and another of his trusted advisers. On Wednesday morning, June 24, 1936, Corcoran, who was still a lawyer in the general counsel's office at the RFC, was summoned to the Oval Office. When he arrived, Raymond Moley, the president's close adviser and the editor of *Today* magazine, was already there. Sitting behind his desk, the president announced that he needed a speech for the upcoming Democratic National Convention in Philadelphia.

Roosevelt was enjoying great popularity as Congress, which had achieved a Democratic majority in 1934, enacted some of the most important New Deal legislation during the second hundred days of 1935. As the date of the convention approached, Roosevelt gathered his advisers in the Oval Office and announced that he wanted something "only fifteen minutes long," which rose "to a serious note." Moley suggested that the speech incorporate some of the themes that Bernard Baruch, the Wall Street financier, had been sounding, specifically "serenity and service." The president called the idea "splendid," adding that he'd also like to "bring in reference to hope, faith, charity — with charity being interpreted as love." Moley and Corcoran nodded, picked up their papers, and spent the rest of the day in a rented suite at the Mayflower Hotel working on the speech. In the evening they walked back to the White House and were joined by speechwriters Sam Rosenman and Stanley High, as well as Missy LeHand. The president then invited everyone to dine with him in the small family dining room.

The talk at dinner that evening was mostly light and nonpolitical. At one point High kidded Moley about having rich friends. Moley paid him no attention, but then the president picked up on the teasing and said he'd noticed that Moley was becoming more conservative. Moley was not amused; as Corcoran remembered, "Moley being an Irishman fought back." Suddenly the good-natured banter turned serious and, according to Rosenman, "the exchanges between them became very bitter; Missy did her best to change the subject but failed. The words became acrimonious." Moley was not invited back to the White House, and his long association with the president ended.

Roosevelt delivered the speech Corcoran and Moley had drafted, with input from Rosenman and High, on June 26 at Franklin Field in Philadelphia before a hundred thousand people. The scene was a dramatic one: It had rained all day, but by evening the sky cleared, revealing a deep blue backdrop. As the Philadephia Orchestra under the direction of Leopold Stokowski played Tchaikovsky, Roosevelt, just offstage and out of sight, fell to the ground when one of his leg braces snapped. The president recovered and was helped to the stage, where he was greeted with a thunderous ovation. Roosevelt delivered his speech with his usual patrician eloquence. The words that would be most remembered that evening — indeed that would forever be emblematic of the Roosevelt presidency — were written by Tommy Corcoran. Gripping the podium, the president intoned in his stentorian voice: "There is a mysterious cycle in human events. To some generations much is given. Of other generations much is expected. This generation has a rendezvous with destiny." It was a phrase meant to inspire, and the crowd reacted with sustained applause. For Corcoran, who was sitting in the audience, it was an important lesson on not only how powerful a speech could be if delivered by the right messenger, but also how influential a speechwriter could be in shaping the message.

With his legislative and speechwriting skills, Tommy Corcoran was quickly becoming one of the president's most important political advisers. Felix Frankfurter recommended to Roosevelt that he make Corcoran his de facto chief of staff: "Very, very rarely do you get in one man such technical equipment, resourcefulness, personal and persuasive style, unstinted character, wide contacts and rich experience, in legal, financial and governmental affairs." In the end Corcoran only added the title of assistant attorney general. He continued to work as a lawyer at the RFC and made no attempt to obtain a position on the White House staff even though increasingly he acted as a political aide and troubleshooter for the president.

Sensitive to the fact that many of Roosevelt's advisers had been with him for a long time and that "as in any administration, many of the entourage were very jealous," Corcoran had an almost surreptitious relationship with the president. Each morning he would show up at the White House gate, and after admission, walk through a lower passage in the West Wing to a private staircase and then to the office of Missy LeHand, which adjoined the Oval Office. According to Corcoran, "In that way I avoided crossing paths with any of Roosevelt's old guard and kept the jealousies down to a manageable level." Corcoran would tell LeHand anything he felt the president should know, and she in turn would inform the president. If Roosevelt wanted some action taken on an issue, then, as he described it, "she showed me in." Indeed, Corcoran's close friendship with LeHand was central to his rising influence. Norman Littell, a Justice Department official, later complained that Corcoran "used his influence with the White House secretaries" to "block off access to the president because it was LeHand who ultimately decided."

There was some truth to Littell's view of how one gained access to the Oval Office. Eventually Corcoran began to bring Cohen along with him: "I simply showed up in the office one day with Cohen and told Missy this was my friend Ben and he was the best lawyer I ever knew. . . ." From that point on Ben Cohen also became a trusted adviser to the president.

The closeness of the relationship between Corcoran and FDR was evident not only in the amount of time Corcoran was spending at the White House, but also in the personal friendship the two men developed. Roosevelt often gave nicknames to associates for whom he developed a personal affection. Henry Morgenthau, a cherished friend who served as the secretary of the Treasury, was cheerfully known by FDR as "Henry the Morgue." Corcoran came to be known in time by Roosevelt as "Tommy the Cork." He, in turn, referred to the president as "Skipper."

Roosevelt enjoyed Corcoran's company. Whenever they were together after hours, whether relaxing with a drink in the White House, having dinner with Secretary of the Interior Harold Ickes, or at some other social occasion, the president would ask Corcoran to play the accordion or the piano. FDR loved ballads and ditties; Corcoran was familiar with most of them, and could play by ear the ones he hadn't played before after hearing only a few bars. Roosevelt's most frequent requests were "The Yellow Rose of Texas" and "Father O'Flynn."

The president also loved political gossip and humorous stories, and Corcoran had plenty of both to offer. Through his network of contacts he always knew the latest scuttlebutt, which he relayed to Roosevelt. He also both recognized a good story and excelled in telling it. His training in the theater during college had given him the timing and polish of a professional comedian.

President Roosevelt briefly considered appointing Corcoran director of the budget, but Treasury Secretary Morgenthau quashed the idea. Morgenthau, who'd known Corcoran when the young RFC attorney had worked in the Treasury Department, wrote in his diary that he told the president that appointing Corcoran to such an important position was "out of the question" because Corcoran "was an intellectual crook. I would not trust him as far as I could see him." Roosevelt deferred to Morgenthau as far as his choice for budget director went, but continued to utilize Corcoran. It was one of Roosevelt's great strengths that he understood how to extract the best from each individual on his staff.

Alongside Ben Cohen, Corcoran had drafted some of the New Deal's most important legislation. Now the president began to use Corcoran as his special emissary to Capitol Hill — the first-ever White House liaison. Not only did Corcoran convey the views of the White House, but he could also help particular congressmen who needed to navigate the federal bureaucracy, or even set up a meeting with the president. During the 1930s senators and representatives did not have professional staffs, but instead relied on the professional Congressional Research Service to research and write bills. Because Corcoran was such a skilled draftsman, his talents were in demand. For congressmen friendly to the administration, Corcoran helped craft legislation, wrote speeches, and even prepared letters to important constituents.

Stanley High, one of the president's speechwriters, claimed that "the role of chief adviser is undoubtedly held at present by Thomas Corcoran, 'Tommy the Cork.'" The president's second oldest son, Elliott, would later write in even more superlative terms about Corcoran: "Apart from my father, Tom was the single most influential individual in the country." According to Elliott, Corcoran, along with Cohen, "had a major hand in most items of New Deal legislation, tightening it to match the increasingly leftist mood of Congress, adjusting it under protest to appease conservative old timers on Capitol Hill."

There were numerous examples to support Elliott Roosevelt's view. When the Social Security bill was being considered in 1935, Senator Bennett Clark of Missouri offered an amendment to exempt those businesses that already provided retirement plans. A businessman from Philadelphia named Forester who sold corporate retirement plans spent fifty thousand dollars — a considerable amount of money in those days — to lobby Congress to support the Clark amendment. When the president heard this, he assigned Corcoran four senators to bring around: Corcoran convinced them all to defeat the amendment. Members of Congress began to perceive Corcoran as a direct line to the president. One New Deal senator, who wanted to ensure that a particular member of the Maritime Commission was not renominated, sent a letter to the president proclaiming, "I talked to Thomas Gardner Corcoran about this and he will talk to you later." And Stephen Early, the president's press secretary and a jealous competitor of Corcoran's, scribbled on more than one memorandum to Roosevelt, "A commitment was made to the congressman through Tommy Corcoran."

When Sam Rayburn of Texas, a liberal Democrat, decided to run for Speaker of the House against the more conservative John O'Connor of New York, Roosevelt, believing it would be politically unwise to throw his support openly behind any candidate, enlisted Corcoran to provide behind-the-scenes assistance to the Texan. Corcoran went about sewing up the support of two important political bosses in O'Connor's backyard: Bronx boss Ed Flynn and Tammany leader Tom Cullen. But, Corcoran remembered, "The big task was to block Jim Farley from helping O'Connor."

James Farley had managed Roosevelt's 1932 presidential campaign. To reward his efforts, the president appointed him both postmaster general and chairman of the Democratic Party. A native New Yorker, Farley was also the former chairman of the state Democratic Party and continued to have enormous influence in New York State politics. In the fall of 1936 he had been visiting Europe on vacation. On the day that he was scheduled to arrive back in New York on a large ocean liner, the city hall bosses hurried down to the docks to greet him and give him the latest news about the leadership contest. Corcoran worried that the city hall crowd would get to Farley before he had a chance to explain to the chairman the president's wishes. From his days working on Coast Guard matters at the Treasury Department, Corcoran still had many friends in that branch of the service. He thus managed to persuade one of his buddies to take him out to sea in a launch to meet Farley's incoming ship. According to Corcoran, "I climbed a ladder up the side of a ship and found Farley. 'Rayburn's our man,' I told him. Then I beat it back to the dock. When Farley met the Tammany bunch, he knew what to say." Indeed, when House Democrats caucused on the afternoon of January 4, Rayburn was elected by a margin of 184 to 127. Eight members from the New York delegation had voted for the Texan.

Part of Corcoran's success on Capitol Hill stemmed from his close relationship with Rayburn. Rayburn genuinely liked both Corcoran and Cohen, and every six weeks or so he would invite the two young men over to his little apartment in the Kalorama area of Washington for a Sunday breakfast. Rayburn would put on a large white apron and cook scrambled eggs and bacon, all the while talking over the issues of the day, political strategy, and inside gossip with his two young friends.

On one occasion Rayburn told Corcoran, "The President ought to be having a meeting every week with his House and Senate leaders so we could tell him what we are planning, and he could tell us his plans. It could eliminate a lot of confusion. See what you can do. But don't dare to let him know I suggested it 'cause he thinks he 'borned' every idea that ever was." Corcoran laughed and said he would see what he could do. A few weeks later Rayburn was at the White House and the president said to him, "Sam, I've been thinking. Maybe it would be a good idea if I had a meeting with Bill [Bankhead] and you and Jack [Garner] and Alben [Barkley] about once a week to talk over what all of us are planning." Rayburn nodded his head seriously; "Mr. President," he said, "that's one of the smartest ideas I've ever heard."

Corcoran effectively mediated between powerful Democrats in Washington, but even Republicans on the Hill admired his energy and determination. Bruce Barton, a Republican congressman and former advertising executive, once told a crowd of young Republicans that the way to revive the fortunes of their party was to emulate Corcoran. Barton noted Corcoran's intelligence and charm, but he maintained that the secret to his success, "divested of legend and fairy tale, is that he works sixteen hours a day in a town where six hours is the normal work day." Corcoran had never slept much. He often had worked through the night during college, and he continued the practice during his professional career. The president was aware of Tommy's work ethic and frequently ordered him to take a "holiday," particularly after some arduous task had been completed.

Corcoran was also becoming a liaison with some of the big financial contributors in the Democratic Party. In 1936 Corcoran visited David Dubinsky, the powerful head of the International Ladies Garment Workers Union, who later recalled that he gave around forty thousand dollars to the Roosevelt campaign, "the first time our union financially supported a Democratic candidate." When John L. Lewis, president of the United Mine Workers, offered to contribute to Roosevelt's 1936 reelection campaign, Tommy was sent to pick up the check, an eye-popping $465,000. He also solicited contributions from wealthy businessmen, such as importer Sam "the Banana Man" Zemurray and department store magnate Lincoln Filene.

Corcoran even assisted the president with certain personal matters. During the New Deal, according to the historian Doris Kearns Goodwin, "there was an odd assortment of single men occupying bedrooms on the third floor" of the White House. One of those was the first lady's brother, Hall Roosevelt. Hall was considered by all who knew him as supremely intelligent, but he drank too much and had difficulty holding down a job. When drinking, he could be loud, truculent, and out of control. The president's son, Elliott, recalled that at one White House formal dinner, Hall pinched Missy LeHand just above her knee. According to Elliott, "[A] shriek rose above the conversation of the fourteen other guests, and she leaped from her chair." As the guests looked on in horror, Eleanor Roosevelt gently chided her brother, "I wish you wouldn't do those things."

The president apparently decided that the best way to get Hall out of the White House was to find him employment far from Washington. Roosevelt needed someone who could be completely trusted to perform this delicate task, and Tommy Corcoran was assigned the job. Corcoran learned that Hall had an interest in a mining venture in Alaska that was seeking a $2.5 million loan from the Reconstruction Finance Corporation, and so Tommy went to confer with his boss, Jesse Jones. According to Jones, Corcoran "said that the President was very anxious for us to make this Alaskan loan, that Hall Roosevelt could get a job with the company as chief engineer, and that the President wanted to get Hall as far away from the White House as possible." Jones authorized a loan of $1.25 million, although he later claimed somewhat unconvincingly in his memoirs that Corcoran's visit had had nothing to do with his decision. The mining project ultimately failed, but at least for a short time the president, with Corcoran's help, had rid the White House of his unpredictable brother-in-law.

If the president appreciated the multitalented Corcoran, the first lady was not so enamored. According to Elliott Roosevelt, "Mother did not take to Tom. He was too pungent a personality to suit her. He was also one more Catholic in the President's entourage and his views were too radical for Mother's taste at that time." On one level Elliott Roosevelt's comment about his mother's view of Corcoran is puzzling, for she was, if anything, more radical than Corcoran. Her political activism was unprecedented for a first lady, and she brought a zealotry to reform that caused at least one member of the president's own cabinet, liberal Harold Ickes, to remark, "I wish that Mrs. Roosevelt would stick to her knitting and keep out of the affairs connected with my Department."

It is more likely that the first lady's scorn for Corcoran was based on his sexist treatment of women — he ignored them — and her dim view of Catholicism. Mrs. Roosevelt, who clearly abhorred intolerance and prejudice in most forms, was nevertheless wary of Catholics. According to her cousin, the political columnist Joe Alsop, "Eleanor still believed the anti-Catholic nonsense she had heard during her childhood." If Corcoran sensed her disdain, he may have considered it just one more example of the barely-beneath-the-surface bigotry he had encountered in so many of the powerful people he'd met.

Even though Corcoran became one of the president's closest advisers, he never joined the White House staff, finding it more advantageous to be able to freelance from the Reconstruction Finance Corporation. The director of the RFC, Jesse Jones, understood that Corcoran's growing influence was a benefit to the agency. The RFC had become the nation's largest lender, its largest investor, and had expanded to include a large number of subsidiaries, including the federal mortgage agencies, the Export-Import Bank, the Electric Home and Farm Authority, and the Commodity Credit Corporation. In short, there was very little economic activity in the country at the time in which the RFC didn't play some role. The conservative Jones and the liberal Corcoran were not particularly close, but each respected what the other could do for him.

At the RFC Corcoran had everything he needed to operate effectively on a practical level: an office, secretarial help, telephones, and mimeograph machines. Jones recognized that Corcoran increasingly understood how to navigate the federal bureaucracy and served as a magnet for talented staff. As historian Arthur Schlesinger has written, "A fluid and emergency-minded organization, RFC was a reservoir of expert talent for any contingency. It provided not only lawyers, but comptrollers, treasurers, bank examiners, personnel experts, public relations experts, not to speak of telephone operators who could get anyone anywhere in the world."

And when Tommy couldn't get what he wanted from within the RFC, chances were he knew someone in the government who could help him. His contacts were numerous because he continued to play the role he had learned at Cotton and Franklin of placing people in key positions around the government. Ironically, one of the most important young men he tried to help find a job wanted to work not in government, but at the Appalachian Mountain Club, where Tommy had spent so many happy summers during college. Joseph Kennedy had asked Corcoran to find his son Joe Jr. a place with the organization. The problem was, there were no openings. Still, Tommy — recognizing Kennedy's vast influence — wrote to the club's president and offered to pay the young Joe's wages and living expenses if a position could be found — and if the arrangement could be kept quiet.

Around this time Corcoran himself was offered a position in the Department of Justice as deputy to the solicitor general. Corcoran would write major legal briefs for the administration and would have the opportunity to argue before the Supreme Court. While such a prestigious legal job must have held interest for Corcoran, he turned it down because he recognized that, in fact, his political power and ability to maneuver within the government would have been greatly diminished.

Corcoran increasingly used his position at the RFC and his access to the Oval Office for purely political purposes — always in support of the president. By 1936 support for the New Deal had waned in some rural communities, and freshman Democratic congressmen, such as D. J. Driscoll of Pennsylvania and Edward C. Eicher of Iowa, faced stiff opposition. Corcoran did everything he could to assist the representatives, soliciting campaign contributions from union bosses, writing speeches, and even arranging for surrogate campaigners. When both men lost, Corcoran arranged for Driscoll to be appointed to the Pennsylvania Public Utilities Commission and Eicher to be named a commissioner of the Securities and Exchange Commission.

Corcoran also became more than just a source for some in the press, such as Isador "Izzie" Feinstein, the leftist chief editorial writer for the *New York Post*, who later adopted the nom de plume I. F. Stone. When Corcoran first met Stone, the journalist-*cum*-liberal-activist was looking for leadership from the administration on civil rights cases. Corcoran subsequently used Stone to write speeches about the Supreme Court, which Corcoran provided to supportive members of Congress. The New Deal lawyer also asked his journalist friend to editorialize on the Court and to support Robert Jackson for governor of New York. Stone, in turn, used Corcoran to help get his father a permanent job at the Philadelphia mint. Corcoran even helped Stone secure funding, from Felix Frankfurter and the retailer Edward Filene, to write a book on the Constitution and the minimum wage legislation, which Corcoran had helped draft.

Even though his stature in Washington had greatly risen, Tommy Corcoran maintained his old office, a standard-sized room with government-issue battered wooden furniture. He had no pictures of himself with the president on the walls. In fact, the only picture he had there was a photograph of Oliver Wendell Holmes that the justice had given him after his year as a clerk. Holmes had inscribed the photograph for Corcoran: "A man may live greatly in the law as well as elsewhere; there as well as elsewhere his thought may find its unity in an infinite perspective; there as well as elsewhere he may wreak himself upon life, may drink the bitter cup of heroism, may wear his heart out after the unattainable."

Holmes's words resonated with Corcoran, for he was a lawyer who loved the intellectual rigor and stimulation of the law. Corcoran often recalled his year clerking for Justice Holmes and the many evenings they spent together discussing concepts of law and the vagaries of justice. He had often expressed to President Roosevelt his desire to become the U.S. solicitor general, the chief litigator for the Department of Justice. Although Corcoran turned down the deputy solicitor general position, he knew that the appointment to the solicitor generalship itself was a critical step on the road to attaining what he'd really secretly wanted since the day he'd been introduced to Justice Holmes in his study on I Street — an appointment to the Supreme Court.

9

The Second New Deal

On Election Day, November 4, 1936, Tommy Corcoran was among a small number of advisers who had accompanied the president and his family to Hyde Park, New York, to await the returns. After dinner that evening the president went upstairs while friends and family mingled in the study and listened to the radio. The Roosevelt women played collective hostess. The president's daughter-in-law Betsey Cushing Roosevelt offered everyone an after-dinner drink, while his mother, Sara Delano Roosevelt, sat regally in an overstuffed chair and received her guests with evident delight. Wearing a white chiffon gown with a huge red rose in her belt, Eleanor Roosevelt busied herself by making sure that the hors d'oeuvres were passed. As the results trickled in from across the country, Corcoran played the accordion, improvising one tune with the words "Oh, Landon is dead" — a reference to the all-but-certain defeat of the Republican nominee, Governor Alfred M. Landon of Kansas. Then around nine o'clock, the doors of the study flew open and a triumphant Roosevelt was wheeled in. As the president greeted his family and supporters, Corcoran played "Happy Days Are Here Again" — the Democrats' theme song — on his accordion.

President Roosevelt had run a spirited and optimistic campaign, often speaking from the back of a train and greeting supporters by telling them, "You look happier than you did four years ago!" Indeed, with the economy improving and as many as six million of the unemployed back at work, Roosevelt could point to a solid record of accomplishment. Landon, a moderate Republican, had attacked the president for "reckless spending," but he lacked the personal charisma of Roosevelt and his campaign never really captured the imagination of the electorate.

Around ten o'clock Corcoran's accordion music was interrupted by the shrill horns of a brass band. Outside, a throng of supporters from town was marching down the avenue to the president's house with red-fire torches and calcium flares. When Roosevelt came out to greet them, they cheered wildly. Upstairs, the Roosevelt grandchildren, who had never really fallen asleep, looked down excitedly from their bedroom windows.

The congratulatory telephone calls began to pour in. Jim Farley, the head of the Democratic Party, called from New York City and asked, "Who are the fourteen persons in Warm Springs who voted against you?" He was referring to the small town of Warm Springs, Georgia, where the president owned a small house and often vacationed. Farley then said facetiously, "You ought to raise hell with them."

The victory was overwhelming. Roosevelt had won 61 percent of the popular vote and carried all but two states, Maine and Vermont. He won an astounding 523 electoral votes as compared to 8 for Landon. It was, at the time, the most lopsided victory in American political history.

At two o'clock in the morning the president received Governor Landon's concession telegram. "The nation has spoken," Landon wrote. "Every American will accept the verdict and work for the common good of the country." An elated president promptly replied, "I am grateful for your generous telegram and I am confident that all of us Americans will now pull together for the common good." A short time later Elliott Roosevelt telephoned from Texas to congratulate his father. And finally, at around three o'clock in the morning, a tired Franklin Roosevelt went to bed.

President Roosevelt didn't have long to savor his victory. Although he had stabilized the financial markets, secured the passage of significant legislation during his first term, and won an impressive reelection, the depression was far from over. The industrial sector of the economy, in particular, continued in turmoil as labor clashed with management and class conflict seemed to be growing. One month after the election, the United Auto Workers shut down production at General Motors with a series of sitdown strikes at plants in Flint and Detroit, Michigan, and in South Bend, Indiana. In Flint police fired on protesters armed only with wrenches and crowbars, but they were unable to break the workers' resolve, and on February 11, 1937, General Motors relented to the union's demands for better wages and working conditions.

Labor's victories, however, were short-lived. The president, counseled by Secretary of the Treasury Henry Morgenthau, slashed government spending in order to quell any threat of inflation. Morgenthau worried that deficit spending and the prospect of rising prices might stall the economic recovery that was under way. But the medicine may have been worse than the malady. When the president cut the federal work rolls, yet continued to collect billions in new Social Security taxes, a deep recession ensued. In late 1937 the gains from the previous year were reversed when unemployment rocketed from 14 percent to 19 percent; two million people lost their jobs between Labor Day and Christmas. Confidence in the financial markets began to wane yet again as the Dow Jones Industrial Average lost nearly 50 percent of its value in a three-month period. Inventory was piling up in business after business. Roosevelt seemed temporarily at a loss, telling his cabinet, "Everything will work out if we just sit tight and keep quiet."

Liberals within the administration thought Morgenthau's economic strategy was wrong and advocated increased deficit spending. But beyond government spending there was a sharp division among the liberals, some of whom, such as the influential Adolf Berle, believed that the administration needed to find a way to work with business, while others, such as Corcoran, believed that the government should move more strenuously to curb monopoly.

Berle, an unofficial adviser to Roosevelt, was a member of the president's brain trust. A graduate of Harvard College and Harvard Law School, he was a professor at Columbia University and considered a brilliant advocate of government planning. Berle believed in the inevitability of corporate concentration and argued that instead of trying to break up large companies, the government should control them, because, in fact, big business brought an efficiency to the economy that was greatly beneficial.

In late 1937 Berle, who had a wide network of contacts in New York, reached out to Thomas Lamont, the elegant and highly respected chairman of J. P. Morgan and Company. A few days before Christmas, 1937, Berle and Lamont convened an extraordinary meeting of business, government, and labor leaders at New York's Century Club. Besides Lamont, Owen Young of General Electric represented the interests of business. Berle's former colleague at Columbia, Undersecretary of Agriculture Rexford Tugwell, and Charles Taussig, another official at the Agriculture Department, came on behalf of the Roosevelt administration. Philip Murray, president of the Steelworkers Union, as well as John L. Lewis and Lee Pressman of the Council of Industrial Organizations were there for labor. After several hours of discussion, the eight men endorsed the broad outlines of an agreement supporting a national industrial policy under which big business, government, and labor coexisted.

Along with other prominent liberals in the administration, Tommy Corcoran believed that Berle's efforts were misguided on both economic and political grounds. Corcoran favored the Brandeisian school of liberal thought that embraced a small-scale competitive economy. Corcoran, joined by Ben Cohen, Harold Ickes, and Robert Jackson, the assistant attorney general for the Justice Department's antitrust division, felt it was time to revive the attacks on business that had characterized Roosevelt's first term. Corcoran had written the memorable speech that Roosevelt delivered at Madison Square Garden on October 31, 1936, in which the president warned, "Only desperate men with their backs to the wall would descend so far below the level of decent citizenship as to foster the current pay-envelope campaign against American's working people."

Members of the Corcoran group, without the stated support of the president, launched their own trust-busting public relations drive, perhaps with the belief that if the American people responded favorably, the president would join them. The day after Christmas, 1937, Assistant Attorney General Jackson delivered a radio address that had been drafted by Corcoran and Cohen. Jackson laid the blame for the recession on the monopolists who "have simply priced themselves out of the market and priced themselves into a slump."

Four days later, Ickes delivered another speech crafted by Corcoran and Cohen. Appearing on NBC's radio network, the interior secretary warned that America was dominated by a "ruling class" of extremely wealthy families who numbered less than one hundred. Ickes's populist message was that America risked becoming a plutocracy unless the country's wealth was distributed more evenly. Roosevelt's silence on the issue caused many of his former Brahmin classmates from Groton and Harvard to declare that he was "a traitor to his class."

But criticism of the president was not confined to the WASP elite. Some in the administration who knew Corcoran to be the wordsmith for these speeches considered his emphasis on class warfare dangerous and objected to his seeming continuing vendetta against business interests. The day after the Jackson speech, Harry Hooker, a former law partner of the president's, told Jim Farley, the chairman of the Democratic National Committee, that Mrs. Roosevelt was irritated by Jackson's antibusiness rhetoric. According to Farley, the first lady believed he was damaging the president. But she blamed Jackson less than Corcoran, whom she felt was increasingly a reckless presence in her husband's inner circle. Nevertheless, in his State of the Union message on January 3, 1938, the president included two paragraphs — written by Corcoran — promising that a special message on the issue of monopoly would be delivered in the near future.

Adolf Berle was exasperated and wanted the president to rein in Corcoran. Berle labeled Corcoran a member "of the Frankfurter group which is extremely powerful because it satisfies the President's desire for some personal villains." Berle, twelve years older than Corcoran and extremely arrogant, described Corcoran in his diary as "fundamentally an ambitious politician" who had "very little else in his head."

Berle tried to appeal to the president directly by arranging a meeting with his new advisory group. Lamont and the others agreed to attend and were led to believe that the meeting would be private, discreet, and substantive. Instead, when Lamont arrived at the White House, he and the other participants were forced to run a gauntlet of photographers and reporters. Someone, perhaps Corcoran, had tipped off the press to the meeting; the next day there were front-page stories with headlines such as MR. BERLE'S ECONOMIC ZOO.

As he did so often when confronted by a series of choices, the president continued to send mixed signals as to which economic approach he favored. In March he named Thurman Arnold, an aggressive and highly skilled lawyer, as chief of the antitrust division at the Department of Justice. And a month later he urged Congress to undertake "a thorough study of the concentration of economic power in American industry and the effect of that concentration upon the decline of competition." But he also continued to hold a series of conferences with representatives of big business and to make favorable statements on the concept of national planning. Ickes complained in his diary that "the President . . . is pulling petals off the daisy with the representatives of big business."

Meanwhile the recession deepened. In seventeen southern states Harry Hopkins, head of the Federal Emergency Relief Administration, reported that people were starving. All across the country emergency relief funds were being depleted. The press was full of stories such as the death in New York City of Sarah Goodman, the sixty-year-old mother of a WPA worker, who died of malnutrition and anemia. The president and his advisers, including Corcoran, were being blamed for the economic downturn. With human suffering on the rise in America, Bernard Devoto, the "Easy Chair" columnist for *Harper's Magazine,* opined to a friend, "Tommy Corcoran's depression is a hell of a lot worse than Herbert Hoover's."

10

Corcoran and Court Packing

On February 4, 1937, a few weeks after Franklin Roosevelt's second inauguration, Corcoran rushed into the president's outer office where Missy LeHand sat at her desk. Waving a sheaf of papers at her, he said, "We've got to stop this." Corcoran had just received a copy of the president's drastic proposal to alter the composition of the Supreme Court.

Fed up with the Court's resistance to change and emboldened by his recent reelection, Roosevelt had approached Attorney General Homer Cummings about what could be done to reform the Supreme Court. Cummings, aware that the number of Supreme Court justices was not constitutionally mandated and, in fact, had varied considerably during the nineteenth century, devised a scheme to balance the many conservatives on the Court by appointing liberal ones.

LeHand looked up at Corcoran from her metal typewriter and said, "It's too late." Corcoran hadn't fully realized it at that moment, but the seeds for Roosevelt's plan had been planted nearly two years before — and in some measure by himself.

On May 27, 1935 — later known as "Black Monday" by those who worked in the Roosevelt White House — the Supreme Court handed down its decision in *Schechter Poultry v. United States*. The Court effectively struck down the cornerstone of the New Deal by declaring the National Industrial Recovery Act unconstitutional. The act had established the National Recovery Administration as a central planning agency to regulate pricing, production, and trade practices for industry. By developing more than five hundred specific industrial codes, the president and his brain trust had hoped to diminish "destructive competition" and encourage the formation of unions and organization of workers.

But the Court ruled in three separate decisions that the code system represented an illegal expansion of federal power over interstate commerce, noting that "extraordinary circumstances do not create or enlarge constitutional powers." Corcoran had been in the courtroom when the decisions were read. A few minutes after the justices recessed, he and Ben Cohen were summoned by a page as they prepared to leave. The two young lawyers were admitted to the Court's robing room, where Justice Louis Brandeis, seventy-eight years old, greeted them. Although highly irregular in light of the constitutional separation between the judiciary and executive branches of power, Brandeis felt that the *Schechter* case made it necessary for him to give the president some friendly legislative advice. "Visibly excited and deeply agitated," according to Corcoran, Brandeis told the young government lawyers that the president had been living in "a fool's paradise," and that the decision just handed down meant that "everything that you have been doing must be changed." Gesticulating, Brandeis declared, "This is the end of the business of centralization, and I want you to go back and tell the President that we're not going to let this government centralize everything. It's come to an end."

For many in the administration the Court's decision meant that what they had worked so hard to achieve during the last three years had been thrown out the window. Moreover, liberals within the administration, such as Corcoran, deeply resented the conservative makeup of the Court. Indeed, not one justice had been appointed by President Roosevelt. Ironically, even Justice Brandeis, one of the three liberals on the Court, had by his own admission "declared war" on the New Deal because he believed that it favored big business. At a press conference four days after the decision, Roosevelt declared the ruling the most important since the *Dred Scott* case, which had precipitated the Civil War, adding that the Court had turned the Constitution back to the "horse and buggy days." After the president had vented publicly, he approached Attorney General Cummings and privately asked him what could be done.

Homer Cummings had known Roosevelt for more than twenty years. He had helped plot the strategy that catapulted the relatively obscure Roosevelt to a spot on the national ticket in 1920 as the running mate to the Democratic nominee for president, Governor James M. Cox of Ohio. Even though Roosevelt had lost that election, he always believed that the exposure he gained during the 1920 campaign enabled him to win the presidency in 1932, and he was forever indebted to Cummings.

When Cummings presented his scheme to Roosevelt to change the makeup of the Supreme Court, the president, who perhaps trusted his attorney general too much, agreed to adopt it.

The "Court-packing plan," as critics called it, gave the president the power to appoint one new justice (up to a total of fifteen) for each member of the Supreme Court who refused to retire at full pay within six months of reaching the age of seventy. At the time, six of the nine justices were over seventy.

Corcoran knew the proposal was constitutional, but he anticipated a political maelstrom. Several months earlier, with the knowledge and encouragement of the president, he had floated a similar plan with Burton K. Wheeler, the powerful Democratic senator from Montana. One day in early 1936 Corcoran and Ben Cohen had dropped by the office of the Senate Interstate Commerce Committee, of which Wheeler was chairman, with a speech they hoped the senator would deliver. Wheeler was out of town, so they left the speech with Joe Wright, secretary to the committee. The speech criticized the Court's interpretation of New Deal policies and by implication warned the justices to watch their step. But when Wright showed the speech to Wheeler, the senator immediately decided against delivering it.

A few months later, in May, Corcoran again went to see Wheeler, this time to urge him to introduce a bill that would add three members to the Supreme Court. Again Wheeler demurred, facetiously telling the New Deal lawyer that if he wanted to defeat the president in the 1936 election, a proposal to alter the Court would be the surest way to do it. Wheeler argued that the Court was like a religion with the American people and recalled that when he ran for vice president on Bob La Follette's Independent Progressive ticket in 1924, their platform had proposed a limitation on the high bench. He told Corcoran that this plank of the Progressive platform had been "used devastatingly" against them "from one end of the country to the other." Corcoran respected Wheeler's political acumen and dropped the idea — at least temporarily.

Corcoran knew that any plan to tamper with the Court would engender great anger from the older justices, particularly Brandeis, as well as from Cohen, who had proven to be generally sympathetic to the New Deal. Ben Cohen's biographer, William Lasser, has convincingly argued, however, that Corcoran had been aware of the president's efforts to enlarge the court all along. Attorney General Cummings, for instance, scribbled in his diary two weeks before the plan was made public, "The president also told me that he had tried it [the court-packing plan] on Tommy Corcoran and the latter agreed it would work." Whatever the state of Corcoran's knowledge at the time the plan was unveiled, he agreed with Roosevelt that the future of the New Deal was at stake. Corcoran decided that this was a critical time to rally around the president — or, as he put it, "tails in heads out." At a few minutes before noon on Friday, February 6, 1937, Corcoran hurried over to the Supreme Court and managed to catch up with Justice Brandeis in the robing area. With Roosevelt's permission, Corcoran briefed the justice on the president's plan so that he would not have to learn about it from the press. Brandeis listened attentively and, when Corcoran finished, told him to thank the president for his courtesy. He then resolutely said that he opposed the president's plan and warned Corcoran that Roosevelt was making a serious mistake.

Meanwhile, the president had summoned congressional leaders to the White House to explain his plan. Roosevelt did not even mention the fact that the Court had invalidated much of his New Deal legislation, but chose instead to emphasize that the justices were overworked. He noted that the Court's caseload was rising and implied that the Court was falling behind since 87 percent of the petitions for writs of certiorari had been turned down with no explanation. The congressmen sat in silence, seemingly stunned by the boldness of the plan and the baldness of the president's presentation.

Later that afternoon Corcoran went to see his old friend Senator Wheeler. Wheeler had been a staunch supporter of the New Deal in its early days, and he and Corcoran had worked closely together on the Public Utility Holding Company Act of 1935; the Montanan had directed the floor strategy in the Senate. But Wheeler had grown increasingly wary of what he perceived to be the president's accretion of power. When Corcoran entered the senator's office, he immediately realized that Wheeler was in a state of agitation. Wheeler motioned for Corcoran to sit down, and Corcoran later recalled a somewhat bizarre exchange between them.

"Do you remember Huey Long?" Wheeler asked. Corcoran said that, yes, he did recall the late senator from Louisiana.

"Did you see what Roosevelt did to Huey?" Wheeler sneered.

Corcoran was startled by the implication of the question. "You don't think Roosevelt had him killed?"

"I say, did you see what he did to Huey?" Wheeler asked again, still not explaining himself. "Now, I've been watching Roosevelt for a long time." Wheeler raised his eyebrows. "Once he was only one of us. Now he means to make himself the boss of us all. Well, he's made the mistake [for which] we've been waiting a long time — and this is our chance to cut him down to size."

"But Burt, the Court," Corcoran implored, trying to turn the subject away from Wheeler's conspiracy theory. Corcoran then tried to co-opt the senator by telling him that he could play a role in naming any new justices. Wheeler wouldn't listen and insisted that the president was going to lose support in the Senate. Corcoran left Wheeler's office knowing that he could not change the senator's mind by himself. Corcoran called on others in the Democratic Party, and several days later Wheeler was visited by Charles Michelson of the Democratic Party's national headquarters, along with Sidney Hillman and John L. Lewis of organized labor. Wheeler refused to change his position.

Notwithstanding Wheeler's opposition, Corcoran believed that the president's only chance of passing the bill was in the Senate, which had traditionally proven more loyal to Roosevelt. The president and Corcoran were encouraged when the majority leader, Senator Joseph Robinson of Arkansas, agreed to help. Robinson knew that the legislation would split the Democratic caucus, but he agreed to shepherd the bill on behalf of the president.

Corcoran immediately set about persuading other senators and congressman to support the legislation. In doing so, he used every means at his disposal. For instance, Senator Claude Pepper of Florida, a supporter of Roosevelt's, needed the names of Department of Agriculture employees in his home state of Florida in order to challenge a House bill that had implications for the citrus industry. However, the Department of Agriculture in Washington, following standard procedure of privacy protection, refused to provide the names. When Corcoran called the senator to have lunch to discuss the president's plan for the Court, Pepper mentioned the difficulty he was having with the department. A few days later the list was delivered to Pepper's office in an unmarked brown envelope. Pepper wrote in his diary, "Isn't that something," and after meeting with

Corcoran he scribbled, "No commitment my position on the court matter." At least Pepper was keeping an open mind.

Corcoran focused much of the pressure on members of the judiciary committee, who confirmed appointments to the Court. Senator Marvel M. Logan of Kentucky learned that his coveted flood control legislation was assured if he supported the plan. Corcoran used the Kelly-Nash machine of Chicago to nudge Senator William H. Dieterich of Illinois, who had expressed a deep ambivalence about the bill. Both men ultimately voted for the proposal. Corcoran, however, was discovering what Senator Wheeler had learned many years before — the American people considered the Supreme Court to be above any political meddling.

The nation's newspapers were especially vociferous in opposition to Roosevelt's plan. The *Chicago Tribune* accused the president of trying to "command a majority of the Supreme Court," raising the question, "Shall the Supreme Court be turned into the organ of the President?" The *Tribune* claimed that the plan jeopardized "an impartial and independent judiciary," and that if successful, that principle "in all probability . . . will be abandoned for all time."

Corcoran was also increasingly being singled out in the press as the driving political force in the White House. Writing in the *Saturday Evening Post*, Alva Johnson claimed that Corcoran had risen "to a position of power vaguely resembling that which the Duke of Buckingham held under James the I, or which Oliver the barber held under Louis XI." The article claimed that Corcoran knew how "to turn the heat up" on behalf of the president. As the battle lines were drawn in the Court plan, *Washington Post* business columnist John T. Flynn wrote, "As soon as a fellow gets close to the throne around here, the whispers start and the knives come out. . . . Thomas Corcoran had better watch out."

On Sunday, March 20, the Roosevelt plan ran into a major roadblock. Taking the highly unusual step of publicly criticizing proposed legislation, Chief Justice Charles Evans Hughes prepared a letter to the president that was also signed by Justices Brandeis and Willis Van Devanter, the only two justices with whom he shared it. The letter consistently referred to "the Court," giving the impression that all nine justices opposed the plan, even though the other six justices were not even aware of Hughes's letter.

For Corcoran the Hughes letter had greater significance than putting members of the Court on record in opposition to the plan. He was deeply upset that Brandeis, who had been such an important intellectual leader for the New Deal, had joined Hughes as a signatory. Corcoran felt Brandeis had been disloyal, even treacherous, and vowed never to talk to the justice again. When Ben Cohen visited him six months later, Brandeis expressed "deep disappointment" that Corcoran had not visited him. According to Cohen, "He mentioned Tom several times. . . . He hoped he would come soon." Brandeis had served as a mentor to Corcoran, particularly during the writing of the Securities Exchange Act of 1933 when Professor Frankfurter had been on sabbatical in England. Brandeis was genuinely fond of Corcoran, and while he may have disapproved of some of the younger man's political tactics, he admired his political acumen and reformist impulse.

But when Cohen carried the message of reconciliation back to Corcoran, his partner said, "I am not going to see him. He did not shoot straight with us last year, and it is best not to renew the relationship. The Skipper [FDR] is very bitter, and I think it is best that he not think that we are in touch with him."

With the Hughes letter and the Wheeler-led opposition in the Senate, Roosevelt's plan was in serious trouble. Majority Leader Joe Robinson warned the president that he could muster only forty votes for the bill; the divisions within the Democratic Party, he continued, were becoming so intense that any future New Deal legislation might be threatened. Still, Robinson vowed to fight on, in the hope, some of his colleagues believed, that he himself might one day be considered for a place on the Court.

The battle dragged on for several weeks. During the period in which the Senate Judiciary Committee convened hearings, Corcoran neglected his daily exercise regime and his weight ballooned from 175 pounds to 200. He was overextended. Besides working to save the Court plan, he and Cohen worked on a comprehensive fair labor standards bill as an epidemic of sitdown strikes swept the nation. Their proposal included a board with unlimited authority to set the minimum wage at whatever it deemed appropriate and also to set different standards on the workweek. Senator Hugo Black, however, was not satisfied with the bill, knowing that such broad discretion would draw strong criticism from southern Democrats and most Republicans. Corcoran and Cohen came to discuss it several times in May. "The four of us sat around the table" recalled Lee Richards, one of Black's assistants. "I was the mark-up man, taking notes. They would play Harvard lawyer, use legalese. Black told them he thought these things could be said in simpler language. Neither got his full way on the bill. The Senator said they couldn't get through everything they wanted. They'd question him on that, and he'd look at them with a smirk, as if to say, 'you guys don't know what you're talking about here.' They didn't see eye to eye on everything and would discuss things pretty strongly sometimes."

In late May, as the administration's prospects for a victory on Court reform dimmed, the fair labor standards proposal was ready. The president hoped it would reinvigorate the party. Black introduced it in the Senate, and William Cronnery in the House. Besides empowering Congress to set minimum wages and maximum hours and prohibiting child labor under sixteen, the proposal called for the president to appoint an independent five-member Fair Labor Standards Board. If collective bargaining failed in a labor dispute, the board would have the authority to increase minimum standards. A final sticking point was whether there should be a national minimum wage of twenty-five or thirty-five cents an hour, or if the rate should be flexible and allow for differences among occupations. Corcoran, Cohen, and Reed debated with the president for a while in the Oval Office before Roosevelt finally declared, "Let's have a flat minimum."

From its inception, wage-hours intertwined with Court reform. As early as March 9, the night before Senate hearings on the Court bill were to open, the president gave a fireside chat — one of his periodic radio addresses to the nation — on the issue. Roosevelt said, "We need a wage and hour law, and we need it now," hitting the word *now*. Court packing absorbed his time and emotional energy, and depleted his political capital with Congress. And Corcoran, for one, felt that Roosevelt's heart, for whatever complex of reasons, was not truly in the wage-hours measure. "I don't want the bill," Roosevelt told him. "I want the issue."

Even though the chances for passage of the Court reform legislation seemed to grow weaker day by day, Corcoran remained loyal and continued to fight and to scheme. He asked his friend Izzie Stone at the *New York Post* to write on the interaction of the Court and states' rights. He instructed his assistant Milton Katz to find a quote about the fallibility of lawyers from Voltaire. Katz couldn't find anything under Voltaire, but he came up with this line from Erasmus: "Lawyers are the most learned species of profoundly ignorant men." He lined up highly regarded academics such as Robert Wilson of Cornell, Calvert Magruder of Harvard Law School, and Edwin Corr of Princeton to provide testimony in support of the president's plan. He asked his staff to prepare memoranda for senators such as Bob La Follette of Wisconsin and administration officials such as John G. Winant. He wrote speeches for others to deliver, telling the New York lawyer and former Securities and Exchange general counsel to make an "appeal to Catholics on the issue of religious liberties."

Corcoran used his friend William O. Douglas, the chairman of the Securities and Exchange Commission and a future Supreme Court justice, in a somewhat creative fashion. Although Douglas never took a position on the plan, Corcoran used him indirectly to support it. He asked Douglas, a former Columbia Law professor, to solicit such former colleagues as University of Wisconsin dean Lloyd Garrison to provide testimony. And Douglas recalled, "When they were bringing men to Washington, and lining them up as witnesses before the Senate Committee, they would occasionally deposit one of those clients in my office at the SEC. I gave the man a comfortable chair and reading material." For Corcoran, any implication that Douglas supported the legislation might help bolster the testimony of a wobbly witness.

At the request of the president, Corcoran also went to see his nominal boss at the RFC, Jesse Jones, to ask him to lobby his friends in the Senate. Corcoran wanted to know whether Jones would support increasing the Court by just two members if the current plan didn't pass. Jones, by his own admission, "had no sympathy to pack the court," but he went to Capitol Hill anyway, where he discovered that the president and Corcoran "probably could have gotten the two additional members" if they had not so embittered the lawmakers through their heavy-handed approach.

One of the biggest problems facing the president was that even his vice president, John Nance Garner, who was still immensely popular in the Senate, opposed the legislation. Vice President Garner reportedly told Senator Wheeler that he was "a real patriot" for opposing the bill. And at one point, after Senator Vandenburg, a conservative Republican, denounced the Court plan on the floor of the Senate, Garner, who had been presiding, stepped down from the rostrum and hugged him. Corcoran believed Garner was "off the reservation," and that he was "doing a lot of damage," but there was nothing that could be done about it.

President Roosevelt's plan was proving to be a political disaster. During the summer of 1937 Corcoran watched as his boss "was getting the shit kicked out of him over the Court plan." But Corcoran recalled that the president was extremely grateful for the support he received from one young congressman: "It made him angry that so many people were against it and along comes this new guy who's backing him. Naturally he's impressed." The new guy was a tall, scrawny twenty-nine-year-old from Texas named Lyndon Baines Johnson.

The Tenth Congressional District, like the rest of the Lone Star State, was traditionally Democratic; during President Roosevelt's first term it had been represented by James Buchanan. When Buchanan died in February 1937 of a heart attack, the president asked Corcoran to find a good Democratic candidate to replace him. Corcoran settled on Dr. Bob Montgomery, whom he had first met during the debate over the Holding Company Act. Montgomery was a riveting speaker who had campaigned hard for Roosevelt in Texas in 1936 and was known as a strong advocate of government-owned utilities. As Montgomery contemplated a run for Congress, Corcoran secured financial commitments totaling nearly thirty thousand dollars for his campaign — the equivalent of several hundred thousand dollars today. In the end, however, Montgomery's wife did not want to move to Washington and so the doctor withdrew his candidacy. Corcoran and Roosevelt, without a candidate, temporarily despaired.

Johnson, who was running the National Youth Administration in Texas, decided to pursue a long-shot candidacy. President Roosevelt was extremely popular in the Tenth Congressional District, Texas hill country, and Johnson, an engaging and tireless campaigner, warmly embraced the New Deal at every opportunity. In fact, the principal issue among the candidates was who would work harder to continue the New Deal programs in Texas. Johnson campaigned in part by suggesting falsely that none of his opponents supported Roosevelt. On April 10, 1937, just weeks after Roosevelt launched the Court-packing plan, Johnson polled three thousand votes more than his nearest opponent in a special election and was elected to the U.S. House of Representatives.

A few days after the election, Johnson was invited to meet with

President Roosevelt, who was on a cruise in the Gulf of Mexico. When the presidential yacht docked at Galveston, the young congressman-elect came aboard. The two men immediately established a rapport. Johnson, knowing that FDR had been a former assistant secretary of the navy, talked about his interest in battleships, and stressed to the president the importance of maintaining a powerful navy. At the conclusion of their meeting FDR told Johnson, "I can always use a good man to help out with naval matters in Congress." He scribbled something on a sheet of paper and handed it to Johnson: "Here's a telephone number. When you get to Washington, ask for Tom."

Shortly after Johnson arrived in Washington, he did call Corcoran, who had already been relayed the message that it was important to the president that Johnson be given a seat on the esteemed naval affairs committee. Corcoran contacted Carl Vinson, the chairman of the committee. According to Corcoran, "there were others who had been around for a while and were in line," but "naturally Lyndon got the appointment."

Corcoran and Johnson quickly became friends. Lady Bird Johnson recalled that they often saw each other at brunch at the apartment of their mutual friend Sam Rayburn: "It was our introduction, Lyndon and I, as a young Congressional couple, to a pretty heady society of people that were cabinet members, Supreme Court justices, really important folks around town." Lady Bird was often the only woman there, explaining that "Lyndon just sort of carried me along and nobody said I had to stay home." She would ultimately become even closer to Corcoran than her husband was. For his part, Corcoran recognized that Congressman Johnson had outstanding political skills: "He was smiling and deferential, but, hell, lots of guys can be smiling and deferential. Lyndon had one of the most incredible capacities for dealing with older men. I never saw anything like it. He could follow someone's mind around, and get where it was going before the other fellow knew where it was going. I saw him talk to an older man, and the minute he changed subjects, Lyndon was there ahead of him, and saying what he wanted to hear — before he knew what he wanted to hear." It was that same ability Johnson had used to charm the president in their very first meeting aboard the presidential yacht in Galveston Bay. Corcoran, of course, had a similar ability.

Just eleven days after Johnson's arrival in Washington, on May 24, the tall, lanky congressman was faced with his first major challenge: obtaining funding for a huge public works project in his district, the Marshall Ford Dam. The dam project had been under way for several years; however, some of the appropriated funds were not being released because the project was behind schedule and, according to the comptroller general's office and the Budget Bureau, money was being wasted. Senator Wheeler, the chairman of the rivers and harbors subcommittee, was scheduled to issue a report on the project.

Johnson feared that the Wheeler report could further delay construction and might even lead to a full-scale congressional investigation. To break the logjam, Johnson knew he would need help from the White House. Although he had made a favorable first impression on the president, Johnson could not — as a freshman congressman — have called the president directly. So he turned to Corcoran. One day, after Corcoran had briefed Roosevelt on another matter, he raised the issue of the Marshall Ford Dam and explained how important the project was to Johnson. Roosevelt thought it over a few moments and then said, "Give the kid the dam."

With the president's blessing, and with Johnson pleading for his continued assistance, Corcoran helped shepherd the project through the bureaucracy. Corcoran later recalled that he "made a hell of a lot of calls on that dam" and successfully persuaded the comptroller general and Budget Bureau to resume funding. With the president's support and the funding spigot turned back on, Corcoran was able to blunt the impact of Senator Wheeler's negative report on the project.

On July 14 the president's legislation to reorganize the Court suffered its most severe setback when its most prominent proponent in the Senate, Majority Leader Joe Robinson, was found dead in his apartment. He had suffered a heart attack while reading the *Congressional Record*. The president turned to Garner to rescue him through a compromise. The vice president managed to rush through an emasculated bill that made some minor reforms in the federal court system but did not even mention the Supreme Court. Corcoran believed the vice president had "betrayed the President."

Before the bill could be signed into law, Court reform would be debated one more time — this time in the context of the battle to elect a new majority leader. Pat Harrison of Mississippi, who had vigorously opposed the plan, was running against Alben Barkley of Kentucky, who had remained loyal to the president.

Once again, Corcoran went into action on behalf of FDR to help Barkley. Senator William H. Dieterich of Illinois was revisited by Chicago's Kelly-Nash machine, and in a telephone call to the chieftains of the Pendergast machine in Kansas City, Missouri, Corcoran enlisted help in persuading freshman Senator Harry Truman. Truman had been leaning toward voting for Barkley, but he was so incensed by what he perceived as Corcoran's heavy-handedness that he ultimately sided with Harrison. Barkley nevertheless emerged the winner — by only one vote. President Roosevelt, who had been so publicly humiliated on the Court-packing issue, felt a modicum of redemption, but Harry Truman was angry and would never forgive Corcoran.

11

The Price of Loyalty

In August 1937, the very month that the president's Court reform plan was finally laid to rest, Roosevelt nominated Senator Hugo Black of Alabama to the Supreme Court to replace the retiring conservative justice Willis Van Devanter. Corcoran, who himself had been mentioned in the *New York Times* as a possible successor to Van Devanter, was thrilled. Black had been an enthusiastic supporter of the New Deal and he had worked closely with Corcoran on several pieces of legislation. Moreover, Black had chaired numerous Senate investigations, including the one that exonerated Corcoran in his dispute with Owen Brewster of Maine during the debate in 1935 over the Public Holding Company Act. Although some of Black's colleagues in the Senate felt he was overly partisan and were not especially fond of him, he was confirmed by a vote of 63 to 16, with 17 members not voting.

Just weeks after his confirmation, a rumor began to circulate that Justice Black had once been a member of the Klu Klux Klan. As it turned out, the rumor was true, and when it was revealed just days before the Court was to open a new session, the White House was thrown into a tailspin. Black and his wife had been vacationing in Europe when they received a wire from the White House asking them to return at once. The president's son, James, and Interior Secretary Harold Ickes advised Roosevelt to ask for Black's resignation.

Roosevelt, however, wanted Black to fight, and he asked Tommy Corcoran to help him. Black, having returned from Europe, decided to issue a statement to the press and public explaining his past. As the senator sat writing his statement with his lawyer in borrowed offices at the RFC, Corcoran looked in on them. The senator had drafted a statement that bordered on defiance: Instead of apologizing for his past association with the Klan, he planned to explain it as an obligation to friends. Corcoran persuaded him to tear up the statement and start over, this time condemning the Klan and asking for forgiveness from his colleagues for his past association with the organization. Following Corcoran's advice, Black delivered an explanation that was accepted by the American people and by the press. He seemed to assuage his former colleagues in the Senate, thereby avoiding impeachment, and the controversy passed.

After Justice Van Devanter's retirement, the next vacancy on the Court occurred when Justice George Sutherland, age seventy-seven, submitted his resignation. Corcoran's old boss at the RFC, Stanley Reed, was named to replace Sutherland on January 15, 1938. Reed, solicitor general since 1936, was tall, quiet, and somewhat eccentric in that he reportedly ate an all-rice diet, three times a day, every day.

Corcoran was delighted for Reed. He also began to think that maybe it was time for him to make a move. He contemplated approaching the president and asking to be appointed solicitor general.

Tommy Corcoran was elated when he heard the news on January 4, 1939. The previous evening Felix Frankfurter was at his home in Cambridge, Massachusetts, dressing for dinner when the telephone rang. It was President Roosevelt, who told the professor that he was nominating him to the U.S. Supreme Court. Overcome by joy, all Frankfurter could manage to mumble was, "I wish my mother were alive." He would later record the moment in his diary by noting that "this nomination came like a bombshell." But according to Ben Cohen, it should not have been a complete shock: "I don't know why Felix was so surprised. Tom [Corcoran] was vigorously lobbying for the appointment and would call him every night to report what had been done. And he did it on my phone!"

Corcoran had indeed expended considerable effort and political capital to help his mentor. To show Roosevelt that there was support outside government for Frankfurter, Corcoran persuaded the columnist Drew Pearson to write several columns about the professor, "praising him to the skies," as Pearson remembered it. Attorney General Homer Cummings had told the president that Frankfurter was too liberal and that he would lay himself open to charges of "red" sympathizing. Moreover, wealthy influential Jews led by *New York Times* publisher Arthur Hays Sulzberger lobbied against Frankfurter, fearing that his appointment would stimulate even more of the anti-Semitism that Hitler was championing in Germany. The president was also concerned about opposition in the Senate.

Some western senators wanted the seat to go to someone from their region. Corcoran helped break the logjam when he met privately with Senator George W. Norris of Nebraska and persuaded him to support the nomination. A liberal Republican and a westerner, Norris was the former chairman of the judiciary committee; his support carried great weight. Corcoran even drafted a letter for Norris to send to the president expressing his position. Corcoran, according to one of Frankfurter's biographers, "kept friendly senators supplied with damaging information about other potential candidates," and "wavering senators . . . found their mailboxes stuffed with pro-Frankfurter wires from Harvard Law School alumni, old progressives, law professors and leaders of local bar associations." Roosevelt finally agreed to appoint Frankfurter after reviewing a poll conducted by George Gallup that had been commissioned by Corcoran on behalf of the White House. Gallup found that lawyers would overwhelmingly endorse the appointment.

Corcoran was of course thrilled by the appointment of Frankfurter, as were other prominent liberals in the administration, who viewed the professor as a committed progressive. On January 4, the day Roosevelt sent Frankfurter's nomination to the Senate, Harold Ickes organized a small party in his office that included presidential adviser Harry Hopkins, Attorney General Frank Murphy (who had recently replaced Homer Cummings), Securities and Exchange Commission chairman William O. Douglas, presidential assistant Missy LeHand, and Corcoran, who arrived with two magnums of champagne. Ickes's diary entry for that day summed up the sentiments of those present in his office: "All of us regard this as one of the most significant and worthwhile things the President has done."

A few weeks later, in late January, Frankfurter took his seat on the Court. Emerging from behind red velour drapes, he looked out at the assembled guests in the small chamber and saw many friends: Harold Ickes, Harry Hopkins, Missy LeHand, Ben Cohen. And next to Cohen, beaming, sat Tom Corcoran. What neither Frankfurter nor Corcoran fully appreciated at that moment was the extent to which they viewed their friendship in different ways.

Felix Frankfurter was fifty-six years old, while Corcoran was just shy of forty. For the last seven years Corcoran, working with Ben Cohen, had drafted and helped pass some of the most important legislation in history. Moreover, Corcoran and Cohen were by now well known in

Washington circles: They were owed favors for the jobs they had secured for others. Their contacts and protégés — numbering in the hundreds of mostly young men — now occupied influential positions in agencies and departments throughout the government. Ben Cohen once observed that Frankfurter related very well to his mentors, men like Brandeis and Holmes, and very well to his students, but never to his peers. Cohen, and particularly Corcoran, once students of Frankfurter, now viewed themselves as his peers.

Only a few weeks after Frankfurter was sworn in as an associate justice, Louis Brandeis on February 13, 1939, sent his notice of retirement to President Roosevelt. Brandeis urged President Roosevelt to replace him with the chairman of the Securities and Exchange Commission, William O. Douglas. That evening at a party, Arthur Krock of the *New York Times* told Douglas that "tomorrow morning there will be a box on the front page of the *Times*, saying that a White House source says William O. Douglas will succeed Brandeis." Krock added, "He [the president] thinks I'm poison, so if he knows I'm for you, he'll be against you." The box appeared without Krock's byline and had the intended effect: Douglas was soon being discussed as a serious possibility for appointment to the Court.

But President Roosevelt had reservations about Douglas, who at the time was only forty years old. Although a westerner by birth, Douglas was a registered voter in Connecticut, and there were no justices represented west of the Mississippi. In March the president decided to appoint Senator Lewis Schwellenbach of Washington State, who had campaigned vigorously for FDR's Court reform plan. Before Roosevelt could make his announcement, Douglas's "friends," including Corcoran, approached William Borah of Idaho, then ranking member of the Senate Judiciary Committee. Borah and others ultimately persuaded the president to change his mind and to settle on Douglas. On April 4 William O. Douglas, age forty, was confirmed by a vote of 62 to 4.

Even though he had never run for elective office or served with justices who were former politicians, Justice Douglas was perhaps the most political member of the Court. As chairman of the Securities and Exchange Commission that Corcoran had helped create, Douglas administered the securities laws that Corcoran and Ben Cohen had played such an important role in crafting.

A few months after Douglas's appointment, Chief Justice Charles Evans Hughes decided to create a new position for the Court: an administrator, someone who could manage the daily routine of the Court's work and would police the district courts and their dockets. Corcoran, as always, thought he knew just the man: his friend Stuart Guthrie, who had lived with him on R Street in "the Little Red Schoolhouse." Corcoran had helped place men all over the government, including the Supreme Court, and he knew Guthrie could be another important ally.

Corcoran implored Frankfurter to help Guthrie get the job. Frankfurter floated Guthrie's name among his colleagues, but a former Tennessee congressman, Walter Chandler, appeared to have the inside track with Chief Justice Hughes. Corcoran then asked Justices Douglas and Black to support Guthrie. Douglas agreed to help, but Hugo Black refused. According to Philip Graham, a clerk to Frankfurter at the time and later the publisher of the *Washington Post*, Corcoran raised his voice to Black in frustration: "I put you on this Court."

"Yes," said Justice Black, "but I'm here now and I'm going to stay."

When Guthrie did not get the job, Corcoran was angry with Black, but he seemed to blame Frankfurter more for not having been insistent enough in encouraging Hughes to hire Guthrie. The anger passed, but it was an indication that Corcoran viewed himself less as the professor's student than as someone of equal stature. It was also an indication that Corcoran, who had once revered the Court on which Justice Holmes served, viewed it increasingly as nothing more than another political institution.

President Roosevelt — and Tommy Corcoran — had failed miserably in the Court reform plan; still, events had unfolded in such a manner as to allow them to leave a profound imprint on the makeup of the Court. What Corcoran had been unable to achieve in one fell swoop with the Congress, he had painstakingly accomplished one justice at a time by helping redefine Hugo Black, lobbying for Felix Frankfurter, and promoting William O. Douglas. It was Corcoran's own version of a Court-packing plan.

Although well known throughout the government and by the Washington press corps, Tommy Corcoran was by no means a household name. Rather, he had remained a government lawyer working from an anonymous office in a large agency. But the changing composition of the Court, perhaps more than any other event during his government service, showed that he held real power. Only a very few people understood the extent of his power, but none understood better than the president himself.

Tommy Corcoran had helped the president achieve some significant legislative victories during his first term, but as Roosevelt's second term came to a close, Corcoran was playing an increasingly active political role in the White House. The landscape was changing rapidly both at home, where many of the early victories of the New Deal had been reversed, and abroad, where the rise of Adolf Hitler in Germany darkened the skies over the European continent. The president called on Corcoran because as he confronted the changing times, he needed a pragmatist who could get things done; someone who was completely loyal.

Roosevelt was still seething over the defeat of his Court reform plan. He especially resented those elected officials in the Democratic Party who had opposed the plan; he vowed privately to retaliate. The president was even concerned about the coalition forming between Republicans and conservative southern Democrats that threatened to undermine the successes of the New Deal. As Corcoran remembered, the president felt he was being forced "into a position of political impotence and antagonism incredible to him," and he wanted to return the party to its core Democratic values. With the midterm elections of 1938 approaching, he set about to purge the party of its conservative wing. Corcoran came up with the term *Copperheads* to describe the disloyal Democrats — a phrase that harked back to Civil War politicians who had betrayed President Lincoln by advocating peace at any cost, even dissolution of the Union.

The plan was simple. With the assistance of his most trusted and savvy political aides, Corcoran, Ickes, and Hopkins, Roosevelt targeted certain House and Senate races, identifying officeholders he believed had betrayed him. Roosevelt then intervened in the Democratic primary and openly supported the insurgent candidate while his aides worked behind the scenes to ensure the incumbent's defeat. In the Florida Senate race, for instance, Roosevelt supported Congressman Claude Pepper, a staunch supporter of the New Deal in the House of Representatives. Pepper later credited Corcoran with his victory in the primary after the White House aide funneled contributions to his campaign from Boston department store magnate Lincoln Filene and United Fruit Company president Samuel Zemurray. In Iowa the White House target was Senator

Guy Gillette, who was opposed by a thirty-five-year-old congressman named Otha Wearin. Secretary of Agriculture Henry Wallace, who was from Iowa and followed the race closely, later recalled that he "didn't like Tommy Corcoran's maneuvers" in the campaign, but at the time there was little Wallace or anyone else could do to stop him. In Maryland the president opposed the renomination of Senator Millard Tydings, who had fought the White House on almost every important piece of reform legislation. When a reporter asked Corcoran about White House interference in the Maryland race, he quipped, "I never have anything to say. Professionally, I am deaf, dumb and blind." But Corcoran helped orchestrate a two-day blitz of the state by the president in support of David J. Lewis, a liberal congressman from the western part of the state.

Of the several purge campaigns being directed from the White House, Corcoran was most involved in the effort to unseat New York congressman John O'Connor, who represented Manhattan and who had opposed President Roosevelt on the death sentence provision in the public utilities holding company bill. Ironically, O'Connor had close ties to both Roosevelt and Corcoran: He was the brother of a former law partner of Roosevelt's and a distant cousin of Corcoran's. Congressman O'Connor's opponent, James H. Fay, was a war veteran and well known in the Irish community. Scorned by the Manhattan Democratic machine, Fay was personally courted and persuaded to run by Corcoran and Harry Hopkins.

During the New York Democratic primary campaign Corcoran did everything he could to ensure Fay's election, including raising money, researching issues, and writing campaign speeches. In mid-September Jim Farley, the chairman of the Democratic National Committee and an opponent of the Roosevelt purge, had lunch with Treasury Secretary Henry Morgenthau. Morgenthau told Farley that he had been stunned when Corcoran had called him and asked him to get "internal revenue collectors to come out for Fay against O'Connor in New York."

Farley was fed up with Corcoran's scheming and publicly referred to him and his allies as political "amateurs." Corcoran, however, was unfazed by the criticism and spent the last month of the 1938 election season helping direct field operations for the Fay campaign. On Election Day his candidate won easily, although most of the other Roosevelt-supported candidates lost.

◆　◆　◆

During the midterm elections, Corcoran took time out to help one of his protégés. Congressman Lyndon Johnson had another public works project that he wanted to fund. This time he managed to wangle an appointment with the president by himself. According to Johnson, "I had visions of damming the Colorado and Pedernales rivers, of building a simple, rural electrical line out to the farmers that lived in my Hill country." After being led into the Oval Office, the young congressman prepared to make his case, but he was quickly interrupted by Roosevelt, who asked him, "Did you ever see a Russian woman naked." When a puzzled Johnson drawled a tentative "no," Roosevelt proceeded to tell him about White House aide Harry Hopkins's recent trip to Russia and how the Russian women were so strong because they did so much of the physical labor. Johnson listened politely, if somewhat bewildered, and before he knew it, "my fifteen minutes was gone . . . and I found myself in the West Lobby without ever having made my proposition."

Johnson again sought out Corcoran for help. Corcoran told him, "Roosevelt likes pictures, the bigger, the better. That's where you made your mistake. You should have gotten a picture of some dam and pictures of your transmission lines to the big cities, Houston and Dallas and San Antonio. That would have gotten his attention." Johnson dutifully obtained large photographs of the Buchanan Dam and the transmission lines under construction for Austin. He then scheduled another meeting with the president.

A few weeks later Johnson found himself back in the Oval Office. This time he avoided any small talk. After shaking hands with FDR he rolled out a big map and laid a number of photographs on the president's desk. Johnson made his case about the dam project as Roosevelt listened attentively. When the congressman finished, Roosevelt reached for the telephone and called John Carmody, the head of the Rural Electrification Administration. Johnson later remembered, "[H]e made old John give me that first loan, which resulted in the Pedernales Electric Cooperative. I walked out of there with a million-dollar loan. That was about one of the happiest moments in my life." It also secured Johnson's reputation in West Texas as someone who could deliver for his constituents.

Tommy Corcoran had been thinking for several months that perhaps it was time for him to leave government, or at least to change his career within the government. Indeed, after Roosevelt's reelection in 1936, Corcoran had contemplated returning to the Cotton and Franklin law firm in New York, but he didn't want to leave Ben Cohen behind — he knew he couldn't persuade the white-shoe firm to accept a Jewish lawyer. President Roosevelt told him that he had an important legislative agenda and that Corcoran would be central to getting it passed. But Corcoran had spent most of the second term in political dogfights, and he was weary.

Moreover, Joe Kennedy had made Corcoran a very tempting offer, which he mentioned in a letter to his father. Although Corcoran wasn't specific about the Kennedy proposal, it was clear that it would mean a great deal more money. Corcoran's father wrote back that the president's enemies "would rejoice at your departure." And his father wondered how his son would feel if "accused of turning turtle on the liberals?"

Corcoran approached Roosevelt about becoming the solicitor general of the United States, the government's trial lawyer before the Supreme Court. According to Corcoran, the president beseeched him to stay in his current position, telling him that there "would be lots of chances in the future to be Solicitor General," and that someday he and Ben Cohen would "take over any New York law office" they wanted. Corcoran's father agreed, writing his son that his work for the president carried with it "honor and glory" and that it would be "a stepping-stone" to greater heights.

Corcoran decided to stay put and later recalled the depth of his loyalty to the commander in chief: "I could not refuse to do anything Roosevelt told me." But in truth, he had other reasons for staying. "Subconsciously, I didn't want to lose my secretary, Peggy Dowd, whom I would later marry. She was a beautiful immigrant daughter born in San Francisco of immigrant parents and wouldn't fit into a New York law office and I knew she wouldn't go." Peggy came from a modest background. After living briefly in San Francisco, her parents had moved to Washington, DC, where her father joined the post office and her mother raised Peggy and three other children. Like Corcoran, the green-eyed, red-haired Dowd was Catholic; she had been educated by nuns at the Convent of Immaculate Conception in Washington. She never attended college, but she took a course in typing while still a teenager and landed a job at the Reconstruction Finance Corporation. Ben Cohen observed that she was the only person he knew who could keep up with Corcoran.

Tommy soon found that he and Peggy had more in common than work. Although not well educated, she was intelligent and politically astute; like him, she loved music and was an accomplished singer. Corcoran was spending more and more time with Dowd, having meals with her and escorting her home after work. He was falling in love.

Just weeks after the midterm elections, Corcoran was working on another political problem for Roosevelt. When Cardinal George Mundelein of Chicago told the RFC lawyer that he planned to travel to the Vatican in 1938, Corcoran arranged for him to stop over in Washington and visit with Roosevelt. During his stay, Mundelein discussed with the president the initiation of formal diplomatic relations between the United States and the Vatican. The president, although noncommittal, seemed receptive to the idea, and the cardinal set off for Europe.

Mundelein had been outspoken in his opposition to the rise of the Nazis in Germany. However, the Vatican had been substantially less vocal in its opposition. As the decade of 1930s came to a close, the Vatican also had not yet condemned the Catholic hierarchy in Spain and its affiliation with the fascist movement headed by General Francisco Franco. Franco had revolted from the Spanish Republican government in 1936 and by 1939 had established a dictatorship over all of Spain.

In the United States, the Roosevelt administration initially favored the reestablishment of Republican rule, but conservative leaders in the Catholic Church conducted an effective lobbying operation that reversed American foreign policy. Their main contact in the White House was Corcoran, who managed to persuade the president to maintain the arms embargo on both sides in the Spanish Civil War. Corcoran may have favored a progressive domestic agenda, but his foreign policy views were decidedly reactionary: He believed that the political left in Europe, which included the Communist Party, threatened the church and was therefore dangerous.

While the embargo did deny American arms to the Spanish loyalist government, it did not hinder the flow of weapons to Franco from Mussolini and Hitler, both of whom provided material support to their fellow fascist. Roosevelt would later acknowledge to his cabinet that he had made a "grave mistake" with respect to neutrality in the Spanish Civil War.

In early October, two weeks after Mundelein's trip to the White House,

Corcoran boarded a tugboat that chugged out into New York Harbor to greet the cardinal, who was returning on an Italian ocean liner. Mundelein was delighted to see Corcoran, but his mood was one of grave concern. He showed little interest in pursuing his original conversations concerning diplomatic relations with the Vatican. The cardinal had been alarmed by what he had seen in Europe; he now believed that fascism posed a serious threat not only to the church, but to democracy itself. Convinced that he must shore up national support for President Roosevelt, Mundelein decided to confront one of the president's most vociferous Catholic critics, Father Charles Coughlin.

Father Coughlin had been born in Ontario, Canada, and was ordained as a Catholic priest at the age of twenty-two. In 1926 he moved to a suburb of Detroit, where he arranged with a local radio station to broadcast one of his Sunday sermons. From that point on he enjoyed a meteoric rise in popularity; his audience ultimately reached an estimated forty million people. The writer Wallace Stegner, a frequent listener, attributed Coughlin's appeal at least in part to "a voice of such mellow richness, such manly, heart-warming, confidential intimacy, such emotional and ingratiating charm, that anyone tuning past it on the radio dial almost automatically returned to hear it again."

In the early years of the Roosevelt presidency, Coughlin aligned himself squarely with the New Deal. He was scornful of "predatory capitalists," particularly the private bankers whom Corcoran believed were bent on creating a plutocracy. Corcoran admired Coughlin not only for his support of the New Deal and his calls for financial reform, but also for the prominence he was receiving as a Catholic spokesman. Senator Burton Wheeler described Coughlin and Corcoran as close friends, but as Coughlin became more strident and critical of the administration, Corcoran increasingly shared the president's view that Coughlin was a dangerous self-promoter.

By 1937 Coughlin had renounced Roosevelt. His speeches became laced with bigotry and anti-Semitism. He also railed against communism while expressing some cautious admiration for the European fascism of Adolf Hitler and Benito Mussolini. Despite his controversial views, Coughlin still had a large following among Catholics. Cardinal Mundelein considered him a serious threat to the church.

Mundelein asked Corcoran if he would help prepare a radio address that the cardinal wanted his auxiliary bishop, Bernard Sheil, to deliver. Corcoran worked closely with Mundelein and Sheil to craft a speech that was very supportive of the president's foreign policy. In the late fall of 1938, just before Sheil was to deliver his speech, Corcoran left a message at the White House press office that Sheil "publicly raked Coughlin over the coals for Cardinal Mundelein," and suggested that "this information ought to leak out so they will know who Sheil is." If Sheil was going to align the church with the White House, Corcoran wanted to maximize the political impact.

On December 11, 1938, Bishop Sheil's speech, largely written by Corcoran, was carried nationwide over the radio by the National Broadcasting Company. In declaring that Coughlin "does not speak for the Roman Catholic Church or express its doctrines or sentiments," Sheil added his voice to the increasing number of critics, including Jewish organizations, members of the press, and Catholic leaders such as Archbishop Edward Mooney of Detroit. Corcoran's involvement in politics now extended to the highest reaches of the Catholic Church. It was undoubtedly a heady feeling for someone who so strongly identified himself as an Irish Catholic. Growing up in Pawtucket, his family had consciously set themselves apart from other Irish families by their abstinence from alcohol, which his parents believed had corrupted many Irish Americans. Tommy's tribal identification was reinforced by the closed and often bigoted world that he had encountered at Harvard Law School, on Wall Street, and within the Roosevelt administration. In each setting he found himself viewed somewhat disdainfully as an Irish Catholic, a fact that seemed only to intensify his desire to succeed.

In 1938 Corcoran was thirty-eight years old and had been in government for nearly the entire fourth decade of his life. Although an exceedingly capable lawyer, he was increasingly used by the president as a purely political operative. Corcoran had come to Washington as an idealistic young man, although he had always balanced his idealism with a heavy dose of pragmatism. He had, after all, begun his career in Washington working in a Republican administration. But Corcoran was now circling close to the flame of power, and whether he knew it or not, he was changing.

Idealism had given way to pragmatism, and pragmatism was giving way to arrogance.

12

Time to Make a Million

E ven though the purge of anti–New Deal Democrats largely failed in the 1938 midterm elections, the victory of James Fay in the New York City Democratic primary of 1938 had temporarily raised Corcoran's political profile, particularly in the press. On September 12, 1938, Corcoran and Cohen were on the cover of *Time* magazine. The photograph showed a smiling Corcoran standing behind a seated Cohen. Underneath the photograph, the caption for the story read, THEY CALL THEMSELVES CATALYSTS. The inside article gushed that "The firm of Corcoran and Cohen had started out to do a job for a client — the President of the United States. If remaking the Democratic Party is part of that job, Partner Corcoran is well up to learning and playing politics tooth and anvil."

In the early summer of 1939 Corcoran was briefly talked about as a possible successor to Jim Farley at the Democratic National Committee. At one White House press conference, a reporter asked Roosevelt, "Mr. President, are you going to have corroborations or denials, or other comments on reports that Mr. Corcoran is trying to remove Mr. Farley as Chairman of the Democratic National Committee?"

"I don't know what I can call it," Roosevelt replied. "You can call it tommyrot. Isn't that a good idea?" he continued breezily as the reporters laughed. "That refers to your story, you see, and not to Mr. Corcoran." The reporters laughed again at the president's enigmatic comments. If, indeed, the president was considering appointing Corcoran to lead the party, he never publicly tipped his hand.

It was perhaps FDR's refusal on that occasion to support Corcoran more enthusiastically for a more prominent role in his administration that emboldened the lawyer's detractors. A few weeks after Roosevelt's remarks, Steve Early, the White House press secretary, who had never trusted or liked Corcoran, announced the appointment of six new administrative assistants, including James Rowe, Corcoran's friend and fellow Holmes clerk. In his announcement Early made it clear that the president was orchestrating a changing of the guard at the White House and that

Corcoran and Cohen no longer had unfettered access and unchallenged influence. Early told reporters that "the brain trust is out the window."

Corcoran was irritated by Early's comments, but he recognized that the president's spokesman was at least partially correct. Notwithstanding some of the favorable headlines he had received in the wake of the 1938 midterm elections, Corcoran knew he no longer enjoyed the influence he once had at the White House. Although President Roosevelt liked Corcoran and valued his political skills, speechwriting ability, and legal talent, he knew his aide had accumulated enemies virtually everywhere in the government. On Capitol Hill, Senator Guy Gillette estimated that as a result of his work on the Court reform plan and the Democratic purge, Corcoran had alienated more than thirty-five senators. One of those senators, Walter George of Georgia, excoriated the "little group that was trying to drive me from office." He called them "Communists" and included Corcoran and Cohen, whom he referred to as "two little New York Wall Street lawyers who have arrogated themselves the power of saying who shall be a senator and who shall not be a senator." Secretary of Agriculture Henry Wallace predicted with some satisfaction, "It is obvious that Tommy will have very little value when it comes to wining an election."

Moreover, Roosevelt recognized that his domestic agenda would soon be overtaken by events in Europe. One day the president called Corcoran into his office and told him that he "was calling off the New Deal for the war." Corcoran believed that Roosevelt was doing so because he saw "rearmament and support of our prospective allies as a partial solution to his own domestic dilemma."

By this point in his career, Corcoran had developed a deep ambivalence about Roosevelt. While he believed sincerely in many of the things the president was trying to accomplish both internationally and domestically, he had always harbored a fundamental distrust of politicians. On many occasions, particularly during the Court-packing plan and the Democratic purge, Corcoran displayed extraordinary loyalty to the president. Yet he once observed that "Frankie grew up in New York politics. His was a slick city world, an aristocratic world. . . . Frankie would change his mind every fifteen minutes. He would lie." Although he was hurt, Corcoran was not particularly surprised that the president hadn't come to his defense after Early's comments.

◆　◆　◆

As his own star dimmed, Corcoran watched as the influence of another trusted aide, Harry Hopkins, increased. In many ways Hopkins was an unlikely political operative. Born in a small town in Iowa in 1890, Hopkins attended Grinnell College, where he studied social and political sciences. After college, he settled in New York to pursue a career in social work. Appalled by the housing conditions, the lack of health care, and the general absence of opportunity and hope for the city's poor, Hopkins dedicated himself to helping them. In 1931 Governor Roosevelt appointed him the head of the New York Temporary Relief Agency. After Roosevelt became president he appointed Hopkins to run the Federal Relief Emergency Agency. Ironically, Corcoran had helped Hopkins to achieve greater prominence within the administration.

In the late fall of 1938 President Roosevelt asked Hopkins if he would serve as secretary of commerce. Roosevelt knew the business community considered Hopkins practically a socialist and that his appointment would be extremely controversial. The president asked Corcoran to solicit the help of Averell Harriman, the chairman of the Business Advisory Council, a business leaders' association. Though somewhat ineffective, the council was the administration's most important channel to the business community. Harriman, who knew Hopkins, confirmed to Corcoran that he and his colleagues were not enthusiastic about the idea of Hopkins acting as an advocate for American business, but Corcoran nevertheless managed to persuade him that it was smart politics to get behind Hopkins because, as he explained, "Harry has the keys to the White House, not only the front door, but the back door, too."

After Corcoran's visit, Harriman convinced enough members of his council that they could work with Hopkins. On the day before Christmas, 1938, Attorney General Cummings administered the oath of office to Hopkins as the secretary of commerce. Even though he had an important job in the cabinet, Hopkins left the day-to-day running of the department to his deputies and continued to function as one of the key White House advisers.

Hopkins's ambitions were not limited to his admission into the inner circle of the White House or even to a seat in the cabinet. Roosevelt had hinted to several aides, including Hopkins and Corcoran, that he might not run for a third term. He believed that his place in history was secure, and he looked forward to retiring to Hyde Park. He told Dan Tobin of the

Teamsters Union, "I need a rest." When it appeared Roosevelt might not run for a third term, Hopkins approached Corcoran about the possibility of Hopkins's own candidacy.

According to Corcoran, late one evening in the summer of 1939 Hopkins came to his office and asked him to help suppress his involvement with a story that he feared would soon appear in the New York press. Hopkins, as Corcoran remembered it, explained that he had had a relationship with a woman who had just jumped to her death from the window of a New York hotel. Hopkins was married, and he feared that the incident would implicate him in a scandal. Corcoran promised to help. He called New York financier Bernard Baruch, whom he had known from his days on Wall Street, and asked him to use his influence with the New York press. Baruch contacted New York newspaperman Herbert Swope, and while Corcoran never knew what Swope did, Hopkins's name did not appear the next morning in any of the stories concerning the woman's death.

The next morning Corcoran was in his office when Hopkins paid him another visit. The buoyant man thanked Corcoran for helping keep his name out of the newspaper. But Hopkins had returned for another reason: "Tommy, I will be the first to tell you — the President wants me to succeed him." He said he had discussed his candidacy with the president, who had suggested that Corcoran could help secure a fifty-thousand-dollar contribution from his business contacts. Hopkins explained that the money would be critical to launching his campaign.

Corcoran was taken by surprise and thought Hopkins had a delusional view of his own stature and political appeal. He told Hopkins that he would help, but only if the president asked him directly. Hopkins then became concerned. "But you mustn't talk to the President about me or about money. I'm acting for the President, but he doesn't want to be asked about it. You will have to do this on faith." Corcoran said politely that he would wait for the president to contact him.

Hopkins never mentioned his candidacy again to Corcoran, and the president never asked him to raise money for Hopkins. While in hindsight the prospect of Hopkins's candidacy seems far-fetched, others have since confirmed that Roosevelt did, indeed, encourage Hopkins to consider a run for presidency. Roosevelt feared that after he left the Oval Office, a conservative such as James Farley might emerge to capture the Democratic nomination. Hopkins was actually quite well known as the head of the Works Progress Administration and as an international troubleshooter for the president. He also had standing among powerful forces in the Democratic Party, including some of the big-city bosses. In the end, though, Hopkins's poor health prevented him from further consideration.

Corcoran acknowledged in his unpublished memoirs that he had "misread the events in Europe during the 1930's." Indeed, the rise of Adolf Hitler and the unrest in Europe initially seemed to Corcoran as nothing more than predictable tensions among "a patchwork of declining states." In September 1939, however, Hitler, who had already annexed Czechoslovakia and Austria, invaded Poland and defeated its unmechanized army within a month. Soon afterward, Great Britain and France declared war on the Third Reich. Corcoran became convinced that the escalating conflict in Europe threatened to draw in the United States. He also believed that President Roosevelt was the only man with the skill to keep the nation out of war — but if war came, to lead it to victory.

Roosevelt, however, had still not revealed his plans for a third term, and some were beginning to despair. Harold Ickes recorded in his diary that "once in a while a group of us will get together — Frank Murphy, Harry Hopkins, Bob Jackson and Tom Corcoran . . . Ben Cohen and one or two others, and we will talk without having anything to talk about. Word comes to us that the President is going to call us over to the White House, but the call never comes." While Hopkins had obviously harbored his own ambitions during this period, within the administration Corcoran and Ickes were pushing a "Draft Roosevelt for a Third Term" movement.

Some in the administration resented the fact that Corcoran had thrust himself into such a prominent position with regard to the president's political future — especially since they believed that in the wake of Early's comments, Corcoran was being eased out of the inner circle. David Lilienthal, a founding director of the powerful Tennessee Valley Authority, kept a detailed diary during this period, and in one entry he complained that Corcoran continued to view himself as "a kind of watchdog of the President's mind and conduct." Adolf Berle, skeptical of Corcoran's motives, wrote to New York mayor Fiorello La Guardia that "some sort of organization" would "emerge . . . nominally to perpetuate New Deal ideals but really for strictly political purposes."

Ironically, it was in large part due to his continuing loyalty to the president that Corcoran seemed to be accumulating enemies around Washington. At dinner one night in late July 1939, President Roosevelt heard an earful about Corcoran from Jim Farley, the politically ambitious chairman of the Democratic National Committee. The president mentioned that Corcoran had criticized Farley for not supporting the purge in 1938, particularly in the O'Connor race. Farley reminded the president that he had approved of his decision to stay neutral. "Getting back to Corcoran," Farley continued, "there is no reason why he should expect the party chairman, whose first consideration is to maintain party harmony, to do his dirty, party-splitting work." Farley told Roosevelt that he was getting "fed up with Corcoran and his crowd," and he cautioned the president that "they haven't got the influence with you that is attributed to them, but I don't think it is healthy that such an impression of their influence prevails. . . . They are merely peanuts in a sugar barrel." As usual, the president listened without agreeing or disagreeing.

In truth, Farley was intensely jealous of the vastly more intelligent and resourceful Corcoran. Though Farley was chairman of the Democratic National Committee, Corcoran controlled patronage within the administration. Edward Flynn, boss of the Bronx, wrote in his autobiography that Corcoran "short-circuited the National Committee." Flynn noted that "many of the appointments went to men who were supporters of the President and believed in what he was trying to do, but who were not Democrats in many instances, and in all instances were not organization Democrats." This was completely in keeping with Corcoran's view that a civil service should be marked by excellence and not political affiliation, but it infuriated Farley.

Corcoran further enraged the chairman by directly challenging him over a key patronage job in Farley's own state of New York. When the position of U.S. attorney for the Southern District of New York — one of the most visible law enforcement posts in the country — became available, Farley proposed two possible candidates, Charles T. Murphy and Gregory F. Noonan. But Corcoran pushed for an old friend from Cotton and Franklin, John T. Cahill. When Cahill was chosen, rumors again surfaced that Corcoran would be replacing Farley at the Democratic National Committee.

Another prominent member of the administration with whom Corcoran clashed was the TVA's David Lilienthal. Secretary of the Interior

Harold Ickes believed that from an organizational point of view the TVA should be within his bailiwick. It clearly would have enhanced Ickes's already powerful position within the administration. By siding with Ickes, Corcoran ran squarely into Lilienthal. Lilienthal, also a graduate of Harvard Law School, admired Corcoran's energy but believed Corcoran was "throwing enough knives" into his back "to make him "look like a porcupine." On October 4, 1939, Corcoran and Cohen met with Lilienthal in an attempt to persuade him that the TVA could simply be folded into the Interior Department. Lilienthal recorded in his diary that he became "somewhat warm behind the collar" at what he called their proposal for "back door administration," and he noted that he was consistently "interrupted by Corcoran with some highly personal reference or some wisecrack about the next election and its effect on TVA." Lilienthal wearily recorded in his diary that "Tom doesn't seem to realize that the method of which he is so extensively a practitioner of trying to slip things through, without adequate consideration and discussion, may have a good deal to do with the growth of that practice among others."

Corcoran's enemies, those who actively plotted against him, were gaining in numbers: Secretary of Agriculture Wallace, Chairman Farley, economic adviser Berle, and Press Secretary Early were just a few. Hopkins and Lilienthal were not enemies, but neither were they friends. They were unlikely to defend Corcoran when others disparaged him.

The pressure on Corcoran was building.

As rumors swirled that the president had become disaffected with Corcoran, Harold Ickes, one of the few in the administration who provided a different point of view on Corcoran, wrote to Roosevelt, "As I look back over the last two years I can honestly say that Tom has been invaluable. Some of us could write and speak for the cause . . . but it was Tom who did most of the practical work." To emphasize his point, Ickes, who had taken time out from his vacation in Maine to write, reminded Roosevelt that Corcoran had been invaluable when "Farley was holding back in the traces." Ickes insisted that Corcoran was "badly needed" in the upcoming campaign.

Corcoran had dozens of loyal supporters throughout the government — men for whom he had found jobs — but he had few defenders in the White House. James Roosevelt, the president's son, had been an important ally. In early June 1939 an article appeared in the *Saturday Evening Post* accusing James of being a war profiteer who had helped Joseph Kennedy to obtain the ambassadorship to Great Britain. According to the magazine, "Jimmy has helped Kennedy to reach the great positions he now holds as that of Ambassador to London and that of premier Scotch whiskey salesman in America." Kennedy had known the article was coming, but despite his best efforts had been unable to suppress it. When it appeared, James asked Tommy how he should respond. Corcoran advised him to check into the Mayo Clinic and not talk to anyone from the press. Young Roosevelt followed his advice. Not only did the story die, but while he was out in Minnesota, Roosevelt fell in love with his nurse, whom he later married. Although Corcoran had once described young Jimmy as "naive and inexperienced," he was still the president's son and had been a loyal supporter of Corcoran's. When James Roosevelt left Washington and moved to Hollywood with his new bride, there was one less person in the White House to defend Corcoran.

No one else in the president's family stood up for Corcoran. FDR's daughter, Anna, believed Corcoran had ably served her father, but she was influenced by her close friend Norman Littell, a high-ranking Justice Department official who intensely disliked Corcoran. Littell often criticized Corcoran to Anna and once told her, "No quality is so essential in government as simple integrity and forthrightness." Then, referring to Corcoran, he added, "Ability and brilliance of mind are not enough." Anna tended to think Corcoran had become a liability to her father.

Corcoran's chief ally in the White House, Missy LeHand, would suffer a stroke in 1941, but even in 1939 she could no longer protect Corcoran's interests and shield him from his detractors. Littell claimed that LeHand had represented one camp in the White House and the "Tommy Corcoran school worked through her and did everything they could to court the influence of Mrs. Roosevelt." But the first lady, never a fan of Corcoran's, was now becoming increasingly unfriendly. Although Corcoran's charm was legendary, the grande dames of Washington increasingly found him cocky and abrasive. Secretary Ickes noted in his diary that Marion Frankfurter, the wife of the Supreme Court justice, "has never really liked Tom and she likes him even less these days."

Then, in the summer of 1939, Raymond Moley, formerly the top aide to Roosevelt, published his memoir, *After Seven Years,* in which he portrayed the president as having been manipulated by Corcoran. Corcoran wrote to his brother David, now in Buenos Aires, ". . . [Moley is] sore because I wouldn't play stooge for him inside the White House. There has been so much swill poured on me in the last couple of years . . . the Moley stuff is only part of a lot more." Some of it, however, Corcoran had brought on himself.

Jim Rowe, a friend of Corcoran's and an administrative assistant to Roosevelt, recalled that the complaints about Corcoran rang true because the president himself was getting fed up with Corcoran's behavior: "The problem between Tom and the President was that Tom would stand in front of the President and insist on a course of action and pound on the desk." Rowe added, "Now you know, no one ever pounded the desk with Roosevelt."

Some of the Irish charm had seemingly given way to impatience and truculence. Perhaps Corcoran thought the extraordinary loyalty he had shown the president deserved more than a simple hearing on issues that mattered to him.

Roosevelt's secretary, Grace Tully, recalled that Corcoran's exclusion from the inner circle of the White House came at some point in 1939 "without a single drum or flourish being heard." There was an impending speech, and the president had asked for speechwriters Sam Rosenman and Robert Sherwood. As they worked on the speech in the Oval Office, Roosevelt looked at Tully and said, "Where's Tommy?" Tully told the president that since he had not specifically asked for him, she had not called him. Roosevelt replied, "Well, never mind then. There's no time right now to get him." According to Tully, "That speech was prepared without Tommy's help. So were the ones from that day forward."

After his health began to fail, Secretary Hopkins's plans for a presidential run in 1940 were permanently derailed. Roosevelt did not have to look far for other potential candidates: Senator Burton Wheeler, Chairman Jim Farley, and Vice President Garner were all interested. Roosevelt also encouraged Secretary of Agriculture Henry Wallace, Supreme Court justice William O. Douglas, and Attorney General Robert Jackson to consider candidacy. Corcoran's friend Justice Hugo Black even entertained the notion of picking up the liberal mantle if Roosevelt stepped down. But as the war in Europe intensified, the pressure on Roosevelt to run again became enormous.

The first public calls from within the administration for a third term came from Attorney General Jackson. They were quickly echoed by Corcoran, who persuaded state party leaders to rally around the commander in chief. Corcoran's good friend Mayor Ed Kelly of Chicago addressed a convention of young Democrats in August 1939 and told them that they must not accept the president's "no" to a third term.

In the fall of 1939 Roosevelt finally decided to seek reelection, although he did not tip his hand until the following summer. U.S. entry into the European war now seemed inevitable, and Roosevelt simply did not believe he could walk away from such a crisis. Corcoran advised him to be careful not to move in the direction of what he termed "the European quagmire." Corcoran was isolationist for a number of reasons. He felt that the American public was not ready to engage in a foreign war. He also worried that by taking sides, Roosevelt would alienate a large segment of the American electorate, what he called the "hyphenated American": German-Americans, Italian-Americans, and Irish-Americans. In many ways, his concern for the last group colored his view of the war.

Corcoran claimed that Roosevelt, "like most Episcopalian patricians . . . believed a free Europe was the center of liberal civilization." The president was not only Episcopalian, he was an Anglophile. Corcoran had strong objections when in 1940 Roosevelt invited the king and queen of England to Hyde Park for what was termed a "hotdog" picnic. In his unpublished memoirs, Corcoran explained that Irish Americans remembered their parents' repression at the hands of the British, and "were even more adamant about the sanctity of the Old Sod's moral neutrality." He recalled that Harry Hopkins once told him, "Tom you're too Catholic to trust the Russians and too Irish to trust the English."

"You're right, Harry, and so I am," replied Corcoran. "So I am."

As the preparation for war intensified, Corcoran and Hopkins, who had both seen their ambitions thwarted by the president, now clashed more frequently, especially in the counsel each offered to Roosevelt over the desired relationship between government and business. Hopkins advocated a rapprochement with business, believing that the industrial sector was essential. Corcoran, on the other hand, proposed to extend the early New Deal by keeping Republican industrialists out of the war business: Indeed, he favored government planning and production. On this and other issues, the president clearly favored Hopkins, who now lived in the White House and boasted to Corcoran, "Remember Tommy, anything you spend an entire day doing I can undo in ten minutes after supper." Within the White House Corcoran and Hopkins continued to work together on various projects, but Corcoran's friends believed Hopkins did nothing to discourage, and may have actually surreptitiously encouraged, the mounting criticism of Corcoran from outside the White House. As William O. Douglas put it, "Hopkins was adept at 'throwing sand in the gears' of any potential competitor for influence over FDR."

Many Democrats heaved a collective sigh of relief about Roosevelt's decision to seek a third term — although it was unprecedented and controversial, and support for the president was by no means unanimous. Since Roosevelt's nomination was not in doubt, the question most often asked was who would occupy the second place on the ticket. Corcoran had long believed that during the debate over the expansion of the Supreme Court, Vice President Garner had been disloyal; Corcoran not only encouraged Roosevelt to drop Garner from the ticket but actively disparaged the vice president to his friends throughout the government. Adolf Berle complained to House Speaker Sam Rayburn that Corcoran's treatment of Vice President Garner was just another example of his arrogance. Rayburn, who liked Corcoran, was nonetheless angry that Garner, a fellow Texan, was "being put up to every kind of insult and obloquy."

Garner himself had had enough of the job and mused about a possible challenge to Roosevelt. Working with Harold Ickes, Corcoran used Congressman Lyndon Johnson and Texas attorney Alvin Wirtz to engineer a face-saving deal for Garner: The Texas delegation would support his favorite-son candidacy for the presidency, but would also refuse to join in any stop-Roosevelt movement. After he made his decision, Garner appeared to harbor no lasting resentment of Corcoran, telling one colleague, "If I was going to rob a bank, I'd want to go along with Tommy Corcoran."

Corcoran initially promoted Attorney General Frank Murphy as a smart choice to replace Garner on the national ticket. Born in a small farming community in Michigan in 1893, Murphy served abroad as a U.S. Army officer during the First World War and was later elected a judge in Michigan. He gained national attention in 1926 when he ruled in favor of the celebrated lawyer Clarence Darrow, who was defending a black man accused of murder. Four years later he was elected mayor of Detroit and became one of President Roosevelt's most prominent supporters. Murphy, at the suggestion of President Roosevelt, ran and was elected governor of Michigan in 1936, but was defeated two years later after he failed to support the automobile industry during a strike. Roosevelt admired Murphy and in late December 1938 appointed him attorney general. Corcoran also admired Murphy who, like himself, was loyal to Roosevelt, politically astute, and a Catholic.

The Catholic identification seemed increasingly important to Corcoran. Although anti-Irish and anti-Catholic sentiments were still prevalent in certain parts of the country, the phenomenal success of men like Corcoran, Kennedy, and Murphy had softened the rigid barriers that once kept the Irish from assuming positions of national importance. William Shannon, a historian on the Irish in America, has written, "These and others like them, men in their thirties and early forties when Roosevelt came to power in 1933, were the first generation of American Irish to play significant roles on the national stage." Corcoran knew Roosevelt would win and may have figured it was time to break down the barrier that Al Smith had not been able to twenty years earlier.

For a brief time the potential candidacy of Murphy also seemed to be gaining currency in the press. Corcoran's friend columnist Joseph Alsop argued that if Roosevelt chose his Catholic attorney general as vice president, the Democrats would have a "dream ticket" for 1940. But when Justice Pierce Butler died in November 1939, Roosevelt nominated Murphy to the Supreme Court.

Ultimately Roosevelt chose Henry Wallace, his two-term secretary of agriculture, as his running mate in 1940. Corcoran opposed the selection because he believed Wallace lacked the necessary political skills. Like many in Washington at the time, Corcoran thought that Wallace was soft on communism and something of a dreamer. For his part, Wallace viewed Corcoran as a dangerous political operator who had demonstrated terrible judgment in both the Court reform plan and the Democratic purge. The secretary of agriculture told Jim Farley that he was disturbed by Corcoran's influence on matters of vital national interest. And he complained to Adolf Berle that "the politics of the Corcoran crowd [are] as completely disastrous as anything could possibly be." But neither the presence of a new vice president nor the carping of rivals for the president's attention could dissuade Corcoran from practicing politics in the White House. He was still pulling strings, calling in a chit, cajoling a congressman, or placing a public servant in a critical job. Politics was in his blood. And he was still mixing it with the Catholic Church.

Father Coughlin had briefly suspended his attacks on the president following Bishop Sheil's speech in late 1938, but by early 1939 he had resumed his scathing criticism of Roosevelt and his foreign policy. Mundelein and Sheil again enlisted Corcoran, who traveled to Chicago to prepare a speech endorsing the president's proposed neutrality legislation. Mundelein, however, was gravely ill; on October 1, 1939, he died. Notwithstanding the loss of his friend, mentor, and cardinal, the next night Bishop Sheil again went on national radio to denounce Father Coughlin and to strongly support the president. Roosevelt termed the radio address "a grand speech."

According to several accounts, following Bishop Sheil's speech in October 1939, President Roosevelt decided to send a message to Cardinal Francis Spellman of New York that Coughlin was a liability. Roosevelt allegedly asked a prominent professor at Catholic University to convey to Spellman that if Coughlin were not taken off the air, the Internal Revenue Service would be ready to look into the personal taxes of each of the nation's Roman Catholic bishops. Corcoran, who had once before suggested using the IRS for such a purpose against Roosevelt's political enemies, confirmed the outlines of the scheme to one journalist by acknowledging, "That sounds about right."

As it turned out, the IRS was not needed. In early 1940 the National Association of Broadcasters implemented new rules limiting the sale of airtime to "spokesmen of controversial public issues." Coughlin's access to the airwaves diminished, and his influence dwindled. Although he continued to write articles that promoted American neutrality and praised the German people, he was completely discredited after the attack on Pearl Harbor and returned to an anonymous life as a parish priest outside Detroit. Tommy Corcoran had played a small, but important, role in his demise.

After Mundelein's death, Corcoran worked to ensure that Sheil succeed the liberal cardinal. Corcoran spent several days in Chicago advising Sheil, and upon returning to Washington he told David Lilienthal and Ben Cohen, "I have good news. We managed to get Bishop Sheil elected to take Mundelein's place . . . tough fight but we made it. See how important that is for 1940." Lilienthal recorded his horror in his diary: "This was the most dangerous of all kinds of politics — the mingling of the Catholic church and the city machine operations. Somehow I have difficulty in believing Tom has been authorized to participate in this sort of thing."

Even though Sheil replaced Mundelein as head of the archdiocese of Chicago, it was Cardinal Francis Spellman of New York who emerged as the country's most prominent Catholic. Spellman was not nearly as liberal as Sheil, but he was nonetheless close to Corcoran. Spellman's mother had been raised in Taunton, Massachusetts, the same small town as Corcoran's mother, and while they barely knew each other growing up, this common heritage served as a bond between them. Corcoran claimed that he was the first to introduce Cardinal Spellman to President Roosevelt and his family. James Roosevelt became close friends with the cardinal, and by 1936 Spellman was a familiar figure at both the White House and Hyde Park. Indeed, that year he became the first priest ever to celebrate a Mass in the White House.

Corcoran and Spellman shared an innate love of politics. A few years earlier Spellman had tried unsuccessfully to have James Michael Curley, the controversial former mayor of Boston, appointed ambassador to Italy. When Roosevelt rejected the idea — likely because Curley had served time in jail — Spellman privately criticized the president and later wrote in his diary, "The President and James Farley had heard that I was displeased." Perhaps Spellman now felt that he was owed a favor, because he and Corcoran discussed the possibility of Spellman representing the church in Washington on a full-time basis.

Spellman was not popular with many in Roosevelt's inner circle. The president noted that the administration's highest-ranking Catholic official, James Farley, "doesn't like Spellman." James Rowe, a Roosevelt aide, recalled, "Nobody liked Spellman, but everyone listened very closely." Most considered him, in the words of Drew Pearson, to be nothing more than "a hard-boiled politician." It didn't help Corcoran's standing in the White House that he was associated with the cardinal and so visibly involved in the politics of the church. To some of his colleagues in the White House, Harry Hopkins began referring to Corcoran as "that little Jesuit."

◆ ◆ ◆

In anticipation of the 1940 Democratic convention, held that year in Chicago, Corcoran, ever the loyal political soldier, was still plotting strategy. William O. Douglas remembered attending a meeting in the Oval Office just before the convention with the president, Corcoran, Harry Hopkins, Speaker Alben Barkley, and Senator James Byrnes of South Carolina. After a few minutes of small talk, Corcoran announced, "Alben should give the keynote address." The president ignored the remark for a moment, but then he turned to Barkley and asked "Alben, how are your vocal cords these days?"

Notwithstanding Corcoran's continuing loyalty, experience, and political skills, President Roosevelt gave him a relatively minor role in the 1940 campaign. In September Senator George Norris of Nebraska and Mayor Fiorello La Guardia of New York jointly announced at a White House ceremony the creation of "Citizen's Committee for Roosevelt." Norris stated that the country needed President Roosevelt because, as he put it, "These are no ordinary times." Perhaps with this in mind, Roosevelt suggested that Corcoran leave Washington and move to New York to work with the liberal New York mayor on the Citizen's Committee.

Corcoran served as vice chairman of the committee and spent several months in New York, meeting daily with La Guardia and organizing independent voters around the country. The president clearly didn't want to offend the party regulars who so resented Corcoran. Arthur Krock, the *New York Times* correspondent, would later tell Corcoran that he had done the president "an incalculable service by removing the cause of frustration for so many others." For the man who had spent weeks traveling the country by train with the president during the 1936 campaign, it was a clear signal that his influence had largely evaporated.

One day in early October 1940, Roosevelt pulled aside his secretary of the interior, Harold Ickes, and told him that it was time for Tommy Corcoran "to resign from the legal staff of the RFC, and then, after the election, either come back into the government or do whatever he may feel like doing." The president recognized Corcoran's considerable talents, but he wanted them directed to a specific project and felt it was too politically dangerous to allow him to continue serving as a virtual minister without portfolio at the RFC.

◆ ◆ ◆

Not long after the 1940 convention, Corcoran confided to speechwriter Sam Rosenman that it was time for him to leave government, at least temporarily: "I want to make a million dollars in one year, that's all. Then I'm coming back to the government for the rest of my life." Corcoran had said this once before — a decade earlier when he left his clerkship with Justice Holmes to pursue his fortune on Wall Street. Then it was the challenge of making money that attracted him, but now his motive was more practical. In truth Corcoran had been contemplating leaving the government for more than a year. The man who had scorned the institution of marriage had fallen in love and wanted to start a family.

In the winter of 1940 Corcoran, thirty-nine years old, asked his long-time secretary, Peggy Dowd, who was twelve years his junior, to marry him. Corcoran had wanted to marry her for some time, but the pace of his work and opposition from his mother and his mentors, Frankfurter and the president himself, had caused him to wait. Josephine Corcoran, Tommy's mother, had once referred to Peggy as your "warmed over french fried potato of a secretary." The president, ever the patrician, thought Corcoran could do better than to marry a working Irish girl whose father was a mailman in the District of Columbia. Frankfurter simply wanted his student to marry someone with money so that he could continue to devote his energies to public service.

Corcoran hoped to convince Roosevelt that he was making the right decision and he arranged through Missy LeHand to formally introduce his new bride to the president. Peggy bought a new dress and hat for the occasion, and she and Tommy arrived at the White House family quarters at the appointed time. But after they'd waited for well over two hours, Harry Hopkins came into the reception area to tell them that the president could not, in fact, see them. Corcoran was furious and later claimed that the incident contributed to his decision to leave public service.

Tommy and Peggy exchanged vows at a simple ceremony in a small Catholic church, St. John's, in Leesburg, Virginia, on March 4, 1940. They had delayed the event several times due to changes in the congressional calendar. Only the couple's immediate family and a few close friends attended the service. Ben Cohen, of course, was there. Corcoran's first roommate in Washington, Ed Foley, now general counsel for the Treasury Department, was the best man. Cohen was Corcoran's best friend, but Foley was his closest Irish American, Catholic friend. While neither

Corcoran nor Cohen ever seems to have commented on Tommy's choice for best man, Corcoran apparently believed that it was more appropriate to have Foley at his side.

Tommy placed on Peggy's finger a ring that she had picked out by herself because he had been too busy to accompany her to the jeweler. The society pages of the newspapers ran a photograph the next day showing the young couple laughing after the ceremony. They were photographed examining a rabbit's foot that a family member had given them for good luck.

After a brief honeymoon skiing in Canada, Tommy and Peggy bought a house on Garfield Street in the District and, as if to signal that Tommy wasn't quite ready to give up the Little Red Schoolhouse, the newlyweds were joined by Corcoran's old roommates, Ben Cohen and Stuart Guthrie, who would live with them for next several months. Clearly Corcoran, whose life had been so dominated both professionally and socially by male companionship, continued to have a somewhat unusual view of women.

Corcoran began to consider his options. He had been inclined to leave government anyway, but he wanted to have a family and his government salary of nine thousand dollars a year at the Reconstruction Finance Corporation simply wasn't enough. He resurrected the idea that he and Ben might join Cotton and Franklin in New York. Corcoran talked it over with the partners in the firm, but they were not ready to accept Ben because he was Jewish. Then Peggy became pregnant.

Peggy had never wanted to move to New York, and now with a baby on the way they decided to remain in Washington. Tommy knew that the best way to take advantage of the knowledge he had gained in government, and the vast network of contacts he had cultivated, was to help his prospective clients understand how Washington worked. Corcoran would use his legal, political, and personal skills as a Washington lobbyist.

PART THREE

The War Years

13

A New Stage

Late one evening in the fall of 1940, Tommy Corcoran answered the telephone in his house and an operator told him that he had a long-distance call from his brother in Mexico City. Over the static on the line, Tommy heard the anxiety in his brother's voice as David told him that his company, Sterling Pharmaceutical, was in serious trouble. David, who was unable to return to the United States for several weeks due to business commitments, asked him to catch the next plane to Mexico City. As it happened, the inauguration of Mexican president Manuel Avila Camacho was just days away, and Tom managed to wangle an appointment as a member of the U.S. delegation.

David Corcoran was three years younger than his brother but possessed of similar energy, acumen, and ambition. Growing up in Pawtucket, he was constantly finding ways to make money: delivering newspapers, tending the cash register in a grocery store, handing out dinner pails to mill workers, and selling the *Saturday Evening Post* door to door. He was a fine athlete who starred as quarterback on his high school football team and held the state's broad-jump record.

At Pawtucket High School David was president of his high school class, head of the school's athletic association, and editor of the school newspaper. During the summers he joined his older brother as a hutboy with the Appalachian Mountain Club in New Hampshire's White Mountains. Together Tommy and David assisted hikers and mountain climbers, cooked and cleaned for guests at the huts, and cleared and maintained the range's wooded trails and hiking paths.

At seventeen David was accepted to both Princeton and Brown. Although both his father and Tommy had attended Brown, David left the gritty streets of Pawtucket for the Gothic arches and refined eating clubs of Princeton. In his junior year he decided that he wanted to be a doctor, and after completing the necessary pre-med course work in his last two years he was accepted at both Johns Hopkins and St. John's College,

Oxford University. Before making a choice, he decided to gain some practical experience and arranged an internship with the family doctor in Pawtucket. While he had enjoyed studying medicine, David found practicing it on a daily basis unrewarding. Indeed, he was bored by the stream of patients complaining of the flu or skin rashes or indigestion. He decided to pursue a career in business and enrolled at the Harvard Business School. Excelling in the classroom, his brilliance caught the eye of Professor Phillip Thayer, who, much as Professor Frankfurter had done for Tommy, helped set the stage for young David's future.

After graduation, Professor Thayer gave David Corcoran his first opportunity in international business, offering him a position as treasurer of an exporter, the Asiatic Selling Company. Thayer had been brought in to help rescue the money-losing firm. While the professor traveled through Asia promoting Asiatic Selling, David manned the New York office.

Although the company ultimately went bankrupt, Corcoran's marketing and management skills did not go unnoticed. Another export firm active in Asia, Dodge and Seymour, offered him a position in 1928. Only twenty-five years old, Corcoran moved to Osaka, Japan, where he sold everything from Palmolive soap to Del Monte canned goods to automobiles. Although Asian consumers were not always receptive to American goods, Corcoran did particularly well selling automobiles, and General Motors hired him away from Dodge and Seymour to manage its Tokyo office. At GM he promoted Chevrolet automobiles, whose sales soon outpaced those of Ford, which had enjoyed a traditional lead.

David was making a name for himself as an international businessman, but he was homesick. He was also growing increasingly leery, as his brother later recounted, "about the military clique's growing influence in Tokyo." After five years in Asia he returned to New York, where he considered several offers before accepting a position with the Sterling Pharmaceutical company.

Sterling was founded as a patent medicine company at the turn of the twentieth century by two Ohio entrepreneurs with only a thousand dollars. It pursued an aggressive growth strategy and acquired several patent medicines; a dozen years later the company was worth four million. Sterling made its most important acquisition when it paid $5.3 million for the American Bayer aspirin company on December 12, 1918, one month after the armistice ending World War I. The Bayer Company, which was German in origin, had been seized during the war under the Alien Property Custodian Act. Sterling now owned a piece of the best-known patent medicine in the world. Instead of trying to fold Bayer into its stable of patent medicines, Sterling created two companies, the Bayer Company to sell Bayer aspirin, and Winthrop Pharmaceuticals to house its sixty-three other patent medicines. Ironically, Sterling's managers discovered that in many places, particularly Latin America, the American Bayer Company could not compete with its more established European counterparts, and so it withdrew its presence.

In 1919 the Bayer Company and I. G. Farben, the German manufacturer of Bayer, entered into a joint venture to divide profits from the sale of Bayer aspirin around the world. I. G. Farben was an enormous company with immense production facilities and a huge workforce, including many Nobel Prize–winning scientists. The company's laboratories and facilities manufactured everything from vaccines to rocket fuel to aspirin.

Although it still held the American rights to Bayer, Sterling's export sales in 1939 were limited to a few markets, including the Philippines, Cuba, and Puerto Rico. In these countries the company's offices were managed by Germans because of its aspirin sales and cooperative agreements with the I. G. Farben industries. At the request of the company's president, Dr. William E. Weiss, David Corcoran traveled around the world to the company's various outposts in order to assess how best to raise export sales for Sterling's products. When he returned, he recommended to Dr. Weiss that Sterling acquire foreign production facilities in Latin America to support a more effective distribution network.

The rise of Nazi Germany meant that Sterling came under scrutiny from many different quarters of the U.S. government for its past association with Farben. In September 1939 a committee appointed by Congress and led by Nelson Rockefeller began to collect information on U.S. companies operating in South America. Sterling was asked to provide detailed information on its activities. A month later the Department of Justice began investigating U.S. companies suspected of having Nazi connections. The FBI subsequently produced reports that accused Latin American subsidiaries of U.S. firms, including Sterling, of employing Nazi sympathizers. More importantly, the Department of Justice began examining whether or not Sterling violated American antitrust laws through its association with I. G. Farben. Rumors swirled that Senator Burton Wheeler would announce that he was planning to appoint a subcommittee to investigate the relations between American and German firms.

After an all-night flight to Mexico City, Tommy met his brother in the lobby of the Hotel Reforma under murals that had been painted by Diego Rivera. They exchanged greetings, then David got right to the point: He was hearing rumors of government investigations into Sterling. With war on the horizon in Europe, David Corcoran was concerned about the relationship between Sterling and Farben and was worried about Weiss, Sterling's president, whom he considered naive and a possible Nazi sympathizer. David was a businessman and a loyal American who wanted nothing to do with the Nazis. He feared that his company was in serious danger.

The British were already boycotting German firms and David worried that if the United States entered the war on the side of Britain, the company, because of its cooperative agreements with Farben, might be seized by the U.S. government under the Alien Property Custodian Act — just as the American Bayer aspirin company had been seized thirty years earlier. The Alien Property Custodian Act stipulated that the assets of the company had to be sold off to the highest bidder.

Tommy Corcoran shared his brother's abhorrence of the Nazis, but he viewed Sterling's problems in a more stark political light. Notwithstanding that German industry was now functioning under Nazi rule and that Sterling's president had continued to do business with them, Tommy believed that his brother's company was a potential victim. As Corcoran explained it many years later: "People with superior political connections appeared ready to legally steal [David's] company." Tommy included on that list Senator Wheeler. Corcoran was friendly with Wheeler, but they had crossed swords on both the Court-packing plan of 1937 and the purge of Democrats in 1938. Corcoran believed that Wheeler, among others, might want not only to punish him through his brother, but also to arrange indirectly for a political payoff. Tommy believed it was possible for a senator such as Wheeler to fix the bidding process and award the assets to a corporation whose future earnings would in turn help finance an expensive reelection campaign. In the aftermath of the Teapot Dome scandal, Wheeler had been prosecuted, albeit acquitted, of taking money from an oilman to pull political strings at the Interior Department.

When Tommy flew back to the United States, he poked around and quickly discovered that Sterling was being investigated on many levels. In addition to Wheeler, the Department of Justice and the Federal Bureau of Investigation had launched inquiries. While Congress focused on the extent of Nazi influence on American corporations by companies such as Sterling, the Department of Justice was taking a different approach: examining whether Sterling had conspired with Farben to control the sale of aspirin — in essence forming an aspirin cartel. For his part, Tommy Corcoran decided early on that, with the exception of his brother, he cared not a whit for the management of Sterling, particularly if they had authorized entering into an illegal relationship with Farben. Corcoran would gladly sacrifice any member of the Sterling's management if it would preserve his brother's company — and reputation.

As the Nazi onslaught continued unabated in Europe, war also raged on another front — in Asia, where Japan's imperialist army marched against China. Japan had invaded China in 1937 and occupied Beijing and the coastal areas of the country. By 1938 the Japanese had moved farther and farther into the Middle Kingdom, occupying large areas of the north, east, and south, and installing a puppet government at Nanking.

Notwithstanding the growing threat of world war, Americans remained, for the most part, decidedly isolationist. During the first two terms of his presidency, Roosevelt had pursued a foreign policy that had been articulated most passionately in his 1936 Chautauqua address in which he proclaimed, "I hate war." After Britain and France reluctantly declared war on Germany, Roosevelt told the nation in a fireside chat on September 3, 1939, that he "hoped the nation will keep out of this war." President Roosevelt privately believed that the United States would at some point be forced to engage both Germany and Japan, but he had seen how twenty years earlier President Wilson had misread the public sentiment leading up to World War I and how he had paid a price after the war in his effort to establish the League of Nations.

In Asia, President Roosevelt was increasingly concerned about Japanese aggression. If Japan were to gain complete control over China, not only would the morale of other Asian nations deteriorate, but Japan would be situated strategically to wrest control of all Asia and the Pacific. The president felt that America's best hope to thwart the Japanese in Asia rested with Chiang Kai-shek, the former military aide to Sun Yat-sen, the founder of the Nationalist Kuomintang Party. For well over a decade Chiang had enjoyed supremacy in the Nationalist movement, attempting to gain control over all China by intermittently fighting regional warlords, communist insurgents, and, ultimately, the Japanese.

By 1940 Chiang had moved his Nationalist government headquarters from Nanking to Chungking. The Chinese communists, led by Mao Tse-tung, operated out of Yenan in the northwest. With the invasion of the Japanese, Mao had shifted his energy to repelling the foreign army, and he and Chiang enjoyed an uneasy coalition. Chiang, however, continued to be most interested in retaining power for himself and recognized that the United States could be a critical ally.

While the United States provided loans to China, it did nothing to halt Japanese expansion until January 1940 when President Roosevelt allowed a forty-year-old trade treaty to expire, thereby cutting off trade and curtailing critical shipments of oil, steel, and iron. Several months later, in the fall of 1940, Japan responded by signing the Tripartite Pact, forming an alliance with Germany and Italy.

Although President Roosevelt was reluctant to be far out in front of the American people in either actions or rhetoric, he began to prepare for war by sending to Congress a bill establishing the first peacetime compulsory military service program. In September 1940 the bill passed by only one vote — a clear indication that many in Congress continued to be in an isolationist mood. Next, the president sent to Congress legislation creating Lend-Lease, a plan to provide weapons and supplies to Britain with the understanding that repayment would be made in kind after the war.

At the beginning of 1941 Corcoran officially informed the president that he was leaving the government to begin a career practicing law. The president had successfully won reelection to a third term, defeating the Republican candidate Wendell Willkie by nearly five million votes. Corcoran had not played a major role in the campaign, and it was clear to him that, like Moley before him, he was no longer a member of the inner circle. Although Roosevelt's reaction is nowhere recorded, he accepted the resignation of his long-serving aide.

When Justice Frankfurter heard of Corcoran's imminent departure, he advised the president to keep Corcoran in the government, although it was clear he thought the RFC lawyer should have far less influence and power. On January 8, 1941, Frankfurter wrote Roosevelt an astonishing letter, claiming hyperbolically that "for a combination of reasons Tom lacks mental health right now. He is, therefore, in great danger of making a wrong turning, with possibilities of vast harm to himself and of undoubted serious damage to the national effort."

Frankfurter believed that "the key to the situation is to gain time by finding the square tile for Tom's square peg." The justice advised the president to send Corcoran a letter "constituting an appropriate blend of affection and direction . . . ordering him to stay here until the right outlet is found for him. In the meantime, Tom must be employed. But it ought not to be difficult to have him temporarily made a Special Assistant to the Attorney General. A command, showing affection for that would compose his troubled soul, is the practical solution."

While expressing apparent personal concern for Corcoran, Frankfurter actually was more worried that Ben Cohen would leave government if Corcoran did. In his memorandum to the president, Frankfurter wrote, "That is the last thing Ben wants to do — leave here — but Tom's leaving would operate as a coercion of Ben because of the latter's devotion to him." Frankfurter feared losing Cohen because "of his extraordinary talents and imagination and his rare gifts of character."

On January 19, 1941, the day before her father attended Roosevelt's inauguration to an unprecedented third term, Margaret Gardner Corcoran, seven and a half pounds, was born at Sibley Hospital in Washington. She was christened by the Washington press corps "the inaugural baby." A few days later Corcoran received a letter from Roosevelt, who began by congratulating him and his wife on the birth of their daughter. Roosevelt welcomed him "to the high rank of Fatherhood, " adding, "If the young lady has only some of the loveliness of her mother and some of the fire of her father, she will be a great girl."

The president then made an attempt to persuade Tommy to remain in government: "I know you are troubled about your family responsibilities. But this is the most critical year in our country's history and you simply cannot leave me now. You must know that I understand fully how much your front-line fighting has put you 'on the spot,' and that you can no longer contribute effectively without portfolio. As our plans unfold,

National Defense will have positions of rank and responsibilities where your great talents and powers will be desperately needed."

Roosevelt continued, "All this, as you will be the first to appreciate, takes time. And so, as your Commander-in-Chief, I instruct you to enroll within the next week as a Special Assistant to the Attorney General to await a definite assignment. I need intelligent, devoted and selfless men. You have been one of those few and must continue. Few men have been understanding of the forces of history against which we have contended and against which we must now rally more powerfully and astutely than ever. I have always thought you were one of those few. Today I need such men more than ever."

The president closed the letter by noting that Corcoran had been "fond of quoting Holmes as your great exemplar. Fundamentally, he was a great soldier in life and not merely on the battlefield. Ask yourself how he would have answered this call." This final appeal was a direct and very personal effort to tug at Corcoran's heartstrings, for Holmes continued to be Corcoran's greatest source of inspiration. Little did Corcoran know that while the president had signed the letter, it was largely written by two of Corcoran's closest friends, Ben Cohen and James Rowe.

For his part, Corcoran liked and admired Roosevelt, but he had watched the president drop other advisers. He later recalled an amusing incident from the 1936 campaign. Corcoran had traveled with the president to Hyde Park and was working on a speech with Roosevelt, Peggy Dowd, and Missy LeHand when a Hudson River neighbor brought the president a pheasant that he had shot. Roosevelt loved game and he ordered the bird prepared for lunch. Corcoran remembered that "we worked well that morning," but "the pheasant was never out of his thoughts and he kept dropping asides about lunch. A fat pheasant, he pronounced, was the perfect dish for four companions." But just a few minutes before the meal was to be served, Mrs. Roosevelt arrived unexpectedly with her secretary and the president's mother. Three additional places were set at the table and as the president was being wheeled into the dining room, he whispered to Corcoran, "Tommy, I am about to perform a small miracle. There might be a political lesson in it for you. I am going to carve and serve that bird so that each lady at the table is convinced she is favored with the choicest portion. Sorry, boy, there won't be anything left for you but the

Pope's nose." At the dawn of his third term, the president was carving up the choicest assignments for others. Corcoran had enjoyed eight exciting, productive years in the government, and perhaps he would return, but for now he wanted to make some money.

As Corcoran prepared to leave government, David Lilienthal observed that Tommy was not the same man he had first met nearly a decade before: "Then he had the appearance and the lingo of a campus leader — very youthful, full of zest and fun, but essentially the sophomore. There is something hard and tough in his appearance and manner now and it all came back to me — the resemblance to the hard-bitten, tough guy cynical ward leaders in Chicago." Corcoran was more cynical than he had been a decade before, and with good reason. He had never shied away from a fight and always ably defended the president, even to the point of accepting responsibility for debacles, such as the Court reform scheme, that he had not created. But he had no regrets about his government service, for he had been involved at the highest level in some of the most important decisions of the administration and had accomplished an extraordinary amount. Corcoran had displayed unswerving loyalty, but like his boss, the president, he was also a pragmatist. He had learned the degree to which the president's pragmatism eclipsed his loyalty.

Only a few weeks after Corcoran left the government, Lauchlin Currie telephoned him and asked if he could drop by his office. Currie, who had been appointed one of the president's six administrative assistants in the 1939 reorganization plan, was an economist by training and an early advocate of war preparation. Currie and Corcoran certainly knew each other, but they were not particularly close friends. Nevertheless, Currie walked the four blocks from the White House to Corcoran's rented office to convey a request directly from the president. Roosevelt, according to Currie, fervently believed that the United States must help the beleaguered government of Chiang Kai-shek. The president feared that if China fell, Japanese imperialism would go unchecked in the region. Conversely, if the United States could bolster Chiang, perhaps the mainland could provide air and naval bases for an eventual Allied invasion of Japan. Currie told Corcoran that the president wanted to provide Lend-Lease assistance to Chiang, but he first wanted Corcoran to discreetly sound out his friends on Capitol Hill.

Corcoran had long believed that the European powers had deep-seated differences rooted in their history and would have to sort out their own problems. He felt that the greatest threat to America came from Japan, and he was intrigued by the president's plan to arm Chiang quietly. As he put it, "It was an interesting question: would the Congress allow executive action in the Pacific theatre under the aegis of Lend Lease, which had been written with Europe in mind? Or would Congress bolt the doors and hobble the President before the first ship for China loaded with arms bought with nominal loans to the Chungking government?" Corcoran knew that Chiang had powerful friends in the United States, including the publisher of *Time* magazine, Henry Luce. He decided that the answer to the question depended on how it was posed, and that any public opposition to future assistance to China depended on how the plan was implemented. If the aid were provided quietly and not overtly as a first step to American military engagement, he believed the American people would not object. Corcoran, ever the loyal soldier to Roosevelt, agreed to help and visited his old friends in the Senate, including Senators Burton Wheeler of Montana, Worth Clark of Montana, Paul Douglas of Illinois, and Robert La Follette of Wisconsin. A few weeks later Corcoran reported to the president that while these men were opposed to involvement in Europe, he did not believe that a modest aid program to China would cause them serious concern.

After evaluating Corcoran's optimistic assessment, Roosevelt conveyed to him, again through Lauchlin Currie, that he wanted to establish a private corporation to provide assistance to the Chinese. Corcoran thought the president's idea was ingenious, and later wrote that "if we'd tried to set up a government corporation per se, or do the work out of a Federal office, there would have been devil to pay on the Hill." Instead, Corcoran set up a civilian corporation, which he chartered in Delaware and, at the suggestion of the president, named China Defense Supplies. It would be, as Corcoran later recalled, "the entire lend lease operation" for Asia.

In order to provide the company with the stamp of respectability, Roosevelt arranged for his elderly uncle, Frederick Delano, who'd spent a lifetime in the China trade, to be co-chairman. The other chairman was T. V. Soong, Chiang's personal representative who frequently visited Washington to lobby for aid to his government. Soong, a Harvard graduate, was also Chiang's finance minister, as well as his banker and his brother-in-law. And he was a close friend of David Corcoran, whom he had met when the younger Corcoran was working in the Far East.

After getting the green light to proceed with the establishment of China Defense Supplies, Corcoran hired a staff to run the company. With Delano and Soong as the chairmen, Corcoran went about appointing a politically savvy management team. First, he asked his brother David to take a leave of absence from Sterling to become president. Although David Corcoran was an extremely competent manager, Sterling was then under investigation by the Department of Justice, and David's appointment could be cynically viewed as an attempt by Tommy to protect his brother from the investigation by shielding him with a quasi-government role. Next he appointed a bright young lawyer named Bill Youngman as general counsel. Youngman had previously clerked for Judge Learned Hand, and after Ben Cohen recommended him, he landed a job as general counsel at the Federal Power Commission. To direct the program from China, Corcoran chose Whitey Willauer, who had been his brother Howard's roommate at Exeter, Princeton, and Harvard Law School. Corcoran had previously helped Willauer get a job at the Federal Aviation Administration and he knew Willauer was "crazy about China." After helping to establish and run China Defense Supplies, Willauer moved over to the Foreign Economic Administration, where he supervised both Lend-Lease to China and purchases from China. Lastly, Corcoran arranged for the Marine Corps to detail Quinn Shaunessy, who, like Corcoran, was a graduate of Harvard Law School. Shaunessy was given the task of locating and acquiring goods, supplies, and weapons for the Chinese. Corcoran took no title himself other than outside counsel for China Defense Supplies. He paid himself five thousand dollars to set up the company, but didn't want his affiliation with it to interfere with his incipient lobbying practice.

Secretary of State Cordell Hull summed up Chiang Kai-shek's dilemma over the war when he told Treasury Secretary Henry Morgenthau, "If we could only find some way to have them [the Chinese] drop some bombs on Tokyo." Hull's view was shared by a retired American Army Air Corps captain in China named Claire Chennault. Chennault, a tall, lanky Texan, had grown up in Louisiana and was descended from southern Civil War heroes Stonewall Jackson and Robert E. Lee, as well as one of the Marquis

de Lafayette's revolutionary compatriots. In 1917 he was commissioned in
the U.S. Army, and during World War I he earned his wings. After the war
Chennault served in a number of peacetime assignments flying fighter
aircraft. During the 1930s he became an instructor at the Air Corps
Tactical School, where he first advocated the controversial view that the
United States needed an air force comprising aircraft constructed for
speed, range, and firepower, instead of the traditional heavy bombers.

Chennault left the U.S. Air Corps in 1937 due to partial deafness. He
approached Chiang Kai-shek and offered to help his meager and poorly
trained Nationalist air force. Chiang immediately appointed him his aviation adviser. Since the United States refused to provide air defense of
Chungking and Chennault knew that it would take years to train and
equip a Chinese air force, he seized upon the idea of creating a volunteer
air force made up of former U.S. airmen. He also knew that he was not
well regarded by the military brass — his military tactics were considered
suspect, and his management of soldiers was known to be lax. Bypassing
the generals, Chennault came to Washington to talk to the politicians.
According to Corcoran, he received orders from the president through
Missy LeHand to meet Chennault and "size him up."

Tommy recalled that in his first meeting with Chennault, he initially
wondered whether or not the general was "mad," because he actually
believed his small air corps could defeat the massive Japanese air force.
But if Corcoran was skeptical of Chennault's views on the war, he was
attracted by the general's charisma and recognized a soul mate of sorts in
his doggedness. As Chennault's Chinese-born wife, Anna, would later
write, "The Chennault-Corcoran association was easy. Differing in their
abilities, they were temperamentally much alike; they were both almost
naively incapable of believing anything was impossible and . . . they would
both fight a fight through the last ditch and beyond."

Chennault had carefully studied Japanese tactics and strategy. Like the
U.S. generals, the Japanese high command believed in the invincibility of
state-of-the-art bombers in any air war. Chennault, however, believed in
swift and maneuverable fighter planes, which on the one hand could be
used offensively to attack bombers and, on the other hand, could be used
defensively to protect cities and armies. Chennault told Corcoran that if
he were given the resources, he could actually maintain an air force within

China by taking advantage of areas where the local population was sympathetic. He also promised that his air force would deplete the Japanese bomber fleet and harass Japanese supply lines. Corcoran was impressed by Chennault's plan to ultilize "a new combination of the fierce loyalty of the population and the mobility of air power." He reported back to President Roosevelt that Chennault was the "most original fighting man" he had ever met.

After his meeting with Chennault, Corcoran described himself as a member of the "Chennault entourage." From a political standpoint, Corcoran realized that if Chennault's plan to save Chiang failed, the United States was far enough removed that it would not be held responsible, and yet if it succeeded, the U.S. would be credited with having saved China.

Within the administration Corcoran lobbied two powerful cabinet members, Treasury Secretary Morgenthau, with whom he had suffered poor relations ever since the gold-buying decision of 1933, and Navy Secretary Frank Knox, a Republican. Although Morgenthau and Knox were skeptical, they agreed not to oppose Corcoran. Along with T. V. Soong, Corcoran presented the president with a plan to utilize Lend-Lease in support of Chiang.

Roosevelt was greatly impressed by the concept and approved the Chennault proposal for the creation of the American Volunteer Group. Now came the hard part: Chennault needed planes and pilots. He asked Corcoran to help him.

Quinn Shaunessy, Corcoran's detail from the Marine Corps, discovered that the War Department hoped to consign one hundred P-40 fighters, built by the Curtiss-Wright Corporation, to Britain. The British, however, did not want the planes since newer, faster ones already were being built in Britain. Because the P-40s were considered too heavy and too slow to engage the Japanese air force effectively in dogfights, the War Department sold them to Chennault at a greatly reduced cost. During a conversation with T. V. Soong, David Corcoran, a Princeton graduate, suggested using the name *Flying Tigers* for the American Volunteer Group. Walt Disney, a friend of Chennault's, then designed a tiger emblem for the planes, which soon became famous.

Next, Corcoran worked out an arrangement with his friends James Forrestal — the undersecretary of the navy — and Frank Knox that

Chennault would not cherry-pick pilots from any one branch of the armed forces, but rather would seek volunteers from all the branches and select a few men from each. However, General George Marshall, the supreme Allied commander, opposed the idea of uniformed Americans joining the Flying Tigers, where they would serve in a mercenary capacity rather than being in the service of the United States. According to Corcoran, he counseled Roosevelt, who "was troubled by the soiled label that Chennault's irregulars might wear," to "act as forcefully as political constraints allowed." Nevertheless, on April 13, 1941, the president signed a secret executive order authorizing the American Volunteer Group to recruit reserve officers from the army, navy, and marines. In July ten pilots and 150 mechanics were supplied with fake passports and sailed from San Francisco for Rangoon, where Chennault had established a training base.

By the early fall Chennault's air force was proving remarkably successful. Although the P-40s were not light and maneuverable, Chennault deployed them with great effectiveness. His pilots often flew in close formation with their guns bearing down on a single target. As Corcoran later explained it, "In combat, they could double-team any adversary, single out one enemy plane at a time, attack it in concert, destroy it, then single out another." Chennault's pilots also flew from a higher altitude than their enemy and would dive downward, breaking up orderly Japanese flight formations, and then attack while enemy planes scattered in confusion. The Flying Tigers were extremely effective in their raids on Japanese positions and forestalled the closing of the Burma Road, a key supply route to China.

Tommy Corcoran had left the government, but in many ways he continued to be involved in the affairs of the nation, particularly with his work on China Defense Supplies. But he was also signing up other clients, and just as he had developed the reputation of a skilled operative in government, he quickly became known as a "fixer" in private practice.

Corcoran may have been motivated by the thrill of a new challenge, the opportunity to operate on an international stage, or simply the need to make more money to support his growing family. One thing was certain, however: He had no interest in making sure that the New Deal was either expanded upon or even preserved. Indeed, not long after he left government, Corcoran told Congressman Johnson, "Lyndon, my boy, the New Deal is dead." One Corcoran observer at that time told the former New Dealer Jonathan Daniels, "It hurts to be dropped as Tommy was dropped, especially in Washington. And he can't prove he still has power except in fees."

14

Peddling Influence

Preparing for war rapidly changed the physical landscape of Washington. After practicing law out of the offices of friends for a few months, Corcoran rented his own law office in the Investment Building not far from the White House on the corner of Fifteenth and K Streets. Despite the construction of temporary buildings all over the city, the street was largely undeveloped, and Corcoran "had a beautiful view of K Street, right down to the Potomac River." He wasn't listed in the telephone directory and his office didn't even have a nameplate on the door, but clients seemed to have no trouble finding him.

The U.S. entry into the European conflict seemed inevitable. American industry had not had a particularly close relationship to government, but now it was being asked to convert quickly to war production. As David Brinkley pointed out in his book *Washington Goes to War,* "Everyone knew the government had to act. But except briefly during World War I, the government had never done anything like this before." As the nation's capital geared up for war, there was inevitably some degree of chaos. For Tommy Corcoran, who had friends scattered throughout the government and who knew the intricacies of the bureaucracy better than almost anyone, the rapid changes in Washington brought opportunity and with it, some unwanted notoriety.

Corcoran had only been out of the government for a short time, but he was "running" the Asian Lend-Lease program and working to defend against both the Justice Department inquiry and a potential congressional investigation into Sterling Pharmaceutical. Corcoran assembled a defense team led by John Cahill, his former classmate at Harvard Law School and an associate of his at Cotton and Franklin. Cahill was the U.S. attorney in New York and, not coincidentally, had been working with Thurman Arnold, the assistant attorney general for antitrust matters, supervising the Department of Justice's inquiry into Sterling. At Corcoran's urging,

Cahill resigned his post on February 10, 1941, to enter private practice. There were no laws prohibiting him from representing a client in a case on which he had been working, and notwithstanding a clear conflict of interest, Cahill immediately began representing Sterling Pharmaceutical.

Now that he had help on the Sterling case, Corcoran began to take on new business. His first major client was Henry J. Kaiser, a West Coast businessman who had made a fortune from government contracts, primarily in helping build the Boulder and Shasta Dams. Corcoran had first met Kaiser when Corcoran was an attorney at the RFC and he, Harold Ickes, and David Lilienthal established the the Bonneville Power Administration. Now as the country prepared for war, Kaiser recognized that the government's procurement program offered many exceptional business opportunities. Kaiser needed to know the people in Washington who were making the decisions, and he called on Tommy Corcoran for assistance.

Corcoran was able to open doors for Kaiser all over town.

At the White House, Corcoran introduced him to several people, including Lauchlin Currie. At the Federal Reserve, Corcoran arranged a meeting with the chairman, Marriner Eccles, who had been introduced to Kaiser several years earlier when Eccles was a construction magnate in Utah. Corcoran later boasted that through his contacts at the Interior Department he denied the Bonneville Power Administration to Alcoa, the giant aluminum company, and helped secure it for Kaiser.

Corcoran also helped at the War Department, where he introduced Kaiser to William Knudsen, the former chief executive of General Motors who had been appointed at the end of 1940 to command the Office of Production Management to coordinate defense preparations. Over the course of the next few years, Kaiser arranged for $645 million in building contracts at his ten shipyards, eight of which were located on the West Coast. He netted a profit on each ship of between $60,000 to $110,000 and made millions with his assembly methods. He pioneered group medicine at his companies, creating what eventually became Kaiser Permanente, a precursor to today's health maintenance organizations.

Corcoran's representation of Kaiser was featured prominently in a March 1941 story in the *Washington Times-Herald* that included a photograph of Kaiser chatting with Knudsen. As author Joseph Goulden would later comment, the picture said "this is the sort of entrée Tom Corcoran has in high-level government; hire him as your lawyer and you, too, can walk right into Knudsen's office and ask for big defense contracts."

Although he had left the Reconstruction Finance Corporation only a few months earlier in January 1941, there were no restrictions on Corcoran's lobbying his former employer; he helped Kaiser to arrange a loan at the RFC, which was heavily involved in financing the war effort. At the time, magnesium, a scarce light metal, had wide application in the aircraft industry and would be critical to any war effort. Corcoran encouraged Kaiser to go into magnesium production, and the industrialist decided to build a plant in San Jose, California. Corcoran arranged a meeting for Kaiser with Corcoran's old boss, Jesse Jones, the RFC's director, to discuss financing future plans.

With Corcoran at his side, Kaiser outlined his proposal to Jones, who was somewhat taken aback by the fact that while Kaiser wanted to borrow several million dollars, "the private capital he proposed to put up to go into magnesium manufacturing was only $100,000." According to Jones, "Mr. Kaiser knew nothing about manufacturing magnesium, so I was a little skeptical. . . . The whole thing looked a little screwy to me, one that would be of doubtful outcome." Notwithstanding Jones's skepticism, the RFC wound up lending upward of twenty-eight million dollars to Kaiser. Although the loan was collateralized, it is doubtful he could have obtained such financing elsewhere.

Corcoran had been placed on retainer for twenty-five thousand a year by Kaiser. But after the RFC loan was secured, Corcoran sent Kaiser a bill requesting $135,000 in cash and a 15 percent stake in Kaiser's magnesium enterprise. Undoubtedly Corcoran was working from the knowledge he had gained fifteen years earlier at Cotton and Franklin when his mentor at the time, Joseph Cotton, told him that the best way to make money was not by lawyering, but by getting a piece of the equity. Kaiser was shocked, but Corcoran pointed out that the magnesium deal was potentially worth millions. A frugal businessman, Kaiser ultimately paid Corcoran his retainer and an additional sixty-five thousand for his work on the RFC loan, but he never gave Corcoran any stock.

As Corcoran's caseload, fees, and reputation grew, so did the stories about him. In a town where everyone knew everyone, the rumor mill about Corcoran was churning fast. In May 1941 the newspapers reported that a House appropriations subcommittee had questioned Secretary

Ickes about Corcoran's role in seeking financing for the Iriskin Oil Company in Alaska. Although there were no details provided, the allegation was that Corcoran had somehow used his close friendship with Ickes to get Iriskin a sweetheart deal. Weeks later, more details trickled out. Corcoran had allegedly presented Ickes with a draft letter that he wanted sent to Secretary of War Frank Knox, imploring Knox to provide government financing to Iriskin for the drilling of oil in Alaska.

It was not surprising that some of Corcoran's activities on behalf of his clients were reported in the newspapers — often in a negative light. Corcoran had many friends and admirers in Washington, but he also had many detractors. For instance, one senior official at the Department of Justice told Kaiser's top corporate officers that Assistant Secretaries Robert Patterson and Robert Lovett of the War Department "were greatly disturbed to learn that Mr. Kaiser was connected to Tommy Corcoran."

As the de facto Lend-Lease czar for China, Corcoran played an important role in making sure the spigots of U.S. assistance were turned on for Chiang Kai-shek. On March 11, 1941, the president signed a directive formally establishing the Lend-Lease program, which enabled any country whose defense was deemed critical to the security interests of the United States to receive wartime aid by sale, transfer, exchange, or lease. Almost immediately the United States increased its allocation of supplies to China from three thousand tons a month to ten thousand. Besides military hardware, the assistance included large quantities of Sterling Pharmaceutical's Atabrine drug to combat malaria in the Chinese army. China Defense Supplies was responsible for getting the aid to the beleagured troops fighting in the mountains of western China.

For the first time in his career, Corcoran could see how he could have an impact on public policy from outside government and be more independent than when he was on the inside. He wrote his old friend Jim Landis, ". . . You were a million times wise in choosing to build where you were entirely your own master." But Corcoran's aggressive management of the Asian Lend-Lease program and his support for the American Volunteer Group was sparking controversy within the adminstration.

In effect, Corcoran was running an off-the-books private war in which a private company, China Defense Supplies, was diverting some of the war matériel destined for China to a private army, the American Volunteer

Group. Henry Morgenthau, who had long considered Corcoran untrust-
worthy, complained to China's Ambassador Hu Shih and to T. V. Soong:
"I don't like it. The President doesn't like it. I have never worked that way
. . . and I am not going to work that way." Morgenthau was undoubtedly
miffed that Corcoran was succeeding so publicly when President
Roosevelt had initially suggested that Morgenthau himself might lead the
China relief program and that Corcoran work under him as a federal
employee.

Asian Lend-Lease also met resistance from the American high command in Europe, who were less concerned about Corcoran than about
Chiang Kai-shek. General George Marshall and General Joseph Stilwell,
the American commander in Asia, believed that Chiang was completely
corrupt and that his army needed drastic reform, not more war matériel.
Stilwell, in particular, felt that Chiang's heavy reliance on the air effort
was a flawed military strategy. Stilwell wrote to Marshall, "The continued
publication of Chungking propaganda in the United States is an increasing handicap to my work. . . . We can pull them out of this cesspool, but
continued concessions have made the Generalissimo [Chiang] believe he
has only to insist and we will yield."

Corcoran's problems with the Asian Lend-Lease effort were largely
political, but he also had serious problems with his other major client,
Sterling Pharmaceutical, and those were of an increasingly legal nature.

Assistant Attorney General Thurman Arnold, a former Yale professor and
expert on constitutional law, was ready to prosecute any American company aiding and abetting a German company in any part of the world. He
was convinced that I. G. Farben and Sterling had created an aspirin cartel and believed he could prove it. On April 10, 1941, the Department of
Justice issued subpoenas to Sterling and to the company's subsidiary,
Winthrop, as well as to other firms associated with Farben. Tommy
Corcoran immediately decided that Sterling should fully cooperate with
Arnold's investigation. He was only too happy to have the relationship
between Sterling and Farben severed so long as Sterling avoided indictment on criminal charges. Cahill took on the responsibility of releasing
documents to the Justice Department, while Corcoran mapped out a
strategy to prevent the presentation of evidence to a grand jury in the
hope that the government ultimately would file only a civil case. Meanwhile,

Sterling endured a spate of negative publicity. The liberal newspaper *PM* splashed across its front page the headline THESE FIRMS EARN MONEY FOR HITLER, and claimed that Sterling was helping the Nazi propagandist Joseph Goebbels fulfill his pledge that "Americans would help Hitler win the Americas." Other negative stories followed in newspapers such as the respected *New York Herald Tribune*.

Then, on June 2, the company appeared to catch a break when President Roosevelt nominated Attorney General Robert Jackson to the Supreme Court. The new acting attorney general, Francis Biddle, was a close friend of Tommy Corcoran's. Like Tommy, Biddle had clerked for Oliver Wendell Holmes. The day after his appointment, Biddle accepted a settlement offer from Sterling in which the company would plead nolo contendere to a criminal "information" and pay a nominal fine of five thousand dollars. It amounted to a slap on the wrist. For Sterling a major legal cloud had been lifted, although the company was still being investigated for its ties to the Third Reich.

With Jackson gone and Biddle poised to be the new attorney general, Corcoran thought it might be time to return to government. He had been in private practice for less than six months, but Roosevelt had promised on several occasions that he would make him solicitor general. Corcoran, as he later remembered it, arranged through Missy LeHand to see the president, telling her that "he had never asked for a favor before." On June 6 he met with Roosevelt in the Oval Office and expressed his interest in the appointment. Roosevelt was noncommittal, but indicated that he hoped Corcoran would return to government service.

The next thing Corcoran did was line up political support. Inside the White House, Jim Rowe, one of Roosevelt's administrative assistants, wrote a single-spaced memorandum to the president: "Most people have forgotten it, but Tommy is a brilliant legal scholar and, what is more important in a Solicitor General, has a felicity and clarity of expression both in formal and informal talk surpassing any other lawyer I have ever met." House Speaker Sam Rayburn, a longtime political ally, recommended Corcoran without hesitation. So did Mayor Ed Kelly of Chicago and many other prominent Democratic politicians and administration officials. But Corcoran knew that this wasn't just any political appointment; the support of mayors and congressmen was not enough.

The solicitor general had to be an extremely accomplished lawyer — someone who not only knew the law but would defend the Constitution and would do so eloquently and without a political agenda. Although it was unusual and irregular for members of the Supreme Court to take a public postion on a presidential appointment, the position of solicitor general was the exception, and justices had historically recommended candidates for the job. Corcoran had friends on the Supreme Court, men whom he had helped to be confirmed. He believed an appointment was within reach.

Corcoran managed to persuade four justices to write personal letters on his behalf. Justices Stanley Reed and William O. Douglas sent letters directly to the President. So did Justice James Byrnes, who as a senator from South Carolina had called on Corcoran many times for advice. A month later Justice Hugo Black, who had mended fences with Corcoran over the Guthrie nomination, followed suit and wrote a glowing letter of recommendation.

Corcoran still needed one more letter to show the president that a majority of the Court viewed his appointment favorably. In late September he went to see his closest friend on the Court, Felix Frankfurter. Corcoran had been deeply disappointed by Frankfurter's lackadaisical support for Stuart Guthrie, but he was nevertheless confident that after all the battles they had fought side by side, he could secure a strong recommendation from his onetime mentor.

Justice Frankfurter greeted Corcoran warmly in his chambers. After the two men sat down, Corcoran got right to the point. He explained that four of Frankfurter's brethren had already sent letters and that he only needed one more to clinch the appointment. Frankfurter listened attentively and then said that he was sorry, but didn't feel he could offer any assistance. Corcoran was stunned. He pressed the justice for an explanation, but none was forthcoming. Corcoran became agitated. Joe Rauh, a former clerk to Frankfurter and a close friend of Corcoran's, later said that Corcoran then wagged his finger at Frankfurter and in much the same tone as he had reproached Justice Black only months earlier, said, "I put you here, now produce." Whatever the case, the meeting ended awkwardly, with a distinct chill, and with no recommendation.

A few weeks later, according to Corcoran, Frankfurter asked him to drop by his office. In the interim Corcoran had been considered but

rejected by War Secretary Frank Knox as a possible assistant secretary for
naval affairs. According to Corcoran, the "story had gotten all over town
that [Frankfurter] had blocked my appointment as solicitor general."
Frankfurter both encouraged and offered to help Corcoran to find job in
war production because it would then look as if Corcoran hadn't been
nominated for solicitor general "because he preferred something else."
Corcoran was outraged that it seemed "more important that his judi-
cious and honorable reputation should stay intact than that my career
should take a course I'd chosen." Corcoran later recalled that he indig-
nantly replied that he wasn't interested in Frankfurter's help. Then,
according to Corcoran, the justice became irritated, calling Corcoran "an
ungrateful Irishman."

Corcoran was deeply hurt by what he viewed as Frankfurter's betrayal,
but according to Rauh, Frankfurter had two reasons for opposing
Corcoran. First, Frankfurter told Rauh he didn't believe that the Court
should interfere in such matters as the choice for solicitor general — an
absurd suggestion since there was clear precedent for recommendation of
a candidate and since, as Rauh noted, Frankfurter "interfered in everything." The second reason, according to Rauh, was that the administration was preparing for war and Corcoran's nomination would lead to a
confirmation fight that would damage the president. There was some
merit to this concern. Roosevelt had recently sent up to the Senate the
nomination of Ed Flynn to be the ambassador to Australia. Flynn was an
affable and competent individual, but he was also a partisan Democrat
and had been rejected by the Senate. Corcoran still had many enemies in
the Senate on the Democratic side as a result of his role in the Court-
packing plan and the 1938 purge. And Republicans, the minority party in
the Senate, would have liked nothing better than to hand the president
another defeat.

Rauh also acknowledged the possibility of a third reason: Frankfurter
"simply did not want Tom to have the job." Indeed, according to Rauh,
some in Washington felt that Corcoran had gotten "too big for his
britches," a view that may have been shared by Frankfurter. Ed Prichard,
a Washington lawyer who had clerked for Frankfurter and worked for
Corcoran, later claimed that "Felix repeatedly said, to me and to others,
that if he thought Tom was going to dedicate himself to the job of solicitor general, he would support him cheerfully, and go to bat for him, but

he felt that Tom viewed the solicitor general's position as just another post from which he could operate politically. Felix felt that the solicitor general's post was not appropriate for that. I think, way down underneath, Felix had some apprehensions about the general direction Tom's life was taking — he was becoming more reckless." In fact, Frankfurter told his colleague Justice Douglas that Corcoran had become little more than a political hack and that he would "never want a fixer . . . as Solicitor General."

President Roosevelt wanted Corcoran back in the White House and offered him a position in the counsel's office. He promised Corcoran he would enjoy the power and latitude that he'd had before at the RFC. But Corcoran felt that he deserved a position with more prestige. He also worried that his most important ally in the White House, Missy LeHand, had suffered a stroke; he recoiled at the thought of fighting pitched battles with Harry Hopkins, who not only had the president's ear but now actually lived at the White House.

After it became clear that Corcoran would not be nominated for solicitor general, Ben Cohen was briefly considered for the job. Corcoran kept a low profile for fear of hurting his friend's chances, but he worked quietly behind the scenes to support the nomination and encouraged his friend to take the position if it was offered. As he had for Corcoran, Roosevelt received many letters of support for Cohen. Wendell Willkie, who had been defeated by Roosevelt the year before, wrote of Cohen that he "had disputed with him much and disagreed with him more. . . . but I have come to have a powerful respect for his ability and character." Charles C. Burlingham, the elegant, blue-blooded New York lawyer considered by many at that time to be the patriarch of the American bar, believed that Corcoran was not qualified because he was "coarse and crude," but that Cohen deserved serious consideration because he was "the type of lawyer I like best, a gentleman."

Nevertheless, Roosevelt worried that appointing a Jewish lawyer would be politically controversial and turned instead to the assistant solicitor general, the mild-mannered and extremely capable Charles Fahy. Fahy, a southerner, had been general counsel to the National Labor Relations Board for five years before becoming assistant solicitor general. He was noncontroversial, had a stellar reputation as a lawyer, and was easily confirmed. Like Corcoran, Cohen was discouraged by the treatment had received, but instead of leaving government, he left the country, accepting a position as an aide to Ambassador John G. Winant in London.

Before Cohen sailed for England, he witnessed a scene that revealed the depth of the rift between Frankfurter and Corcoran. Several months had passed since Corcoran's rejection for the solicitor general post. Indeed, the country was at war; Joe Rauh had enlisted in the army and was leaving for the South Pacific. As several of Rauh's closest friends, including Cohen and Corcoran, gathered on the platform at Washington's Union Station to bid him farewell, Justice Frankfurter walked toward them. Corcoran turned and saw Frankfurter approaching. They briefly made eye contact and then Corcoran walked away in the opposite direction without even stopping to say good-bye to Rauh.

Following the appointment of Biddle as attorney general, the apparent respite for Sterling was short-lived. Hitler's armies now occupied most of Europe and President Roosevelt, increasingly alarmed, announced that financial transactions in the United States involving U.S. firms operating in continental Europe would be blocked. Because Sterling's subsidiary Winthrop was half owned by the U.S. branch of I. G. Farben, its transactions were included in the order. Then, on Friday, June 20, the Treasury Department froze the firms' assets.

With Sterling's assets frozen, sales dropping from bad publicity, and the various investigations still proceeeding, Tommy Corcoran was desperately looking for a way to extricate the company from its problems. In mid-July he thought he had found one. On the evening of July 18, 1941, Corcoran tracked down Assistant Attorney General Arnold at a party and told him that he had a plan. Corcoran proposed that the Justice Department provide immunity to Sterling on the grounds that it was in the interests of national security for the company to compete with I. G. Farben in Latin America. In fact, he had prepared an unsigned, undated memorandum stating as much. Corcoran argued that he could get the secretary of interior, his close friend Harold Ickes, to sign the memorandum and provide political cover for the Department of Justice.

Arnold was skeptical, but agreed to run it by Attorney General Biddle later in the week. Corcoran insisted they show it to him that evening — even though Biddle was at his country house, Skyland, ninety miles away in Virginia's Blue Ridge Mountains. Driving in a pelting rain, Corcoran and Arnold arrived there sometime after midnight. Biddle read Corcoran's memorandum, but even though he and Corcoran were close friends, he could not agree to such a circumvention of the judicial process. He refused to sign. Syndicated columnist Thomas Stokes later referred to the incident as "the midnight ride of Paul Revere Corcoran."

Corcoran now feared that Arnold and his staff would bring the evidence before a grand jury and ultimately seek indictment. Corcoran decided it was time to cut Sterling's losses and offered the Justice Department a "civil information" on the part of Sterling, meaning that the company would bypass the grand jury procedure and accept a civil charge rather than a criminal one. Corcoran hoped to limit not only the potential monetary penalty but also additional negative publicity. In exchange, Corcoran committed that Sterling would sign a consent decree canceling the Farben contracts and would wage an aggressive campaign to sell its own brand of aspirin in Latin America.

Instead of first negotiating with Arnold's staff, Corcoran arranged to meet with an interdepartmental committee of Treasury, State, and Justice Department officials that had been overseeing the investigation of Sterling. One of those officials was the general counsel to the Treasury, Ed Foley, Corcoran's old friend, roommate in Georgetown, and the best man at his wedding. Early in August Tommy and David Corcoran made a presentation to the committee. Following the advice he had once given to Lyndon Johnson to use visual props when making a case to President Roosevelt, Tommy arrived at the committee's conference room with a map of South America — "the biggest map anyone had ever seen," according to David, who proceeded to explain how Sterling would introduce a new aspirin tablet, called Mejoral, to compete with Bayer in South America. David displayed impressive salesmanship and considerable charm in arguing to the committee that Sterling should be let off off the hook so that it could beat the Germans in South America.

As part of the consent decree, Sterling agreed to abrogate all contracts with I. G. Farben. Sterling not only lost its trademarks but received no indemnity from the lawsuits that were sure to be filed by Farben for breach of contract. In essence, Corcoran had avoided a prosecution by the Justice Department for illegal contracts to sell aspirin in Latin America by promising to sell a carbon copy of that aspirin in the region. Although he hadn't succeeded in getting immunity for his brother's company, he had cut a deal with the federal government that was strikingly similar to the one that had been rejected by his friend, Attorney General Francis Biddle, during the "midnight ride."

Thurmond Arnold was furious that Corcoran had circumvented his department and signed off on the deal only after the company agreed to replace its president and chairman. On September 4 Biddle was confirmed as attorney general; the next day he publicly announced the consent decree. Some in the press, including Thomas Stokes, believed that once again Tommy the Cork had put in the fix. In Congress there was a cry for an investigation of the matter. Republican congressman Lawrence Smith of Wisconsin declared, "It is common gossip in government circles that the long arm of Tommy Corcoran reaches into many agencies; that he has placed many men in important positions and they in turn are amenable to his influences." But Smith's insinuations stirred little interest, and Sterling proceeded under the consent decree.

Even though Corcoran had left the government and was busy defending Sterling and promoting Chiang Kai-shek, he continued to dabble in politics. Following the death on April 4, 1941, of Texas senator Morris Sheppard, who at the age of sixty-five suffered an intracranial hemorrage, Lyndon Johnson decided that he would run for the Senate in the special election. Corcoran later said that President Roosevelt encouraged the young congressman because he knew Johnson was "a man that he could count on." But Johnson faced a stiff challenge from W. Lee O'Daniel, a former flour salesman who was elected governor in 1938. In the three years since then, O'Daniel had become an extremely popular figure in the state, earning the nickname "Pappy" — which referred to *pap,* a term New Dealers used to describe federal projects and largesse dispensed by the administration. Johnson knew that, in contrast to the popular governor, he was not well known outside his congressional district. The campaign would be an uphill struggle.

Corcoran promised to help Johnson in any way he could. He worked with his friend Eliot Janeway, an economist, journalist, and political activist, to help Johnson raise money from Roosevelt supporters on Wall Street. Jim Rowe later recalled that "it was all cash in those days." Corcoran always arranged for the funds to be hand-delivered to Johnson personally in Texas by a trusted lieutenant. Corcoran also reached out to labor, specifically to the New York garment district. When David Dubinsky, head of the International Ladies Garment Workers Union, questioned why it was in labor's interest to contribute to an obscure Texas congressman, Corcoran told him, "You'll be getting a liberal from Texas! What do you want for a nickel?"

During the campaign Corcoran spread the rumor with the Washington press corps that the president was going to Texas to campaign for Johnson. The story was picked up by the Marsh newspapers, a syndicate in the Southwest, and by the dozens of weeklies in the region that subscribed to the syndicate. The rumor became so embellished as it was rewritten in the press that it was widely believed that the Texas legislature had passed a resolution inviting the president to come to the state. Corcoran later recalled that "the trip didn't happen," but the rumor had successfully burnished the reputation of Johnson as a close friend of the president's.

John Connally and Herbert Henderson, the congressman's two most trusted young aides, returned to Texas to run the campaign. Johnson's Capitol Hill office was essentially shut down, although he left behind a shy twenty-three-year-old named Walter Jenkins as his Washington representative. Jenkins had no experience, and LBJ was constantly asking him to get something from various federal agencies. Jenkins relied heavily on Corcoran: "I talked to him lots of times. He was still very powerful and when you asked him something, he could do it."

Corcoran for his part remembered that "we gave LBJ everything we could; we wanted him to win over O'Daniel." On the day that Johnson left to campaign in Texas, he requested approval of another rural electrification project from the Rural Electrification Administration. A bureaucrat at the agency told the young congressman that approval of the project on such short notice was impossible. A few hours later an REA official received a phone call. "This is Tom Corcoran at the White House. Congressman Johnson wants this today, and the White House wants him to have it today." Corcoran had left the government several months earlier, but no one he talked to seemed to know it, or if they did, they figured that he still had the support of the White House. Congressman Johnson got the approval.

During the campaign O'Daniel suggested that Texas form its own army and navy to protect its southern border from invasion — presumedly from Nazi sympathizers in Mexico and other parts of Latin America. At

Corcoran's urging the president said nothing at the time. Months later, on election eve, Roosevelt denounced the plan as "preposterous." As voters picked up their morning papers on the way to the polls, the headlines featured the president's denunciation of O'Daniel.

Notwithstandng O'Daniel's gaffe, Johnson lost, falling 1,311 votes short of victory. The young congressman's defeat was portrayed in the press as a blow to the credibility of the Roosevelt administration. One headline in the *New York Times* read, DEFEAT OF HAND-PICKED ROOSEVELT MAN HAS WASHINGTON WONDERING. The story went on to describe how O'Daniel's victory "was a stunning reversal to the ambitions of Tommy G. Corcoran." Corcoran was portrayed as looking to the Johnson election as a way to ingratiate himself with the Democratic Party and propel himself back into the government, perhaps as a future attorney general. Privately, however, he must have known that if the president had decided against appointing him solicitor general, his chances of ever becoming attorney general were remote.

Perhaps Corcoran took sustenance from Johnson, who told him shortly after his defeat, "Well, Tommy, in the political business, if you're counted out, you're never a crybaby in the public about it." Still a congressman, Lyndon Johnson had no discernible prospects for political advancement, but he didn't complain. Johnson knew he would get another chance at some point. He asked Corcoran, "Did you ever see a shooting gallery with its circular, rotating discs with lots of pipes and rabbits on the circuit? Well, when you miss one the first time, you always get a second chance. And the sonofabitch who trimmed you will always come up again. And then you can get him."

Because he had only lost a special election, Johnson had not lost his seat in the House of Representatives. And while he returned to Washington to pursue a legislative agenda, he largely turned his attention to other matters.

Johnson had not been born to wealth and had not managed to accumulate any capital on his modest salary in the Congress. However, Lady Bird had inherited thirty-six thousand dollars from her mother. After her husband's defeat in the Senate race, she agreed to use the money to invest in a radio station. At the suggestion of his good friend Alvin Wirtz, Johnson looked into acquiring KTBC, a station in Austin that had been optioned to two wealthy Texas businessmen.

In late 1941 Johnson approached E. G. Kingsbery, an ultraconservative Austin businessman who owned a half interest in KTBC. Kingsbery had opposed Johnson's candidacy, but after the congressman helped Kinsbery's son gain admission to the U.S. Naval Academy at Annapolis, the businessman was indebted to him. Johnson told Kingsbery, "I'm not a newspaperman, not a lawyer, and I might get beat sometime. I did have a second-class teacher's certificate, but it's expired, and I want to get into some business." Impressed by Johnson's energy and initiative, Kingsbery told Johnson that he wanted to pay his "obligation" to him and simply gave him his half-interest option.

The option to buy the other half was owned by the Wesley West family, who had extensive holdings in the oil industry and owned the *Austin Daily Tribune*, a conservative daily. Just a day or two before Christmas, Johnson traveled to Plano County to work out a deal with Wesley West at his ranch. Johnson charmed the older man, who later recalled, "I didn't like Lyndon Johnson," but said after meeting him, "He's a pretty good fellow. I believe I'll sell it to him."

With the two half-interest options, Johnson had only one more obstacle to overcome in his purchase of the station — approval from the Federal Communications Commission. To help navigate the process, Johnson called Tommy Corcoran.

When Corcoran left government and had been looking for clients, Johnson made sure that he was placed on retainer by the Houston contracting firm of Brown and Root, owned by George and Herman Brown, who had financed Lyndon's previous campaigns. Corcoran had been paid as much as fifteen thousand dollars for "advice, conferences and negotiations" related to shipbuilding contracts. Now it was Johnson looking to Corcoran to help him with a business proposition. Corcoran did not disappoint. As Corcoran later told Johnson's biographer, Robert Caro, "I helped out all up and down the line."

Corcoran had an important contact at the FCC: James Fly, the chairman of the commission, had been his classmate at Harvard Law School and owed his appointment in good measure to Corcoran. Justice Frank Murphy later told Felix Frankfurter that he had helped get Fly the position as a favor to Tommy Corcoran. According to Murphy, "[It] was at Tom's request that I gave the former Chairman a ten thousand dollar a year job so as to create a vacancy into which Fly was placed."

Corcoran also knew how to work the staff at the FCC. William J. Dempsey, a former general counsel, also owed his government appointment to Corcoran. They had shared an office when Corcoran first left the government, and Dempsey now helped Corcoran to lobby the staff at the FCC. When Robert Caro asked Corcoran whether Johnson's status as a congressman had helped his wife obtain the radio license, "Corcoran reacted at first with only silence, and a look of contempt that someone should ask so obvious a question. Finally, he growled, 'How do you think these things work? These guys [FCC staffers] have been around. You don't have to spell these things out for them.'"

The FCC approved the transfer almost two years later, and Johnson became the owner of a radio station with liabilities of nineteen thousand dollars and accounts receivable of eight thousand dollars. He would ultimately turn KTBC around and use it to amass a fortune of more than twenty-five million dollars. The station was placed in the name of Lady Bird, a fig leaf that would protect her husband from conflict-of-interest charges in his political career.

In Washington after the FCC approved the license, Johnson threw a cocktail party. All of the Texas delegation came: Senator Tom Connally arrived with his wife, a platinum blonde who had been married to another senator. Speaker Sam Rayburn was there. Corcoran, of course, was also in attendance, and played his song "The Good Old Rebel":

> I'm a good old Rebel
> And that's just what I am
> For this fair land of freedom
> I do not give a damn
> I'm glad I fought against it
> I only wish we'd won
> And I don't ask no pardon
> For anything we done.

The southerners laughed heartily as Corcoran, a son of Pawtucket, belted out the tune in a mock southern accent.

A couple of days after the party, Johnson visited Rayburn in his "hideaway," the small private office in the Capitol where the speaker retired to read or relax with friends. Jonathan Daniels, an assistant to Roosevelt, was also there. At one point the conversation turned to Corcoran. They all liked Tommy, and Rayburn still couldn't understand why the president had let him go. Johnson, however, thought he understood what had happened. He reckoned that Corcoran had become too arrogant and too public; that he had alienated his supporters and begun to believe that he was indispensable to the president. As Johnson put it, "Anybody can get along without anybody."

15

Under Investigation

On December 7, 1941, Corcoran was spending a quiet Sunday relaxing at home. That morning he read in the *New York Times* what he had privately known for several days: He had been asked finally to testify before Senator Truman's defense investigation committee. Early in the afternoon he telephoned his friend and client, T. V. Soong, Chiang Kai-shek's Washington representative, at his house in Chevy Chase, Maryland. Corcoran wanted to discuss the *Times* article with him, but Soong greeted him with startling news: "Your fleet is at the bottom of Pearl Harbor." Corcoran was shocked and turned on the radio to hear for himself how Japanese naval and air forces had sunk several American battleships at Pearl Harbor and killed hundreds of sailors and soldiers. The next day President Roosevelt and Congress declared war on Japan, and three days later Germany and Italy declared war on the United States.

The challenge of waging a two-front global war rapidly transformed Washington from a sleepy town into a bustling, sprawling military camp. Almost overnight new agencies, bureaus, and departments were created to manage the war effort. Hundreds of prefabricated structures were erected all over the city, even on the National Mall, the half mile of green lawn between the Washington Monument and the Capitol. Every day thousands of soldiers and new government workers poured into Union Station. While the army enlisted soldiers, the government enlisted workers to staff the burgeoning bureaucracy.

Corcoran's impending testimony before Congress had come about as a result of the publicity he received in the newspapers. His work as a lobbyist had caught the eye of Senator Harry Truman of Missouri in early 1941. In his second term in the Senate, Truman, a Democrat, had successfully obtained an appropriation of fifteen thousand dollars to launch an investigation into waste and mismanagement in the construction of army camps. The Senate Special Committee to Investigate the National Defense Program — or the Truman Committee, as it was commonly known —

began hearings in April. As the hearings turned to the issue of defense production, an important theme emerged concerning how defense contracts,
expected to exceed thirteen billion dollars in 1941, were awarded and the
role Washington's lobbyists played in that process.

Corcoran's name first surfaced in the hearings in July 1941 when a representative from the Todd Shipyards testified before Senator Truman that
contrary to recent news reports, his company had not hired Corcoran to
help it win government contracts. Then in September, a story about
another case involving the former New Deal lawyer appeared in the press:
The *New York Times* reported that Corcoran might have received favorable
treatment in the settlement of a Justice Department case brought against
his brother David's company, Sterling Pharmaceutical. In October syndicated columnist Thomas Stokes revealed that President Roosevelt had
asked Vice President Wallace to find a position for Corcoran on the
Economic Defense Board, which the vice president controlled, but that
Wallace had demurred. Stokes wrote that "Wallace disapproves of the way
Mr. Corcoran has capitalized on his government associations to promote
his lucrative 'law' practice."

Corcoran may have then gotten wind that more bad publicity concerning his law and lobbying practice was imminent. In any event, by
September he had had enough and he wrote to Senator Truman requesting to appear before his committee in order to clear his name. Senator
Truman responded that the committee would consider his request at
some point in the future. In the meantime the committee subpoenaed a
former New Deal colleague of Corcoran's, Charles West, to testify.

Charles West, a former member of Congress, undersecretary of the
interior, and White House congressional liaison, had filed suit against
Frank Cohen, chairman of the Empire corporation, for seven hundred
thousand dollars, or 1 percent of the defense contracts obtained by
Empire from the government. West denied that he had sold influence,
but he testified that Cohen had offered to contribute fifty thousand to
the Democratic National Committee. Moreover, according to West,
Cohen had sought to hire Corcoran in order to obtain the government
contracts. When Cohen eventually testified, Senator Truman wagged his
finger at the witness and in his midwestern drawl sardonically characterized Cohen's decision to retain West and Corcoran, "You were after anyone with influence." After the West and Cohen testimony, Corcoran

again wrote to Senator Truman and asked to testify. This time his request
was granted.

On December 16, just nine days after the attack on Pearl Harbor,
Corcoran appeared before the Truman Committee — the first time he
had testified before a congressional committee in his capacity as a private
lawyer. Sitting at a long table with a six-inch microphone propped in
front of him, Corcoran provided a vigorous defense of his law practice in
his opening statement. He began by noting that he was appearing voluntarily and not under subpoena. Corcoran declared that he wanted to
explain the "innuendos" that he had somehow used "influence" with government agencies.

"I do not know, and I feel quite sure that no one else knows," he said,
"just what 'influence' means. If with respect to me it means experience in
knowing what the government likes and does not like, I cannot understand why it should not be utilized to make the burden of government
lighter. If it means confidence in my ability to get performed what I
undertake to get performed by corporate officers and others outside the
government in return for commitments within the government, I cannot
remember when I have betrayed that confidence."

Within the context of this definition Corcoran acknowledged that business had been exceedingly good since he hung out his shingle ten months
earlier, in February 1941. He testified glibly that he had turned cases away
by the hundreds and that he probably had not worked for anything less
than five thousand dollars. He claimed that he had worked on only five
defense-related projects and that he had never worked as a defense contract
broker. In Corcoran's view, brokers increased the cost of government and
the burden on the taxpayer, and their profiteering was "an outrageous evil."
But Corcoran, who admitted he had made at least a hundred thousand dollars on his defense-related work, claimed that he had never received as a fee
a fixed percentage for soliciting defense-related contracts. Nor, he claimed,
had he ever received a fee that in any way either directly or indirectly
increased the cost of the government's preparation for war.

Corcoran testified about each of the five defense-related cases on
which he had worked. He discussed his work for China Defense Supplies,
which supervised all Lend-Lease arrangements for China. For that work
he received only five thousand dollars. In the case involving Henry Kaiser

and the magnesium plant at San Jose, California, Corcoran alluded to the sixty-five-thousand-dollar fee he received for helping establish the plant. He raised the case involving Havenstrike Oil mentioned in the newspapers and claimed he never received a fee from the oil company. In another case involving the Vilalert corporation, Corcoran's work consisted of reducing an eight-million-dollar order of the British Purchasing Commission to one million, which, he noted, "is not the way a percentage broker operates." He received twenty-five thousand in legal fees.

And finally, he explained his role in the Savannah Shipyard case, which was a subsidiary of the infamous Empire Ordnance Company. Corcoran allegedly helped the company to gain a contract with the Maritime Commission to build twelve cargo ships for twenty million dollars. The Maritime Commission invalidated the contract on the basis that Savannah had neither the financial nor the managerial capacity to carry out the contract. Corcoran testified that he had assessed the problems facing the shipyard and then referred the company to another Washington law firm, Kloplovitz and Dempsey. Corcoran's fees amounted to five thousand dollars. He never mentioned that his brother-in-law was an officer of the Empire Ordnance Company.

Although Corcoran had answered the committee's questions thoroughly, some members of the panel were convinced that Corcoran's lobbying activities pointed up the need for more stringent lobbying restrictions. One senator, Carl Hatch, a Democrat from New Mexico, introduced a bill in late 1941 to prohibit former government employees from practicing before any government department or agency for two years after they had left government service. In introducing the bill, Senator Hatch argued that legislation was needed because he estimated that some two thousand former employees representing sixteen government agencies had appeared before those same agencies in the previous five years.

President Roosevelt complained privately to his assistant Jim Rowe that ". . . the cause of good government is not helped by the stories . . . published about Tommy Corcoran." And the administration went on record when Attorney General Cummings wrote Senator Hatch that he approved of the proposed legislation. However, the bill never made it out of the Judiciary Committee, presumedly because Washington lobbyists persuaded their friends on the panel to kill it.

◆　◆　◆

Although Corcoran had been under a cloud of investigation, and had been bitterly disappointed by the president's decision not to appoint him solicitor general, he remained very much involved in the affairs of the nation. Corcoran's two most important clients, the Flying Tigers and Sterling Pharmaceutical, were not only successful business enterprises but were also playing a role in the Allied effort.

For the first few months of the U.S. war with Japan, the only Allied successes in the Pacific came from the Flying Tigers. In February 1942, following the Japanese capture of the islands of Guam, Wake, and Hong Kong, the U.S. Congress approved a five-hundred-million-dollar Treasury loan to China. In a fireside chat on the twenty-third of that month President Roosevelt explained that "it is essential that we help China in her magnificent defense and in the inevitable counteroffensive — for that is one element in the defeat of Japan."

Chennault's air force had already been waging combat in Burma a full year before any American troops arrived on the Asian continent. Chennault's pilots shot down more than fifty Japanese planes with only minimal losses. In the first seven months of the war, they were officially credited with destroying ninety-nine enemy planes and downing more than three hundred, while sustaining losses of only twelve.

The overall American effort began to show strength at the battle of the Coral Sea in May 1942 when the United States checked the Japanese advance in the southwestern Pacific by sinking or damaging three Japanese carriers. A month later the fleet prevented the Japanese conquest of Midway Island by destroying four Japanese aircraft carriers. Within two months of these battles, the United States was on the offensive and the marines had landed on Guadalcanal.

By early 1942 David Corcoran was mounting Sterling's offensive in Latin America with the Mejoral brand of aspirin. With Corcoran directing the advertising blitz, company representatives handed out eighty-one million handbills, twenty-seven million samples, and four million posters. In the first eight months of the campaign the company spent more than half a million dollars on advertising, much of it devoted to radio. In Argentina, Sterling hired local singers to perform its jingle, *"Mejoral le quita el mal"* (Mejoral makes the pain go away), live on the radio several times a day. On one occasion the firm hired an unknown performer, Maria Eva

Duarte, to sing the tune; she was subsequently fired when she became sick and missed work. Without explanation, the radio station was abruptly shut down and local government officials threatened to run the company out of the country altogether. David Corcoran then learned that his company had fired "Evita," the mistress and future wife of the military leader Juan Perón. David and Tommy Corcoran quickly boarded a plane to Buenos Aires, where they personally apologized to the young chanteuse. "They were practically on their knees," one company official recalled.

Evita agreed to come back to work, and the Mejoral marketing blitz continued. With Evita singing the Sterling jingles, Argentina became the biggest per-capita consumer of aspirin in the world.

Tommy seemed to have made the transition from public life to private practice. He was proving to be as good an advocate for his clients as he had been for his president. Indeed, Corcoran's law practice was thriving, and with the exception of his testimony before the Truman Committee, he had managed to sidestep controversy. He was still involved with the Roosevelt administration, and, in fact, his work with the Flying Tigers meant that he had was playing an important role in the war effort.

Things were also going well on the home front. Peggy had given birth to their second child, Thomas Jr., and they were preparing to move to a larger house. But just as things seemed to be calming down, an old colleague dragged him back into the spotlight.

Norman Littell was born in Indianapolis, Indiana, the son of a Presbyterian minister. He graduated from Wabash College and was the first Indianian ever awarded a Rhodes Scholarship. After attending Christ Church College at Oxford for three years, Littell entered Harvard Law School, but, unable to afford the tuition, he transferred after his first year to the University of Indiana Law School. After graduation, Littell made his way to Washington and worked in a variety of jobs. Littell was an unabashed liberal and committed New Dealer and had developed a network of like-minded friends, including the president's daughter, Anna, and Vice President Henry Wallace. He also befriended Ben Cohen, who encouraged him to accept a position as assistant attorney general for the lands division. With more than five hundred attorneys, the division was the largest and in some respects the most important in the Justice

Department. Cohen hoped Littell would help break up what many liberal New Dealers viewed as improper control over federal land litigation and land acquisition policies.

Littell quickly developed an antipathy for Cohen's friend, Tommy Corcoran. Littell was bothered by the fact that Corcoran seemed to have so many tentacles into the Department of Justice. Although he admired Attorney General Frank Murphy, Littell had been bothered by his cozy relationship with Corcoran. Littell alleged that Corcoran had tried to have Murphy fire him. This would not have been surprising given that Littell was a member of Henry Wallace's ultraliberal circle, which Corcoran so disdained. The friendship between Murphy and Corcoran soured, according to Littell, when Murphy "refused, point blank, to take orders from Tommy. . . . Ironically, only a few months later Murphy was appointed to the Supreme Court and replaced by Francis Biddle." Biddle and Littell initially seemed to work well together, and Biddle even encouraged Littell to lend his support to Corcoran when he was being considered for solicitor general.

In 1941 Littell was particularly bothered by Corcoran's role in the Savannah Shipyard case. After the Maritime Commission invalidated its contract with Savannah on the basis that the company had misrepresented its financial and managerial capacity, the company sued the U.S. government. The case fell to Littell, who brought a condemnation, or seizure of property, against the company. Within the Department of Justice, however, Littell felt pressure to settle the case, especially from Jim Rowe, the assistant to the attorney general, whom he knew was a close friend of Tommy Corcoran's.

Corcoran and Rowe had been friends since they had first met at the home of Oliver Wendell Holmes. In 1938 Rowe had been appointed an administrative assistant to the president. While serving on Roosevelt's staff, Rowe's primary responsibility was congressional relations. He was also concerned with patronage and the recruitment of talented candidates for federal office, and so he often consulted with Corcoran. President Roosevelt was extremely impressed with Rowe's political acumen as well as his legal and administrative skills; by the beginning of the fourth term, as Corcoran's career in government had begun to wane, Jim Rowe's had ascended.

In 1941 Rowe became assistant to the attorney general. On May 13, 1942, he telephoned Littell to inform him that Savannah Shipyard's attorneys,

William J. Dempsey and William C. Kloplovitz, "had taken up with the Attorney General the matter of effecting a settlement." Littell told Rowe that he couldn't "settle anything as a matter of principle," and that his office was "re-examining the whole matter, including the effect upon the appraisal of grossly defective construction work, and collateral accounting matters which reach into the subsidiary company."

Nine days later Littell and Rowe were at a cocktail party at Biddle's house when Rowe took him aside and asked, "What are we going to do about settlement of the Savannah Shipyard case?" When Littell didn't answer, Rowe, according to Littell, told him that "Tommy Corcoran represented Savannah Shipyard through Dempsey and Kloplovitz" and that "those fellows are our friends." Although it is doubtful that Rowe would have said anything so overtly political to Littell, Corcoran did have an interesting history with Kloplovitz and Dempsey. He had helped both lawyers obtain positions at the Federal Commerce Commission. After the two lawyers left the government, they formed their own firm, and when Corcoran exited the Roosevelt administration, he temporarily rented office space from them. Even more interesting, Dempsey's father had served as a member of the Maritime Commission, which may explain in part how Corcoran was able to obtain the contract for Savannah in the first place.

Rowe told Littell that he had been asked by the attorney general to look into the matter, and added, "I've got to do something," which Littell inferred to mean that he intended to settle the case.

Rowe did do something. On June 30 Littell was summoned to the attorney general's office, where he found Rowe, Dempsey, and Kloplovitz seated around a small conference table with Biddle.

"Sit down Norman," Biddle said. "What is this conference all about?"

"I haven't the slightest idea, Mr. Attorney General," Littell replied increduously. "There are no grounds for a conference that I know about." Littell was stunned, but he suspected that since the meeting was in the attorney general's office and he had been the last one to arrive, Biddle's ignorance was probably feigned.

According to Littell, Biddle then asked the same question to Rowe, who explained that Dempsey and Kloplovitz wanted to appeal Littell's decision not to open settlement discussions. The attorney general looked again at Littell: "You settle most of your condemnation cases, don't you? You told me you did."

"Yes sir, but there are additional factors in this case," Littell explained. Staring directly at Dempsey and Kloplovitz, he added, "And I do not think it is appropriate to discuss them in the presence of opposing counsel."

Biddle was a close friend of Tommy Corcoran's, but he was also an excellent lawyer and he knew that Littell was correct. He agreed that opposing counsel should not be present for what was really a discussion of internal strategy.

A few days later, Littell met with Rowe and Biddle again to discuss the case. This time Littell was ready. He bluntly warned Biddle and Rowe that because of their intimate connection with Tommy Corcoran, and following on the heels of the settlement of the Sterling Pharmaceutical case in which Corcoran had been involved, any settlement in the Savannah Shipyard case would create a scandal. If this was a veiled threat, it worked. Biddle turned to Rowe: "Norman is right. This could be another Sterling Products case." Ultimately the case went to trial, and a jury awarded Savannah Shipyard $1,285,000 — about $200,000 more than the company had been prepared to accept before the trial. Self-rightous and pompous, Littell proclaimed in his diary that "the net gain is in the realm of principle — an imponderable that cannot be evaluated in terms of dollars."

Littell's and Corcoran's mutual contempt remained dormant until November 1944. What respect Littell did have for Corcoran dissipated after Biddle, again at Corcoran's urging, tried to remove him. Littell believed that Corcoran and the attorney general were scheming on behalf of their close friend Jim Rowe, the assistant to the attorney general. Littell was aware that Corcoran, Biddle, and Rowe had all been clerks of Oliver Wendell Holmes, and Littell believed that the plan was for Biddle to receive a spot on the Supreme Court and for Rowe to replace him as the attorney general. If such a plan did exist, it backfired when Littell not only refused to resign but also submitted a twenty-five-page memorandum, accompanied by a letter, to the defense investigation committee formerly chaired by Truman and now chaired by Senator James Mead of New York. The memorandum alleged, among other things, that Corcoran had intervened with Biddle on several cases under review by the Justice Department.

In the memorandum Littell was especially critical of the way in which Corcoran had interfered with the Justice Department's handling of the

Savannah Shipyard case. Three years earlier, Corcoran had explained his role in the Savannah Shipyard case to the Truman Committee, testifying that he had been paid about five thousand dollars by Washington lawyers Kloplovitz and Dempsey to assist the Savannah Port Authority in the legal work required to issue revenue bonds. But Littell argued that Corcoran's role had been much greater and that, in fact, Savannah Shipyard was a fly-by-night enterprise that had tried to hoodwink the federal government.

In his letter to the committee, Littell also recalled an instance when he was meeting with Attorney General Biddle on an important matter at the Department of Justice and the Biddle's secretary interrupted to say that Corcoran was holding on the telephone. According to Littell, Biddle abruptly ended the meeting and took the call, telling Corcoran, "No — you don't need to come over here. I'll come over there if you wish." The attorney general's obsequiousness caused Littell to ask the committee, "What has Tommy Corcoran got on Biddle?"

After the testimony of Corcoran in late 1941, the Truman Committee had considered the Savannah case closed and, now, three years later, the same committee under Mead did not want to insert itself into an internal Justice Department dispute. Members of the committee refused to comment on the allegations, but maintained that either the attorney general or his assistant, Littell, should resign. When neither man blinked, President Roosevelt entered the fray and fired Littell, calling his insinuations of Biddle's corruption "inexcusable." Like Roosevelt, Biddle had gone to Groton School, and they were bound by a strong "old boy" network that Littell underestimated at his peril. Moreover, the president was still fond of his former aide, Tommy the Cork. Several months earlier he had told Vice President Henry Wallace, "I wish I had Tommy back." And only weeks before, Roosevelt told Biddle that he would consider appointing Tommy to the U.S. attorney position for the Southern District of New York, one of the most powerful jobs in the Department of Justice.

Perhaps most importantly, President Roosevelt believed that Littell's charges of improper interference in Department of Justice matters, if given credence, might drag his administration into scandal at a time when the nation needed to focus on only one thing: winning the war. When Littell learned that he had been fired by the president, he told reporters that at least he had managed to block the appointment of "a

Tommy Corcoran henchman" — presumably Jim Rowe, who had been mentioned as a possible successor to Biddle. Littell may also have succeeded in scuttling any plans that the president had to bring Corcoran back into the adminstration.

Senator Mead had hoped to avoid any more hearings, but Littell's memorandum was leaked to the press and appeared in newspapers around the country. Littell charged that Corcoran's influence over Biddle had caused the attorney general to seek a settlement in the Savannah Shipyard case, even though the facts, in Littell's view, strongly supported taking the case to the grand jury. Littell also charged that Dempsey and Kloplovitz had acted as "Tommy Corcoran's front law firm."

But Littell's most sensational allegation had nothing to do with the Savannah Shipyard case, but rather with the Sterling case. Littell claimed that the settlement of the antitrust charges against Sterling on September 5, 1941, the day after Biddle was appointed the acting attorney general, had been "completely dominated by Tommy Corcoran. . . ." Littell accused Sterling of being "an agent of Nazi Germany," and he called Biddle's settlement of the case "the lowest point in the history of the Department of Justice since the Harding administration."

There was an immediate outcry in the press that the relationship between Biddle and Corcoran be investigated. Some in Congress joined the chorus calling for an examination, but they were largely ignored. Writing in the *Washington Post,* reporter Charles Van Devander observed, "Strong influence is being brought to bear to block an investigation by Congress into the affairs of the Department of Justice, including Attorney General Biddle's allegedly close relationship with lawyer lobbyist Tommy Corcoran." In the House, Speaker Rayburn made certain that no committee held a hearing on the issue.

Although there was no formal investigation of the Savannah Shipyard case, Attorney General Biddle testified before the Senate Judiciary Committee on December 10, 1944. Over the objections of Chairman Richard Russell, he was asked about Littell's charges of improper influence. The attorney general defended Corcoran without reservation, calling him "a completely honest man." Biddle then added for effect, "If there is any question about that, I want it on the record." Biddle went on to claim that Littell had too often refused to consult with him before pronouncing a department position and that Littell had been fired for disloyalty "in circulating vicious stories about me." Littell later claimed that Biddle had "lied," but nothing came of his allegations.

In fact, Republicans were not clamoring for more investigation of Biddle or Corcoran. Corcoran was no longer perceived as having direct access to Roosevelt. Moreover, through his lobbying activities he had developed a close relationship with a number of Republican members of Congress whose campaign coffers had benefited from his personal largesse or that of his clients. More importantly, the Republicans had close ties to oil and real estate interests and were delighted to be getting rid of Littell, whom they viewed as an activist in his role as director of the department's public lands division. Tommy Corcoran had once again successfully dodged an investigation of his lobbying activities.

As a young man in the New Deal, Corcoran had been outraged by the heavy-handed lobbying of big business. But now as a lobbyist for big business, he refined and used many of the same tactics that were once used against him. His growing reputation as a fixer ensured that the future president would never call on him for advice or counsel; more significantly, it brought him into direct conflict with one of the most powerful and vindictive men in the annals of American government.

16

The Wiretap

Corcoran was still embittered by the solicitor general experience and often complained to friends that the administration was in a state of "political and moral collapse," while the White House was being run "entirely by Frankfurter and Hopkins." Yet Corcoran's criticism of the men surrounding the president was tinged with a certain ambivalence because he recognized that his law and lobbying business would clearly benefit from the continuation of the administration.

Corcoran was also ambivalent about President Roosevelt's decision to run for a fourth term. With the nation at war, Corcoran believed that Roosevelt was the best man to lead the country. Still, he feared that "the Skipper" was failing physically. He saw it in his face, which was increasingly gaunt, and in his eyes, which on many days were dark and tired. Corcoran worried about who could succeed Roosevelt if he became ill or stepped aside.

Before becoming vice president, Henry Wallace had served with great distinction as Roosevelt's secretary of agriculture. Corcoran, however, intensely disliked Wallace, whom he had long considered politically inept. Wallace was from the extreme liberal wing of the Democratic Party, and Corcoran derided his vision of a global New Deal and the creation of an American social service state. Moreover, Corcoran believed he was the wrong person to hold together the fragile New Deal coalition of northern liberals and southern conservatives, and knew that within Democratic Party circles there was significant dissatisfaction with the man — an ineffectual vice president with no apparent political muscle. There may also have been a business component to Corcoran's feelings about Wallace: The secretary had opposed the prewar drug cartel from which Sterling Pharmaceutical had greatly benefited.

With Roosevelt's health so clearly failing, Corcoran believed it was important not only to have a strong vice presidential candidate in the upcoming election, but to have one with whom he had a strong personal relationship. With all these considerations in mind, Corcoran promoted the idea of placing Justice William O. Douglas on the ticket.

Douglas was fiercely ambitious, and Corcoran knew that while he enjoyed serving on the Court, he secretly harbored the desire to one day run for national office. In his unpublished memoir Corcoran wrote that Douglas "wanted the presidency worse than Don Quixote wanted Dulcinea." But Douglas had no natural base of support and very few political contacts. Since he had been in private practice, Corcoran had been helping Douglas expand his political and business network around the country. Indeed, according to his biographer Bruce Allen Murphy, Corcoran had even arranged for various honorary degrees to be presented to Douglas in order to gain favorable attention in the press. Sometimes Corcoran even wrote Douglas's acceptance speeches.

Corcoran also tried to create a groundswell of support for Douglas within the Roosevelt administration. He talked up the justice to his old friend Leon Henderson at the RFC. He told Jerome Frank at the SEC that he believed Roosevelt would drop Wallace and pick Douglas and that Frank should jump on the bandwagon. He enlisted the support of Abe Fortas at the Department of the Interior, and he persuaded Fortas's boss, Harold Ickes, to agree to support Douglas if Wallace was dropped. He also talked to his congressional friends Lyndon Johnson and Sam Rayburn. He asked for assistance from Ernest Cuneo, associate general counsel at the Democratic National Committee, who had wide political contacts and shared his concern about Wallace. Corcoran enlisted Jim Rowe, one of Roosevelt's administrative assistants and someone who commanded increasing respect as a political thinker within the party. Finally, Corcoran tapped Eliot Janeway, business editor at *Time* magazine, to be the inside man for Douglas in the press.

Felix Frankfurter complained to Harry Hopkins that "subterranean skill" was being used by Corcoran in "managing the Douglas candidacy." Frankfurter now disdained Corcoran, and he believed Douglas was improperly using his position on the Supreme Court as a springboard to political office. This was somewhat ironic given that Frankfurter, who never aspired to elective office, remained intensely political.

As the date of the opening of the convention neared, it appeared that Corcoran's plan might actually succeed. After a luncheon with the president, Secretary Ickes reported that Roosevelt intended to pick Douglas as his running mate. Corcoran also learned that Robert Hannegan, now chairman of the Democratic National Committee, had received from the

1. Thomas Corcoran, age nine. (Collection of Thomas Corcoran Jr.)

2. The Corcoran brothers (left to right) — David, Howard, and Thomas — circa 1906. (Collection of Thomas Corcoran Jr.)

3. The Corcoran brothers — Thomas, Howard, and David — in an undated photograph. (Collection of Thomas Corcoran Jr.)

4. The Corcoran brothers—Thomas, David, and Howard—in an undated photo. (Collection of Thomas Corcoran Jr.)

5. Thomas Corcoran (far left) with unidentified coworkers in the White Mountains of New Hampshire, circa 1919. (Collection of Thomas Corcoran Jr.)

6. Tommy "the Cork" Corcoran in an undated photograph from the New Deal years. (Collection of Thomas Corcoran Jr.)

7. Franklin D. Roosevelt presents his pen to Thomas Corcoran after signing the Public Utility Holding Company Act in August 1935. Behnd the president are (left to right) Senators Alben W. Barkley (D-KY), Burton K. Wheeler (D-MT), and Fred H. Brown (D-NH); Dozier Devine of the Federal Power Commission; Congressman Sam Rayburn (D-TX); Corcoran; and Ben Cohen. (Collection of Thomas Corcoran Jr.)

8. Thomas and Peggy Corcoran examine a rabbit's foot given to them by a friend on their wedding day, March 4, 1940. (Harris & Ewing photo, collection of the *Washington Star*, reprinted by permission of the District of Columbia Public Library)

9. Corcoran appears before the Senate defense investigating committee at his own request on December 16, 1941, telling the senators that he had never received a fee that in any way increased the cost of the government's preparation for war. (AP Wide World Photos)

10. Margaret (Peggy) Corcoran with her daughter Margaret Gardner Corcoran, circa 1941. (Collection of Thomas Corcoran Jr.)

11. Digna Gomez with her daughter Alice in a passport photo from the 1940s. (Collection of Alice Howard)

12. Margaret Corcoran as a debutante, 1957. (Glogan Photos, collection of the *Washington Star*, reprinted by permission of the District of Columbia Public Libary)

13. On May 19, 1960, Corcoran appears before the House Legislative Oversight Committee to discuss his off-the-record meetings with Federal Power Commission members. (AP Wide World Photos)

14. Benjamin Cohen, Thomas Corcoran, and President Lyndon Johnson, circa 1965. (Collection of Thomas Corcoran Jr.)

15. Tom Corcoran with Anna Chennault in the Presidential Box of the Opera House in Washington's John F. Kennedy Center for the Performing Arts. (Collection of Anna Chennault)

16. "Tommy had the reputation of an indefatigable, rascally rogue." — Harry McPherson (Collection of Thomas Corcoran Jr.)

president a postdated, scribbled message to the delegates that he wanted Hannagan to deliver at the opening of the convention: Roosevelt would be happy to run with either Justice William O. Douglas or Senator Harry Truman. It's not clear from whom Corcoran learned of the note, but he took credit for it with Douglas, who was overjoyed and told Corcoran that he had scored "a ten strike."

Corcoran believed that Roosevelt's message was significant because the president mentioned Douglas's name before Truman's. In Corcoran's mind, the order of names only confirmed the intelligence he had received from Ickes — Roosevelt intended for Douglas to be his running mate.

But Corcoran was wrong. The letter actually listed Truman's name first. More importantly, notwithstanding Corcoran's best efforts to organize leading Democrats on behalf of Douglas, the party bosses, Hannegan included, wanted Truman. The senator from Missouri was, after all, the product of a political machine and more like them.

On Wednesday, July 19, the Democratic convention opened in Chicago. Justice Douglas was at his home in Washington State ready for the telephone call telling him that he'd been chosen as the president's running mate. While Corcoran remained in Washington, DC, to work the phones and coordinate the effort, Ernest Cuneo was in Chicago rounding up delegates. As a final coup for the Douglas candidacy, Corcoran persuaded Joe Kennedy to back the ticket with substantial financial resources if the justice was on it. But it was all to no avail. Hannegan released the president's letter with Truman's name listed first. And Cuneo discovered that the delegates were all for Truman.

The general election in 1944 pitted Tom Dewey, the governor of New York, and his running mate, John W. Bricker, the governor of Ohio, against President Roosevelt and Senator Truman. Dewey refrained from attacking the president's conduct of the war or foreign policy. Indeed, the Republican platform in 1944 abandoned its previous call for isolationism in favor of postwar organization of states similar to what Roosevelt had advocated. Dewey also embraced many New Deal programs, such as Social Security, but he claimed that many of them were being run incompetently. And he indirectly raised the issue of the president's failing health by constantly referring to the "tired old men" who were running the government. On Election Day Roosevelt won the electoral votes of thirty-six states, and 53 percent of the popular vote, the slimmest margin of victory in his four elections.

Six months after the president's reelection, Corcoran's worst fears were realized when Roosevelt collapsed dead in Warm Springs, Georgia. Suddenly the decision in Chicago to put Harry Truman on the ticket had taken on lasting historical significance. For Corcoran, it was the end of an era. He had left the Roosevelt administration and government nearly five years earlier, but had remained close to the Roosevelt family of public servants, New Dealers like himself who believed in the power of government to make a difference in people's lives. Now that he was in private practice, it also helped that he could get virtually any member of the administration on the telephone. Corcoran had little regard for Truman and the men who surrounded him. For one thing, he didn't know them. Not long after seeing the new president and his cronies in the White House, Corcoran remarked, "A gang of crooks has hijacked the funeral train of a great man."

When he assumed the presidency in 1945, Harry Truman was largely unprepared. Although Roosevelt liked Truman, FDR had not taken him into his confidence, failing, for instance, to even inform his vice president that there was a project under way to build an atomic bomb. But Truman, a plainspoken midwesterner, had good political instincts and knew he had to move quickly to take control of the government. He didn't trust Roosevelt's Ivy League–educated eastern friends and advisers, and shortly after he became president, Truman placed his Missouri cronies Harry Vaughan, John Steelman, and James Vardaman into key positions in the White House.

As the war in Europe drew to a close, the president was particularly concerned about the spread of communism, increasingly a subject of speculation and discussion in the press. In late May and early June Truman became alarmed when a series of cables written by Harry Hopkins describing his meetings with the Soviet leader Joseph Stalin were reported in some detail by columnist Drew Pearson. Truman considered Pearson a potential threat to national security, but he was more worried by the apparent breach of security in the White House. The president turned for assistance to the director of the Federal Bureau of Investigation, J. Edgar Hoover.

Hoover, the son of a Washington civil servant, had in 1917 joined the Justice Department's division of investigation, the forerunner of the FBI, and only seven years later, at the age of twenty-nine, was appointed the director of the FBI. Ironically, in announcing the appointment, Attorney General Harlan Fiske Stone stated that the division's investigative activities would be greatly scaled back, including the banning of wiretapping. During World War I the division had engaged in domestic political surveillance, and dossiers had been compiled on more than two hundred thousand organizations and individuals. Then, in the 1924 Teapot Dome scandal, the Department of Justice illegally gathered information on perceived political opponents. Attorney General Stone, who was headed for a seat on the Supreme Court, declared, "A secret police may become a menace to a free government. . . . because it carries with it the possibility of abuses of power which are not always quickly apprehended or understood." Echoing Stone, Hoover vowed that "wiretapping will never be done in this bureau." But after the election of Franklin Roosevelt, that was to change.

In 1937 President Roosevelt's attorney general, Homer Cummings, authorized wiretaps in the investigation of gangsters and kidnappings. Cummings cited authority under a 1928 Supreme Court case, *Olmstead v. U.S.*, arguing that the Constitution did not specifically prohibit wiretapping. It did not take Hoover long to overcome his previous misgivings about listening in on others' conversation. The FBI director had the full support of the president and, indeed, Roosevelt personally liked Hoover, who often supplied him with political gossip. Hoover never looked back, and for the next forty years he wiretapped hundreds of people in and out of government, often for purely political purposes.

Hoover was able to justify almost any action he took as consistent with national security interests. In 1945 Hoover decided to order a wiretap placed on the telephone of Ed Prichard, a liberal New Deal lawyer and close friend of Corcoran's, who had clerked for Felix Frankfurter and was a top aide in the Department of the Treasury. Hoover had no evidence that Prichard had done anything wrong, but he was friends with Drew Pearson and, more importantly, his agents had learned from White House aides that Prichard held a "dim view" of Truman's abilities and had referred to several of the president's top aides as "numbskulls." That was enough to suggest to the director that Prichard might be involved in activities detrimental to the security of the nation. The wiretap was installed, and the FBI quickly learned that one of the people Prichard talked to most frequently was Tommy Corcoran.

Only a month after the Prichard wiretap was installed, President Truman's chief administrative aide, Edward McKim, told the FBI director that the president was concerned the leaks had not been curtailed. Hoover asked one of his top agents, Myron Gurnea, to meet with McKim. Gurnea later recorded in a memorandum that McKim told him, "Thomas Corcoran had been engaged in questionable activities and he wanted a technical placed on his telephone line." A *technical* was another name for a wiretap.

McKim was also concerned that Corcoran had too much influence in the Department of Justice and told Gurnea that for all practical purposes, Corcoran "has been Attorney General." McKim wanted to know, too, "of any sources Drew Pearson has." Both Pearson and Corcoran had been recorded on the Prichard wiretap, although there was no evidence that any sensitive information had been passed among any of the three men.

After Gurnea briefed the director on his conversation with McKim, Hoover approved the tap on Corcoran, although not on Pearson. It was understood that the wiretap was highly secret and, according to an FBI liaison, "White House aide Harry Vaughan warned 'if the [wiretap on Corcoran] should ever become known it would be our [the FBI's] baby.'" In order to protect the White House, Vaughan made it clear that he would deny any knowledge of the operation.

Hoover, a ruthless and vindictive man, believed that Corcoran was part of an informal cabal dedicated to embarrassing him. The director had come under attack in the press in the spring of 1940 for cracking down on the anti-Franco forces in the United States when he ordered his agents in Milwaukee and Detroit to arrest radicals accused of having signed up volunteers for the International Abraham Lincoln Brigade, the batallion of three thousand Americans who fought on the side of the Spanish Republicans. Hoover learned that Max Lowenthal, a protégé of Corcoran's who worked for Senator Wheeler, had been spreading the word around Capitol Hill that the FBI had acted precipitously and recklessly. Hoover's anger intensified when Senator George Norris, Corcoran's close friend and collaborator in the third-term drive for President Roosevelt, sharply criticized Hoover and demanded hearings.

During the late summer and fall of 1940, a series of reports carried over the radio and in newspapers claimed that Corcoran wanted a New Dealer to replace Hoover as FBI director. Typical of these was a story carried by the *Chicago Herald-American* on November 14, 1940, headlined NEW DEAL PURGE PLANNED, which stated flatly that "the inner circle of the White House planned to bring about sweeping changes in the government," and claimed that Corcoran and Cohen were the leaders of a White House effort "to force the retirement of J. Edgar Hoover." One of Hoover's top lieutenants, Edward Tamm, complained to Ugo Carusi, an assistant to the attorney general, that "there was an attempt by Mr. Corcoran to make the FBI free of Hoover next year."

Susequently, one of Hoover's palace guards reported to Corcoran that Attorney General Robert Jackson had been told the FBI was keeping him under surveillance and maintained an investigative file on him. If Jackson was correct, Hoover was spying on Corcoran even before he left the government. Whatever the case, the FBI wiretaps on Prichard and Corcoran produced no clues as to who in the White House was leaking to Drew Pearson, but they did reveal that Corcoran was involved in another case with national security implications.

In early 1945 FBI director Hoover believed he was on the verge of uncovering a massive espionage scandal. He learned from the wiretap on Corcoran that the former New Deal lawyer was assisting John Stewart Service, a career State Department employee, who had been arrested for possible communist activity in what came to be known as the *Amerasia* case.

Amerasia was a biweekly journal devoted to Asian affairs that was begun in 1937 by a leftist intellectual, Philip Jaffe. The journal operated on a shoestring budget, with Jaffe serving as both editor and publisher. In February 1945 Kenneth Wells, an agent in the Office of Strategic Services with a background in Asia, was reading the magazine when he made an alarming discovery: It included an article clearly based on a secret memorandum that Wells himself had written. Indeed, much of the article had been lifted verbatim. The OSS was the predecessor of the Central Intelligence Agency and was the agency mainly responsible for counterespionage activity. Wells feared that someone had infiltrated the OSS, and he went straight to the FBI to report the breach in security.

The FBI determined that the information contained in the article, if acquired by the Japanese, had the potential to harm Allied interests by revealing critical sources. The bureau immediately launched an investigation, and in order to discover the source of the security breach, agents secretly broke into the offices of *Amerasia* one night in June. They discovered hundreds of classified documents, many lying out in the open.

The bureau subsequently installed wiretaps in the *Amerasia* offices and in the homes of Jaffe and others associated with magazine. After gathering information for three months, Jaffe and five others, including John Stewart Service, were arrested on June 6, 1945. While Jaffe and his colleagues were clearly communist sympathizers — Jaffe himself planned to become a Soviet spy — Service was a dedicated foreign service officer, an expert on Asia raised in China by missionaries, who had hoped to use *Amerasia* as a vehicle to influence policy toward China by exposing Chiang Kai-shek's government as both inept and corrupt.

Service's arrest alarmed his close friends, among them Lauchlin Currie, who — as it turned out from documents discovered in the Kremlin many years later — had been a Soviet spy. Currie had been first sent by Roosevelt to China in 1941 to help Chiang Kai-shek with his economic problems and to demonstrate the American commitment. On a subsequent trip, Currie met Service, then living in Beijing, who confided to him that he was not impressed by Chiang and had serious doubts about the sustainability of his government. The two men began a correspondence, and Service later claimed that Currie passed on information "to people like Drew Pearson . . . to spread any news he wanted to spread about China."

Currie was also a close friend of Ben Cohen, now the State Department's legal adviser. Only hours after Service was arrested, Currie called Cohen and told him he wanted to help Service. Cohen did not particularly know Service, but he liked Currie and indicated a willingness to help. Besides the fact that Currie was an old friend from the New Deal, Cohen was interested in protecting the State Department from the taint of scandal. He also may have been concerned about gaining congressional approval for the United Nations charter, which was being debated at the time. Whatever the reason, Cohen knew the best man to advise John Service about his legal problems: Tommy Corcoran.

Corcoran and Currie knew each other well from their days in the Roosevelt White House and their more recent work on Lend-Lease, and so after being approached by Cohen, Corcoran called Currie directly. Currie told him that several well-known civil rights lawyers had offered to represent Service and turn the case into a cause célèbre. But Corcoran argued that publicizing the case would be a terrible mistake, stressing that the goal should be "to get the guy out," and not "making a Dreyfus case out of it." After all, Corcoran added, "The Dreyfus case was wonderful for the lawyers and tough on Dreyfus. . . . Let someone else be hanged for the wearing of the green." Corcoran told Currie that he was not "going to let them push this kid around," referring to the twenty-five-year-old Service. While not formally representing Service, Corcoran promised to "work around the edges of this thing for a day or so and see if I can liquidate the whole damn thing."

After talking to Corcoran, Currie went to see John Service. He suggested to the diplomat that he talk directly to Corcoran, but Service demurred. He already had an attorney, Godfrey Munter, a well-respected lawyer who was the former president of the District of Columbia Bar Association. Moreover, Service knew that Corcoran was an officer of China Defense Supplies, the company that had been formed to channel American aid to the Chinese Nationalists. If anything good was going to come of his arrest, Service felt it would be exposing the corruption of Chiang Kai-shek. Service later wrote that contacting Corcoran "seemed like going into the enemy's lair." He wanted time to think it over.

Corcoran, however, didn't wait for Service to make up his mind. He began making inquiries around town about Service's lawyer of record, Godfrey Munter. The FBI was wiretapping Corcoran when he asked one associate whether or not Munter ". . . is a Jewish fellow?" When informed that Munter was Scandinavian, Corcoran inquired, "Is he a Red?" When told that Munter was a former president of the District of Columbia Bar, Corcoran still wasn't satisfied, and over the course of the next few days he spoke to several attorneys about replacing Munter — even though he had not been authorized to do so by Service. Moreover, Corcoran was coming to the conclusion that he was the best person to replace Munter.

On June 10, 1945, four days after Service's arrest, Hoover learned of Corcoran's efforts to assist Service and of Cohen's and Currie's interest in Service's exoneration. The FBI director also learned that Corcoran had used his influence at the Justice Department in an attempt to quash a possible indictment of Service. Corcoran had direct contacts with such high-level officials as Assistant Attorney General James McGranery, who had supervisory responsibility for presenting the case to the grand jury; Jim McInerney, one of the Justice Department officials directly involved in presenting the case to the grand jury; and even Attorney General-designate Tom Clark. Indeed, Corcoran was friendly with all three men, particularly McInerney.

The wiretap revealed that Corcoran strongly opposed having Service testify before the grand jury or agree to any joint defense strategy. Corcoran was not interested in the fate of the other defendants and did not want to cast Service as simply one of the victims in a political witch hunt. Corcoran believed that the best strategy was to offer no additional information until lawyers at the Justice Department offered some sort of deal. At the time, Corcoran's friend Jim McInerney was seeking to persuade Service to appear before the grand jury to make a statement that would clear his name, since the Justice Department had nothing on him. Corcoran, however, had serious reservations about the risks involved whenever inexperienced witnesses appear before grand juries. But McInerney pressed him. The Justice Department lawyer promised that the only reason for insisting on Service's testimony was that "they didn't want any doubt about this because of the FBI." Moreover, McInerney assured him, Service "puts up a hell of a fine appearance,"and his testimony before the grand jury would be "the best way of clearing it up."

Corcoran acceded to Service's appearance before a grand jury only after Assistant Attorney General McGranery promised to "take care" of the matter. To reinforce the deal Corcoran also cleared it with Attorney General-designate Tom Clark, who assured him that Service would not be charged with any crime, but would be required at some later date to appear as a witness in the trial involving the other *Amerasia* defendants. Corcoran received further assurances from Clark that the Justice Deparment lawyers questioning Service would not be "antagonistic."

Clark was facing a potential fight over his nomination, primarily from two senators, Burton Wheeler of Montana and Kenneth Wherry of Kansas. On June 11 Corcoran called Clark to assure him that "arrangements were being completed whereby his nomination would not be opposed." The next day Corcoran called Clark again and told him that Wheeler was in Europe and "Wherry was all for him." These conversations were picked up by the FBI wiretap, and Myron Gurnea recorded them in a memorandum to Director Hoover, noting: "It is obvious that Corcoran is making every effort to develop Tom Clark and by inference has taken the credit for having Tom Clark's nomination approved by the Senate Committee."

Corcoran, of course, had sources within the Department of Justice, and it was not long before he learned of the taps. Henry Grunewald, a private investigator who had first done work for Corcoran at the RFC and now regularly assisted him, called him on June 14 and told him that Hoover "is gunning for you now." Grunewald, who referred to Hoover as "that SOB," told Corcoran that since Attorney General Biddle had left the Justice Department, the FBI director believed that Corcoran could no longer be protected. Corcoran brushed aside Hoover's threat, pointing out to Grunewald that the new attorney general, Tom Clark, was "also a good friend."

Through the wiretap, Hoover learned not only of Corcoran's activities, but also of the collaboration among Currie, McGranery, and McInerney. The FBI director wanted to have Corcoran indicted. But the wiretap had been installed without the approval of the attorney general, which was required under President Roosevelt's 1940 directive. Hoover knew that if the existence of the unauthorized wiretap ever became public, the White House would deny any knowledge of it. Reluctantly, he remained silent.

Harry Vaughan, one of President Truman's top aides, was outraged by Corcoran's behavior in the Service case. Vaughan went to see Assistant FBI Director Gordon Neese and told him that he was thinking about suggesting to John Snyder, the secretary of the Treasury, that he conduct a very complete investigation of Corcoran's income tax returns because he was "certain that Corcoran did not declare his full income." But Vaughan demurred, perhaps hoping to learn even more negative information about Corcoran.

Corcoran, however, aware that he was being wiretapped, became much more circumspect in his telephone conversations, even to the point that he openly taunted the eavesdroppers. On one occasion Corcoran called Justice Douglas and, as they traded political gossip, tapped the telephone receiver with his pencil and said, "I'm doing my own tapping now." Douglas and Corcoran both laughed.

Many years later Corcoran wrote in his autobiography, "The phone taps were a nuisance and they cost me considerable sums on tailor bills. I'd start each day with a huge pocket full of nickels and make all of my sensitive calls from a wide assortment of phone booths. With three major hotels and a couple of drug stores within a block of my office, there were plenty of public phones available. . . . The worst of it was that my pants pockets kept wearing out for the wear and tear of all those nickels."

At some point during the summer of 1945 Vaughan showed President Truman some of the transcripts of the wiretap from Corcoran's home telephone. Vaughan was surprised because even though the president disliked Corcoran, he was horrified by the invasion of privacy. One of the transcripts dealt mainly with Mrs. Corcoran making appointments with her hairdresser. Truman reportedly asked Vaughan, "What the hell is this crap?" When Vaughan answered, "It's a wiretap," Truman became angry. "Cut them off. . . . Tell the FBI we haven't got any time for that kind of crap."

But the wiretap on Tommy Corcoran was not removed, either because Vaughan did not convey the message to the FBI or, more likely, because Hoover wanted it continued. Ironically, Attorney General Clark actually authorized a wiretap on Corcoran on November 15, 1945. The ostensible purpose was to ensure that Corcoran's lobbying "did not interfere with the proper administration of government." Clark's real reasons for the wiretap were never made clear, but Hoover may have let the attorney general know that Corcoran claimed some control over him.

While the wiretap continued to pick up much mundane information, on several occasions the FBI did glean a better understanding of how Corcoran conducted his lobbying business and how close he came to the edge of impropriety. Corcoran was clearly concerned about making money, but he seemed equally motivated by the thrill of making a deal. He had once derided what he viewed as the corrupt, poker-playing cronies of President Truman, but the wiretaps made clear that Corcoran had become a Washington fixer. While the bureau did not pick up anything incriminating on Corcoran, the wiretaps did reveal Corcoran had been less than forthcoming in one congressional inquiry.

In the summer of 1945 the FBI was listening when Corcoran was contacted by Alva Johnson, a staff writer for the *Saturday Evening Post* who wanted to interview him about his lobbying practice. Johnson was interested in a number of cases, but told Corcoran he was particularly curious about the recent sale of a radio station, WMCA in New York. The station had been sold in 1943 by Donald Flamm, a businessman, to Edward V. Noble, a former undersecretary of commerce. The transaction, which on its face had seemed both straightforward and proper, resulted in a lawsuit and a congressional investigation after Flamm charged he had been pressured to make the sale. Flamm's allegation was supported by Leslie Roberts, a former midlevel official in the commerce department, who claimed that the "deal had been greased from the White House down." Roberts specifically mentioned the involvement of Tommy Corcoran.

In the fall of 1944 Clarence Lea, a Democratic congressman from California, held a hearing to review the transaction. His commerce subcommittee then issued subpoenas, including one to Corcoran. Corcoran managed to delay his testimony for several months, but on December 14 he appeared before the committee in closed session. After several hours he emerged from the hearing room and told reporters that he had played no role in pressuring Flamm to sell the radio station. Indeed, Corcoran noted that during almost the entire period during which negotiations for the sale of the station were being conducted, he had been in Mexico on business. And he claimed that he had been surprised when he returned to learn that the sale price was $850,000, an amount that he considered "three and a half times the sum of the physical assets and thirty times the station's earnings." As was often the case, however, Corcoran's version of events was incomplete and self-serving, but it would be another year before Alva Johnson's exposé in the *Saturday Evening Post* provided additional detail.

In his October 1945 series of articles, Johnson claimed that the "facts of the sale of WMCA station are interesting in themselves. The greater interest however, is what happened to the men that attempted to investigate the case." Johnson explained that the subcommittee had been originally chaired by Democratic congressman Edward E. Cox of Georgia, who at one time had been charged with improperly seeking a favor from the Federal Communications Commission involving a Georgia radio station. The Department of Justice ultimately dropped the investigation, but, according to Johnson, after Cox scheduled hearings and issued subpoenas related to the WMCA case, the department indicated it might be interested in pursuing its prior investigation of the Georgia radio station.

Cox resigned from the subcommittee with the blessing of Sam Rayburn, who went to the floor and praised him for his "bigness of mind and heart." Cox was replaced by Clarence Lea.

Johnson also wrote that after the subpoenas were issued the subcommittee's chief counsel, Eugene L. Garey, was "invited to a wild-turkey dinner at the home of Speaker Sam Rayburn. Tommy was there with his accordion . . . the next day Tommy called at Garey's office and said he wanted the WMCA case dropped." Then, according to Johnson, Garey learned that "a close friend and business associate of his would be investigated by the Department of Justice unless he resigned." When the new chairman, Lea, postponed the hearings, Garey seized the opportunity to resign, claiming that he didn't agree with the direction of the investigation. As reported by Johnson, the inquiry had been effectively thwarted.

After the article appeared in the *Saturday Evening Post*, Corcoran was worried that his reputation would be damaged, and he called his friends to gauge their reaction. One of the first people he called was Ernest Cuneo, a close friend and adviser to New York mayor Fiorello La Guardia and an independent newspaper publisher and editorial writer. Corcoran had met the voluble Cuneo during the 1940 campaign, and the two men had become close friends. When Corcoran asked Cuneo what he thought of the articles, Cuneo replied that "the net effect of the articles was nothing." As he put it, "I mean, they are forgotten. Drew Pearson says you can't even understand them." Two days later Corcoran and Cuneo talked again, and a relieved Corcoran reported that "the articles have done no real harm."

Corcoran never denied the story as reported in the *Saturday Evening Post*, although in a private conversation with Senator Lister Hill of Alabama — wiretapped by the FBI — he elaborated on what had really happened. Corcoran told Hill that the chief counsel, Garey, was going to expose the corrupt business practices of the president's son, Elliott: ". . . he was gonna burst it in connection with the WMCA thing and that's why Larry [Fly, the FCC chairman] and I were fighting it so furiously. We were covering the boss."

In 1933 Elliott Roosevelt, whom his father, referred to as "Bunny," had joined the Hearst radio chain. Elliott had never shown any great acumen for business, but a few years later he started a radio station company with the help of a number of investors. By 1940 the company was bankrupt, and as Roosevelt biographer Ted Morgan has written, "The entire investment capital of $500,000 had gone down the drain, and not a penny had been paid back to investors." None of this, however, had been made public and, as Corcoran explained to Senator Hill, "If this had broken during the last election — that's when they were trying to pull it — I tell you it could have thrown the election." According to Corcoran, "I had my own fingers pretty badly mashed, but I did keep it dead for a year."

PART FOUR

The Lobbyist Years

17

The Key to Lobbying

Lever Brothers was a major manufactuer of soap products and, like many companies during World War II, was forced to comply with certain quotas on raw materials. In 1945 Lever retained Corcoran to lobby the Department of Agriculture to increase the company's quota on fats and oils, enabling it to use more in the production of its soap. Corcoran knew that if he was successful, Lever Brothers stood to profit handsomely, so he told his partner Worth Clark that he wanted a hundred-thousand-dollar fee.

By chance Corcoran bumped into Secretary of Agriculture Clinton Anderson at a party. Corcoran had known the secretary from his days as a House member during the New Deal. "After enough drinks," according to Corcoran, Anderson confessed that the staff had recommended that Lever's request be denied, but that it was irrelevant since the war was over and he planned to lift all restrictions anyway. Corcoran saw an opening and a few days later told Worth Clark, "Now I think that gives us a way of going to them [the staff at the Department of Agriculture] and say now you know and we know that [quotas are] going to collapse, it's going to be unnecessary, but it's awfully important for us to make this showing so come on and do it for us." Corcoran, of course, would not himself have delivered such a message, but was happy to have Clark, who had good friends in the department, make the request.

As historian Alan Lichtman has written, "The key to lobbying is not getting something done, but taking credit for getting something done."

During the war years Corcoran had largely practiced on his own, occasionally partnering with other firms on big cases. By 1945 he was at something of a crossroads: He had more than enough work for himself and he needed help, but he knew that he didn't want to join a large Washington law firm. So he decided to start his own firm. He reached out to some of his closest friends, Democrats with whom he had served in the New Deal, and asked them to help him build a partnership. He was joined by his younger friend Jim Rowe, who had spent two years as a navy lieutenant in the Pacific; Ed Foley, who had served as general counsel to the Treasury Department and during the war as an army colonel in Europe; and William Youngman, a Harvard-trained lawyer who had worked briefly in the New Deal. Corcoran also brought in former senator Worth Clark of Montana to serve as "of counsel" to the firm. While each of Corcoran's partners was a skilled lawyer, it was clear from the beginning that their practice would entail more lobbying than courtroom work.

Lobbying in the 1940s depended heavily on personal contact with legislators and high-ranking executive branch officials. In order to help a corporate client, a lobbyist needed to be able to pick up the telephone and talk to a senator or congressman. Corcoran and his partners all had excellent contacts on Capitol Hill and at the White House. Part of Corcoran's success stemmed from his continuing ability to move men around the government like chess pieces.

Although he had a more difficult time arranging appointments for his friends with the Truman administration, Corcoran never stopped trying. When Abe Fortas became restless working at the Interior Department under Secretary Ickes, Corcoran tried to arrange an appointment for him on the U.S. Court of Appeals. As it turned out, President Truman had already committed the seat to someone else, so Corcoran urged Fortas to seek appointment to the U.S. District Court for the District of Columbia. The wildly ambitious Fortas agreed, but only if he could be somehow assured that he would be considered in the future for a more prestigous judicial appointment. According to Fortas's biographer Bruce Allen Murphy, Tommy the Cork was "off and running again, talking up the idea with Attorney General Tom Clark."

A year later, in 1946, Corcoran was helping another old friend, James Landis. Landis had been teaching at Harvard Law School, but was clearly unhappy and longed to be back in the government. With the help of John L. Sullivan, the assistant secretary of the navy, Corcoran spread the word that Landis would be the perfect person to be appointed chairman of the Civil Aeronautics Board. By encouraging speculation about Landis's appointment, Corcoran helped create a groundswell of support within the adminstration. In April President Truman called and offered Landis the job. Corcoran was pleased for Landis. It didn't hurt that he was also representing Pan American Airways at the time.

◆ ◆ ◆

While Corcoran was growing rich as a lobbyist, he sometimes seemed less intrigued by making money than operating as a fixer. On one occasion in the fall of 1945, Corcoran was approached by Dick Von Gutard, a wealthy businessman whose daughter was stranded in Russian-occupied Germany. Von Gutard retained Corcoran to secure the young woman's safe release. Rather than work through the State Department, Corcoran contacted his good friend Bishop Bernard Sheil of Chicago, who was going to Europe on other matters, and asked him to use his good offices to help. The prelate agreed. As compensation, Corcoran arranged for Von Gutard to "pay the expenses of the man of the cloth over and back as a contribution to him. . . . If the man of the cloth actually delivers — a $5,000 contribution to the Catholic Youth movement over here . . . for myself, a bond up to the gift limit of three thousand dollars for each of my kids. . . ."

For Corcoran, part of being an effective operator entailed dispensing advice to his powerful friends. Typical was Corcoran's advice to Senator Lister Hill of Alabama on a strategy to pass the Office of Price Adjustment bill, which was favored by Hill but opposed by many industries. Corcoran knew Senate parliamentary procedure better than most who worked in the Congress. He advised Hill that the only way to pass the bill was to allow individual senators to "get their products exempted on the record" by having roll call votes. In other words, a farm state senator would be more likely to support price controls if his constituents were exempted. After the Senate and House conferenced on the legislation, Corcoran explained to Hill, the conferees would "bring out a bill that's a workable bill." "Then," strategized Corcoran, "when it comes to the floor [for final passage], you carefully arrange not to have a record vote." Corcoran further explained, "Every guy who goes out . . . can say, 'Well, Goddamn it, you can see what I did on the record. By Jesus, I voted against the Goddamned thing when it came to the voice vote, but of course there wasn't a record vote and you can't see it there. . . .' " Corcoran acknowledged that this was not an "intellectually honest process," but advised Hill that this was the best method to get the bill passed and still protect himself with important constituencies.

Corcoran's willingness to compromise on the issue of intellectual honesty was tame compared to some of the tactics that he employed as a lobbyist. In late 1945 he teamed with former Democratic senator William H.

Smathers of New Jersey and came close to extorting a fee from a New Jersey sugar company that had been charged with tax evasion by the Department of Justice. After being contacted by company officials, Corcoran called Smathers and told him that he had been handed a case by "people who are awfully scared and might pay you desperately well." He told Smathers that he had informed the company's representatives that they could go to jail, thereby heightening their apprehension so that they would be willing to pay a large fee. "I think you can just take the pants off them," Corcoran said. He also suggested that Smathers, who had served on the Judiciary Committee, might convince his friends in the Department of Justice he was "getting the full tax and fraud penalty out of these people — there's no use in smashing up a local enterprise in my home state. Get it?" A few days later Smathers reported back to Corcoran that "I told them I wanted $5,000 now and $15,000 in January." Smathers happily told Corcoran that company officials had said they would take the train from New Jersey to Washington to personally deliver the money.

Corcoran also helped Joe Kennedy. From the day in 1934 that President Roosevelt had installed Kennedy as the first chairman at the Securities and Exchange Commission, Corcoran had watched him closely. Initially skeptical of one of the richest men in the country, Corcoran grew to admire him and was fascinated with how Kennedy operated the levers of power.

The Merchandise Mart was a massive, limestone building on the north bank of the Chicago River that had been constructed by Marshall Field and Company in 1938 at a cost of thirty-five million dollars. With its twenty-five-story tower, the Mart originally had four million square feet of floor space, making it the world's largest building at the time. Only a few years after the building was completed, however, Field president Hughston M. McBain had decided that the company should get out of the real estate business and concentrate on retailing. Low-paying government agencies occupied more than a third of the space, and the building was not needed for the company's operations. By the company's own estimates, the building was worth only twenty-one million in 1944.

Joe Kennedy bought the Merchandise Mart in July 1945 for just $12,956,516. To cover most of the purchase price, he borrowed $12.5 million from the Equitable Life Insurance Society of the United States. Four years later, Kennedy signed a new loan for seventeen million from Prudential Insurance Company of America. He then collateralized the loan with the Mart, paid off the old loan, and invested the excess funds in other projects. Jim Landis, now a Kennedy adviser, suggested that the Joseph P. Kennedy Foundation buy a quarter interest in the property.

Next, Joe installed Wallace Ollman, a tall, amiable accountant, as manager of the building. Ollman told Kennedy that the rates the government were paying were "submarginal." Kennedy understood that if he could dislodge the government agencies from the building, mostly Treasury Department offices, and sign up some high-rent tenants, he could greatly improve his cash flow. Kennedy called Tommy Corcoran and asked him to devise a plan to get the Treasury Department employees out of the Merchandise Mart. Corcoran enlisted Jim Rowe to work on a legislative fix. Rowe proposed getting an appropriation through the Congress that would permit the Treasury Department to construct its own building. While Rowe worked on lining up congressmen, Corcoran made sure that his friend and former roommate Ed Foley, the general counsel at the Treasury Department, enlisted the department's support. According to attorney John Lane, one of Corcoran's close friends, they pulled it off.

After construction began in 1950 on a new federal building in Chicago, Corcoran and Rowe sent Joe Kennedy a bill for seventy-five thousand dollars — a significant sum of money in those days, but still only a small percentage of what they had saved Kennedy. Kennedy sent the lawyers a check for twenty-five thousand and said he wouldn't pay one more dime. In recalling the incident many years later, Corcoran told Lane that Kennedy was "a cheap son of a bitch." Nevertheless, Corcoran understood Kennedy's power; if he didn't like the man, he at least admired him. In any event, Corcoran was unwilling to cut off Kennedy. He continued to advise him on Washington-related matters and often suggested business opportunities to him. Perhaps he remembered Lyndon Johnson's admonition that in politics you always get a second chance.

In July 1947, following the death of publishing heiress Cissy Patterson, Corcoran suggested to Kennedy that he buy the *Washington Times-Herald* from Patterson's heirs. Corcoran wrote Kennedy, "See what a principality Eugene Meyer built out of the *Post* — he turned it into the 49th state. Why don't you be the 50th and let me [be] part of the shadow?" Corcoran was somewhat cryptic about the role he envisioned for himself if Kennedy were to buy the *Times-Herald*. He may have wanted to broker the deal and, perhaps, to represent the paper afterward. But Kennedy replied to Corcoran that he had made "several efforts" in the past to buy the paper. With Patterson's death, "everybody in the country wanted to buy it," Joe groused. Kennedy figured that the paper would be sold at a premium, and he didn't want to invest in anything that he couldn't get for a bargain.

While Hoover was picking up a lot of information about Corcoran's lobbying practice from the wiretap, he was also gathering some good political gossip. One intercept caught Corcoran talking to William O'Connor, whose uncle, a federal judge in Los Angeles, had close contacts in both the White House and the Department of Justice. Hoover was shocked to learn that Truman was considering having him replaced as FBI director, in part because the president frowned upon his relationship with the gossip columnist Walter Winchell. Hoover immediately wrote a confidential letter to Truman's top aide Harry Vaughan and, without making any reference to the wiretap, professed to never leaking any information; he maintained that he talked to the press only after checking with the office of the attorney general.

Hoover also picked up information on the machinations of the Supreme Court. Despite his falling-out with Felix Frankfurter, Corcoran still had several friends there, foremost among them William O. Douglas. They often talked on the telephone, gossiping about politics, the law, and the Court itself.

One day in the spring of 1946 Corcoran's telephone rang at his home. It was Justice Douglas calling to tell Corcoran that Chief Justice Harlan Stone had died: "Cerebral Hemorage. He passed out on the bench at 2 o'clock and we carried him out."

Corcoran was stunned. "Well, the lightning is striking isn't it."

Douglas had admired Stone dating back to the time when Douglas was a law student and Stone was the dean of Columbia Law School. Douglas summed up his respect for Stone when he told Corcoran, "Another great oak has fallen."

Ironically, when Stone had served as the attorney general in the late 1920s he had helped select Hoover as director of the Federal Bureau of Investigation. In the aftermath of Stone's death, Hoover's FBI picked up from wiretaps numerous conversations between Corcoran, Douglas, and others concerning the behind-the-scenes jostling to fill the vacancy left by Stone.

In a conversation with Ernest Cuneo, Corcoran described the "struggle for the Chief Justiceship in which it's Jackson against Black, with the chances out of it will emerge Jimmy Byrnes." Corcoran then explained that he didn't think "either man will accept the appointment of the other. I think either of them will resign and quit if the other man went in." He blamed the animosity between the two justices on Frankfurter, "who can't keep out of it." Corcoran declared, "It's Frankfurter against Black. That's what it is. . . . And Bob Jackson is being hurt enormously by that factor." Cuneo and Corcoran agreed that Black was their choice.

Two days later Corcoran called his friend Justice Stanley Reed and reported that he had heard that "the new chief justice was Bob Jackson." Corcoran called back the next morning and, after learning that Justice Reed was not at home, talked to Mrs. Reed. Corcoran told her that the rumor was wrong: Jackson would not be nominated. That same day he called Justice Black's home and spoke to Mrs. Black, telling her that he would drive over to pick up the justice later that morning. Then, in the afternoon, Corcoran called Justice Douglas in his chambers and told him that the postmaster general was supporting Jackson. That evening Senator Burton Wheeler called Corcoran and told him that he had recommended Black to the president.

The next night Corcoran received a call from a friend in the White House (unidentified in the wiretap transcripts) who told him that Justice Douglas was now in the running. Corcoran believed that the feud between Black and Jackson had become too acrimonious and too public for either man to emerge as chief justice. Calculating that the president would look to a compromise candidate, Corcoran began to quietly promote Justice Douglas. Two days later, journalist Drew Pearson called Corcoran to discuss the nomination. Pearson told Corcoran that the White House had briefly preferred Douglas for "chief," but that Frankfurter had begun lobbying against him. Corcoran, not wanting to ascribe too much power to Frankfurter, replied that Jackson, Frankfurter's choice, had been the front-runner until the left wing of the Court objected. Corcoran guessed that Truman would go outside the current membership of the Court; he predicted that Fred Vinson, secretary of the Treasury, would be one of the top contenders.

As it turned out, Truman considered Douglas, but he felt he was too young and too liberal — and undoubtedly his association with Corcoran did not help his candidacy. The president appointed Vinson — just as Corcoran had predicted.

18

The Truman Years

W hile Corcoran was extremely active on the international front during the postwar years, he was somewhat frustrated at home — he
knew President Truman didn't like him, and he no longer had access to
the highest levels of the government. One day in late 1946 Cororan telephoned Senator Lister Hill. With the FBI monitoring the call, Corcoran
scornfully described the president to Senator Hill as another Ulysses S.
Grant, "loyal, honest, and dumb as hell." He bemoaned the almost whole-
sale shift of cabinet posts, ambassadorships, and federal judgeships from
New Dealers to people for whom the Roosevelt crowd had little regard. In
a pessimistic moment, he predicted: "This experience is going to prove
institutionally that democracy can't do it; that unless it has an uncom-
mon man in the Presidency, it won't work." To hearten Corcoran, Hill
invoked his father's old rallying cry: "Chin up, tail over the dashboard."

When he had been a senator, Truman had disliked Corcoran: He
resented his arm-twisting tactics on behalf of Roosevelt, and he believed
that after Corcoran left the government he became a war profiteer. Now
as president, Truman's contempt for Corcoran only intensified. Even
though he had ordered the wiretap ended, Truman undoubtedly learned
of Corcoran's disrespect for him, and he let it be known that he wanted
nothing to do with the man who had once been his predecessor's trusted
adviser. After Gael Sullivan was nominated to be the assistant postmaster
general, he met with the president, who told him, "There are just two
things I want you to do. Don't talk to Drew Pearson and stay away from
Tommy Corcoran." Some in the Truman White House, such as Clark
Clifford, the president's young counsel, knew the depth of his boss's
hatred for Corcoran and used it to advantage.

A rising star in Washington, Clifford had been raised in St. Louis,
Missouri. After graduating from Washington University Law School, he
talked his way into one of St. Louis's premier law firms as an associate
trial lawyer. Within a few years he had gained a reputation as one of the
best trial lawyers in the Midwest. He enrolled in the navy during World

War II and served briefly in San Francisco. He was asked by his commanding officer, John Vardaman, if he would be interested in joining him as his assistant in Washington, where Vardaman had recently been assigned as the navy liaison to the White House. Clifford leapt at the opportunity. Within months he and his young wife, Marny, had packed their belongings, moved to Washington, and were living in an apartment on Connecticut Avenue. When the president asked Vardaman to go to Yalta to join the negotiations with the Russians, the navy liaison left Clifford in charge. Soon thereafter, the tall, handsome, exceedingly polite naval officer caught the eye of the President Truman, and in 1945 he became the counsel to the president, a position in which he would serve for the next five years.

On September 17, 1947, Corcoran's law partner Jim Rowe, who had recently returned from several months in Germany where he had assisted Robert Jackson in the Nuremberg war trials, drafted a thirty-page single-spaced memorandum outlining his thoughts on how President Truman might win the 1948 election. Truman's popularity was very low, but Rowe believed the president might yet forge a coalition to defeat the popular Republican candidate, Thomas Dewey, and stave off the quixotic candidacy of the Progressive Party candidate, Henry Wallace. After consulting with a number of labor leaders, Rowe developed a strategy for the upcoming election. It would prove remarkably prescient.

Rowe had the memorandum delivered to Clifford and asked that it be forwarded to the president. Clifford read the memo and was very impressed with Rowe's political acumen. He decided to add a few paragraphs on civil rights and foreign policy and to tinker with some of language. He then had the memorandum retyped, double spaced instead of single, and submitted it to the president under his own name, without reference to Rowe.

Rowe's strategic document proved cannily accurate, both as a predictor of what would happen and as a strategy for countering Dewey and Wallace. But it was Clifford who became known as the man who engineered Truman's come-from-behind victory over Dewey. Indeed, the document became Clifford's calling card for the next several decades. It was years before journalists learned that Jim Rowe had actually written the famous memorandum. Clifford explained in his memoirs, published in 1991, that he believed at the time that submitting the memorandum to the president under Rowe's name would have undercut the message because of Rowe's association with Tommy Corcoran, whom Truman so deeply despised.

Although Corcoran played no role in Truman's presidential reelection, he did have a role that year in the election of a young man in to the U.S. Senate from the state of Texas.

Lyndon and Lady Bird Johnson had made a significant amount of money on their radio station, and the former congressman was enormously loyal to Tommy Corcoran given his help in matters of both politics and business. In February 1947 this loyalty was tested when Corcoran represented investors bidding against Johnson's most important financial supporters, George and Herman Brown. Brown and Root, the Brown brothers' investment company, had joined a group of oil investors to form the Texas Eastern Transmission Company to purchase the Big Inch and Little Inch pipelines. The consortium offered $143 million — $12 million more than the Tennessee Gas Company, represented by Tommy Corcoran, had offered. One of the investors, Charles I. Francis, a Houston oil and gas attorney, later told one of LBJ's biographers, "Lyndon took no part in the original sale. . . . He said, 'Charley, I can't do that. Tommy Corcoran is on the other side.' "

A year later, in the spring of 1948, Johnson decided to make a second run for the U.S. Senate. He wrote to Corcoran to assure him that he hadn't done any damage to his relationship with the Browns: "One U.S. Senator for the next thirty years is worth more than two Big Inches." Johnson asked Corcoran if he would help him with the campaign, and Corcoran readily agreed.

In his effort to win the Senate seat, Johnson faced a formidable opponent in Coke Stevenson, a former lieutenant governor who had served as governor from 1941 until he retired in 1946. Like Johnson, Stevenson had a compelling personal story. He had been born in log cabin in central west Texas and was so poor that friends said he didn't have enough clothes "to dust a fiddle." He had labored as a cowhand as a youth, and then worked his way through law school as a janitor at a bank. After practicing law, he was appointed a country judge, then elected to the state House of Representatives, where he was chosen Speaker in 1933.

Johnson's challenge to Stevenson was made all the more difficult because Johnson did not have the support of organized labor. The leadership of the American Federation of Labor had been incensed by Congressman Johnson's support of the Taft-Hartley Act, which had passed the Congress over President Truman's veto and provided, among other things, that a union had to give sixty days' notice before beginning a strike and could not refuse to bargain collectively. At its June convention, the AFL broke a fifty-year tradition of neutrality and endorsed Stevenson. Organized labor was not particularly strong in Texas during this period, but Johnson needed support wherever he could find it. Tommy Corcoran began working behind the scenes to shore up labor.

First, Corcoran contacted a leading official of the railroad brotherhoods and carried the message that if elected, Johnson would consider "amendments or corrections" to Taft-Hartley. Corcoran made the case that, notwithstanding Taft-Hartley, Johnson was still more pro-labor than Stevenson. Within weeks, four transportation brotherhoods had endorsed Johnson. Next, Corcoran invited Joe Keenan, an AFL executive, to dinner. Corcoran explained to Keenan that Johnson's support for Taft-Hartley was based on purely political factors, since organized labor was unpopular in Johnson's district. Nevertheless, Corcoran explained, down deep Johnson was a genuine liberal and a true friend of labor. After Sam Rayburn made a similar pitch to Keenan, the AFL official promised to "do his best to soften up the effect of the [AFL] endorsement." On August 11 Corcoran told Secretary of the Interior Harold Ickes with evident relief that he had had "a terrible time straightening out labor" in the Johnson campaign, "but it is finally straightened out."

On September 2, after a heavy voter turnout, unofficial results had Stevenson winning by only 362 votes, causing Lady Bird to tell a friend that it appeared "Lyndon has lost." But Johnson was superbly organized, and by the time the results became official, he had reduced Stevenson's total by 205 votes and increased his own by 174. Johnson was declared the winner by seventeen votes.

Stevenson immediately filed suit in U.S. District Court in Washington, DC, charging fraud in the election. On September 24 Judge T. Whitfield Davidson, a conservative anti–New Dealer and friend of Stevenson's, invalidated the results of the election and set a trial date. It now looked as though Johnson would not have his name placed on the ballot for the general election unless he prevailed in court.

The day after the judge's ruling, Joe Rauh was in his office when he received a call from Corcoran: "Joe, we've got to save Lyndon Johnson's seat." Rauh walked over to the law offices of the powerful DC firm of Arnold, Fortas and Porter, where he discovered some of Washington's finest lawyers squeezed into a small conference room. Corcoran later remembered that he and Abe Fortas had assembled "the greatest collegium of legal talent that Washington could supply" to plot a legal strategy for Johnson. Fortas, Corcoran, and Rauh were joined by former attorney general Francis Biddle, Jim Rowe, and Ben Cohen. The decision was made to take the case directly to the Supreme Court, and a motion was drafted on the spot to be put before Justice Hugo Black.

On September 28 Justice Black issued an order suspending the South Texas hearing. The next day, after receiving the order, Judge Davidson ordered Johnson's name put back on the ballot. Although it has never been proved, Joe Rauh later claimed that he "always thought that Tom Corcoran had spoken with Black before the hearing."

On Election Day, November 2, 1948, Lyndon Johnson easily defeated Jack Porter, his Republican opponent, and was elected to the U.S. Senate from Texas. However, the battle with Coke Stevenson was still not over. On October 20 Stevenson had formally requested that the subcommittee on elections and privileges of the Senate Rules and Administration Committee investigate the circumstances surrounding Johnson's victory in the primary. When the Democrats were swept into office, control of the Senate changed hands. Republicans could have continued their investigation until the new Congress was seated in January, but the chairman of the committee, William Jenner of Indiana, announced that he would leave any further congressional action for the next Congress. Jenner's decision was strongly influenced by Senator Styles Bridges of New Hampshire, a conservative Republican, who also served on the committee. Bridges was also a close friend of Corcoran's and one of the China lobby's most important defenders — as well as one of its greatest recipients of financial largesse. "For the record," Corcoran told Johnson, "Styles Bridges got this formal action taken for us. Remember that someday."

After Truman's reelection, Corcoran continued to expand his hugely profitable lobbying business. While he may have been disliked by the president, he still had many friends in Congress as well as sprinked throughout the administration.

Corcoran was also thriving at home, where Peggy was expecting their fourth child. He and Peggy had bought a large five-bedroom house on Woodland Drive, near many of the city's embassies in the affluent northwest section of Washington. The house had a large dining room, and Tommy had installed a fine piano. While he didn't live ostentatiously, he did live well. The children attended private schools, and the family often took expensive vacations.

Forty-eight years old, Corcoran finally had the financial security and independence that so many of his mentors — men like Oliver Wendell Holmes, Joseph Cotton, and Franklin Roosevelt — had enjoyed.

Many of Tommy's friends and former colleagues, however, were not so fortunate. Some were swept up in the nightmare of the McCarthy era, while others made poor personal choices. Ever the loyal friend, Corcoran helped those who came to him with their problems. In some instances, those whom he helped had become pariahs of Washington.

Ed Prichard had been had been a high-ranking official at the Treasury Department and a disciple of Corcoran's during the New Deal. When word reached the White House in 1945 that Prichard was critical of Harry Truman, he was wiretapped, accused of leaking sensitive information, and ultimately eased out of his position. And while nothing was ever proved, Prichard left the federal government in 1946 and returned to his home state of Kentucky.

A former Supreme Court clerk and a capable lawyer, Prichard opened a law practice and, according to his biographer, "was hired to represent several large corporate clients under the auspices of Tommy Corcoran." When Prichard mentioned to Corcoran that he hoped to represent a particular railroad company, Corcoran told him, "I'll get it for you." But in 1949 Prichard, who had remained politically active in Kentucky, was accused by the state's attorney general of voter fraud, allegedly participating in ballot-box stuffing in both the 1943 and 1946 elections. In July the case went to trial; Prichard was convicted and sentenced to prison.

Corcoran wrote to his old friend, offering moral support and, if it was needed, financial assistance. Prichard replied that Corcoran was "the first person in offering help who has mentioned money, and it is a critical factor. . . ." To defray court expenses for the appeal, Corcoran asked other Washington lawyers to pitch in. Ed Burling, esteemed partner at Covington and Burling, was not quite so magnanimous: "I can't see any reason why in the world I should be asked to aid in Prich's appeal."

Prichard's appeal failed. He went to prison and served sixteen months. Upon his release in 1951, he was disbarred and flat broke. Corcoran again came to his rescue, giving him several appellate briefs to research and write and paying him twenty-five hundred dollars for his work from August to December. Prichard wrote Corcoran, "You have been more than generous in my time of trouble and I shall never forget your kindness." Three years later Prichard was reinstated by the Kentucky Bar Association, and while his life had been largely destroyed, he managed to make a living as a lawyer, thanks in large part to Corcoran.

Duncan Lee, a descendant of Conferedate general Robert E. Lee, had been born in China, where his parents were missonaries. After graduating from Yale Law School, he went to work at the New York law firm of Donovan and Leisure, where he became a protégé of Corcoran's Wall Street friend "Wild Bill" Donovan. When Donovan was tapped by Roosevelt to become the first director of the Office of Strategic Services, Lee followed him as his top aide.

During this period Corcoran met Lee and was struck immediately by the young attorney's intellect and courtliness. What Corcoran did not know was that both Lee and his wife had joined the Communist Party in 1939 while Lee was a student at Yale Law School. Jacob Golos, a Russian spy living in the United States and responsible for recruiting new agents, described Lee's activities in a memorandum contained in the famous World War II espionage files, Venona: "[Lee] can bring no documents out of his department, but will remember them as much as possible, then make notes and pass them to 'Dir' "—the code name for another radical activist.

In late 1944 Lee's life began to unravel. He had fallen in love with one of his intelligence liaisons, and his marriage began to deteriorate. Moreover, he had been assigned to a new courier, Elizabeth Bentley, whom he distrusted. The Soviet intelligence station chief wrote of Lee in 1945: "Lee asked us to leave him in peace . . . and explained that his decision to stop working for us with the fact that he cannot have a 'double life,' that his conscience is 'not clean' because he 'deceived the U.S.,' that there is a constant struggle in his soul. . . ."

In August 1948 Bentley testified before the House Un-American Affairs Committee and denounced Duncan Lee, among others, as a communist spy. Three years before, she had provided much of the same information to the FBI, but since the allegations were unsupported by other corroborative evidence, the Justice Department never indicted Lee. In public testimony, which followed that of Bentley, Lee admitted that he knew her, but he denied ever passing information to her. Bentley's public testimony, however, sullied Lee's reputation, and he was unable to get a job.

Tommy Corcoran hired Lee. Corcoran also tried to help him win back his reputation and approached Dean Acheson to ask if he would vouch for Lee. But Acheson, now secretary of state, was himself under assault by Senator Joseph McCarthy. He barely knew Lee and did not want to become involved. Some time later, Acheson asked Jim Rowe about Lee, who told him half jokingly, "You Anglicans have a different kind of loyalty."

Eventually Lee decided to leave the United States and live in Bermuda. Corcoran arranged through a former law partner for Lee to be employed by the American Insurance Group. Lee wrote Corcoran in 1951, "I hope you know how much I appreciate all that you have done to make this situation possible and so much more besides."

Jim Landis and Tommy Corcoran had been acquaintances at Harvard Law School. When they were thrown together by Felix Frankfurter during the 1934 securities legislation, they got to know one another better. Although never close friends, they greatly admired each other, and Corcoran proved to be a loyal friend. Landis was a brilliant lawyer, but he never could manage his personal relationships or finances with the skill and care that he applied to a legal brief.

President Harry Truman had chosen Landis to be chairman of the Civil Aeronautics Board, but after only two years, he failed to reappoint him. Although Truman did not make his reasons known, the airlines resented Landis and opposed his renomination because he was a tough regulator. Pan Am, Tommy Corcoran's client, actually spearheaded the drive to get him fired, because as chairman he had been entirely hostile to the airline's effort to monopolize overseas flights.

According to his biographer Donald Ritchie, Landis's personal life may have caused Truman to turn against him: "The traumas of divorce and separation from his family and friends ate away at him. During the days he worked feverishly at the CAB. After these long hours of toil he drank heavily to relax and required pills to put himself to sleep every night. His excessive off hours drinking became common gossip in Washington, which his opponents turned to their own use."

The day after Christmas, President Truman told Landis that he was not reappointing him. According to Ritchie, Landis "left the White House and wandered about the city and its taverns the rest of the day." Landis's close friend Stanley Gerwitz called Corcoran, who came to Landis's apartment and waited for him. Even though Corcoran had not benefited professionally from his friendship with Landis, he remained loyal to his old law school classmate. When Landis finally showed up late in the evening, Corcoran called Joe Kennedy in Florida and told him, "You've got to take Jim on." Kennedy gave Landis, who had served on the Securities and Exchange Commission with him, a job at Kennedy Enterprises.

By 1950 a committee headed by Representative Frank M. Buchanan, a Pennsylvania Democrat, was investigating a wide range of lobbying activities. Buchanan revealed that even under the weak new disclosure law, the number of registered lobbyists had more than doubled in just two years, to 2,074. "I firmly believe," he concluded, "that the business of influencing legislation is a billion dollar business."

He also noted that lobbying had undergone a transformation that made it hard to track. "In the 1870's and 1880's, lobbying meant direct, individual solicitation of legislators, with a strong presumption of corruption attached," he stated. "But modern pressure on legislative bodies is rarely corrupt. . . . It is increasingly indirect, and [it is] largely the product of group rather than individual effort . . . the printed word is much more extensively used by organizations as a means of pursuing legislative aims than personal contact with legislators by individual lobbyists." Although that was certainly the trend, there were still a handful of lobbyists, Tommy Corcoran foremost among them, who could make things happen in Washington. According to journalist and lobbying expert James Deakin, in the the late 1940s and 1950s it was "often hard to tell where the legislator [left] off and the lobbyist [began]."

Notwithstanding his personal good fortune, Corcoran was not self-absorbed. He recognized that the country faced great challenges, particularly in the area of foreign policy, and he still wanted to serve. Lobbying was just a game to him — a way to keep score. But Corcoran had always been guided by a deep sense of moralism, reflected not only in his loyalty to friends but also in his commitment to public service. What had changed was the nature of the threat facing America. That threat, embodied first in fascism and later in communism, caused Corcoran to align himself with some of the most conservative leaders in the country.

19

Foreign Policy by Other Means

While the end of World War II brought the United States superpower status, it also signaled the beginning of the Cold War and a U.S. foreign policy predicated on "spheres of influence." The Berlin crisis, the fall of China, and Soviet development of nuclear weapons led to increasing apprehension among U.S. policy makers concerned about Soviet expansion around the world. Although now a lawyer in private practice, Tommy Corcoran had clients who became integral to American foreign policy goals in both China and the Western Hemisphere.

One month after the surrender of Japan, in September 1945, Tommy and David Corcoran, joined by a recent addition to Tommy's law firm, William Youngman, created a Panamanian company, Rio Cathay, for the purpose of pursuing business ventures in Asia and South America. Around the same time Whiting Willauer, who had remained in China with Claire Chennault after the Second World War, returned to the United States to seek financing for a business venture.

Chennault and Willauer believed there were enormous economic opportunities in China even though the country continued to be immersed in a civil war. At the time, commercial travel in China was dominated by two small airlines, CNAC and CATC, each of which was backed by powerful political factions within the Nationalist government. Chennault and Willauer seized on the idea of creating a commercial airline to compete with CNAC and CATC. The two China hands believed they could put together a modern airline with bigger and faster planes that would ultimately eclipse their smaller and more inefficient rivals. Sensing that commerical opportunities in China were timely for those who knew the right people, Tommy and David Corcoran entered into partnership with Chennault and Willauer, using Rio Cathay as the legal vehicle for investing in the airline venture.

Notwithstanding Corcoran's contacts in the business community, financing the venture remained elusive. As Corcoran wrote to Willauer, "The romance of China has about worn out in the securities markets," and after several false starts he began to despair, telling Willauer that the project had become "a nightmare for a Cotton [and Franklin] trained banker like me." Willauer, however, persevered and secured a million dollars in operating capital from a combination of American and Chinese investors, including the Chinese government.

Although Corcoran welcomed the financing, it meant that the return on his investment diminished even before the airline was launched. He had anticipated that he would hold nearly 37 percent of the equity in the airline, but Willauer's plan gave a greater percentage to the Chinese government, and Corcoran's share dropped to 28 percent. Corcoran complained to Willauer, and though Willauer was growing weary of the lawyer's carping, he nevertheless pleaded with him to remain committed to the airline, telling him, "If today we had to bear the burden of being underfinanced, we would not have the chance of either temporary or permanent survivial in China." Against his better judgment, and based largely on his fondness for Chennault, Corcoran promised to help.

The next hurdle was to break into the market — to actually find customers — and it was here that Willauer's faith in Corcoran paid off. Corcoran looked to his old friend Fiorella La Guardia, the former mayor of New York, who was the director general of the United Nations Relief and Rehabilitation Administration. UNRRA, as it was known, was delivering substantial relief via ship to the shores of war-torn China, but the supplies were piling up on the docks because there was no means to ferry them to the interior of the country. La Guardia asked the Corcoran group to present him with a proposal. In China, Chennault and Willauer enlisted the support of Madame Chiang, and in Washington, Corcoran received the support of Ambassador T. V. Soong. Nonetheless, it was not enough to convince UNRRA officials, who opposed awarding a contract to an upstart airline owned largely by foreigners. Corcoran, however, went back to La Guardia and pleaded with him. Shortly before he resigned in 1946, La Guardia reversed the decision of his staff and awarded a nearly four-million-dollar contract to the new airline.

Civil Air Transport was officially launched on January 29, 1946, and for several months the UNRRA contract provided a steady cash flow with its planes flying more than four thousand hours a month. But as the civil war intensified, the airline struggled to maintain its routes. By the beginning of 1947 the situation had become so serious that aircraft hours had dropped in half, to two thousand a month. Corcoran used his contacts at his old government employer, the RFC, to arrange for an agreement for the corporation to purchase tin from the Yunnan Tin Producers' Association, but more contracts of this sort were desperately needed. By the end of the year Corcoran began to explore ways in which the U.S. military might contract with the airline. Toward this end he arranged a meeting between Chennault and Rear Admiral Roscoe H. Hillenkoetter, the director of the Central Intelligence Agency.

The CIA, successor to the wartime Office of Strategic Services, was created by executive order on July 6, 1947. The purpose of the new agency was to provide the centralized coordination and analysis of intelligence so that, as Truman explained many years later, the president would not have "to look through a bunch of papers two feet high."

The Hillenkoetter meeting with Corcoran took on added significance in February 1948 when events thousands of miles away from China had an enormous impact on how the U.S. government was viewing the emerging Cold War. After communists staged a coup and took over the government of Czechoslovakia, members of the Truman administration became convinced that it was imperative to meet a perceived and growing threat of Soviet expansion — not just in Eastern Europe, but in Asia as well.

After his meeting with Corcoran, Hillenkoetter introduced the lawyer to Frank Wisner, the director of the Office of Policy Coordination, who, notwithstanding his bland title, was in charge of covert activities for the agency. In their meeting it was clear that Wisner was very interested in China, and Corcoran convinced him that he could help.

In early October 1948 CAT began to fly missions on behalf of the CIA, and on November 1 a formal agreement was signed by a representative of the agency and by Corcoran. The agreement committed the agency to provide up to five hundred thousand dollars to finance a CAT base, to advance two hundred thousand dollars for the airline to fly agency personnel and equipment in and out of of the mainland, and to underwrite any shortfall that might result from a hazardous mission.

Within days of signing the agreement, CAT was airlifting personnel and equipment from the city of Chungking, the last mainland capital of the Republic of China. The airlift was followed by similar ones in 1949 in several other cities, including Kweilin, Luchnow, Nanking, and Amoy. Willauer reported to Corcoran that "each evacuation has cost us heavily, but we have never lost enough equipment or personnel to cripple our operations."

That same year, Corcoran signed up a client who would prove to be one of his most lucrative — and controversial — for the next three decades. Corcoran first met Sam "the Banana Man" Zemurray in the early 1930s when President Roosevelt encouraged his aide to solicit a contribution from the businessman for the 1936 reelection campaign. Zemurray and Corcoran liked each other from the beginning, perhaps based on the fact that they had both achieved success in arenas dominated by a WASP ruling class. Corcoran stayed in touch with Zemurray over the years, introducing him to powerful Washington figures such as Nelson Rockefeller, who had a plan to bring workers from Central America to the labor-starved southern United States. In 1949 Zemurray asked Corcoran to join the United Fruit Company, and the former New Dealer served in the role not only of lobbyist but of inside counsel as well.

The United Fruit Company had been founded in the nineteenth century by three young entrepreneurs: a young Massachusetts ship captain, a banana importer, and a Brooklyn-born businessman. The company prospered through the first three decades of the twentieth century, and by 1930 its board of directors included some of Boston's oldest and most prestigous Brahmin families. That same year United Fruit acquired the Cuyamel Company, owned by Zemurray, a Russian Jewish immigrant who had entered the banana business at age eighteen in Mobile, Alabama. Zemurray owned more than five thousand acres of banana plantations in Guatemala, where he had negotiated important tax and other government concessions. When United Fruit paid him over thirty million in stock for his company, he became the company's largest shareholder. Allegedly, upon greeting the board for the first time, Zemurray told them, "You gentlemen have been f——ing up this business long enough; I'm going to straighten it out."

Guatemala, once the center of Mayan civilization, was a small, poor country with an agrarian economy that early in the twentieth century had been based almost entirely on coffee growing. When the coffee market collapsed during the worldwide depression of the 1930s, the economic elite within the country turned to a strong leader, Jorge Ubico, who opened Guatemala to American corporations including W. R. Grace, Pan American Airways, and the United Fruit Company.

Zemurray aligned United Fruit closely with the government of President Ubico. Ubico gave the company hundreds of square miles of land, and in exchange it employed more than forty thousand Guatemalans and made huge infrastruture investments, ultimately controlling the railroads, electric utilities, telegraph, and the country's only port. United Fruit was so ubiquitous within Guatemala that the company earned the nickname *El Pulpo*, the Octopus.

In Central America the fear that communism might spread was particularly acute in Guatemala, where leftist and progressive elements threatened American corporate interests.

In the summer of 1944 Guatemalan university students and teachers took to the streets and were eventually joined by a coterie of young army officers in deposing the ruling junta. Democratic elections followed; university professor Juan Jose Arevalo was elected and served as president for the next five years. Arevalo implemented sweeping reform by passing a labor code giving workers the right to organize, including those who worked on the large United Fruit banana plantations.

With Corcoran helping guide its Washington strategy, the United Fruit Company developed a close relationship with key people in the government agencies and departments that could affect U.S. policy in Central America. Thomas McCann, an employee of the company, later wrote a book about his experiences, describing how "companies like United Fruit . . . became political instruments and carried out government policies by other means, usually in secret, whereby the government got what it wanted through the use of the company and the company got what it wanted as well." The United States used the company as an American beachhead against communism in Central America, while the company used the U.S. government as a means to protect its vast real estate holdings and cheap labor sources. Corcoran viewed his work for United Fruit as no different in many respects from his work for the Flying Tigers: In both instances, he believed he was promoting the interests of U.S. capitalism and American-style democracy.

20

Corcoran's Cold War

As Mao consolidated his power over mainland China in 1949, the U.S. State Department released a "White Paper" officially declaring that the Nationalist side had "lost the confidence of its own troops and its own people." The paper concluded that the victory of the communists had been beyond the "the control of the U.S. government."

In January 1950 Civil Air Transport relocated its base of operations to the island of Formosa, where Chiang Kai-shek had established his new government. During its three years on the mainland, CAT had ferried more than three hundred thousand personnel and flew over fifty-nine million miles. But with the evacuation of the Nationalists complete and the mainland routes gone, CAT desperately needed new sources of revenue. As the company confronted possible bankruptcy, Willauer flew to Washington, where he and Corcoran scoured the U.S. government for support. Once again, the CIA came to the rescue.

On February 27, just two weeks after the Soviet Union and China signed a mutual defense pact, President Truman signed National Security Directive 64, which stated that "it is important to United States security interests that all practical measures be taken to prevent further communist expansion in Southeast Asia." Frank Wisner at the CIA decided that one of those practical measures should be the acquisition of an airline to give the agency the mobility it needed in the region. Wisner negotiated with Corcoran for the purchase of CAT. In March, using a "cutout" banker or middleman, the CIA paid CAT $350,000 to clear up arrearages, $400,000 for future operations, and a $1 million option on the business. The money was then divided among the airline's owners, with Corcoran and Youngman receiving more than $100,000 for six years of legal fees, and Corcoran, Youngman, and David Corcoran dividing approximately $225,000 from the sale of the airline. Even though Chennault collected only a hundred thousand, he seemed content, writing to Corcoran, "I am quite satisfied with the airline solution. . . . We could not have operated a modern airline without aircraft and we didn't have the capital to buy modern transports."

Corcoran, however, was not entirely out of the airline business in China. A few months before he and his partners sold CAT, they had spun off a subsidiary of the airline.

In the final weeks before the collapse of Chiang Kai-shek's goverment, the British, attempting to negotiate a separate peace with the Chinese communists and thereby diminish American influence in the region, arranged for all the planes of China's two small commercial airlines, CATC and CNAC, to be flown to Kai Tak airfield in Hong Kong. Once under control of the Crown, the British were prepared to recognize communist China and turn the planes over to Mao's air force. The Chinese, according to Corcoran, "desperately wanted these aircraft to help mount an attack on Taiwan." Willauer later observed that "if the communists got those transport planes and put them together with the Red paratroopers, considering the chaos which existed on Formosa at the time, it would have been a pushover for the Reds to have taken Formosa."

In anticipation of the British announcement, Corcoran formed a Delaware partnership called Chennault and Willauer. Corcoran then arranged for the planes, estimated to have a value of approximately twenty million dollars, to be sold to a new corporation owned by the Civil Air Transport partnership. The new entity, a subsidiary of Civil Air Transport, was called Civil Air Transport Incorporated. On December 12, 1949, CATI purchased forty-three planes from Chinese Air Transport for $1.5 million and fifty-one planes from the Chinese National Air Corporation for $2 million. The money was advanced by the Central Bank of China and the bank of Taiwan, but Willauer and Chennault signed personal promissory notes that were later made the obligation of the corporation.

The communists, however, disputed the legality of the sale and claimed that the planes belonged to them. Back in Washington Corcoran scrambled to have the planes registered by the U.S. Civil Aeronautics Authority, an essential step to establish legal ownership in both American and British courts. Next he hired an old friend from his Wall Street days, the former head of the Office of Strategic Services, William Donovan. Donovan immediately called on the Foreign Office in London to inform the British that CATI had purchased the two airlines and that they were owned by an American corporation.

Even though the British government was prepared to recognize the communists as the legitimate government of China, the high court in

Hong Kong initially ruled that the planes could not be transferred to the communists because they were now owned by an American corporation.

Notwithstanding this layering of corporate entities, Corcoran faced serious obstacles in his efforts to salvage the planes. The Chinese counterclaimed, arguing that since the purchases had been carried out under American law, they were not valid in Hong Kong. Adding to Civil Air's problems, the planes, impounded by the British, were guarded in Hong Kong by Chinese employees pending the outcome of a court battle over their ownership. In March most of the airfield's employees defected to the communists and piloted away several planes. A month later several small bombs were denotated at the airfield, and seventeen of the remaining aircraft were damaged.

The dispute over the planes in Hong Kong was fast becoming an international political bête noire. The United States delivered a formal diplomatic protest to the British over Hong Kong's decision to award the planes to the communists. In Washington, Secretary of State Dean Acheson, at Corcoran's urging, denounced the decision. After the planes were sabotaged, the Americans blamed the communists, who in turn blamed the Hong Kong government. When a thousand tons of spare parts were stolen by the communists, the Taiwanese boarded British vessels to search for the parts. The Chinese government informed the British that a settlement in its favor was a prerequisite to the establishment of diplomatic relations.

Then on June 25, 1950, North Korean forces crossed the thirty-eighth parallel in a massive invasion of South Korea. Whereas the administration had previously viewed the conflict between the People's Republic of China and Taiwan as a civil war, it now considered Taiwan an important check on communist expansion in the region.

For the net two decades American foreign policy tended to view communism as monolithic — even though Russia had plundered Manchuria at the end of World War II and Stalin had extended recognition to Taiwan. Chiang's government was the first foreign government to openly lobby for U.S. aid, and it received billions of dollars in government assistance. To assure continued assistance, the Taiwanese government employed better than two hundred agents and lobbyists, including Tommy Corcoran, to propagandize its cause.

◆ ◆ ◆

In 1950, as Corcoran worked to protect his and his partners' interests in Hong Kong, anticommunism hysteria reached a fever pitch in the United States. On Febuary 9, in a speech in Wheeling, West Virginia, Senator Joseph R. McCarthy made the startling claim that he had a list of 209 communists in the State Department. In subsequent speeches he revised the numbers, and notwithstanding that he did not produce a shred of evidence, he convinced a large segment of the American public that communists had infiltrated the government and threatened the future of democracy. For the next four years McCarthy demagogued the issue of communist influence within the U.S. government, denouncing the Roosevelt and Truman administrations for "twenty years of treason."

Corcoran had a complicated relationship with Senator McCarthy. On the one hand, Corcoran had been extremely close to the man McCarthy defeated, Robert La Follette; on the other, he admired the junior senator from Wisconsin. The fact that McCarthy was a successful Catholic political leader may have initially attracted Corcoran to him. If so, Corcoran was no different from the nearly 60 percent of the U.S. Catholics who expressed a favorable opinion of the senator. More importantly, however, according to Corcoran, McCarthy "saw international communism as the awesome threat that it really was, and is. Further, he drew attention to the error of our ways in letting Chiang's government fall."

Corcoran was also concerned about the spread of communism in another part of the globe — Central America, where the United Fruit Company had vast holdings.

Guatemala, the headquarters of United Fruit's Latin American operations, was scheduled to hold its first democratic election for president since the coup six years earlier. Captain Jacobo Arbenz Guzman, one of the heroes of the 1944 revolution, had emerged as the leading candidate. U.S. State Department officials monitoring the election were skeptical of Arbenz, but nevertheless adopted a cautious, wait-and-see approach. However, representatives of the United Fruit Company in Guatemala were certain that Arbenz was a communist and that his election would spell disaster for their company.

In the spring of 1950, six months before the election in Guatemala, Tommy Corcoran went to see Thomas C. Mann, the director of the State

Department's Office of Inter-American Affairs. Sitting in Mann's boxlike office, Corcoran came right to the point. "Tom, I'm concerned about this election in Guatemala. Does our government have any program for bringing about the election of a middle-of-the-road candidate in Guatemala?"

Mann, who barely knew Corcoran but was well aware of his reputation as a Washington fixer, seemed surprised by the lawyer's sudden interest in the political affairs of a small nation in Central America. "No, we don't," Mann later recalled telling Corcoran. "That is for the people of that country to decide."

"Well," Corcoran mused, "I've been kicking around the idea that American companies doing business down there might agree between themselves on some method to bring moderate elements into power in Guatemala."

Mann, a career foreign service officer, was outraged. "Look, Tom, any attempt by American companies to influence the electoral campaign would greatly weaken their position in Guatemala and only add to the present difficulties." Mann, fearing that Corcoran and his friends at United Fruit might be cooking up something, then added, "And it's idle to suppose that a plan of this sort can be kept secret." Corcoran knew that his trial balloon had not gotten off the ground. He and Mann talked for a few more minutes, shook hands, and Corcoran left.

As a result of his work for the Flying Tigers and association with Bill Donovan, Corcoran knew many high-ranking officials in the three-year-old CIA, including Deputy Director Allen Dulles. A few days after visiting Mann, Corcoran paid a call on Dulles. Although Corcoran knew and disliked the deputy director's older brother, the prominent Republican Wall Street lawyer John Foster Dulles, he found Allen more agreeable. Both brothers had worked for the prestigious New York City law firm of Sullivan and Cromwell, which had represented United Fruit during the 1930s.

During their meeting Dulles explained to Corcoran that while the CIA was sympathetic to United Fruit, he could not authorize any assistance without the support of the State Department. Dulles assured Corcoran, however, that whoever was elected as the next president of Guatemala would not be allowed to nationalize the operations of United Fruit.

Corcoran did not give up trying to shape U.S. policy toward Guatemala. He had remained close to Robert La Follette, the fiery progressive from Wisconsin. After losing his Senate seat, La Follette desperately needed a job. Corcoran persuaded United Fruit to retain him, nominally to handle labor relations. Corcoran sent La Follette to lobby liberal members of Congress with whom he had served. He hoped that La Follette's former colleagues would conclude that if a populist found Arbenz too liberal, then the Guatemalan president must be nothing short of a radical.

In the November elections, United Fruit's worst fears were realized. Over the three-day voting period Arbenz, who had run a campaign with a decidedly anti-American tone, received more than 60 percent of the popular vote. Following the election, officials at the State Department worried increasingly about the leftist leanings of Arbenz's closest advisers. Thomas Mann attended the inauguration on March 15, 1951, and "came back pretty well convinced that they were Marxist-Leninists."

Less than a year later, on June 17, 1952, President Arbenz implemented a land reform program that radicalized Guatemalan politics. He promulgated Decree 900, an ambitious program for agrarian reform that expropriated idle land on government and private estates and redistributed it in lots of eight to thirty-three acres. Because the company had huge tracts of undeveloped land, the plan intensified the growing conflict between the Guatemalan government and United Fruit.

In neighboring Nicaragua, President Anastasio Somoza feared that the Guatemalan revolution might spread and that he too might be ousted. Somoza persuaded senior members of the Truman administration to consider covert action against Arbenz. President Truman generally supported the idea of U.S. intervention in Guatemala. He gave the green light to the director of the CIA, Walter Bedell Smith, to initiate a secret plan, code-named Operation Fortune, to overthrow Arbenz. Working with Smith and others in the agency, Corcoran arranged for small arms and ammunition to be loaded on a United Fruit freighter and shipped to Guatemala, where the weapons would be distributed to dissidents. The plan was thwarted, however, when Secretary of State Dean Acheson personally and vigorously protested to the president, who agreed to postpone any covert action.

In February 1953 the Arbenz government confiscated a quarter million acres of United Fruit's land and reimbursed the company a little over one million dollars — a figure in line with the company's own valuation of the property, at least for tax purposes. Officials at United Fruit were never-theless apoplectic and claimed that the actual value of the land was more than ten million dollars.

With the election of Eisenhower in November 1952, the political cli-mate changed, and Corcoran sensed that the new occupant of the White House would be more favorable to his client. John Peurifoy, installed as ambassador to Guatemala in 1953, expressed a view that was gaining cur-rency throughout the government when he said, "Communism is directed by the Kremlin all over the world, and anyone who thinks differently doesn't know what he is talking about." The Arbenz government was no longer just a threat to U.S. corporate interests, but was emerging as a threat to U.S. strategic interests as well.

Corcoran sent former senator La Follette to see the new foreign policy team in the State Department. La Follette first met with Mann, now the acting secretary of state for inter-American affairs, and urged him to per-suade the new administration to join other Latin nations in "a concerted effort" against "communist influence" in Guatemala. But State Depart-ment officials continued to believe that the United States should not intervene directly in Guatemala, and Mann, who now appeared more open to such intervention, was reassigned to Greece.

In 1953 the newly elected president, Dwight Eisenhower, appointed John Foster Dulles secretary of state and brought Walter Bedell Smith over from the Central Intelligence Agency as the new undersecretary. Smith, as CIA director, had been involved in planning Operation Fortune. Corcoran now pressed him to consider how the United States might once again strike in Guatemala to undermine the Arbenz presidency. Smith, however, didn't like Dulles, and he complained to Corcoran that he had less power at the State Department than he'd had at the CIA. He told Corcoran he wanted to help the United Fruit Company and won-dered aloud whether or not he, Smith, might go to work for the company itself. Corcoran agreed to help, and Smith worked to convince his new colleagues in the State Department that Arbenz had to be overthrown.

With Smith as his ally, Corcoran played a critical role in prodding the administration into devising a new plan to topple the Arbenz govern-ment and restore the holdings of United Fruit. Corcoran now acted as the liaison among the State Department, the CIA, and United Fruit. He helped select the principal planners for an invasion of Guatemala, dubbed Operation Success. Smith directed John C. King, a West Point graduate who had spent a considerable amount of time in Latin America identifying Nazis before the war and was now the director of operations at the agency, to assess whether Guatemalan dissidents with help from neighboring Central American dictators could overthrow the Arbenz regime. According to Stephen Schlesinger and Stephen Kinzer, authors of *Bitter Fruit*, an account of the American coup in Guatemala, Corcoran may also have had a role in appointing Whiting Willauer — his friend and partner in Civil Air Transport — U.S. ambassador to Honduras in 1954.

As planning for the U.S. plot progressed, Corcoran and other top officials at United Fruit became anxious about indentifying a future leader who would establish favorable relations between the government and the company. Secretary of State Dulles moved to add a"civilian" adviser to the State Department team to help expedite Operation Success. Dulles chose a friend of Corcoran's, William Pawley, a Miami-based millionaire who, along with Corcoran, Chennault, and Willauer, had helped set up the Flying Tigers in the early 1940s and then helped several years later to transform it into the CIA's airline, Civil Air Transport. Besides his association with Corcoran, Pawley's most important qualification for the job was that he had a long history of association with right-wing Latin American dictators.

CIA director Dulles had grown disillusioned with J. C. King and asked Colonel Albert Haney, the CIA station chief in Korea, to be the U.S. field commander for the operation. Haney enthusiastically accepted, although he was apparently unaware of the role that the United Fruit Company had played in his selection. Haney had been a colleague of King's, and though King was no longer directing the operation, he remained a member of the agency planning team. He suggested that Haney meet with Tom Corcoran to see about arming the insurgency force with the weapons that had been mothballed in a New York warehouse after the failed Operation Fortune. When the supremely confident Haney said he didn't need any help from a Washington lawyer, King rebuked him, "If you think you can run this operation without United Fruit, you're crazy!"

The close working relationship between the CIA and United Fruit was perhaps best epitomized by Allen Dulles's encouragement to the company to help select an expedition commander for the planned invasion. After the CIA's first choice was vetoed by the State Department, United Fruit proposed Corcova Cerna, a Guatemalan lawyer and coffee grower. Cerna had long worked for the company as a paid legal adviser, and even though Corcoran referred to him as "a liberal," he believed that Cerna would not interfere with the company's land holdings and operations. After Cerna was hospitalized with throat cancer, a third candidate, Colonel Carlos Castillo Armas, emerged as the compromise choice.

According to United Fruit's Thomas McCann, when the Central Intelligence Agency finally launched Operation Success in late June 1954, "United Fruit was involved at every level." From neighboring Honduras, Ambassador Willauer, Corcoran's former business partner, directed bombing raids on Guatemala City. McCann was told that the CIA even shipped down the weapons used in the uprising "in United Fruit boats."

On June 27, 1954, Colonel Armas ousted the Arbenz government and ordered the arrest of all communist leaders in Guatemala. While the coup was successful, a dark chapter was opened in American support for right-wing military dictators in Central America.

During the period in which he helped plan the secret overthrow of the government in Guatemala, Corcoran was also working to help the company on another front. Corcoran had known for some time that the Justice Department had been investigating United Fruit for possible violations of the nation's antitrust laws. The company controlled virtually all the bananas and sugar imported into the United States. Shortly after the invasion in 1954, the Justice Department initiated an antitrust action against United Fruit.

Corcoran later told Ed Whitman, United Fruit's director of federal relations, that he (Corcoran) could have settled the suit two years earlier. He claimed that he "had so persistently expressed himself" to the assistant attorney general of the antitrust division that officials at the Justice Department would "scarcely speak" to him anymore. However, according to Corcoran, other advisers counseled the company to wait for a Republican administration, believing it would be more receptive to quashing any claim.

After revelations of American involvement in the coup, the Eisenhower administration was roundly criticized both by members of the press and by congressional Democrats. Neither the White House nor the CIA even issued a statement when, a mere five days after Arbenz's resignation (June

29, 1954), the Justice Department brought an antitrust suit against the United Fruit Company in federal court, charging that the company had a monopoly on banana exports from countries such as Guatemala. Indeed, Corcoran believed that Dulles had actively promoted the suit "just to prove that he wasn't involved with the company."

Corcoran now advised the company to adopt a hard-line stance. He recommended United Fruit "not make any compromises whatever with respect to the jurisdictional matters involving your operations in the tropics." He claimed that the company should demand the return of all expropriated property. Corcoran counseled that while the company might sell large tracts of land to the Guatemalan government at a nominal cost, the precedent of reaching compromise over expropriated property would hurt United Fruit throughout Central and South America. On Corcoran's advice, the company tried to mitigate the suit by donating nearly a hundred thousand acres of its holding in Guatemala to peasants. Even so, by the end of the decade *Fortune* magazine found that United Fruit "in Guatemala, Costa Rica and Honduras," was "still the largest single private landowner, largest single business, and largest corporate employer."

About this time, former CIA director Walter Bedell Smith reiterated to Corcoran his interest in joining United Fruit. Corcoran later recalled, "He told me that he had always liked to watch those pretty sailing ships on the Atlantic — the Great White Fleet" — a reference to United Fruit's cargo vessels. Given Smith's extensive contacts throughout the government, Corcoran liked the idea, and he recommended Smith to company officials. "I told them: 'You have to have people who can tell you what's going on. He has a great background with his CIA association.' Their answer was: 'He doesn't know anything about the banana business. He'd have to take a subsidiary position.' I told them: 'For Chrissakes, your problem is not bananas . . . you've got to handle your political problem.'" Smith ultimately received a seat on the board.

With various parts of the government seemingly at odds with one another over U.S. policy toward Guatemala, Corcoran understood the importance of maintaining congressional support for the role that United Fruit played in Central America. He advised the company to rally the members of the New England delegation, particularly its blue-blooded Massachusetts senators, Christian Herter and Leverett Saltonstall.

However, these men were moderate Republicans, and Corcoran told Whitman that the company needed to "pursue a line of coddling the Liberals." Corcoran did not fear either the right wing or the moderate wing of the Republican Party, but rather, as Whitman phrased it, "the powerful Liberals that we must learn to play ball with."

At one point in 1955 Corcoran suggested to Ed Whitman, the head of public relations for United Fruit, that Bishop Sheil of Chicago lead a trip to Guatemala with several senators, including Sparkman of Alabama and Cooper of Kentucky. Whitman expressed concern to Corcoran about the advisability of inviting Bishop Sheil — who only a year before had publicly criticized Senator McCarthy, then at the height of his power.

In April 1954 Bishop Sheil denounced McCarthy before a rally of twenty-five hundred UAW members. Ironically, that same week, Corcoran's other close friend in the Catholic hierarchy, Cardinal Spellman of New York, praised Senator McCarthy before a communion breakfast in New York City for six thousand policemen and firefighters. Spellman later told the press, "McCarthy is against communism and he has been doing something about it."

According to Whitman, Corcoran told him not to worry about McCarthy because he "says he can control and has controlled Senator McCarthy . . . and that he does this through Senator Dirksen." Everett Dirksen had for number of years been not only Corcoran's close friend but also the beneficiary of significant political contributions from the China lobby. And McCarthy, who'd held enormous power during the previous four years, had been discredited through the so-called Army-McCarthy hearings. Dirksen asked Corcoran to come to his home to help plot a strategy for McCarthy's political rehabilitation. According to Corcoran, however, "He couldn't be saved. He'd already lost himself in the bottle."

For many years Zemurray kept Corcoran's work for United Fruit a guarded secret, and Corcoran himself often took extraordinary measures to hide his association with the firm. On one occasion, several years after he had been hired by the company, Corcoran passed Ed Whitman on the street in Washington, DC. Corcoran nodded to Whitman, but did not speak to him. Only after returning to his office did Corcoran call Whitman and ask to come over and brief him on various issues. Whitman recalled that Corcoran explained "that it was not wise for him to be seen talking to me in public places or conferring too often, even in private." However, in June 1954 — the same month as the coup — the gossip columnist in the *New York Journal-American* reported that "one of the most hush, hush stories of the year has finally leaked. Tommy the Cork . . . has for some time been employed on a huge retainer by the United Fruit Company to look after their interests. . . ."

For those who had served with Corcoran in the New Deal, it was an inexplicable betrayal. But Corcoran saw the world differently now. Even though many of his friends, former colleagues, and contemporaries had been unfairly pilloried, and in some cases ruined, by Senator McCarthy's reckless and outrageous tactics, Corcoran faulted McCarthy more for dragging "the good name of anti-communism through the mud." It was indication of how far Corcoran had traveled along the ideological spectrum that he believed McCarthy had made "anti-communism a dirty word," and that "we have suffered far more from that than from any other legacy of his demagoguery."

21

Family and Friends

Tommy's first decade as a lobbyist in Washington had been extremely successful. Although he remained a controversial figure among many people, he had made the transition from public service to private practice; through a combination of powerful clients, friends in government, and his knowledge of Washington, he still retained an enormous amount of influence. During the 1950s he was listed on four occasions in the magazine *U.S. News and World Report* as one of the one hundred most influential people in America.

While he continued to fantasize about returning to government someday, the truth was that Corcoran felt he needed to make money because his family was expanding rapidly. After Margaret, his first son was born. The boy was named Thomas Gardner Corcoran Jr. but would be known as Tim — at least in part to differentiate him from David's oldest son, also named Thomas. Then came Howard, followed by Christopher, Cecily, and finally David. Peggy and Tommy had six children during a twelve-year time span.

Tim believes Tommy loved having a large brood because his father viewed the Corcoran family as a continuation of "the project his own father had started. Grandpa had been an immigrant and had brought up three very successful boys." His friends and, later, his children believed that he instinctively modeled his family after Joseph P. Kennedy, one of the most successful Irish Americans in the country at the time.

Tommy emulated Joe Kennedy by hiring sailing instructors for the children. He retained a French teacher to come to the house to tutor them, and at dinnertime he made them say grace in French. They had, as one family friend described it, "every kind of lesson you could imagine." While Corcoran sometimes worked six or seven days a week, he could also be an attentive father. He often gave the children phonograph records and encouraged them to read a book a day. The dinner hour was frequently a didactic affair with Corcoran sitting at the head of the large dining table, asking the children about the books they had read or about current events. Occasionally his inquiries could be laced with a touch of Holmesian condescension: He would call on his oldest son Tim to voice his opinion on an issue, telling him, "You always know what the common man is thinking."

Convinced and determined that his children would achieve greatness, Corcoran wanted his family recorded for posterity. He hired a photgrapher to come and film sixteen-millimeter home movies of the children at Christmas and on their birthdays.

"Dad" Corcoran came to visit often during the 1950s, sometimes for weeks at a time. Since the death of Tommy's mother more than a decade before, "Dad" had continued to practice law and stay active in Rhode Island civic affairs. He was a devoted grandfather who took a great interest in all of Tommy's children — particularly his grandsons, with whom he enjoyed engaging in long conversations about baseball. He played the piano, the banjo, and the guitar; like his son, he loved to sing.

From time to time, Dad still told Tommy what to do. When Tommy's brother Howard married for the second time in the spring of 1952, he chose a widow, Esther, who had been raised as an Episcopalian. Because she was not a Catholic, Tommy refused to speak to her, and for several months Howard and Esther had no contact with Tommy. As the Thanksgiving holiday approached, Tommy invited the entire Corcoran family to dinner except Howard and Esther. Dad Corcoran called up his son and told him he wasn't coming unless Howard and Esther were also at the table. They were invited forthwith. A few months later Howard and Esther were back for Christmas luncheon; when Esther walked under a sprig of mistletoe hanging in the archway of the house, Tommy leaned over and kissed her. Esther looked up at him and smiled. "Well I knew I'd make it eventually."

Between 1946 and 1952 Ben Cohen lived with Tommy and Peggy Corcoran at their house on 4640 Hawthorne Street. Known by the children as Uncle Ben, he was, according to Tim Corcoran, "just like a member of the family." Cohen worked at the State Department in the counsel's office. He and Tommy had diverged somewhat in their political views: Tommy had grown more conservative, while Ben remained an inveterate liberal. But they continued to be devoted friends, and Tommy remained convinced that Ben was the most brilliant lawyer in Washington.

The Corcoran family moved to a larger home on Woodland Drive in 1952. The atmosphere at the house was lively; there was always some activity going on, particularly at the dinner hour. Someone might drop by for a meal: Justice Hugo Black, Bishop Sheen (who lived next door), Lowell Mellett (a columnist for the *Washington Evening Star*), and the Chennaults, when they were in town, all showed up from time to time. Esther Corcoran remembers that occasionally Tommy would stop by their house after work and ask her and Howard to come to dinner. They would pile into his car and drive to his house to on Woodland Drive, where he would open the front door and yell, "Peggy! Esther and Howard are having dinner with us tonight." As Esther remembered it many years later, "Peggy was always so gracious. She might be upstairs, but she would lean over the banister and smile, 'Nice to see you. I'm so glad you're here.' "

Tommy and Peggy also carried on an active social life outside the house. They often saw Justice Black and his wife, Josephine; Senator Lister Hill and his wife, Henrietta; and Senator Claude Pepper and his wife, Mildred. Sometimes they would go to the Olney Theatre to take in a show, although Tommy would be fidgeting after the first half hour. They took turns having cocktails or dining at each other's houses. Claude Pepper recalled, "We'd talk about everything and just have a lot of fun." And Tommy still played his accordion, once accompanying Senator Happy Chandler, the future commissioner of baseball, as he sang "Take Me Out to the Ball Game" to the delight of the guests assembled in Justice Black's living room.

Peggy was always charming, informed, and seemingly happy. But if she was all smiles on the outside, she was inwardly feeling the pressure. She was bringing up the six children largely by herself. Tommy was active with the children when he was there, but he was working very hard, always late into the evenings during the week and often on the weekends as well, sometimes traveling for days or weeks at a time. Peggy had begun to drink, first at social events and then increasingly at home. Tim remembers that from time to time, "Mummy was just a little funny in the afternoon."

In the autumn of 1955 Corcoran received an unexpected telephone call from Joe Kennedy asking him to come to New York for an important meeting. Corcoran had not had a close relationship with Joseph P. Kennedy since the millionaire businessman had stiffed him over the Merchandise Mart bill. Even though he had no idea what Kennedy was up to, he readily agreed to the meeting. They arranged to get together at a swank restaurant on the Upper East Side of Manhattan. When Corcoran arrived he was greeted not only by Joe but also by his twenty-nine-year-old son Bobby. The elder Kennedy got right to the point. He wanted Corcoran to carry a message to Lyndon Johnson. He believed that the Texas senator wanted to run for the presidency. If Johnson would publicly announce his candidacy and privately pledge to take Jack Kennedy as his running mate, then Joe promised, "I have friends who will help finance the ticket." Corcoran was intrigued by the idea, and while he believed that Jack Kennedy was too inexperienced to seek national office, he knew Joe Kennedy should not be underestimated. He agreed to carry the message to Johnson.

A week later Tommy flew to the LBJ ranch in Texas. Johnson listened carefully to Corcoran as the lawyer outlined the Kennedys' proposal. The senator understood the national political landscape as well as anyone and knew that while Eisenhower had not declared his intention to seek reelection, he probably would be a candidate again — and he would probably win again. Johnson understood that Kennedy wanted his son John, a senator from Massachusetts for only four years, to receive the national exposure of a presidential campaign. Following the Roosevelt model — FDR filled the number two spot on the 1920 Democratic ticket — Kennedy, if chosen as LBJ's running mate, would be positioned to seek the presidency in either 1960 or 1964. Johnson never discussed his own plans with Corcoran, but told him to politely decline Joe Kennedy's offer.

Corcoran returned to New York to relay the message to the Kennedys. Corcoran later remembered, "Young Bobby . . . was infuriated. He believed it was unforgiveably discourteous to turn down his father's offer." John Kennedy, who had not been a part of the discussion with Corcoran, received the news with more reserve. One day not long after Corcoran's trip to Texas, the Massachusetts senator asked Corcoran to come to his office on the third floor of the Senate Office Building. "Listen, Tommy," the senator began in his distinctively Boston accent, "we made an honest offer to Lyndon through you. He turned us down. Is Lyndon running without us?"

Corcoran looked at the ambitious young politician and chuckled. "Does a fish swim? Of course he is. He may not think he is. And he certainly isn't saying he is. But I know God damned well he is. I'm sorry he doesn't know it."

The truth was that Johnson was eyeing the presidency, but he didn't believe this was his only opportunity to make a run. And while Corcoran

had been the intermediary between Johnson and the Kennedys, he was
not the adviser to whom Johnson would have revealed his plans. As their
individual status in Washington had changed over the years, so had their
relationship. While they continued to respect and personally like each
other, Corcoran no longer acted as a mentor to the Texan, who had far
surpassed him in terms of political power.

Nearly two decades after they had first met, Corcoran, the lobbyist, and
Johnson, the politician, had very different agendas, and they used each
other to advance their own interests. Their symbiotic relationship was
revealed in the 1956 election. Journalist Drew Pearson had lunch with
Corcoran right after the California primary in which Adlai Stevenson had
swept to an impressive victory. Pearson recorded in his diary that Corcoran
"has been masterminding Lyndon Johnson, but says he is actually for
Stevenson." Stevenson, of course, had been a classmate of Corcoran's at
Harvard Law School, and Tommy knew him well. Pearson, clearly amused
by Corcoran's ability to play all sides, noted that Corcoran was "an amaz-
ing man" who "hasn't lost his vivaciousness despite the years."

When Stevenson captured the Democratic nomination for the presidency a few months later, the question became whom he would choose as
his running mate. Johnson initially conveyed to Stevenson that he wasn't
interested. After being encouraged by Corcoran and others, however, the
Texan changed his mind and let it be known that he would accept a place
on the ticket. Corcoran believed that the strategy Joe Kennedy had laid
out for his son was as sound for Lyndon Johnson as it was for Jack
Kennedy: Even if President Eishenhower won reelection, which seemed a
likelihood, the Democratic vice presidential nominee would gain important experience and national exposure, laying the groundwork for the
next election. Stevenson ultimately allowed the delegates at the
Democratic National Convention to choose his running mate; in a close,
open contest Estes Kefauver defeated John Kennedy. But Johnson's brief
fliration with the vice presidency confirmed Corcoran's views of the
Texan's ambition to seek higher office.

After the election, in which Eisenhower handily defeated Stevenson for
a second time, Johnson settled back into his duties in the Senate. He had
decided that if he could not be president or vice president, he would be
the most powerful man in the Senate; in December 1956 he became the
Senate majority leader. To help guide him on policy matters, he reached
out to the man he wanted as his chief of staff — James Rowe, Tommy

Corcoran's law partner. Rowe had been Roosevelt's last administrative assistant and was considered one of the most brilliant strategists of the Democratic Party. Johnson undoubtedly knew that Rowe would also benefit from the political wisdom of Corcoran, a savvy strategist in his own right. And Rowe, despite his run-in with Norman Littell a decade earlier, had an unblemished reputation. Corcoran, on the other hand, as Johnson well knew, was someone who had to be handled carefully. Harry McPherson, a Senate aide at the time and later White House counsel to Johnson, said, "I had the feeling that Tommy had the reputation of an indefatigable, rascally rogue. In light of that, I think Johnson was a little edgy about him . . . didn't want to be too closely associated with him."

Rowe was unwilling to take the job. He had a young family and finally was making a little money in private practice; he had no real desire to return to government. Johnson telephoned Corcoran and appealed to him to convince his law partner to come back into the fold. Corcoran told Rowe that he could return to the firm at any time, but that he needed to help the majority leader. Rowe, always the good soldier, reluctantly agreed.

22

The Late 1950s

The children knew something was wrong. In the middle of their sailing vacation off the coast of Newport, Rhode Island, Skipper Bob Perry — who also happened to be their sailing instructor and a Corcoran legal associate — told them they had to return to shore. They had been sailing in a rented, forty-five-foot yawl for four days around Cape Cod and the islands off Rhode Island under brilliant blue skies when Perry had taken a dinghy into harbor to get supplies. He had returned in the evening, and although he'd been unusually quiet during dinner, the children hadn't noticed the sadness in his face.

The next morning the yacht docked in Newport Harbor and the children were driven to a local airfield. They boarded a private plane, Tenneco's corporate jet, and were flown to Washington, DC. They were driven home to the house on Woodland Drive, where they discovered their Uncle Howard sitting in a chair in the living room somberly awaiting them. He took the children aside one by one and told them privately that their mother had died. The children ranged in age from Margaret, who was eighteen, to eight-year-old Cecily. Howard told each of them how much their mother had loved them. Tommy, who was not home, had been too distraught to break the news to them.

Peggy Dowd Corcoran died in 1957 at the age of forty-four of a cerebral brain hemorrhage. She'd had extremely high blood pressure and had been drinking too much for many years. Peggy and Tommy had often argued, usually over the children, and particularly over their oldest daughter Margaret, favored so clearly by Tommy. Notwithstanding the arguments, he was very much in love with his wife. Peggy was widely liked and admired by all those who knew her, and condolences flooded the house on Woodland Drive. Felix Frankfurter, who had not spoken to Tommy for several years, sent flowers.

The wake was a somber, well-attended affair. As Peggy's cousin, Margaret Dowd, viewed the body lying in the open coffin, she noticed flecks of plaster around the hairline of Peggy's forehead. Corcoran had hired a sculptor from New York to make a death mask of his beloved wife.

Tommy was suddenly a single father with six children. He wrote one friend, "While little children may mean 'petite soucie,' big children surely mean 'grand soucie.'" A few years after Peggy's death, he told a friend that he was "just beginning to realize how much buttoning and unbuttoning there is to bringing up children." He doted on the children, continuing their sailing lessons, tennis lessons, and French lessons. On weekends he drove them to the country for long walks. Because Washington had limited cultural activity beyond its museums, he took them to New York to attend concerts and plays. After Peggy's death, Tommy used to tease his children, "I know, I know, I know that I'm nagging, but I'm your Jewish mother." Tim, the oldest son, remembered that for the most part his father was loving, but also recalled that "when he was in a bad mood, he could be an Irish father." According to Tim, he "could be nasty; he had a temper."

Tim was enrolled at Phillips Exeter Academy in Exeter, New Hampshire. Tommy was determined that his children have a superior education, and Exeter was the oldest and one of the finest preparatory schools in the country. Just six months after the death of Peggy, Tommy wrote his son a chastising letter complaining that the boy had received a D in science. The single-spaced, four-page letter ended on a wistful note: "My whole life is now wrapped up in the future of you children as the only purpose left to me." The next year, Tim, now a junior, received an encouraging letter from his father about his college prospects, noting that an Exeter C "is good enough to get into Brown or Harvard."

Tommy pushed all his children to achieve, but none harder than Margaret. In writing to Tim, Tommy boasted that Margaret "is graduating first in her class." It seemed that Tommy lavished Margaret with praise and attention at every opportunity. She was extremely bright and pretty with strawberry-blond hair and green eyes.

Only months after Peggy died, Tommy presented Margaret to Washington society at a New Year's Eve debutante ball. Tommy invited Margaret's aunts and uncles to attend the ball, as well as old friends of his and Peggy's. Tommy also made sure that Margaret's younger brothers and sisters were there to pay tribute to their sister as she debuted in an oyster-white silk ball gown. Margaret's younger brother Tim remembered that "we didn't resent her. She was smart and very pretty and we knew Daddy favored her."

Soon after Peggy died, Corcoran's good friend General Claire Chennault succumbed to lung cancer, on July 23, 1958. Before he died, Chennault had asked Corcoran to look after his wife, Anna. Anna and the general had two young children. They were living in Louisiana, where the general had bought a house after returning from Asia. After Chennault's death, Anna and her two daughters moved to Washington, DC, and Corcoran watched over them until she could determine where she would live and what she would do. She decided to remain in Washington "largely by default."

Born in Beijing — then known as Peking — in 1923, Anna Chennault came from a cultured and successful family. Her father had been ambassador to several countries, and was the Chinese consul general in San Francisco throughout World War II. He had also been the dean of the prestigious Peking University and the founder of the first English-language newspaper in Peking, the *North China Morning Post*.

Anna followed her father into journalism. At nineteen she became the first female war correspondent for the Central News Agency in war-ravaged China. She was immediately assigned to cover the Fourteenth Air Force, headed by that swashbuckling American commander, Captain Claire Chennault. Chennault, who was a friend of Anna's father, was thirty-three years her senior and had a wife and eight children living in Louisiana. He became captivated by Anna almost immediately. When Chennault was relieved of his command by General Stilwell in 1937, he was ordered to return to the United States. Before leaving, he pledged to Anna that he would come back for her. Within six months he had divorced his wife and returned to China to marry Anna. Soon thereafter, Chennault founded the Flying Tigers. For the next several years the Chennaults lived in Asia, working primarily in the service of Chiang Kai-shek.

In 1949, the year Chiang fled the mainland and established his government on the island of Formosa, the Chennaults moved back to the United States to live in Louisiana. A year later Anna became an American citizen. Throughout the next decade until his death, the Chennaults traveled frequently to Asia and the general continued to run his airline, Civil Air Transport.

Almost immediately after her arrival in Washington in 1958, Anna and Tommy became inseparable. He escorted her to numerous parties and social events around town and she, in turn, invited him to increasingly lavish dinner parties at her stylish apartment at the Watergate Hotel. Only five foot two and barely one hundred pounds, she looked tiny next to the broad-shouldered Irishman.

Anna had other male friends as well and rejected numerous proposals for marriage, telling her suitors that "I'm never going to get married again. I want to be buried next to my husband in Arlington Cemetery." This may well be true, but Anna and Tommy were often seen together. In his book *Tangled Web*, William Bundy, the assistant secretary of state for East Asian affairs to President Kennedy, referred to Corcoran as Mrs. Chennault's "constant escort." Esther Corcoran, Tommy's sister-in-law, claims that "if Tommy had asked, Anna would have married him in a second."

Even though Corcoran was raising a family by himself, and helping the widow of a dear friend, he still had time to offer assistance to a longtime associate. In 1958 Henry Grunewald, one of Corcoran's more shadowy friends and associates, was indicted for tax evasion. Grunewald was a swarthy German American who had worked for New York insurance executive Henry Marsh during the first half of the 1930s. Corcoran described Marsh as "a mover, a shaker, and a manipulator" — which, coming from Tommy, meant something. According to Corcoran, Marsh used Grunewald "for certain errands, such as delivering cash to members of Congress." Corcoran claimed that Marsh once told him, "Henry is utterly amoral. He just doesn't know right from wrong. Tell him what to do and he'll do it."

Grunewald also provided significant support to President Roosevelt's 1936 presidential campaign, and afterward Marsh asked Corcoran to find his assistant a federal job. Corcoran seized upon the idea of sending Grunewald to Omaha, Nebraska, where there was a sizable German American population. He secured him an appointment as regional director for the Office of the Alien Property Custodian, a largely inactive federal office, but one where Grunewald could, according to Corcoran, "serve as Marsh's representative with insurance interests" and "help

Senator Norris in a difficult reelection campaign." Senator George Norris had been an important supporter of many New Deal initiatves.

Grunewald's stay in Omaha was short-lived. Corcoran wrote in his unpublished memoirs that "no sooner had Grunewald reached Omaha, than he checked into a fine hotel and hosted an extraordinary party. Almost every prostitute in town was there and he had a bottle of gin for each. The party was loud, but the hotel manager was even louder when he called the police to throw Grunewald out. The scandal was loudest of all and Grunewald had to be fired. Senator Norris was not reelected."

Grunewald returned to Washington and from time to time performed work for Corcoran. In 1939 he broke into the Swiss consulate in New York City and stole secret plans of the German high command. Corcoran may have used Grunewald — who was known as the "mystery man of Washington" — in the same manner that Marsh had once used him, to deliver cash from the China lobby and from powerful corporations such as Pan American Airways to elected officials on Capitol Hill. Indeed, in 1952 Grunewald suffered an embarrassment when it was revealed that he had acted as a funnel for an illegal contribution to Richard Nixon's 1950 California Senate campaign. (Ironically, the contribution was made at the behest of Owen Brewster, who had tangled with Corcoran fifteen years earlier.)

After Grunewald was indicted for tax evasion in 1958, he turned to Corcoran for help. Grunewald was not a wealthy man and did not have the resources to defend himself adequately. Corcoran knew that any overt assistance would help the reputation of neither Grunewald nor himself, so he arranged for his brother-in-law George Foulkes, who worked in the firm, to loan Grunewald fourteen thousand dollars, a sizable sum of money in those days. Corcoran kept the promissory note in his own files. It was apparently never repaid; Grunewald died before the case was settled.

As the decade came to a close, Tommy Corcoran had reached the pinnacle of the lobbying profession — he still had friends in every branch of the government, he had influence over policy matters, and he had made a great deal of money. But the decade had been a tough one for him personally. Not only had his wife died, but so had his business partner and close friend Claire Chennault. Those losses were followed by the death of his father, who in 1958 passed away at the age of eighty-seven. Tommy had remained close to his father until the end even though the older man refused to move from his home in Pawtucket. Dad Corcoran once told a reporter that he liked to think of Tommy as the young boy who wanted most of all to be a "one man band." As Tommy entered his fourth decade in Washington, he still had a few songs to play.

23

Using the Back Door

Although lobbying in Washington continued to be a profession that conjured up the image of backroom deals, by the late 1950s things had changed: The number of decision makers in Congress had increased, public policy issues were more complex, and communications had been enhanced by the advent of television. Lobbyists still needed to establish personal relationships with members of Congress, and they often provided money for campaigns — and for personal use. But the really successful lobbyists also had genuine expertise and knowledge about a particular issue, or perhaps a broader understanding of government. Members of Congress had very small staffs, usually just a secretary and an administrative assistant. The Congressional Research Service provided background on legislation, but its analytic capabilities were limited. In a 1958 *Cosmopolitan* magazine article, a lobbyist is quoted as saying, "The Congressman would be completely at the mercy of the damn bureaucrats if it wasn't for us furnishing him with information."

Joe Goulden, author of *The Superlawyers,* wrote that "By most scorecards, the most powerful lobbyists in the nation's capital were the most powerful lawyers: Abe Fortas, Clark Clifford and Tommy Corcoran." Although their personal styles differed, they shared a common approach to their craft. All three men maintained a vast network of contacts. They preferred to work behind the scenes and they shunned publicity unless it was in the context of providing counsel to a powerful public figure.

Corcoran, in particular, liked to work alone, although he often partnered with other lawyers, allowing them to serve as the attorney of record or registered lobbyist for reporting purposes.

He preferred to charge on a retainer basis, like his friend and competitor Clark Clifford. Pan American Airways paid Corcoran a retainer of thirty thousand dollars even though he never appeared on the airline's behalf in a formal proceeding before the Civil Aeronautics Board. That sort of work was for lawyers of lesser stature; Tommy was there to provide strategic advice and, where necessary, appropriate pressure.

But in some ways Corcoran was very different from his competitors. Clark Clifford used to provide his clients with a rehearsed disclaimer, telling them, "If you want influence, you should consider going elsewhere. What we can offer you is an extensive knowledge of how to deal with the government on your problems. We will be able to give you advice on how best to present your position to the appropriate department and agencies of the government." Clifford tried to imbue his lobbying with the patina of statesmanship. He had gained the reputation of a wise man in Washington and recoiled at the thought of being labeled an influence peddler.

Tommy Corcoran never gave such a disingenuous speech to his clients. He knew that the only reason they hired him was to get the job done, and he was determined to get it done any way he could. But that didn't mean Corcoran ever did anything illegal, and if occasionally he skirted the edge of propriety, he made sure to leave no footprints. Corcoran knew that his style of legal practice required that he not leave a paper trail, so he didn't keep a logbook, a list of visitors, a record of long-distance calls, or time sheets. Corcoran had been a "wise man" during the New Deal, but he had also been an implementer and, most of all, an operator.

By the late 1950s came mounting evidence to indicate that some agencies within the federal government were being manipulated by lobbyists such as Corcoran, Clifford, and Fortas. In 1959 the chief counsel to the House Commerce Committee, Professor Bernard Schwartz of New York University, began an investigation into the Federal Communications Commission and other independent regulatory commissions. He obtained documents and identified witnesses whom he believed could testify about the undue influence of Washington lobbyists. When Schwartz was unable to persuade the chairman of the committee, Oren Harris of Arkansas, to launch an investigation and hold hearings, he copied all his investigative files and presented them to Senator Wayne Morse, a Republican from Oregon with a reputation for uncomproming integrity.

Morse reviewed the documents and kept them for a day and a half as he pondered the next step. Only after a pleading telephone call from House Speaker Sam Rayburn did he return them. Morse did not copy the documents, but before returning them to Schwartz he did allow Drew Pearson and his young partner, Jack Anderson, to take notes from them.

The documents showed widespread abuse within the administration, which Morse characterized as "honeycombed with immorality." After Morse went to the Senate floor and excoriated the Congress for what he believed was a cover-up, Pearson and Anderson wrote a series of articles laying out the improprieties committed by bureaucrats, political appointees, and business executives. Corcoran was not accused of any illicit or unethical behavior in either the Schwartz investigation or Pearson columns, but on August 15 he called Drew Pearson "to beg that something be done regarding Morse. . . ." If Corcoran feared that he might eventually become the subject of a new congressional investigation, he was right, but it was not to come for another two years.

In the meantime, Corcoran wound up one of his most lengthy and complicated legal cases. On July 21, 1959, almost ten years after General Chennault had (with Corcoran's help) purchased the aircraft of China's two small commercial airlines, CNAC and CAT, Sir Hartley Shawcross, a former Labor Party attorney general, rose before the Privy Court in London, the highest legal authority in the United Kingdom. As Shawcross presented his argument on behalf of Civil Air Transport Inc., his American legal advisers, Tommy Corcoran and William Donovan, were seated next to him.

Given the duration of the appeal, the decision came relatively quickly. After only a few weeks, the Privy Court ruled that the transfer of title to the aircraft from Chiang to Civil Air Transport Inc. had been legitimate. Any cause for celebration on the part of CATI was short-lived, however. Since the government of Taiwan had largely financed the sale of the planes in the first place, it quickly demanded that they be returned and that CATI's promissory note be paid off.

The government of Taiwan was making life difficult for Chennault, Willauer, and Corcoran. Corcoran pointed out to Taiwanese government representatives that CATI had advanced $10 million in counterclaims and that it was owed at least $2.5 million in legal fees. Corcoran, negotiating on behalf of his partners, indicated that they were willing to settle for $1.25 million; the Taiwanese refused. Corcoran then threatened the government of Taiwan, his client on other matters at the time, telling the Taiwanese lawyers that he would wait for the outcome of the 1960 election. Should a Democrat be elected to the White House, he said, he would advocate for less assistance to the island nation. At this point the State Department became concerned, and Secretary of State Dulles let it be know that he wanted Corcoran and Chennault to settle the matter. On September 14, 1959, an agreement was signed to liquidate the obligations arising out of the $4.55 million promissory note. CATI agreed to pay $1.3 million in claims, but it received credit for claims more than $1.9 million. In sum, the Chinese settled for about two million dollars in real value. Corcoran received past-due legal fees, but his partner Duncan Lee later claimed that he was sure "the shareholders netted very little from the operation in terms of money. . . . certainly nothing commersurate with the talent and time they put into it."

The next problem was how to remove the planes from Hong Kong and deliver them to Taiwan, since many of them had rusted and parts had been pillaged during the long legal battle. Corcoran, who had remained close to the top brass in the navy, managed to "rent" an aircraft carrier for the Taiwanese. *Cape Esperance,* stationed in Manila, steamed into Hong Kong Bay and docked in the harbor, where a ramp was built. The planes were then hauled aboard, and the carrier sailed back to the United States. The aircraft were rebuilt and then delivered to the Nationalist air force in Taiwan. Many years later, Corcoran displayed in his office a large photograph of himself, Willauer, and Donovan aboad the carrier in Hong Kong Harbor. He quipped in his unpublished memoirs, "You don't just call Hertz for that sort of conveyance, especially when the national interest is involved."

Early in 1960 an obscure oil and gas trade magazine, *Oildom,* published an article alleging that the previous year Tommy Corcoran had improperly lobbied the chairman of the Federal Power Commission, Jerome Kuykendall, for a rate increase on behalf of the Tennessee Gas Company. The magazine did not have a wide circulation, but when Kuykendall saw the article he decided to inform a congressional subcommittee of the ex parte communication before someone pointed a finger and accused him of wrongdoing. Kuykendall had indeed met with Corcoran, even though he knew that federal regulations prevented him from having contact with anyone connected to a case outside the hearing process — an administrative procedure akin to a judicial hearing.

Kuykendall telephoned the chief counsel to the House Interstate and

Foreign Commerce Committee, who immediately informed his boss, Chairman Oren Harris, of Corcoran's alleged activities. Although not a friend of Corcoran, Harris was a loyal Democrat who recognized that it was an election year and that Corcoran was perceived as a close ally of the Senate majority leader, Lyndon Johnson, a likely candidate for president. But the chairman also knew that he risked exposing the entire Democratic Party to a scandal if he failed to investigate. Harris ordered the staff to gather all the facts surrounding Corcoran's contacts with the commission and prepare for hearings.

The Federal Power Commission, created during the New Deal, was authorized to regulate the electric and natural gas industries, and had broad authority over consumer prices — and therefore the profits of natural gas companies. In October 1959 the commission was preparing to rule on an application by the Midwestern Gas Transmission Company, a subsidiary of the Tennessee Gas Company, to build a five-hundred-mile pipeline to import gas from Manitoba, Canada, to Marshfield, Wisconsin. Tennessee Gas had been represented in Washington by Corcoran for many years. Indeed, some of the company's earliest financing came from the Reconstruction Finance Corporation, where Corcoran had worked in the 1930s.

The FPC needed to make a decision on Midwestern's application for pipeline construction by November 1, 1959, or the trans-Canada company could terminate the contract and theoretically renegotiate it at a higher cost. More significantly, the company wanted the FPC to ensure the economic viability of the project by guaranteeing a 7 percent return on its investment. The staff of the FPC, however, had recommended a 6.25 percent rate of return. On October 20 Midwestern presented its case to the commission in an open session. Accompanying Midwestern's president, Nelson W. Freeman, were the company's attorney of record, Harry S. Littman, and its "adviser," Tommy Corcoran. While no commissioner voiced any objection to the construction of the pipeline, the commission was uncertain as to how to deal with the rate structure.

While Freeman presented the oral arguments before the commission on that day, it was Corcoran who ultimately persuaded the commissioners to adopt the higher rate. Before the case was decided, Corcoran had off-the-record conversations with three of the five commissioners, including Kuykendall, who had been inclined to support the staff recommendation.

On October 31 the commission overruled its staff and approved the 7 percent rate of return advocated by Corcoran and his client.

Three months later, the article in *Oildom* magazine appeared. Republicans on the Harris Committee believed that Corcoran's contacts with Kuykendall had been inappropriate and, after a committee staff investigation, pressed Harris to hold hearings. They whispered to the press that Tommy Corcoran, the infamous New Dealer, would be exposed finally as a corrupt influence peddler. One of Corcoran's friends, Washington lawyer John Lane, remembered, "There was going to be a major hanging. The press was chasing Corcoran everywhere."

On March 24 Chairman Harris announced that the subcommittee on legislative oversight would hold hearings the following week, with Kuykendall as the lead witness. Corcoran knew he would eventually be asked to testify and set about establishing his defense. He asked his law partner Jim Rowe to help, as well as John Lane and former FBI agent James McInerney, who was asked to find out whether or not the Department of Justice had launched its own investigation. Corcoran also asked his brother Howard to come down from his law firm in New York — Corcoran, Kostelanitz and Gladstone — to oversee the defense.

Like his older and more famous brother, fifty-seven-year-old Howard was a skilled lawyer, although somewhat less impetuous. After Harvard Law School, he had joined Tommy in the New Deal, working for a number of government agencies, including the Department of Agriculture, the Securities and Exchange Commission, and the Tennessee Valley Authority. He also worked as an assistant U.S. attorney in New York until 1943, when Tommy helped arrange his appointment as the U.S. attorney for Southern District of New York. Tommy had never been as close to Howard as he had to David, but he thoroughly trusted his younger, quieter, and more studious brother.

FPC chairman Jerome Kuykendall and the other four commissioners had all been appointed by Eisenhower. As he stood at the witness table with his hand raised, Kuykendall, tall and balding, gave the appearance of Republican rectitude. He acknowledged that Corcoran had telephoned him on one occasion and had visited him on another, but he denied any impropriety. Several members of the committee, however, were skeptical. One young Democrat, John Dingell of Michigan, complained that the commission's decision would cost consumers in the upper Midwest in excess of sixteen million dollars a year. Dingell also harshly criticized Kuykendall for even taking Corcoran's telephone call. The FPC chairman seemed exasperated: "Well, how could I prevent it? Someone calls you on the phone, you don't know what they are going to say, do you? By the time I knew what he was talking about, he had said it. I didn't talk to him. He talked to me."

After three days of intense questioning and debate, Kuykendall was forced to concede that his meeting with Corcoran had been "improper" because Corcoran had touched on the merits of the case. Kuykendall should not have spoken with anyone outside his staff about the case, and he certainly should never have consulted with someone such as Corcoran, who had a direct interest in its outcome. He stated that during his seven and a half years as chairman of the commission, there may have been half a dozen or so such incidents, but that no one, including Corcoran, had ever influenced his vote in a case. As always, the members of the committee had the last word. Republican congressman John Bennett of Michigan told Kuykendall, "The most charitable thing that could be said about your conversation with Mr. Corcoran, both on your part and his, was that it was not only unfortunate, but foolhardy and indiscreet."

The appearance of scandal continued to worsen for Corcoran over the next few weeks. It was revealed that even though he had never been the attorney of record for Tennessee Gas before the commission, the gas company had paid him more than three hundred thousand dollars for legal services during the two-year time period in which the application was pending. The other FPC commissioners whom Corcoran had lobbied, William R. Connole and Arthur Kline, also testified. Kline revealed, in stark contrast to Kuykendall, that Corcoran had visited his office eight times over a two-year period. Kline also stated that he initially had opposed the Midwestern application because he believed its parent, Tennessee Gas, could arrange favorable financing for building the pipeline. At the time of the FPC hearing, Kline had made no public statements on his position, but Corcoran apparently knew how he was leaning. He told the commissioner that Tennessee was planning to sell its stock in Midwestern, thereby making financing a less certain event. A few days after Corcoran's visit, Kline changed his position and agreed to leave the rate question open.

When members of the subcommittee on legislative oversight heard Kline's testimony, their concerns about Corcoran deepened. Corcoran had managed to persuade Kline to change his vote, but, more significantly, he seemed to have been able to learn of Kline's precise objections to the Midwestern application — objections that had been expressed only in closed commission meetings. Corcoran, of course, had friends on the staff level at the FPC, and someone had undoubtedly advised him on how to lobby Kline.

The star witness of the hearings was to be Tommy Corcoran. His testimony was delayed for several days as he and committee lawyers wrangled over what documents he would provide the committee. The committee staff had conducted numerous interviews before the testimony of other witnesses, and they invited Corcoran to be interviewed as well. They also wanted Corcoran to turn over his private appointment books for inspection. John Lane had become one of Corcoran's principal advisers in the FPC case, and he counseled him not to accede to an interview or to turn over anything voluntarily. "No way, just be quiet," Lane said.

But Corcoran was nervous. According to Lane, Corcoran's partner Jim Rowe contributed to the anxiety; he believed that Corcoran may actually have violated the law. "Tommy, it was unethical," Lane recalled Rowe telling Corcoran during one strategy session. Corcoran thought he should consider an aggressive public relations campaign; according to Lane, "Every day he would have a different version of events. Every day he would have a press release and I would tear it up." The stress was weighing on Corcoran. One day in April after returning from a trip to New York by airplane, he fainted on the tarmac and was taken to the hospital. He was diagnosed with a bleeding ulcer and spent the next several days resting in bed.

On May 19, 1960, Tommy Corcoran, fully recovered, made his long-awaited appearance before the committee, accompanied by his brother Howard and his partner Jim Rowe. A young reporter for the *New York Times*, Anthony Lewis, was covering the hearing and described the scene: "Tanned with prominent ears and eyebrows and blue-gray hair, the 59 year old witness spoke in a resonant and cultivated voice. Once started he hardly stopped talking. The committee members and counsel had trouble getting in questions." Indeed, Corcoran maintained that there was nothing improper or even surreptitious about his contacts at the commission. "I walked down the corridors of the Commission," he said, "and I have always walked down the corridors of the Commission — in broad daylight with a brass band behind me."

Congressman Bennett, who had been so derisive of Kuykendall's version of events, was no more convinced by Corcoran's. He pressed the witness on why he needed to engage in any ex parte communication with members of the commission when the president of the company had already given a full presentation to the FPC in public testimony. Corcoran searched among the papers on the table in front of him, then ostentatiously waved before the committee a letter that Bennett himself had written to the Federal Power Commission in support of the pipeline. Corcoran declared that Bennett had been "part of our support," and he thanked the blushing congressman for "your ex-parte, very desirable, and very proper and very welcome help in an ex parte communication to the Commission." The frustrated Bennett asked no more questions.

Corcoran then lectured the committee members on administrative law, telling them at one point, "I think I know as much about the Federal Power Commission as most people." He maintained that, in fact, he could legally have gone much farther than he did in his lobbying efforts. "We did have the right under the law to go and talk about the merits if we chose to talk about the merits," Corcoran said, " but we carefully avoided that." And near the end of his first day of questioning, he seemed to be trying to actually provoke his attentive questioners. "I'm wondering if it isn't improper if a lawyer doesn't take care of his client up to the limits of the law on the books at the time."

The second day of Corcoran's testimony didn't go much better for the congressmen. Anthony Lewis reported in the Times that "unabashed, he lectured the members of the Subcommittee on Oversight. Sacrcasm, piety, wit and condescension poured from him." The biggest uproar came in the exchange with Stephen B. Derounian, a Republican of Nassau County, Long Island. The New Yorker pressed Corcoran on why he kept no office record of his work for the Tennessee Gas Company. The subcommittee knew he had been paid handsomely, but Corcoran's records did not actually describe the nature of the work.

"Mr. Derounian," the witness said, "I know I am not like your friend Tom Dewey. I don't come down here in the same kind of a case as your friend Tom Dewey, who is also a friend of mine, with a long, long

timesheet justification as to how he charged more than I did in the case."
(Corcoran was referring to fees charged by former governor Thomas E.
Dewey's law firm in another natural gas case.)

Derounian looked exasperated. "Tom Dewey is not my friend," the
congressman said. He then looked at Chairman Harris and, turning back
to Corcoran, sputtered: "And stop winking at the chairman with your left
eye. Maybe he is your friend, too."

At one point, near the end of the day, Corcoran curtailed his filibus-
tering and clearly stated that the backlog of cases at the commission had
necessitated off-the-record visits by him. It was his job as a lawyer to cut
through procedural difficulties in order to serve his client. He advised the
members of the panel to increase the size of the commission staff, clarify
the rules, and eliminate the backlog of cases.

"I don't see why anybody takes the job of being chairman of the FPC,"
he added. "Certainly, if we [Democrats] should be so fortunate as to
become the new Administration, I do sincerely hope that nobody asks me
to take that job."

Tommy had once again masterfully acquitted himself. The case for
ethical misconduct that had seemed to be building against him collapsed
after his testimony. Corcoran, who had seemed so nervous just days
before his testimony, had answered the questions with a confidence and
ease that almost suggested he had known what was going to be asked of
him. In fact, a member of Corcoran's defense team had obtained the transcripts of interviews conducted by the committee staff from a friendly
lawyer on the committee. While Corcoran hadn't known the exact questions the congressmen would ask, he had the great advantage of knowing
in advance the extent of their knowledge.

Seven months later, the Democratic staff of the commerce committee
issued its report, which completely cleared Corcoran of any impropriety
in his contacts with the Federal Power Commission. The report had
actually been written by one of Corcoran's lawyers, John Lane, who submitted it to the staff. Lane cited language in the Administrative
Procedures Act that cleared Corcoran of any wrongdoing. Lane argued
that since FPC staff and members of Congress had been a party to the
proceedings concerning Tennessee Gas, lawyers for the company also
had that right. In fact, the report, signed by the Democrats on the committee, stated that Corcoran's contacts with commission members had

been not only "proper" but "necessary." The Republicans on the committee fervently disagreed, calling the majority's conclusion "the most shocking political whitewash to come out of a congressional committee in many years."

While Democrats and Republicans on the House Commerce Committee bickered over the propriety of his activities, Corcoran was in Mexico negotiating agreements for a joint U.S.-Mexican pipeline on behalf of the Tennessee Gas Company. The press reported that "officially his visit was described as a vacation, but it was understood that he was in conference with various government officials concerning the projected pipeline."

Tommy Corcoran had successfully gamed the system, but in the process he had raised some important questions about how government was operating — the same types of questions that reformers such as Professor Schwartz and Senator Morse had raised two years earlier. Federal agencies were set up not only to regulate, but also to nurture and promote industries essential to the U.S. economy. These agencies were becoming overwhelmed by an ironic combination of too much bureaucracy and too few resources. Moreover, the ethical rules applied to the agencies were murky, since they operated on one level as judicial bodies, but on another as policy makers. And Corcoran had astutely raised the question of what a lawyer's obligation was to his client vis-à-vis the federal regulatory system. Corcoran understood the dilemma better than anyone — but instead of trying to fix the problem, as he might have thirty years before, he profited from it.

In an editorial on the FPC case, the *New York Herald Tribune* noted that the important thing was "not the strange role Mr. Corcoran seems to have played over the years," but rather "the light it focuses on the vulnerability of vastly powerful regulatory agencies to the secret pleadings of private interests, to influence peddling, to pressure of all sorts." The *New York Times* put it more succinctly: "Federal regulatory agencies should have no back doors."

24

LBJ for the USA

During the 1960 presidential election, Tommy Corcoran's behind-the-scenes advice to candidate Lyndon Johnson earned him the sobriquet in the press as the "Washington mastermind" for the campaign. In fact, Corcoran played a relatively minor role and only surfaced at the Democratic convention, where he joined with other Johnson advisers to persuade the Texan to accept the vice presidency.

In February 1960 the *New York Times* reported that while Senator Johnson "stubbornly contends that he has no plans, or expectations of becoming a candidate, several aides, including Corcoran, were working for him behind the scenes." The article quoted Corcoran as suggesting that he was used for "the testing of new ideas."

Three months earlier Corcoran's good friend, the seventy-eight-year-old Speaker of the House, Sam Rayburn, had returned to his home state of Texas to announce the formation of an "unofficial Johnson for President campaign." Rayburn's announcement followed that of Senator John F. Kennedy, who had declared his candidacy for the presidency in the Senate caucus room a month earlier, and Senator Hubert Humphrey, who had tossed his hat into the ring at the beginning of the new year. Sensing that he had a greater name recognition than any of the declared candidates, and desperately seeking vindication after two stinging previous defeats, Adali Stevenson allowed others to present his case. Senator Stuart Symington had decided to wait in the wings, hoping that in a deadlocked convention he would become the consensus alternative.

Corcoran was one of a number of prominent New Dealer–era luminaries, including Eliot Janeway, Dean Acheson, and William O. Douglas, who were supporting Lyndon Johnson. Presidential chronicler Theodore White later called the group "a loose and highly ineffective coalition," which was not entirely fair since it did manage to raise nearly $150,000 for Johnson's undeclared candidacy. LBJ himself decided not to campaign actively; as majority leader he believed he couldn't neglect his Senate duties to mount a full-scale campaign. Moreover, he reasoned that there were already three senators either contemplating or in the race, none of whom equaled his stature. He anticipated that no clear, consensus candidate would emerge from the primaries and that at the July convention, the delegates would turn to him as the obvious choice to top the ticket in November. Johnson figured that, as the only prominent southerner, he could count on more than three hundred delegates without writing one campaign check.

Johnson's political theories proved dead wrong. In March Senator Kennedy won the New Hampshire primary. On April 5 Kennedy surprised the country by winning two-thirds of the delegates in the Wisconsin primary. When he defeated Humphrey a month later in West Virginia, Kennedy became the undisputed front-runner. With his youthful image and father's millions, Kennedy was picking up endorsements and delegates across the country. In early July, as Democrats were poised to convene in Los Angeles to choose their nominee, Kennedy appeared to have amassed enough delegates to win the nomination, but the outcome was still not certain. There was strong opposition to Kennedy among the party's elders, including not only Rayburn but also Mrs. Roosevelt, who faulted Kennedy for having missed the vote to censure the anticommunist demagogue Joseph McCarthy. The former first lady favored Adlai Stevenson. Former president Truman supported Missouri favorite son Stuart Symington. On July 7 Lyndon Johnson, hoping to capitalize on the potentially deadlocked convention that he had envisioned several months earlier, announced that he would seek the presidency.

The Johnson forces frantically visited the state delegations in the hope of stimulating a rush to the Texan. They also tried to sow doubts about Kennedy: that he was sick with Addison's disease, that a Catholic couldn't win nationally, that old Joe Kennedy had been pro-Hitler. Johnson stressed that he was a self-made man and told delegates, "I haven't had anything given to me." But he was too late. On Tuesday, July 12, Senator John F. Kennedy of Massachusetts was nominated on the first ballot with 806 votes, nearly twice as many as his nearest competitor, Lyndon Johnson, who received 409 votes. The only question that remained to be resolved was who would occupy the second spot on the ticket.

On the next evening Tommy Corcoran was waiting for an elevator in the Biltmore Hotel when the doors opened. There, standing behind a phalanx of advisers, was the nominee, Senator Kennedy. According to

Corcoran, he stood in the elevator door before it could close and explained to Kennedy that he should pick Johnson as his running mate. "Tommy, you are a most unusual man," Kennedy laughingly replied.

In fact, Kennedy had been contemplating his choice for vice president for some time. On the first night of the convention, he had met privately with Clark Clifford, Stuart Symington's chief adviser, at his suite in the Biltmore Hotel. Kennedy told Clifford that if he got the nomination, he was seriously considering putting Symington on the ticket. Like Johnson, Symington had forgone the primary process in the hope of emerging as a dark-horse candidate. On July 14 Kennedy telephoned Clifford and offered Symington the vice presidency. Clifford enthusiastically told Kennedy that he would convey the proposition to Senator Symington.

In the meantime Kennedy decided — notwithstanding opposition from his brothers and other key advisers — that he needed the southern vote to defeat Richard Nixon, the Republican nominee, in the general election, and that he should probably ask Lyndon Johnson to be his running mate. Moreover, the senator from Massachusetts believed that Johnson would lend stature to the ticket. Kennedy retracted the Symington offer and now offered the vice presidency to Johnson, who said he would have to think about it. That evening Tommy Corcoran telephoned his old friend Ed Foley, who had been his first roommate in Washington thirty years earlier. The two former New Dealers agreed that Kennedy could not win the general election unless Lyndon Johnson was on the ticket. Corcoran then telephoned Johnson to urge him to accept Kennedy's offer.

Johnson replied that he would not even think of taking the number two spot unless he could be chosen unanimously and unless Speaker of the House Sam Rayburn — a fellow Texan and his political mentor — recommended it. Corcoran knew that before he took another step he needed to check with one other person: He telephoned Lady Bird, who seemed sympathetic to the idea.

Corcoran and Foley next decided that it was up to them to persuade Rayburn to recommend to Johnson that he consider the vice presidency. Rayburn was also staying at the Biltmore, and Corcoran and Foley went to see him in his suite. Corcoran went in alone to talk with the Speaker, while Foley waited outside. The Speaker argued that the nomination of a Catholic for president was a recipe for disaster. Moreover, he argued that

Johnson would have to give up his leadership post in the Senate, which would be injurious to the Democratic Party in the long run. Corcoran listened attentively and then outlined an astonishing proposal to Rayburn: Johnson could accept the nomination for vice president, and if he won, he could resign before taking office, thereby maintaining his leadership position in the Senate. Next in line of succession to the vice presidency would be Rayburn himself. Whether or not Corcoran actually considered this a viable plan is not clear. He may have been simply trying to flatter the Speaker. Whatever the case, Rayburn recognized it for what it was: a preposterous plan.

As Corcoran and Rayburn huddled inside the suite, Representative Hale Boggs of Louisiana happened to walk down the hallway and bumped into Ed Foley. When Foley told him what was going on, Boggs said that if Johnson were on the ticket, he felt Louisiana would go Democratic. Corcoran emerged from his meeting despondent, but now Boggs, who was a close friend of the Speaker's, went in to make one last try. Rayburn remained reluctant, but his steadfast opposition faded when Boggs kept pressing upon him the question, "Do you want to see Richard M. Nixon in the White House?" Finally Rayburn agreed that if Kennedy asked him, he would go along with it. Boggs and Foley shook the Speaker's hand, left the room, and excitedly told Corcoran the good news. Corcoran, in turn, rushed to the Kennedys' suite and informed the Democratic nominee that Rayburn was behind his choice. Then he ran back to Rayburn's suite to tell him that Senator Kennedy was coming over to thank him — a gesture, later described by journalist Arthur Krock, "that seemed to please the Speaker very much."

Notwithstanding Rayburn's blessing, Johnson harbored a deep personal resentment of his younger Senate colleague and was not convinced that he wanted to run on the ticket. Likewise, some of Kennedy's closest advisers didn't want Johnson: Bobby Kennedy continued to fight against putting the Senate majority leader on the ticket, and some prominent liberals, including top labor officials, also objected to Johnson. The deal was sealed only after *Washington Post* publisher Phil Graham, close to both Kennedy and Johnson, helped broker an agreement.

The Kennedy-Johnson ticket went on to victory that November, winning by a margin of only 112,000 votes out of nearly 70 million cast. Kennedy had run a tough campaign and had displayed extraordinary personal appeal as well as a keen intellect, but in no small part the success of Irish Americans like Corcoran, who had been influential on the national stage for thirty years, helped pave the way for the election of the first Irish Catholic president in American history.

After the election Corcoran called Joe Kennedy to congratulate him on his son's victory. Corcoran knew that the elder Kennedy would play an important role in helping the president-elect chose his cabinet, so he recommended Jim Rowe to be the next attorney general and Ed Foley as secretary of the Treasury. According to Rowe's son, his father would never have been presumptuous enough to think that he had a chance to be attorney general in a Kennedy administration. And even if he had, Corcoran would not have been the right person to make the case. But that didn't stop Corcoran. Joe Kennedy listened politely, but he had already made up his mind that his other son Robert would be the next attorney general. Still, the Kennedys liked Jim Rowe, who was designated an unofficial talent scout for the Department of Justice. He both interviewed and recommended a number of young, highly capable lawyers who became key figures in Bobby Kennedy's Justice Department. Foley had played an active role in the campaign and had served as undersecretary of the Treasury from 1948 to 1953. Kennedy, however, believed he needed a Republican in his administration and turned to Douglas Dillon. The only position the president-elect gave Foley was head of his inaugural committee.

Although not a member of his firm, Corcoran's old friend Jim Landis landed a job in the administration. Landis, now remarried, returned to Washington to help the president with his reorganization of the federal bureaucracy. His recommendations were controversial and he rubbed people the wrong way, as he had during his entire professional life, but Kennedy recognized the man's enormous talent: After the president was sworn into office, he asked Landis to stay in the White House and handle negotiations with the USSR on the first direct air service between New York and Moscow. There were even rumors in Washington at the time that if Justice Frankfurter resigned, the president was considering Landis for a Supreme Court assignment.

Then, in September 1961, reporters called Landis's New York law office to ask about a divorce suit in which he had been named as a correspondent.

The woman in the case was Landis's Washington secretary, and her litigious husband had somehow obtained some flirtatious love notes that Landis had sent her. Mortified and certain that his wife would leave him, Landis shut himself up in his Washington apartment and went on a drinking binge. Once again, Corcoran calmed him down, telling him, "You can get something on anybody." Corcoran promised to help. Four months later, the litigation was dropped.

Landis's troubles were not over. Two years later he pled guilty to income tax evasion, served a short jail sentence, and was disbarred.

Even though Corcoran had been friendly with Joe Kennedy, and even though he was Irish Catholic and from the Northeast, he had never really been part of John Kennedy's inner circle. The Kennedys correctly identified him as a Johnson man. Indeed, during the Kennedy presidency, a full portrait of Lyndon Johnson dominated the reception room at Corcoran's law office. And while Kennedy consulted with lawyer-lobbyist Clark Clifford, perhaps Corcoran's best-known comptetitor in the lobbying profession, the president never called on Corcoran. Part of the reason may have been, as Arthur Schlesinger Jr. claimed, that "despite their Irish Catholic affinity," Bobby Kennedy "somewhat disapproved of Tommy."

Corcoran wasn't particularly concerned that Jack Kennedy didn't value his advice. After all, he had access to the White House through Lyndon Johnson. On November 5, 1960, election eve, Corcoran had written Lyndon and Lady Bird that they were "back on the main trail of political service and political growth in this country and in the world." He flattered Johnson by telling him that he was "free to be a national statesman, free to be a world statesman, free to free the greatness that FDR saw in you." And for several months after his inauguration, Corcoran recalled in his memoirs that "Lyndon started out being one of the most influential vice presidents in history — for a while at least. Certainly things were going well enough for everybody."

Then, on November 22, 1963, President Kennedy was assassinated. As Corcoran later wrote, "The young president was cut down long before his time . . . and now by the twisted deed of a mad assassin," Lyndon Johnson, who had lost the race for 1960 nomination, realized his life's ambition of becoming president.

◆ ◆ ◆

It was early in 1964. The black bunting honoring John Kennedy had been removed from the White House, and LBJ had settled in as the nation's thirty-fourth president.

As usual, Tommy was in a hurry. The young woman behind the counter carefully placed the legal pads and pens in a brown paper bag. Years later she remembered that after she handed her customer the bag, he smiled at her. The woman has a vague recollection, or perhaps just a romantic delusion, that after the man left the store, the manager told her she'd just helped "Tommy Corcoran, one of the most famous lawyers in Washington."

It would be another thirty years until her mother showed her a birth certificate indicating that her father was named Tommy Corcoran. The daughter, who had long supected that she was adopted, listened while her mother described her father as "a very famous lawyer who had been close friends with more than one American president."

The story is sketchy, and only a few details can be confirmed. Apparently Corcoran traveled in July 1942 to Panama City, Panama, where he had business, most likely on behalf of Sterling Pharmaceutical, which had interests throughout Central and South America. While in town Tommy met a successful local lawyer, who invited him to a party; there he met the lawyer's daughter, a ravishingly beautiful young woman named Digna Rosa Gomez. Gomez was petite with brown eyes, shoulder-length black hair, and fair skin. She spoke English fluently, although with a decidedly Spanish accent. Corcoran, married just over a year, had a brief, romantic affair with Gomez.

In May 1942 Gomez gave birth to a baby girl and christened her Victoria, but later changed the name to Alice — allegedly because Tommy liked the name. Little is known of the relationship between Gomez and Corcoran. There are no letters or records of any contact between them, and neither Alice nor any of Tommy's children with Peggy know whether or not he continued to see Digna, although for at least three years he provided her and their daughter with some financial support. Alice does assert that her mother told her that Tommy used to call her from the Capitol and from the White House.

When Alice was only three years old, her mother married a U.S. naval officer stationed in Panama named Vaughn Howard. Howard had enlisted in the navy and quickly risen in the ranks to become one of the youngest chiefs in the service.

In 1946 Howard legally adopted Alice; that same year he was reassigned to the U.S. Navy Bureau of Medicine and Surgery in Washington, DC. The family moved to an apartment on Barnaby Street in southeast Washington, where Howard and Gomez had two more daughters in quick succession. Digna stayed at home to raise the three girls.

According to Alice, her mother said that Corcoran desperately wanted to see his daughter, but Digna forbade it because she knew it would bother Vaughn. She also believes that her adoptive father and Corcoran may have met on a few occasions — a distinct possibility, because Howard acted as a navy liaison to the U.S. Congress. The Howard family lived in Washington for the next four years, but in 1954 moved to Camp Pendleton, California. Six years later the Howards returned to Washington. For a short time Alice worked at Ginn's Office Supply on Connecticut Avenue, just blocks from the White House and from Corcoran's law office.

Peggy Corcoran seems never to have known the story. Tommy's children themselves learned of it only in the late 1990s.

In late 1964, however, Corcoran was preoccupied with a political scandal. Only weeks after Johnson was sworn in as president, Bobby Baker got into trouble for fraud and tax evasion. Baker had been LBJ's closest aide and most important adviser in the Senate. He and Corcoran had known each other for many years, and although never close friends, their mutual respect for Lyndon Johnson and the fact that they were both political operators meant that they saw one another often.

Tommy had actually helped Baker buy his house in the affluent section of Washington known as Spring Valley. Corcoran had learned that Baker and his wife, who was expecting their third child, were looking for a larger home. At the time, Tommy was representing Tenneco, and he knew that a house under construction — originally intended for one of the company's vice presidents, who had been recalled to Texas — was slated to go on the market for $175,000. Baker was encouraged to put in a bid of $125,000, which was accepted. Although Baker never recalled doing any special favor for Corcoran in return, Tommy always knew that he was owed one.

In January 1964 Baker was indicted by the U.S. attorney in Washington for tax evasion. The former Capitol Hill aide sought out John Lane, whom he had known in the Senate and who by now had established a small but highly regarded law practice. Lane did not have a white-collar defense practice, but he knew that Tommy Corcoran's brother, Howard, practiced in New York with Boris Kostelanitz, a respected attorney who had handled several criminal tax cases. Lane and Baker went to see Corcoran in his office. As they sat and talked on Corcoran's leather couch, Corcoran's secretary came in and told Baker that Attorney General Robert Kennedy was on the telephone. Kennedy wanted to assure Baker that he had not personally ordered the case against him and that his knowledge of the case came only from newspaper clippings.

Baker retained Kostelanitz to defend him on the charges of tax evasion and retained Edward Bennett Williams, the renowned criminal lawyer, as his counsel. The case was assigned to Judge Oliver Gasch of the district court after several judges reportedly rejected it because they personally knew Baker. Ironically, Gasch, a close friend of Howard Corcoran's, owed his appointment to Tommy Corcoran. But much to Baker's chagrin, Corcoran didn't intercede on his behalf, probably because Lyndon Johnson never asked him. The president, according to one lawyer close to the case, "didn't want to touch Baker with a ten foot pole."

By the middle of May the Baker scandal had faded as a political problem. Nevertheless, during the summer of 1964, with the Democratic convention in Atlantic City only weeks away, President Johnson was seriously considering not running for reelection.

Johnson had become increasingly discouraged by his inability to shake off Bobby Kennedy, who had picked up the mantle of his fallen brother and was viewed by many as the true heir to President Kennedy. The president was also growing increasingly concerned about the direction of events in Southeast Asia, where a communist insurgency was gaining intensity. He was most unhappy about his inability to make more progress on a domestic agenda, centered on his War on Poverty, that he had hoped would be his legacy as president.

He told his wife he might just leave Washington and politics behind and return to his beloved ranch in Texas. The president's press secretary, George Reedy, remembered that as the convention began Johnson remained conflicted and seemed in a near-manic state. On two occasions the president told Reedy that he was not going to run; he even drafted a speech saying that he would not accept the nomination.

Tommy Corcoran and a young clerk he had hired for the summer, Robert Bennett, a Georgetown University law student, had driven to Atlantic City on July 28 to witness the opening gavel of the Democratic convention. Bennett remembered that only a few hours after they arrived they were lounging around their hotel room when the telephone rang. Corcoran asked Bennett to answer it. The voice at the other end said, "This is President Johnson. I'd like to speak to Tommy Corcoran?" Bennett thought it was a joke, perhaps one of Corcoran's friends imitating a Texas accent, and he handed the telephone to Corcoran, chuckling, "It's for you — some guy who says he is the President." Bennett then heard Corcoran say, "Hello, Mr. President," and realized that, in fact, the voice at the other end of the telephone had been none other than the president of the United States. Although he only heard one side of the conversation, he saw Corcoran grow more and more agitated. Bennett remembered Corcoran raising his voice and telling Johnson, "Dammit, Lyndon, you cannot do that. No, no, no. You cannot do that." Corcoran never revealed to Bennett what the president had said, but it seems plausible that Johnson was conveying to Corcoran what he had earlier conveyed to Reedy: his decision not to seek reelection.

In the end, of course, Johnson did become a candidate, and the convention became little more than a coronation. On the third day of the convention, however, Tommy was distracted by terrible news. On July 30 Corcoran's friend James Landis was found floating facedown in his pool. An autopsy revealed a significant level of alcohol in his blood. The insurance company asked that any funeral be delayed until a thorough investigation could establish whether or not he had committed suicide, which if established would have eliminated a payout to his widow. Outraged by the prospect of more publicity, Corcoran worked with two of Landis's friends — Bobby Kennedy, who had recently stepped down as attorney general, and Tom Dewey, the New York attorney and former Republican presidential nominee — to protect the legal rights of Landis's widow. According to Corcoran, "We hit on a way to dissuade the insurance company from its insulting intentions. . . . If the company wriggled out through the loophole of a suicide clause they might face the embarrassment of being investigated for something else." The company acceded and Corcoran, Kennedy, and Dewey joined numerous others at a private funeral in Rye, New York.

Then in October 1964, just weeks before the election, another close Johnson associate embarrassed the president. Walter Jenkins, an aide to Johnson for more than thirty years, was arrested in the men's room of the downtown Washington YMCA, a well-known meeting place for homosexuals. District of Columbia police had staked out the restroom, using peepholes for surveillance. Jenkins had been booked on a disorderly conduct charge and released on bail. There had been no publicity, but almost a week after the incident, a reporter for the *Washington Evening Star* received a tip-off from an official with the Republican National Committee. The reporter called the White House for comment. President Johnson was out of town, but asked Lady Bird to call an emergency meeting at the White House with Clark Clifford and Abe Fortas.

Clifford and Fortas tried to have the story killed in the press, but they failed when at eight o'clock on October 14, United Press International put the story out on the wires to hundreds of newspapers across the country. After talking with Jenkins's wife, Marjorie, Corcoran telephoned the president in New York at one-thirty in the morning and pleaded with him not to fire Jenkins: "All I hope is [that we don't] just admit to everything and throw an old retainer overboard too easily. . . . Particularly a Catholic retainer. . . ." Corcoran suggested that perhaps the incident could be portrayed as "a great frame-up." When Johnson was noncommittal, Corcoran resorted to his favorite tactic: flattery. He told the president, "I'm sure nobody will think they see any signs of distress in your face about it. I'm sure that the impression they'll get is the true impression that you're a leader to whom a blow like this doesn't hurt." And in a parting shot at his competitors, he said, "All I'm concerned is that the master's touch be on this and not just a bunch of amateurs like me, or amateurs like Clark [Clifford] or Abe [Fortas]."

But Johnson was clearly more comfortable with the advice of Clifford and Fortas, although he suggested to Lady Bird that Corcoran, because he was Catholic, should be the liaison with the Jenkins family. The president wanted Tommy to go to Jenkins's house and inform his wife of the facts of the case. When Lady Bird suggested that Jenkins be offered the number two position at KTBC, the radio station in Austin, the president responded, "I'll just let them know generally through Tom that they have no problem in that regard."

In the end Jenkins was forced to resign. Corcoran had known Jenkins from the time the young Texan had first arrived in Washington, and he wrote him a comforting letter, telling him, "You have done a great job for America and I am on your side." And on November 2, 1964, election eve, Corcoran wrote Jenkins that "for Lyndon's ultimate attainment of the greatest power in history no other human contribution will have been more responsible than your sweat and blood. . . ."

The election of 1964 pitted President Johnson against the conservative Republican senator from Arizona, Barry Goldwater. It was a contest, as characterized by presidential chronicler Theodore White, whose outcome was a foregone conclusion; as the campaign wore on, the only question was "how large, how broad, how deep, would be Lyndon Johnson's sweep." Johnson waged a brilliant campaign that capitalized on the aspirations of John Kennedy by offering a domestic program embodied in "the Great Society" and simultaneously exploiting fears that Goldwater was an extremist who would lead the country into nuclear war. In the end Johnson won over 61 percent of the more than seventy million votes cast. It was the greatest margin of victory that any president had ever received from the American people.

A few weeks later Corcoran wrote the president that his reelection made "his heart sing again as in the Thirties." He went on to distinguish Johnson from John Kennedy: "Catholic though he was, he was a Harvard skeptic. But you are an Old Covenanter 'true believer,' and 'faith makes the fact.'"

With Johnson now firmly esconsed in the White House, Corcoran told friends that he was finally going to "cash in." Everyone in Washington knew of the history between Corcoran and Johnson, not to mention Rowe and Johnson. The general belief was that Corcoran and Rowe had access to the White House; indeed, lots of business came through the door, and the firm had more work than it could handle. Nevertheless, in the fall of 1966, after Nicholas Katzenbach resigned as attorney general, Corcoran recommended to the president that he appoint Jim Rowe to the position. Corcoran wrote the president that he "had seen to it that [Rowe] is financially able" to leave the firm and that it was "his last chance to get what I think he wants." But Rowe was ultimately passed over in favor of Ramsey Clark. He continued to practice law with Corcoran.

Corcoran and Rowe became one of the preeminent lobbying shops in the city. Business during the Johnson years was so good, in fact, that Tommy briefly considered taking over another law firm. One day the owner of Corcoran's building walked into John Lane's office down the street and spread out architectural plans across his desk. Lane and Corcoran had remained close friends, and Lane had built up a small but highly successful firm with a blue-chip client base. The owner told Lane that he was pleased Lane's firm was becoming a part of the Corcoran firm. According to Lane, the owner told him that Corcoran had said that "he was going to make a lot of money for Lane and the lawyers in his firm." The problem was, Lane had no intention of merging his firm into Corcoran's, and had indicated as much to Corcoran on several occasions.

President Johnson didn't fully trust anyone and had been wary of Corcoran for years. He nevertheless repaid Tommy for his longtime loyalty by appointing his brother and law partner, Howard, to the U.S. District Court in Washington. At Howard Corcoran's confirmation hearing before the Senate Judiciary Committee, he was asked how much court-room experience he had. "Zero," he replied. He was nevertheless con-firmed by the Senate and went on to serve with distinction. In the very first months after his confirmation, he presided over the high-profile murder trial of the man accused of killing Mary Meyer, the Washington socialite who allegedly had carried on an affair with President Kennedy.

While Corcoran had no official position in the administration, he often saw the president and first lady on a social basis. Lady Bird had always enjoyed Tommy, and she and the president made sure that he was included at many intimate White House gatherings, including the wed-ding of their daughter Lynda, a party celebrating the thirtieth anniver-sary of Hugo Black's appointment to the Supreme Court, and the first couple's anniversary parties. Tommy's second oldest son, David, dated Luci, escorting her on more than one occasion to a Princeton football game.

Corcoran was also friendly with Vice President Humphrey. In 1960 Corcoran's partner James Rowe had been referred to in the press as the "local mastermind of Hubert H. Humphrey," a role he resumed in 1968. During Humphrey's years as vice president, Corcoran often visited him at his suite in the Executive Office Building. According to one White House staffer, "The visits were so frequent that it was damned obvious — to us anyway — that Tom got along with Humphrey. I know I would have

remembered that fact had Humphrey ever gotten to be President."
Corcoran, ever the operator, was always thinking ahead.

There is no evidence that Corcoran ever actually asked the president to
do anything on his behalf, but Corcoran never apologized for having
access to the White House. George Reedy, President Johnson's press secretary, put it well when he described Tommy's lobbying technique: "If
Tommy was going to steal a hot stove, he'd tell you about it, and then
when he went back for the ashes, he would also tell you he was going back
for the ashes."

PART FIVE

The Late Years

25

Lobbying the Court

"Tommy, we cannot discuss this case," Justice Hugo Black said in a stern southern drawl. "I think you should leave. Right away."

The justice stood up from behind his desk and showed his old friend the door. Black was indeed shocked. He and Corcoran had been good friends for nearly forty years, since they had worked together in the Roosevelt administration, but Black thought his friend had gone too far this time. In October 1969, as Corcoran and Black sat together in the justice's office, there was before the Court a petition to rehear the *El Paso Natural Gas* case. Corcoran clearly had come to lobby on behalf of the company.

Black was familiar with the case. El Paso was one of the world's largest gas pipeline ventures, having aggressively built out its distribution lines in the western half of the United States. For several years the company had attempted to merge with the Pacific Northwest Pipeline Company, but it had been blocked by the Justice Department. *El Paso* had been in the federal courts for a dozen years, and it seemed that every prominent lawyer in Washington had made money off the case at some point. Corcoran's rival for the sobriquet of Washington's most influential power broker, Clark Clifford, had represented El Paso and successfully negotiated with the Justice Department the eventual approval for a merger. But under Chief Justice Earl Warren, a liberal, the Supreme Court had subsequently overturned the department's ruling, accusing it of having "knuckled under" in its negotiations. Moreover, the Court ruled that El Paso had established a monopoly and must divest itself of many of its holdings.

The Supreme Court, a gleaming marble structure modeled on a Greek temple, is located across the street from the Capitol building. While lobbyists often crowded the anterooms off the Senate and House chambers, no one had ever come to the Court to lobby a justice on a case as far as Black knew. The mere mention of a pending case at a social event was enough to cause a justice to consider disqualification from further deliberations.

But Corcoran had acted as though he were simply visiting a member of Congress on a routine legislative matter — not violating a sacred tenet of the legal profession.

Corcoran had represented oil and gas interests for years, but he didn't represent El Paso Natural Gas. In fact, Corcoran's only apparent connection to El Paso was through John Sonnett, a good friend who — like so many in Washington — had been a protégé of his at one time. Corcoran had arranged several important jobs for Sonnett in Washington, culminating in his appointment as head of the antitrust division at the Department of Justice during the Truman administration.

Sonnett, in private practice for several years, had died three months before Corcoran's visit to Black. Sonnett had worked on the oil pipeline case for many years and according to Corcoran deeply regretted that he would never see it resolved. Corcoran, in a gesture of postmortem friendship, had decided to raise the issue directly with his friends on the Court. John Lane later observed that it was "typical" of Corcoran, who "would never have raised the issue if it had affected his own client."

Lane may be correct, but it is also possible that Corcoran was acting as an adviser to El Paso even though Sonnett had been the lawyer of record — a device that Corcoran had used over the years to distance himself from his clients and avoid unwanted publicity. Corcoran often engaged in third-party payments: Even though he was not the lawyer of record, he would perform some service, typically talking to someone in a position of decision-making authority, and then receive a fee from the law firm that officially represented the client.

Whatever the case, *El Paso* had been denied a rehearing before the Supreme Court, and Corcoran told Black that the decision was "a great injustice." Black must have been astounded. He and Corcoran had witnessed great injustices over the years: the hunger of destitute families during the Great Depression, the smearing of reputations during the McCarthy era, and now the insanity of the Vietnam War, which Black so vehemently opposed. El Paso was a huge corporate case whose outcome had less to do with justice than with millions of dollars for lawyers, investment bankers, and oil executives. Corcoran told the justice that he only wanted him to read the brief making the argument for the rehearing. Before he had a chance to explain why the justice should read this brief, however, Black ushered him out of the office.

Black then sat back down heavily in his soft leather chair. He decided not to tell the other justices immediately. He needed time to consider whether or not he should withdraw from the case. Black liked Corcoran and had never forgotten how helpful Tommy had been just after his confirmation when it was revealed that he had once been a member of the Klu Klux Klan. Still, Black felt he had paid back Corcoran a few years earlier by accepting his daughter Margaret as one of his law clerks, even though she hadn't been qualified. Black knew that Margaret was having serious problems. In fact, he had mistakenly assumed that this was the reason for Corcoran's visit. When he'd learned the truth, Black felt that Corcoran had tried to take advantage of him. Nevertheless, he didn't want to publicly humiliate his old friend. Corcoran was sixty-nine years old and had developed a reputation as a political fixer, but Black still remembered him as one of the driving forces in the New Deal.

The incident might have ended there and been forgotten had not Corcoran returned to the Court a few days later and dropped in on Justice William Brennan — a 1956 Eisenhower appointee. Brennan and Corcoran were not particularly close friends, but they were pleasant acquaintances, sharing an Irish heritage, and Brennan, by this time a well-established liberal voice on the Court, had long admired Corcoran's public service and accomplishments. When Corcoran requested an appointment, Brennan thought nothing of it. Brennan, like Black, assumed that Corcoran was simply making a social call.

Brennan, a small man with neatly combed gray hair and blue eyes, offered Corcoran a chair. Corcoran made himself comfortable and then, getting right to the point, asked the justice why the Court was determined to ruin El Paso. He told Brennan the same story he'd told Black: His visit had been prompted by the recent death of John Sonnett. As Corcoran explained to Brennan, Sonnett had told him that the Supreme Court had made a grievous error. Tommy felt obligated to his late friend to try to do something about it.

Not only was Brennan unmoved by Corcoran's appeal, he was outraged. He rose from his chair and told Corcoran that he could not discuss a pending case; Corcoran should leave immediately. Tommy smiled, bade Brennan a cheerful farewell and made his exit as breezily as he had come in. Exasperated, Brennan rushed across the hall to tell one of the clerks what had just happened — that Corcoran had put him in an extremely difficult position, and that he might now have to disqualify himself from the case.

Brennan did not want to do so because he actually agreed with Corcoran. He believed that the Court under Warren might have been too zealous in its desire to break up a monopoly. Perhaps in this instance, Brennan thought, a monopoly was preferable to the alternative — a shortage in natural gas. Brennan knew that Rule 58, one of the standing rules of the Supreme Court, required that for the Court to grant a rehearing, one of the remaining members of the previous majority would have to bring up the petition at a conference. Since Earl Warren had been replaced by the more conservative Warren Burger, that left only Justice William O. Douglas, Black, or himself to present the petition.

Brennan decided to raise the issue of Corcoran's visit at the weekly conference when the justices assembled behind closed doors to decide among themselves which cases to hear, or — in the instance of *El Paso* — to rehear. After Chief Justice Burger noted that there was a petition before the Court to rehear *El Paso*, Justice Brennan told his brethren the details of Corcoran's visit. Brennan acknowledged that it had been highly improper, but he argued that, notwithstanding Corcoran's antics, *El Paso* was perhaps deserving of a rehearing. Justice Black offered no opinion. Indeed, he said nothing.

Justice Douglas and Corcoran had not been close friends since the justice's divorce from his first wife, whom Tommy had represented. Moreover, Douglas was a strong antitrust liberal and didn't believe that *El Paso* deserved a rehearing. As Brennan was making the case for reconsideration, Douglas interrupted him. He argued that Sonnett's so-called deathbed appeal had been only a lawyer's regret at having lost a big case. Moreover, the merit of granting a rehearing had now been overshadowed by Corcoran's improper behavior. Douglas knew Corcoran well, and though he didn't reveal it to any of the other justices, he had been lobbied by him previously on an entirely different matter. Douglas told his colleagues that if the Court granted a rehearing, Corcoran would doubtless go around bragging that he had swayed his buddies on the Supreme Court.

Chief Justice Burger wanted the Court to rehear the case. He was annoyed by Corcoran's visit, but he believed it was of little consequence. Justice Black, who had first been visited by Corcoran, still said nothing.

But Douglas had clearly struck a chord with the other justices. Brennan responded, "If that's the way you're going to look at it, I'll remove myself." The matter was left unresolved.

Justice Brennan returned to his chambers, still uncertain as to what he should do. He decided to seek out Justice John Harlan, whom he greatly respected. Harlan, like Brennan, had been appointed by President Eisenhower and was considered a swing vote on the Court. He was aghast at Corcoran's poor judgment, but also slightly amused. He knew Corcoran was forever bending the ears of senators, and given the proximity of the Court to the Senate Office Building, Harlan figured that Tommy had probably lobbied some senator, then found himself with a few minutes to spare and simply walked over. Even though he didn't ascribe sinister intentions to Corcoran's visit, and even though Brennan had thrown the lawyer out of his office before any substantive discussion of the case could take place, Harlan privately believed Brennan should probably recuse himself. But he told Brennan that in the final analysis, each justice had to make his own decisions in such matters.

Brennan remained ambivalent and decided to ask the advice of another colleague, Hugo Black.

Black was sitting at his desk when Justice Brennan dropped by. Brennan looked grave. "Hugo, I have a terrible problem with the El Paso case . . . I fear that the damage has been done." Brennan explained that he knew of Black and Corcoran's friendship, and he wanted to talk over the incident before making any decision about disqualification. Black then made the startling revelation to Brennan that Corcoran had come to see him, too. Brennan was incredulous.

Justice Black knew that Tommy Corcoran was one of the finest lawyers in the city, perhaps in the country, and yet he had not once, but at least twice within one week brazenly violated his profession's code of ethics. Black went home that evening and told his wife, who later wrote in her diary, "Hugo was furious about it, but said he would not let the incident get him out of case."

Justice Brennan, however, had grown more concerned. The following day he told Chief Justice Burger that he intended to disqualify himself. Burger, who had been chief justice only a short time, believed that a majority of the justices would now support a reversal, yet he was concerned that Brennan's recusal would prevent a rehearing. Burger feared that the Court was on the verge of making a grave error because of a silly mistake by Corcoran, along with an arcane rule.

The chief justice decided that the best solution was to change the rules of the Court. So he drafted a revision to Rule 58 that would have allowed for a rehearing to be called for by any sitting member. When Burger circulated his proposed changes to the other justices, however, Douglas objected. Douglas, the most liberal member of the Court, considered the more conservative Burger an intellectual lightweight, and feared that the move was Burger's attempt to consolidate his power. Douglas refused to permit Burger to prevail. He indicated he would dissent in the rehearing and would not only criticize the change in the Court's rules, but would expose publicly Corcoran's unethical lobbying.

Clearly, Burger and Douglas were headed for a showdown. Unwilling to taint the Court with a potential scandal, the chief justice blinked. On June 29, 1970, the Court announced that the petition for an *El Paso* rehearing was denied.

Had Douglas's dissent been made public, Tommy Corcoran, one of the most distinguished and most successful lawyers in Washington for more than forty years, would surely have been disbarred.

26

Plenty of Action

By the late 1960s and early 1970s several of Tommy Corcoran's protégés from the New Deal were practicing law in some of Washington's most prestigious law firms. Corcoran maintained close ties with most of the prominent lawyers in the city, and many referred cases to him that required his special skills.

One such lawyer, Ed Burling, had cofounded the highly respected firm of Covington and Burling. He was also a major shareholder in a tool-and-die company that had a significant contract with the Pentagon for the production of gun barrels. Burling had recommended that the company retain Corcoran after the Department of Defense threatened to file a lawsuit because of defective welds.

One day in early 1970 officers of the company came and briefed Corcoran on the problem for more than an hour. Corcoran listened attentively and asked one or two questions. When the gentlemen had finished their presentation, he said, "Let me make a telephone call."

"Should we leave?" one of the men asked.

"No, no. Stay put." Corcoran picked up the telephone, dialed a number, spoke briefly with someone at the Pentagon, answered a few questions, thanked the person on the other end of the line, and hung up. "It's settled, your problems are over." Corcoran smiled.

A few days later Burling received Corcoran's bill for ten thousand dollars. Even though the company had saved an enormous amount of money thanks to Corcoran, one of the officers who had briefed him was astonished by such boldness: "He made no pretense of doing anything other than that one phone call. If only he had stalked around for a day or two. The impression was that he was putting the company on notice that he could get things done."

Corcoran remained one of the capital's most influential lawyer-lobbyists. He had built a thriving practice with his small firm Corcoran, Foley, Youngman and Rowe. Corcoran consciously modeled the atmospherics of the firm after Cotton and Franklin, the Wall Street law firm where he had worked more than thirty years before. Like Cotton and Franklin, the offices of the Corcoran firm were simple: Instead of original artwork, the walls were adorned with maps of the world and with framed photographs of Lyndon Johnson, Franklin Roosevelt, and Oliver Wendell Holmes. Corcoran's secretary, Frances Behan, was constantly encouraging him to decorate the place, but a fancy office just wasn't important to him. Too, just as Joseph Cotton had provided an element of eccentricity to Cotton and Franklin, the Corcoran firm comprised an unusual cast of characters.

Beyond atmospherics, however, the similarities ended: While Corcoran's firm was superficially styled after the firm where he had begun his legal career, it was fundamentally very different in its approach to the practice of law. Cotton and Franklin included some of the best legal minds and most able technicians on Wall Street. Moreover, Cotton and Franklin actually operated as a firm, with partners sharing in the profits. Corcoran's arrangement with the lawyers in his firm was much less formal.

Corcoran's firm was a hodgepodge of twenty or so lawyers, many of whose careers had crisscrossed his own long professional path. Corcoran was the clear rainmaker in the firm and he — and, to a lesser extent, Jim Rowe — made all the important decisions. The other lawyers, who varied widely in both acumen and ability, had their own arrangements with Corcoran, with some sharing in part of the profits, others simply renting space. "It was extremely loose," according to Robert Perry, who clerked at the firm while attending Georgetown Law School. "Tommy was clearly at the center of everything that happened, and the others — well, we just did our own thing." Sandra Cuneo, the daughter of Ernest Cuneo, the lawyer, journalist, and publisher who joined the Corcoran firm for a few years in the early 1970s, had a somewhat more comical view of her father's firm. She referred to it as "Bat-Haven," because she considered everyone who worked there "so batty."

Indeed, Ernest Cuneo, a brilliant man, was something of an oddity in the white-shoe, buttondown world of Washington law, but he fit right into the Corcoran firm. He weighed nearly 250 pounds, wore a beret to work, and, after a heart attack, sped around the firm's hallways in a motorized cart. Cuneo had been the chairman of the American Newspaper Alliance and was a strong ally of Corcoran during the New

Deal and later in New York. In the Second World War he had been the liaison between the Office of Strategic Services and British intelligence. During this period he came to know a young British intelligence officer named Ian Fleming, who would later credit Cuneo for inspiring the story lines for two of his famous James Bond thrillers: *Goldfinger* and *Thunderball.*

During the 1950s, because he represented United Fruit and the government of Taiwan, Corcoran befriended numerous intelligence officials, including Robert Amory, the deputy director of the Central Intelligence Agency. Amory was Harvard educated and famous for his volubility. According to Thomas Powers, a chronicler of the CIA during this period, Amory's friends hated to see winter coming because "without Amory puttering in the yard, they never knew what was going on in the world." Amory had resigned from the CIA shortly after John McCone became director in 1961. The story told at the CIA was that he flippped on his "squawk box" line to Director McCone one day and discovered that he had been rewired; he got one of McCone's aides instead. Recognizing this as an obvious sign that he would no longer gain admittance to the inner circle of decision makers within the agency, he asked Corcoran for a job. Amory helped Corcoran represent oil interests while also developing his own international clients.

Also with the firm was Joseph Fanelli, a Harvard-educated Italian American from Brooklyn who had not been offered a position with any of the prestigious Manhattan firms after graduation because of his ethnic background. Fanelli was a brilliant lawyer with great technical skill who did most of the traditional legal work performed by the firm. When there was a brief to be filed or document to be drawn up, Fanelli usually handled it.

Then there was George Foulkes, the brother-in-law of Tommy's late wife, Peggy. Foulkes, an aimiable fellow, was unable to find a job in another firm. Most lawyers in the firm never completely understood what it was that Foulkes did all day, and they assumed that Tommy was just taking care of him. There were a few others like Foulkes who simply wandered into the firm. Corcoran invited his young friend John Lane to join the firm on many occasions, but Lane declined; though he admired Corcoran enormously, he had serious reservations about some of the other lawyers there. As he said many years later, "They all had

some purpose — they could do something for Tommy, but most of
them didn't really practice law."

Robert Perry, who had taught the Corcoran children to sail and whom
Tommy had sent to Harvard for a year of postgraduate legal education,
developed his own practice. Perry had worked in both the Manhattan district attorney's office and the U.S. attorney's office in Washington, and
was a skilled litigator. When he returned to the firm in the mid-1960s
Corcoran helped him develop clients, but by the 1970s Perry had more
than enough work to handle on his own. He stayed for five years and then
joined Lane's firm.

Jim Rowe was also a law partner of Corcoran's. Although he did not
have the network or influence of Corcoran, Rowe's résumé was certainly
impressive: law clerk to Oliver Wendell Holmes, administrative assistant
to President Roosevelt, deputy to Attorney General Francis Biddle, chief
of staff to Majority Leader Lyndon Johnson's Democratic Policy
Committee, and adviser to Johnson's successor as majority leader, Mike
Mansfield of Montana.

Rowe, however, had none of Corcoran's skills at self-promotion, and
according to his son James never made much money in private practice.
This was due in part to the fact that Rowe was somewhat selective in the
clients he represented — at least more selective than Corcoran, who occupied the office next to his. Jim Nathanson — who, like Perry, had taught
the Corcoran children to sail while he attended law school — remembered
a revealing incident about Rowe. Rowe had been retained to represent a
union official who had been asked to appear before the Senate Labor
Committee. Rowe accompanied his client to Capitol Hill and sat behind
him as the union leader delivered testimony that was at odds with what
he had told Rowe he would say. Rowe felt his client had used him and had
lied to him. The day after his appearance, Rowe invited the gentleman to
his office, where he first gave him back his money, seventy-five thousand
dollars, and then showed him the door. Corcoran later told Nathanson
that "Jimmy should have kept the money," but as Nathanson later
remembered, Rowe was "the most ethical man I ever met." Rowe also continued to be active politically, and he took on many causes pro bono.

Ben Ivins, a young legal clerk during the first half of the 1970s, compared the Corcoran firm to a universe in which Corcoran was the sun and
the other lawyers orbited him. "Most of the lawyers were probably just

renting space from Tommy, but he rented the whole sixth floor. He liked having a full law library." Corcoran declined retainers except from blue-chip clients such as ATT, Tennessee Gas, or Pan American Airways, each of which paid him somewhere in the vicinity of five thousand dollars a month. Corcoran, as he later wrote, wanted to avoid the "numbers of young associates who needed to be kept busy." He wanted to keep his firm small so that he could "stay involved with all the interesting action."

There was plenty of action. As a result of his work for Civil Air Transport, Corcoran had gained a reputation in the airline industry. Not only did he represent Pan American, but he also represented Belize Airlines, CAVSA (Mexico's airlines), and Trans World Airlines. And he continued to work on behalf of the airline he had helped create: Civil Air Transport. In 1997 the Central Intelligence Agency produced a short history of the 1954 U.S.-sponsored coup in Guatemala in which it identified Corcoran as someone who "calm[ed] bureaucratic waters when an occasional regulator found peculiarities in the airline's activities." In the same document the agency referred to Civil Air Transport as its "proprietary airline."

Corcoran occasionally teamed up with Anna Chennault, who had become a successful lobbyist in her own right. A CIA memorandum from 1971 described a meeting among agency officials, Corcoran, Chennault, and representatives from Northrop Corporation. The purpose of the meeting was to discuss the sale of Air Asia, Ltd., a subsidiary of Air America, to E-Systems of Dallas, a subsidiary of Northrop. Corcoran is described as pushing for the sale, although the meeting was inconclusive. A few years later, in 1975, Chennault attracted some unwanted publicity when it was reported that Northrop had billed the U.S. government $160,000 for consulting fees to Chennault, including more than $11,000 for lavish parties at her house in early 1972, just a few months after the meetings she and Corcoran held with CIA officials and representatives from Northrop. The parties, according to an article in the *Washington Star,* "were attended by corporate executives, foreign officials and some top US military brass." And it was noted that "Chennault is known as a charming lady with close ties to leading American conservatives and right-wing government officials in Asia."

As a result of his work for Sterling Pharmaceutical, Corcoran had gained particular renown as a lobbyist for the pharmaceutical industry.

Dr. Herbert L. Ley, commissioner of the Food and Drug Administration, called Corcoran's firm "the top drug house in town." One of the most important clients was the Pharmaceutical Manufacturers Association, and in the early 1960s Corcoran tried to eviscerate tough legislation being pushed by Senator Estes Kefauver of Tennessee to regulate the industry more actively. Kefauver — Adlai Stevenson's 1956 presidential running mate — had gained a national reputation in his televised investigations of organized crime. He now chaired the Senate Judiciary Committee's powerful antitrust subcommittee.

Kefauver believed that the drug companies not only charged exorbitantly high prices, but were negligent of the public's safety as well. He proposed legislation that would have required stringent labeling standards for over-the-counter drugs. The ranking Republican on the antitrust subcommittee, Everett Dirksen of Illinois, had been elected to the Senate in 1952 and was now the minority leader. Dirksen admired Kefauver, whom he once said was "as single-minded as an Apache Indian" and "as gracious as a Victorian lady." When the interests of business, and particularly the pharmaceutical industry, came before the Senate, Dirksen was one of their most important and effective defenders and did not hesitate to engage Kefauver on the issues.

Tommy had gotten to know Dirksen because the senator was also a vocal supporter of Taiwan and a close friend of Anna Chennault's. Ironically, Corcoran managed to maintain his relationship with Dirksen, the minority leader, while he simultaneously advised his good friend Lyndon Johnson, the majority leader. After Johnson became president, a member of his cabinet once sneered that "Every pressure group in the country has got it on Dirksen," meaning that the minority leader had often accepted favors from lobbyists. Of course, Johnson owed his wealth in large part to the lobbying expertise of Tommy Corcoran.

After Kefauver introduced his legislation to control the excesses of the drug industry, Dirksen worked closely with Corcoran to thwart him. Bob Bennett, then a young legal clerk in Corcoran's office, remembered that Dirksen often telephoned Corcoran in his office, presumably to discuss strategy. Because Corcoran was a well-known Democrat who had gained a reputation as a fixer, Dirksen, hoping to keep their conversations a secret, used to call under an assumed name. "He would call up and say this is Mr. Smith, or something," Bennett recalled many years later. "He had that gravelly voice, so you always knew it was him, and I would have to catch myself from saying, 'Just a minute, Senator Dirksen.'"

Dirksen also had a law practice in Peoria, Illinois. As Dirksen's biographer Neil MacNeil wrote, "The skeptics assumed that the lobbyists and special interests repaid Dirksen's friendship to their cause through the law firm. To have done so would have been at least unethical and probably illegal, and Dirksen categorically denied any such improprieties." It also would have been very difficult to prove. Tommy Corcoran maintained a vast network of legal contacts and could have easily referred business to Dirksen's law firm; he frequently referred clients to other lawyers, often helping, for instance, former New Dealer Ed Prichard through his hard times in Kentucky. According to Bob Perry, "He was constantly farming out work to other firms and other lawyers." Asked whether or not Corcoran sent business to Dirksen, Bobby Baker, secretary to the Senate majority leader during the late 1950s and early 1960s, declared, "There was no doubt about it."

Whatever the relationship between Corcoran and Dirksen, the senator strenuously fought Kefauver in the antitrust subcommittee. MacNeil has written that "little of this struggle was known even around the Senate, for most of it was fought in the relative obscurity of a judiciary subcommittee's closed hearings. There, Dirksen was a master of the dilatory motion, the obfuscating amendment, and the gamesmanship of mustering the extra votes that meant a majority." In other words, Dirksen was enormously skilled in parliamentary procedure and didn't hesitate to use his knowledge to wage battle. In the end Kefauver marshaled his labeling legislation through the Congress, but only after the country was shocked by a scandal in Germany where a drug known as thalidomide was shown to cause deformity in newborns.

Even after Dirksen left the subcommittee in 1962, Corcoran's influence continued. In 1963 the Democrats controlled the Senate, and Senator Phil Hart of Michigan assumed the chairmanship. Hart was a liberal and an individual of enormous integrity whom many considered the conscience of the Senate. He was prepared to take on the pharmaceutical industry, but the committee was stacked with industry friends such as Tom Dodd of Connecticut and Russell Long of Louisiana. Concerned about price fixing in Latin America by U.S. pharmaceutical companies, Hart wanted authority from the subcommittee to issue subpoenas forcing

drug manufacturers to testify. Corcoran convinced Long to join the
Republicans on the committee to kill Hart's motion, fearing another
probe of Sterling. A year later, according to Drew Pearson, Corcoran
thwarted Hart again when he "pulled the right political switches to side-
track an investigation of the drug [P]ercodan."

Corcoran's representation of drug interests wasn't felt only in the halls
of Congress; he actively lobbied the Food and Drug Administration on a
variety of issues. The FDA was created in 1906 largely as a result of Upton
Sinclair's best-selling exposé of the unsanitary conditions in the meat-
packing industry, especially in the Chicago stockyards. Although *The
Jungle* focused on one industry, it gave impetus to the broader legislation,
supported by President Theodore Roosevelt, that created the FDA.

The agency languished until the 1960s, when Commissioner Herbert
Ley adopted an activist approach to regulating over-the-counter drugs.
After studying the evidence, Ley concluded that many companies were
selling ineffective drugs, and he ordered some three hundred of them
removed from the market. As always, Corcoran represented clients with
varying interests, and he crossed swords with Ley on several occasions.

In 1967 Corcoran represented the sugar industry and lobbied Ley to
take cyclamates, or artificial sweeteners, off the market. Corcoran was
partially successful after his client was able to produce evidence that large
amounts of the chemical caused cancer in rats.

Corcoran also represented Bristol-Myers corporation, and when Ley
considered restrictions on the use of the drug Dynapen, a synthetic peni-
cillin antibiotic, Corcoran undertook a full-scale lobbying effort characterized by Ley as "unmerciful." The FDA commissioner complained that
he "received as many as five phone calls a day from Bristol-Myers or its
representatives" and accused Corcoran of lobbying the undersecretary of
health, education, and welfare, Wilbur Cohen, in an attempt to force the
FDA to change its position. When a reporter from the *New York Times*
questioned Corcoran about his lobbying activities, the lawyer cheerfully
brushed aside Ley's criticism: "We didn't hound him. I just went down
there at that time to listen to what it was all about."

In October 1972 Corcoran enticed Rowland Kirks, chief of administra-
tion for U.S. courts and a top aide to U.S. Supreme Court justice Warren
Burger, to meet with the Democratic Speaker of the House, Carl Albert of
Oklahoma, on a bill before the Congress that would have affected the

entire drug industry. Kirks was an old friend of Corcoran's; they had known each other since Kirks served as assistant attorney general in the Truman administration. The legislation in question concerned the legal remedies in a product safety bill, and Corcoran was working on behalf of the industry to narrow liability. He convinced Kirks that any expansion of the legal remedies would encourage additional lawsuits and potentially overburden the courts. Corcoran also sent around letters and memoranda to various congressmen calling for the defeat of the bill and quoting Chief Justice Burger, who had warned against excessive litigation.

The chief justice was furious when he discovered that Corcoran was both invoking his name and lifting quotations from his speeches to lobby Capitol Hill legislators. He immediately issued a statement claiming that no speech of his "can rationally be construed" as taking sides on any consumer bills. But by the time Corcoran had ceased using Burger's name, he had accomplished his goal of limiting liability in the legislation.

Corcoran also continued to "work" Capitol Hill. He had been friends with Senator George Smathers of Florida for a number of years. Smathers, the nephew of Senator William Smathers of New Jersey, had come to the House from Florida in 1947 and later was elected to the Senate after a celebrated campaign against liberal New Dealer Claude Pepper, who, ironically, was also very good friends with Corcoran. Smathers was a staunch supporter of Chiang Kai-shek and benefited on several occasions from campaign contributions handled by Corcoran. Capitalizing on President Kennedy's "Alliance for Progress" to foster improved relations with Latin America, Smathers cooked up a scheme with a friend of his, Eugene McGrath, the head of an insurance company, to build low-cost housing in Panama. The State Department would underwrite an eight-million-dollar housing project in Panama, and Smathers got the ball rolling by inserting an amendment into the 1961 Foreign Assistance Act guaranteeing investments in housing projects in Latin America. A few months later, Smathers suggested that McGrath sit down with Tommy Corcoran and his brother Howard to discuss which construction company might undertake the project. Tommy Corcoran suggested Gilbaine Building, a well-known company in Providence, Rhode Island. Although the Corcoran firm received a twenty-five-thousand-dollar finder's fee, Smather's plan eventually fizzled after a political firestorm in Panama.

◆   ◆   ◆

During this period Corcoran worked closely with another close friend of Lyndon Johnson's, Senator Thomas Dodd of Connecticut, who served on the antitrust subcommittee and was the chairman of the juvenile delinquency subcommittee. When the documents of a client of Corcoran's were subpoenaed, Corcoran delivered them in person to Dodd, and, according to author Joseph Goulden, exacted the extraordinary promise that they would be shown to no one else. Corcoran was grateful; later, when Dodd was in need of help, it was Corcoran who came to his assistance.

In February 1966 Corcoran's friend columnist Drew Pearson, and Pearson's colleague Jack Anderson, wrote a series of columns alleging that Dodd had diverted to his personal use part of the proceeds from four political fund-raising dinners and cocktail parties between 1961 and 1965, and that he performed favors for several corporations in exchange for money raised at testimonial dinners. Dodd was soon under investigation by the Senate Ethics Committee.

Dodd's chief of staff at the time was Bob Perry, who had previously clerked for the Corcoran law firm. Corcoran thought highly of Perry and had gotten him a job with the antitrust subcommittee. Dodd noticed that Perry's memos were extremely well written, and before long the senator had asked him to try his hand at writing speeches. Again, Dodd liked what he saw and asked Perry to come over to his personal office to be his chief of staff.

Perry had been in his new position only a few months when the Pearson-Anderson stories broke. Anderson had received documents from a disgruntled former Dodd staffer, but according to Perry, the charges were "full of distortions." Perry was responsible for gathering information for Dodd's defense, but it was Tommy Corcoran who orchestrated the legal strategy. As Perry put it, "Corcoran helped Dodd because he liked him, and Dodd was happy to have his help."

Corcoran's initial advice was not to turn over any documents to the committee. He had negotiated with congressional investigating committees before and knew it was often possible to strike an advantagous deal. Moreover, he was fully aware that the committee would not subpoena Dodd personally. But the negative publicity continued, and the committee issued subpoenas to banks, insurance companies, and businesses that had had a connection to Senator Dodd. With a full-scale investigation under way, Dodd, at Corcoran's urging, announced on William F. Buckley's television show, *Firing Line,* that he was making all his files available. It was a last-ditch effort to throw himself on the mercy of his colleagues. Ultimately, notwithstanding the strategic maneuvering of Corcoran, Senator Dodd was censured by the Senate, and later defeated for reelection.

Dodd later complained that he should not have listened to Corcoran and regretted that he did not hire a skilled criminal lawyer such as Edward Bennett Williams. However, the manner in which the Dodd scandal developed was just another indication that Capitol Hill was changing. The advent of an ethics committee, even if it was often ineffective, meant that backroom deals were more difficult to achieve, or at least to keep secret.

Part of the change had come about because power was now more diffuse on Capitol Hill. Congressional staffs were increasing in size. Corcoran, who had previously dealt with members directly, was now forced to cultivate staff as well. On several ocassions, for instance, he telephoned James F. Doherty, a staff member of the House Banking and Currency Committee and the brother of William Doherty, then president of the AFL-CIO's American Institute for Free Labor Development. Corcoran would call James and then feign that he'd actually been trying to reach William, but had somehow gotten mixed up. He would apologize, but then interject that since he had James on the phone, he did have a client who would be affected by certain legislation before the committee. According to James Doherty, "I got the idea that he was emphasizing his friendship with my brother in the thought that it would affect what I was doing in the committee. You know, it was amusing for a while. Eventually, though, it wasn't."

Corcoran also hired attorneys from Capitol Hill to "work" their old bosses, a relatively new phenomenon in the 1960s but later an extremely common practice in Washington. On the Democratic side, Corcoran hired Donald J. Cronin, the fomer administrative assistant to Lister Hill, and on the Republican side, Clyde L. Flynn Jr., counsel to Senator Everett Dirksen.

Although by nature a generous man, Corcoran's help for some of Washington's most powerful people sometimes appeared to have an ulterior motive. Through Anna Chennault, Corcoran had become a close friend of Senator John Tower of Texas. Tower was a Republican and a hard drinker. On one occasion Corcoran was dining alone with Anna Chennault at her apartment when the telephone rang. It was the senator, who wanted to speak to Corcoran. He had been arrested for driving under the influence of alcohol and was sitting in the police station. He was worried that if the arrest became public, he would be disgraced. Corcoran excused himself and went to Tower's assistance. Although Chennault never learned how he did it, Corcoran managed to expunge the arrest record and to keep the incident from ever being mentioned in the press.

One possible explanation is that he had help from his late wife's uncle, Michael Dowd. Dowd was the chief dectective for the District of Columbia in charge of Senate security. A large man with black hair, Dowd was a highly decorated and long-standing member of the police force. When in 1954 a Puerto Rican terrorist entered the House chamber and fired shots, Dowd rushed to the scene, wrestled the man to the ground, and disarmed him. According to Corcoran's sons, he and Dowd worked together on various "projects."

As Corcoran's friend John Lane later remarked, "Sure, they were friends, but Tommy had a 'draw' on Tower."

In the decade after her husband's death in 1958, Anna Chennault, guided by Tommy Corcoran, rose to prominence in the nation's capital. She was an astute businesswoman, a Republican Party activist, and one of Washington's most sought-after hostesses, famous for her elegant parties with eight-course dinners and internationally known guests. When she was not entertaining, she and Corcoran were frequently seen together being chauffered about town in her red Cadillac. Corcoran joked, "I was the first man Anna met when she landed and under Formosan law, I'm her guardian. She's quite a handful."

In 1963 Anna Chennault wrote a book about her late husband titled *General Chennault and the Flying Tigers,* which included an introduction by Corcoran. A decade later Anna wrote her autobiography and dedicated it to "all my teachers, and to the best teacher of them all, Thomas G. Corcoran." In many ways Corcoran and Chennault were Washington's first modern power couple. They had extensive contacts on both sides of the political aisle and had both achieved a measure of fame in their own right. They were also very intelligent, rich, and glamorous by Washington standards.

In 1968 Anna moved to a luxurious apartment in the recently opened

Watergate complex overlooking the Potomac River. Although Chennault held title to the $175,000 penthouse, Corcoran appeared before a DC zoning commission with other Watergate apartment owners and claimed that he had purchased the apartment for her. When the Nixon administration rolled into Washington the next year, it became the address for the most well-heeled Republicans, and invitations to her parties were highly coveted. In the late 1960s and early 1970s, Mrs. Chennault entertained frequently and lavishly the likes of National Security Adviser Henry Kissinger, Securities and Exchange Commission chairman William Casey, Attorney General John Mitchell, and the Joint Chiefs of Staff. According to one published report, her guests entered an "oval foyer of white marble" that led "past marble stairs" to "the roof garden and into the unbelievably spacious living-dining room," described by one visitor as "about 40 feet long."

Corcoran was often in attendance and joked on occasion that he served as "the butler." A young senator from Tennessee, Howard Baker, Senator Everett Dirksen's son-in-law, remembered meeting Corcoran at one party: "Corcoran smiled at me, 'It's nice to talk with someone of normal size — to look at one another eye to eye.'" At five foot seven and a half, Baker was about an inch shorter than Corcoran.

Chennault's parties also always contained a smattering of diplomats. She was particularly fond of Chung Il Kwon of South Korea. In her quest to bolster Chiang Kai-shek and his government in Taiwan and to isolate the communist People's Republic of China, Chennault sought alliances wherever she could find them. Both the Chinese Nationalists and the South Koreans confronted communist adversaries in the region, and both governments sought to maintain a continuing American military and economic presence in East Asia.

It was Ambassador Chung who in 1961 had introduced Chennault and Corcoran to a wealthy young Korean named Tongsun Park. He became something of a protégé to both of them. Although virtually unknown in the United States, Park's family was one of the largest petroleum marketers in the Far East. Chennault subsequently invited Park to many of her parties, and he observed that a great deal of business was accomplished at social settings in Washington.

In 1966 Park founded the Georgetown Club with the help of Chennault and Corcoran. In one newspaper article, Park described the club as a meeting place for people in Washington considered to be "outstanding in their field." There were fourteen founding members and 1,109 charter members. Besides Park, Chennault, and Corcoran, other founding members included Louise Gore, a state delegate in Maryland, Georgetown socialite, and cousin of Senator Albert Gore Sr.; Robert Gray, a prominent lobbyist who was an aide in the Eisenhower administration; and Republican senator George Murphy of California.

The club was located on Wisconsin Avenue between a real estate office and a decorating shop. Although the club's exterior was a simple moss-green-painted wooden facade, Park lavishly decorated the inside with English wood paneling, ancient Oriental pottery and jade, Persian carpets, and yellow brocade sofas. The *New York Times* reported that "$650,000 was spent in building and decorating the club." Park frequently invited Mrs. Chennault and Corcoran to parties where he entertained the likes of Vice President Spiro Agnew, Secretary of Defense Melvin Laird, Kissinger, and Minority Leader Gerald Ford. In 1971 Park threw a farewell party for Chennault and for Senator John Tower of Texas, who were toasted by Corcoran before they embarked for Korea, where Chennault was to receive an honorary doctorate.

Years later, it was revealed by the head of the Korean Central Intelligence Agency that the KCIA had helped to finance the club as a way to influence politicians. There is no evidence that either Chennault or Corcoran knew that Tongsun Park was fronting for South Korean intelligence, although both of them had ties to the intelligence community. Corcoran's links to the world of espionage went all the way back to the Second World War when, as his friend Ernest Cuneo somewhat hyperbolically described it, Corcoran "head[ed] FDR's informal intelligence service and international spy operations long before there was an OSS." For her part, Chennault's advocacy for Taiwan appears to have brought her into close contact with the CIA. In a letter to Corcoran that she wrote from Hong Kong on August 10, 1966, Chennault revealed that her activities had "made the Agency very unhappy," and she referred somewhat mysteriously to her "US connection."

As the cameras clicked and the flashbulbs flashed, Tongsun Park took his seat at the witness table. The day before, Park had been arraigned on a thirty-six-count federal indictment involving alleged influence buying on behalf of the government of South Korea. The main allegations were that Park had been Seoul's principal agent in a six-year-long secret lobbying effort that provided nearly a million dollars a year in gifts, entertainment, and other favors to members of Congress.

When Park's role was uncovered by the FBI in 1976, he fled to London. Several months later he traveled to Seoul and negotiated a grant of immunity with U.S. prosecutors in return for his testimony to Congress. The question that U.S. authorities wanted answered was how a relatively obscure Korean businessman could achieve such social standing and influence in Washington. The answer, in part, was that he had learned his trade from Tommy Corcoran, who acknowledged that "Tongsun couldn't have done what he did without tremendous backing."

When Park was arrested, Corcoran, tongue in his cheek, said, "I always assumed he asked me to his parties because I play the piano." Corcoran then elaborated: "I'm not Tongsun Park's lawyer. I'm his piano player. He had the best piano in Washington." But Tommy laughingly confessed that Park called him "Papa Tom," and it was later revealed that he gave Park entrée into Washington officialdom at the highest level. When South Korean president Park Chun Hee was meeting with President Johnson at Blair House in 1965, Corcoran and Park dropped by unannounced. The two presidents, who had been chatting through an interpreter, took time out from the state visit to shake hands with Park, and Corcoran arranged to have the young Korean businessman's picture taken with the two presidents — a valuable calling card for Park in both the United States and back in Korea.

Corcoran knew that Park was making a fortune in exporting rice from the United States to Korea. When asked about Park's business ventures by a reporter, Corcoran only acknowledged, "I knew somehow that all this rice was going through Tongsun to Korea." The Food For Peace program, commonly referred to in Washington as PL480, required food surpluses, of which rice was a major component, to be sold abroad to developing countries such as South Korea at discount prices as a form of foreign assistance. The surpluses were huge, and some middlemen made significant profits. Much of the rice was grown in Louisiana; Corcoran had strong ties to the state through the Chennaults and his numerous Texas and Louisiana political contacts, including members of the Boggs family. Tommy Boggs, the son of former Speaker of the House Hale Boggs and himself one of the powerful lobbyists in Washingon today, speculated that "Corcoran probably had a piece of some of those rice deals that Tongsun was involved in." Boggs's supposition is more than likely correct because Corcoran had never fogotten what Joseph Cotton had told him about how to how to get rich as a lawyer: You needed more than just lawyer's fees; you needed a piece of the deal.

Wednesday, January 16, 1974, was a raw day. Though no snow lay on the ground, typical of Washington there was a cold, gray sky and biting wind. Inside the Corcoran law firm on K Street, the partners filed into Tommy's office. Some sat on the couch, while others brought in chairs from the lobby area. Jim Rowe began the meeting by announcing that the firm was spending an enormous amount of money on overhead that could not be justified given the revenues. Either the firm would have to cut back or the partners would have to contribute more, and he strongly favored the for-mer course of action. Jim Meers, another of the partners, heartily agreed and made the case that many of the services provided by the firm were not needed. Rowe and Meers proposed cutting many of the library serv-ices and letting go of all the clerks, including the bookkeepers. In their view, only the secretaries should remain on the payroll.

Corcoran sat behind his desk and listened attentively for a few min-utes. Then he interrupted Meers and said that while he would support some scaling back, he couldn't support everything that Rowe and Meers were suggesting. Corcoran picked up the black rotary telephone, dialed a number, and began talking with someone.

All the partners agreed with Rowe and Meers, except Fanelli and Perry, the two lawyers who had the most traditional practices. Both Fanelli and Perry used their clerks to conduct legal research, and for a scholar such as Fanelli, the library was essential.

After about fifteen minutes Corcoran, who had been on the telephone for at least half the meeting, stood up and said that he was sorry, but he had an appointment. He would not be back for the rest of the day, he went on, or the next day, but he would be available on Friday if anyone wanted to discuss the matter further. Then he left and went downstairs to the barbershop, where he had a haircut and his daily facial massage.

The discussion among the other partners lasted for another twenty minutes or so. Near the end of the meeting, Rowe blurted out that during the last year Corcoran had personally subsidized the office with more than $250,000. Corcoran was carrying the other partners, and everyone knew it. Perry scribbled on a notepad that "the entire meeting is academic because TC will do what he wants."

27

Vietnam, Watergate, and Nixon

John Kelly was driving Tommy Corcoran from a meeting on Capitol Hill
when they were suddenly halted by a traffic jam on Pennsylvania Avenue
not far from the entrance to the Department of Justice. An antiwar demon-
stration was under way on the National Mall, and a number of longhaired
demonstrators were crossing the street. As they sat stalled in the car,
Corcoran turned to Kelly and asked scornfully, "What is your generation
trying to do to this country?" Kelly, a Georgetown law student at the time,
was ambivalent about the war and half jokingly replied to his mentor,
"Wait a second — back in the 1930s you were accused of being a socialist."

Corcoran was "all for the Vietnam War," his son Tim has remembered.
The former New Dealer supported American involvement in Southeast Asia
for a number of reasons. First, Corcoran was sympathetic to the plight of
Roman Catholics in Vietnam. Similar to the position he had taken with
FDR regarding the Spanish Civil War, he believed that Catholics in Vietnam
would be persecuted under a communist regime. Indeed, when the French
lost Dien Bien Phu in 1954 and the Vietcong overran the north, hundreds of
thousands of Catholics fled to the south. Claire Chennault's airline, Civil
Air Transport — which Corcoran had helped establish — worked with the
CIA to transport thousands of refugees to the south and to ferry arms, supplies, and personnel to the north. As the battlefield in Vietnam shifted to
the southern part of the nation, Ngo Dinh Diem, a prominent Catholic
leader as well as the president, pleaded for U.S. assistance. Corcoran felt that
the United States had a moral obligation to protect Catholics from the
encroaching communist threat.

Corcoran's views on Vietnam were also undoubtedly influenced by the
Guatemalan coup of 1954. He believed in the fundamental moral goodness of the United States and that America must play a role in transfer-
ring democratic values to the developing world.

Corcoran was probably swayed by the Chennaults, who had worked to
shape United States policy toward China. General Chennault had fervently
believed that the United States had made a great mistake in abandoning

Chiang Kai-shek, and that ultimately it had been myopic foreign policy "experts" who had "lost China." Corcoran did not want to see the example of China repeated throughout Southeast Asia.

During this period Corcoran was also seeing a great deal of Anna Chennault, who was passionately anticommunist. Together they had played a significant role in the U.S. government's support for the Nationalist government of Chiang Kai-shek during the 1950s and 1960s. Through her activities on behalf of Taiwan, Chennault had developed a close affiliation with the Republican Party and counted Senators Everett Dirksen and John Tower among her closest friends. In 1968 Chennault was an official of the Nixon campaign and very close to its chairman, John Mitchell, Nixon's law partner and confidant. Chennault claimed that she and Mitchell talked at least once a day.

By the spring of 1968 the United States had nearly half a million troops committed to the war in Vietnam, which was costing nearly $2.5 billion a month. Eleven thousand Americans had been killed in 1967. As the U.S. continued to suffer nearly a thousand casualties a month, a Gallup Poll found that 49 percent of the American public disapproved of the way in which President Johnson was handling the war. Indeed, Eugene McCarthy, a little-known senator from Minnesota, was electrifying college campuses in his insurgent challenge to Johnson for the presidency.

On March 31 President Lyndon Johnson stunned the nation by announcing that he would not run for reelection and was implementing a partial bombing halt. The next month Johnson's secretary of defense, Clark Clifford, persuaded him to enter negotiations with the North Vietnamese to end the war; after several false starts, the North Vietnamese government sent word on May 3 that it would dispatch negotiators to Paris to meet with American and South Vietnamese representatives. For the first time during his administration, a skeptical and beleaguered president saw the possibility for peace.

Two months after the negotiations began, on July 12, Anna Chennault accompanied John Mitchell and the South Vietnamese ambassador, Bui Diem, to New York City to meet with Republican candidate Richard Nixon, the likely nominee of his party. During the meeting Nixon made it clear that he hoped to use Chennault as his emissary to President Thieu of South Vietnam. In his book on Nixon's foreign policy, William Bundy described what an extraordinary and unprecedented arrangement Nixon had encouraged. "The opposition party's candidate for President," wrote Bundy, "was setting up a special two-way private channel to the head of state of a government with whom the incumbent president was conducting incredibly important and secret negotiations!"

For several weeks during the summer of 1968, Chennault acted as an intermediary between the Nixon campaign and the South Vietnamese government. She actually visited President Thieu in South Vietnam, and she was in constant contact with Ambassador Diem, all the while making John Mitchell aware of her discussions.

On July 31 Anna Chennault and Tommy Corcoran were at a party being given by Washington socialite Perle Mesta at the Sheraton Park Hotel. Just before dinner, Mesta turned on the television to listen to an important address by President Johnson, who declared that he had ordered a bombing halt of North Vietnam, effective immediately. The guests sat down to dinner and discussed the president's stunning announcement. As they were finishing dessert, Chennault was called to the telephone. It was John Mitchell. He asked her to call him back from a more private telephone. As it happened, Tommy's brother David had a suite in the same hotel. David was out of town on business, but Tommy had a key to his apartment, and he let Anna inside. According to Chennault, "I had a sense of needing moral support, or a witness, or both." For his part, Corcoran, who had himself been wiretapped by the FBI nearly two decades previously, may have suspected that someone was tapping Mitchell's calls. In any event, with Tommy listening in on a phone in an adjacent room and taking notes, Chennault returned Mitchell's call. "Anna," Mitchell said in gravely serious tone, "I'm speaking on behalf of Mr. Nixon. It's very important that our South Vietnamese friends understand our Republican position and I hope you have made this clear to them." Chennault knew exactly what Mitchell was talking about: The South Vietnamese should continue to resist peace negotiations. Chennault later claimed that she responded: "Look John, all I've done is to relay messages. If you are talking about direct influence, I have to tell you it isn't wise for us to try to influence the South Vietnamese. Their actions have to follow their own national interests, and I'm sure that is what will dictate Thieu's decision."

Chennault's recollection of her reply to Mitchell sounds stilted and legalistic, probably because she was being advised by Corcoran, who was after all listening on another telephone and may have worried that she would say something that could get her into serious trouble. Bundy characterized Chennault's assertion as "at best a quibble. . . . She may have avoided direct appeals, but her message [to Thieu] was hardly subtle or obscure." Bundy is de facto correct, but Corcoran understood that anything Anna said had potential legal import. Corcoran was wary of being wiretapped, and he knew that the Logan Act forbade a private citizen to engage in negotiations with a foreign government.

President Johnson eventually learned of Anna's activities. According to Bundy, the president and his closest advisers, after realizing that Thieu was being somewhat more reticent and devious in his objections to negotiations, "received a report that shook them." Bundy wrote, "Almost certainly it was based on the deciphered and translated texts of one or more intercepted cables from the South Vietnamese Embassy in Washington," which was under surveillance at the time. While Bundy is undoubtedly correct, Anna Chennault has offered a far simpler and equally plausible explanation as to how the president and his advisers may have come by the information: "Tommy told them." Certainly Corcoran, who had been a Johnson loyalist for more than thirty years, might have contacted the president directly, or perhaps he told his law partner and close friend Jim Rowe, who was effectively running Vice President Humphrey's presidential campaign and had previously been a top adviser to the president. Tommy was sympathetic to the defense of South Vietnam, but as his son Tim pointed out, he "supported Humphrey over Nixon." In any event, on October 30, President Johnson ordered the FBI to conduct "physical and electronic surveillance" of Anna Chennault.

Nixon defeated Humphrey for the presidency in November by the slimmest of margins, with Governor George Wallace of Alabama running as an independent and finishing a strong third. After the election, rumors circulated about Chennault's secret role in the campaign. The *Washington Star* reported that Chennault had referred all inquiries to Attorney General John Mitchell and Senator John Tower, both of whom vehemently denied that she had played any covert role. But fearing that the rumors might gain traction with members of the press and lead to a humiliating public exposure of the campaign's liaison with the South Vietnamese government, Nixon and his advisers shunned Chennault.

Even though Chennault had been an official in the campaign and had

raised an enormous amount of money, she was not asked to play any significant role in the Nixon administration. Corcoran later complained,
"People have used Anna scandalously, Nixon in particular. I know exactly
what Nixon said to her. But Anna said nothing; she kept her mouth
shut." And so did Corcoran.

Chennault and Corcoran also felt that Nixon betrayed them on the
issue of Taiwan. The efforts of the China lobby over the previous three
decades had succeeded in discouraging many nations from entering into
diplomatic relations with Beijing and had been critical in denying the
Chinese government first membership in the United Nations, and later a
permanent seat on the UN Security Council. After Nixon became president, the Taiwanese were replaced by the People's Republic on the council.

Adopting the slogan "Peace with honor," Nixon continued American
military involvement in Vietnam. But the nation was growing weary of
the war: Every evening the American people viewed images on television
of young soldiers wounded and dead on a battlefield ten thousand miles
away from home. Across the country the fabric of American society
seemed to be tearing: Young people differed with their parents over the
war; college campuses erupted into scenes of protest and sometimes vio-
lence; a counterculture movement introduced a new era of flamboyant
dress and music and new, mind-altering drugs. Tommy Corcoran, once a
New Deal firebrand, had nevertheless always worked within the system to
change it, and he could not understand and would not accept the challenge to American institutions. Even more tragically, he did not seem to
understand how the times were affecting his own family.

Tommy had always doted on his daughter Margaret. However, Margaret
and her mother, Peggy, had never gotten along. "They used to have terrible screaming matches," recalled one friend. "I think it was very tough on
Tommy, who loved them both." After Peggy died, Margaret became even
more central to Tommy's life.

Margaret, according to one of Corcoran's law partners, was "cute as a
button." She was also extremely bright, graduating as valedictorian at the
exclusive Holton-Arms School just outside Washington, DC. Margaret
went on to Radcliffe College, where she continued to excel academically,
graduating cum laude in 1962. During the summers, Tommy arranged

challenging jobs for her. One summer she worked as an intern for the Senate Judiciary Committee. A friend of her father's, Carlisle Bolton-Smith, remembered seeing her in the Senate dressed in a kind of cream-colored party dress. She looked like "a frothy little thing," Bolton-Smith later said, but she was "handling serious and complicated issues." Her brother Tim recalled that she had "many of the same qualities as Dad: She was very intelligent and she could read something once and remember it line for line for a couple of weeks." Following in the footsteps of her father, she was accepted to Harvard Law School.

But there was another side to this beautiful and intelligent young woman. During college and then in law school, her behavior became increasingly erratic. Her brother observed that "she would party all year and then a few days before her exams she would study." Like her mother, she had started to drink. Friends and family began to worry she was drinking excessively and that her moods were becoming darker. Ben Cohen once expressed to John Lane that Tommy needed to get help for Margaret. Indeed, things got so bad that the family doctor, Dr. Theodore Abernathy, suggested to Tommy that he have Margaret committed to a psychiatric hospital.

Tommy did try to watch over Margaret by sending Robert Bennett, one of his most able legal clerks, to Harvard Law School for a year to earn his master of law degree. Bennett, who had transferred from the University of Virginia Law School to Georgetown Law School, had an aunt in Washington who was friendly with Corcoran's brother Howard. She'd helped arrange a clerkship for her nephew in the Corcoran firm, where young Bob immediately caught the eye of Tommy Corcoran. After clerking for three years, full time during the summer and part time during the school year, Tommy offered to pay for a year of study at Harvard. "I think in the back of his mind he was hoping that I would look after Margaret," Bennett recalled.

In the early 1960s Harvard Law School was an overwhelmingly male-dominated institution. Of the five hundred students in Margaret's class, only about twenty-five were female. Some professors held women's day, when they would only call on female students. Because she was bright, pretty, and vivacious, Margaret had plenty of suitors. Although they were never romantically involved, Bennett did "date" Margaret from time to time. He enjoyed her company. He found her intelligent and glamorous, the only young woman he knew who wore a fur coat. Still, Bennett also sensed a sadness and fragility about Margaret.

Tommy pushed Margaret to succeed. He helped her with her term papers during the holidays, often taking her into his office so that she could use the law library and the typewriter. On one occasion Margaret had to write a paper on constitutional law. Tommy arranged for her to interview his old friend Supreme Court justice Hugo Black at his home. One lawyer in the firm later recalled his astonishment at the time: "Did you ever hear of such a thing in law school?"

In 1967 Tommy helped his daughter secure a clerkship on the Supreme Court with Justice Black. She became the first female to clerk on the Court. According to one of her contemporaries, "She was not even one of the best students in the class — her father just arranged it." Nevertheless, Tommy was extraordinarily proud of her, but also seemed to have little understanding of the pressure she was under and of the personal demons that continued to haunt her.

Margaret did well for a few months. She arrived early at the Court and worked diligently. Black, according to one of his other clerks, "was very hardworking. He wanted his views on matters to be plainly and clearly stated. There was no room for ambiguity." While Black demanded that his clerks' scholarship be exacting, the justice was also very fatherly, often dining with his assistants in the Court's public cafeteria.

One Friday in the spring of 1967, Black asked Margaret to review thirty-five certiorari petitions over the weekend. According to Black's wife, Elizabeth, the justice came home distraught because Margaret "flew off the handle" and said she couldn't work all weekend because "she had to go to parties with her Daddy." Elizabeth Black adored Tommy, but felt badly that when asked, she had encouraged her husband to take on Margaret Corcoran as a clerk. She knew how "disappointed" Hugo was in his young clerk, but that he would never say anything to his old friend. That night Tommy Corcoran did not go to a party with his daughter but came over to the Blacks' house after dinner. Elizabeth Black wrote in her diary that Tommy talked about "how young people won't work now; they have too many choices." The justice's wife, a wise and sensitive woman, believed Tommy was apologizing "for Margaret without ever mentioning her name or seeming to refer to her at all."

If Tommy sensed Margaret's mounting anxiety, he seemed bewildered as to how to deal with it. He bought her a Mercedes-Benz sports car. Once accused of ghost-writing Justice Black's opinions, he tried to help his daughter by assisting her in writing legal briefs for the justice. One of her friends from law school recalled that he never really believed that "Margaret had ever wanted to go to law school or had any desire ever to practice law." "I think she was confused," said her brother Tim, "because she was given a male role."

Friends begged Corcoran to seek professional help for his daughter. But Corcoran couldn't bring himself to take the step. "I hate to say it, but I don't think he wanted to create a record for the family," said Tim. Tommy tried to help Margaret get away from her problems by sending her on trips to the Far East with Anna Chennault. But Margaret could not run away from her problems. On January 9, 1970, Margaret Josephine Corcoran, only twenty-eight years old, died at her home from an overdose of sleeping pills. It was reported to be an accident, and the funeral, attended only by family, was arranged hastily. According to Tim, his father's "star died on him."

On December 29, 1970, Tommy Corcoran turned seventy. His friends, sensing his continuing despondency over his daughter's death, and wanting to honor him for his years of public service, threw him a big birthday bash. Invitations were sent out by Justice Stanley Reed and John Lord O'Brien to attend a dinner at the Federal City Club in the Sheraton Carlton Hotel. The invitation stipulated that it was black tie and male only. William Campbell, a federal judge in Chicago who had sometimes acted as an intermediary between Corcoran and Cardinal Mundelein, was designated the toastmaster. Guests were cautioned that toasts were to be short and to the point so that the honoree would have time to speak. Jim Rowe called Justice Hugo Black and asked him to make a speech, but Black was still angry about Corcoran's behavior in the *El Paso* case in late 1969 when the lawyer had come to his chambers at the Court and directly lobbied him. As if searching for an excuse not to attend, he also reminded Rowe that the party was the same night as President Nixon's State of the Union address and that he would have to be at the Capitol. Rowe nevertheless asked him to come for a short time.

On January 22, 1971, Washington's luminaries came to honor Tommy Corcoran. Ben Cohen was there, of course. So was Jim Rowe. Hugo Black, prodded by his wife, appeared briefly, but did not speak even though he had been scheduled to do so. Joe Rauh, John Lane, Clark Clifford, Edward Bennett Williams, Justice Bill Douglas, Senators Wayne Morse, Claiborne Pell, and Henry Jackson, and many others came. Tommy was disappointed that I. F. Stone, who had been invited and with whom he had had something of a falling-out, didn't come. Nonetheless, he was in an ebullient mood.

The guests sat down to dinner at eight o'clock, and Judge Campbell called on a number of friends who told stories and sang Tommy's praises. Judge Campbell read a letter from former president Johnson in which he recalled how thirty-five years before, Corcoran had kept "a kindly eye on that country boy from Texas." The most poignant of the evening's tributes came from Ben Cohen. Slightly stooped and in the halting and raspy voice that had been his trademark for forty years, Ben began, "I think we may count the New Deal years among the best years of his life." After describing Tommy's many accomplishments in the New Deal, Ben mused about Tommy's transformation into a powerful Washington lobbyist: "Now his enemies pretend to take seriously his sputterings about power as if he were only concerned with power for power's sake, rather than for the vindication of the humanistic values of life which he cherishes and esteems beyond their ken." Cohen concluded his remarks by saying, "There never has been a better esprit de corps in government than that inspired by Tom in the New Deal years."

During the entire speech, Corcoran sat with his head cocked and a tight smile across his face. "He had a wonderful time, just loved it," remembered Tommy's oldest son, Tim.

As the waiters began to clear the dessert dishes, Judge Campbell called on Tommy to say a few words. Joe Rauh remembered that Tommy "got up to make a speech and one of the first things he said was that he represented one of the largest oil pipeline companies in the country." Rauh, who claimed that "at one time I would have carried his briefcase," looked over to Senator Wayne Morse, who sat quietly shaking his head. Rauh recalled his own disappointment as he later confessed that the thought of this once brilliant, crusading lawyer now bragging about his corporate clients "made me sick."

But Corcoran's law partner Robert Perry had another memory of the evening. "Tommy got up and said, 'Everybody criticizes me for the way I conduct my law firm, for my clients, for the way I conduct my life. I do it that way because I like it that way.'" For Perry, and many others in the room, it was vintage Corcoran — he was fearless and genuine, and lived by his own standards and no one else's.

A few months after his birthday party, in May 1971, Tommy attended the funeral of Peggy's cousin, Michael Dowd, the much-decorated police detective who had become his close friend. Maureen Dowd, Michael's nineteen-year-old daughter and a sophomore at Catholic University, was working as a clerk in Corcoran's law office. Although she was not in training to be a lawyer, she sat with the other law clerks and occasionally operated the switchboard. ("You got the sense he could get it done with just one call," she recalled years later.) She was an extremely attractive young woman with reddish brown hair and green eyes.

After the service at the grave site, Tommy asked Maureen if she would like a ride with him back to her mother's house, where there was a reception for those attending the funeral. Maureen agreed and climbed into the limousine next to Corcoran. As they were being driven to the Dowd family home in Chevy Chase, Maryland, Corcoran told her that he wanted to adopt her. Dowd was stunned. Corcoran said that he wanted her to have the finest education possible and that he would arrange for her to transfer from Catholic University to Smith, the exclusive women's college in Northampton, Massachusetts. He told her that he would take care of all her expenses — that he had given his daughter Margaret a credit card when she was in college and he would do the same for her.

Dowd recalled, "He was serious and he hit with this at a very emotional time. Of course it would have meant a very dramatic change in my life. I didn't come from a wealthy background and Smith was a wonderful college. I half thought about it in the sense that I thought of it as a kind of scholarship. I think he thought I was going to take Margaret's place." When they got to the house on Legation Street, Corcoran raised the issue with Dowd's mother, also named Peggy. Peggy Dowd, grieving over the loss of her husband, looked at Corcoran in horror. As she remembered many years later, "I said nothing flat. No way." She dismissed Tommy to attend to her other guests.

Tommy Corcoran had met John Connally even before he met Lyndon Johnson. Corcoran was first introduced to Connally when the future

Lone Star governor was working for the RFC in Texas in the early 1930s. Connally eventually came to work for LBJ in Washington, where he and Corcoran saw each other often. Connally ultimately left Johnson to seek political office himself, becoming governor of Texas in 1962. He served for two terms and gained national fame when he was wounded in the assassination of President Kennedy in Dallas in 1963. Connally remained governor during the Johnson presidency, but grew increasingly conservative and closer to the Republican Party. Richard Nixon briefly considered him for a spot on the 1968 ticket, ultimately deciding it was too risky to run with a Democrat. But Nixon continued to view Connally as one of the most talented political figures in America, and in 1971 appointed him secretary of the Treasury.

Among Nixon and Connally's biggest supporters were the Hunt brothers of Texas, Nelson and Bunker. In 1973 the Hunt brothers were under investigation by the Department of Justice for attempting to corner the silver market. John Tower, the Republican senator from Texas and an adversary of Connally, quietly tried to help the Hunts. Corcoran, close to Tower, kept Connally informed of Tower's efforts. Connally had gotten to know the brothers through their father, the multimillionaire oil baron H. L. Hunt, whom he had first encountered during the 1960 campaign when the ultraconservative poured money into Lyndon Johnson's presidential campaign.

Corcoran, who still had good contacts in the Department of Justice, obtained transcripts of wiretaps and wrote a memorandum to Connally providing an analysis of the Justice Department's potential case. He alerted the former Treasury secretary that the evidence against the Hunt brothers was serious and action was imminent. After the Hunts were indicted, Corcoran reported somewhat cryptically to Connally, "Senator Tower's people got there last night — too late."

Corcoran was convinced that Nixon was grooming Connally for the presidency. Indeed, Connally had supported Nixon openly in 1972 and had organized Democrats for Nixon during the general election. Nixon had briefly considered replacing his ineffectual vice president, Spiro Agnew, with Connally on the national ticket. In his memoirs, Nixon wrote, "I believed John Connally was the only man in either party who clearly had the potential to be a great president. He had the necessary 'fire in the belly,' the energy to win, and the vision to lead." Connally, however, believed he needed to more firmly establish his Republican credentials to have credibility as a national candidate of the party. Corcoran told a friend that Nixon ultimately acquiesced but set in motion a plan to make Connally the next secretary of state. Corcoran believed that after the second Russian summit with Premier Brezhnev, both National Security Adviser Henry Kissinger and Secretary of State William Rogers would leave the government and Connally would become the nation's top diplomat. Rogers did leave the government, but the ambitious Kissinger, at Nixon's request, added the role of secretary of state to his portfolio, thereby postponing Connally's return to government. The events of the Watergate scandal ultimately overtook Nixon and destroyed his presidency; John Connally, athough not directly involved in the scandal, nevertheless suffered as a result of his association with Nixon.

On July 29, 1974 — only one week before President Nixon would resign from office — John Connally was indicted for taking a ten-thousand-dollar bribe from a Texan named Jake Jacobsen and then lying to a grand jury about it. Connally retained the esteemed Washington criminal lawyer Edward Bennett Williams, also a friend of Corcoran's. Corcoran greatly admired William's courtroom skills and had on more than one occasion been spotted in the front row of the Supreme Court listening to Williams argue a case.

In early August Williams accompanied Connally to the federal courthouse in Washington, DC, where the Texan was fingerprinted and arraigned before Judge George Hart, a Nixon appointee and another of Tommy Corcoran's friends. Indeed, Corcoran was a friend of nearly everyone involved in the case: the defendant, the defense attorney, and the judge.

For the next several weeks Williams engaged in pretrial conferences with Judge Hart while Williams's firm filed a flood of pretrial motions. The attorney's strategy was clear: He was doing everything in his power to delay the trial in order to distance Connally as much as possible from the Watergate scandal.

One day several weeks before the trial was scheduled to begin, Corcoran went to the courthouse to see his son Tim, who was then an assistant U.S. attorney and worked on the third floor of the building. Tommy told his son that he wanted to pay a visit to Judge Hart. Tim walked with his father upstairs to the floor where the federal court judges had their offices. "It was a sort of murderer's row, with Uncle Howard at one end, then Judge Gasch who Daddy had helped get on the bench, and then Hart. Judge Hart and Dad had known each other for a number of years." Tim had tried a few civil cases before Judge Hart and assumed that his father was only making a social call. Undoubtedly, Judge Hart was under the same impression.

The Corcorans were shown into the judge's chambers. After sitting down opposite Hart, Tommy, according to his son, told the judge in "a very ebullient fashion" that "John Connally was a good friend of his and that he was going to attend the trial every day."

Hart smiled and said, "Tommy, I can't stop you from doing that, but please don't discuss the Connally case anymore because your visit here could be a problem." Tim was flabbergasted: "I couldn't have been more embarrassed." After exchanging a few bland pleasantries, the Corcorans left the chambers.

On April Fool's Day, 1975, the trial of former governor John Connally began. Connally climbed the steps of the courthouse looking svelte and stylish, dressed in a pin-striped suit and wearing a gray homburg. He was followed by his wife, Nellie, his son John, and Tommy Corcoran. As Connally's biographer noted of Corcoran's appearance, it "was as though the defendant wanted to display the high level of his friendships." As far as Corcoran was concerned, the man who always liked to work behind the scenes was only too happy to lend his prestige to his friend. For Corcoran, it was a matter of loyalty.

The prosecution put on a strong circumstantial case with bank records that supported its key witness, Jake Jacobsen. The records clearly showed that Connally had made and then withdrawn deposits of money both before and after his meetings with Jacobsen. Corcoran then watched Edward Bennett Williams put on a masterly defense. First he shattered the prosecution's case by his withering cross-examination of Jacobsen. Jacobsen had testified that he had worn rubber gloves and then counted out ten thousand dollars in small bills, which Connally had placed in a safe. But Jacobsen could not remember the color of the gloves; nor could he remember if he had worn one glove or two. He reckoned it was two gloves because that seemed more logical. In other words, Williams observed, Jacobsen was giving testimony not on the basis of memory, but on what logically might have happened.

With Corcoran sitting in the front row, Williams paraded a host of character witnesses on behalf of Connally in front of the jury. Corcoran's partner James Rowe testified, as did Congresswoman Barbara Jordan, a Texas Democrat who on the surface seemed to have very little in common with Connally, but who attested to his high moral character. Lady Bird Johnson also took the witness stand, telling the court, "Some folks don't like him, but I don't think any of them doubt his integrity." The evangelist preacher Billy Graham lent his support, identifying himself to the jury as someone "busy preaching the gospel of Jesus Christ all over the world."

In his summation, Williams was eloquent, labeling Connally's accuser a "self-confessed habitual liar" and ending with the plea that "what you do in that jury room will place an indelible mark on John B. Connally for the rest of his life." The jurors seemed to be mesmerized by Williams, and after a short deliberation voted to acquit Connally. Corcoran, quoted in a magazine article a few weeks after the trial, called Williams's performance "Pure opera, boy."

Watergate and the movement for reform that came on its heels changed the lobbying profession in Washington. The election of 1974 brought to Congress a wave of newly elected members who were not content to do business as usual. No longer would a few dozen members of Congress decide the outcome of most issues. In many respects the caste-ridden seniority system was scrapped, creating an even greater diffusion of power. Moreover, there was an explosion in the number of issues that were being decided in Washington — and with it came a corresponding increase in the number of staff. The feeling that "everyone knew everyone" was waning.

28

The Admiral

"If he shows up, throw Rickover's ass out of the yard," Nelson Freeman, the chairman of Tenneco, yelled as he slammed his fist on the table. Admiral Hyman Rickover, recognized as the father of the modern submarine navy, wanted his missile frigates, and when the Newport News Shipyard, a subsidiary of Tenneco, failed to deliver them, he ordered members of his staff to go to the shipyard and investigate the delay. Freeman, however, was not about to have Rickover's "spies" prowling around his shipyard.

Well before he made Freeman angry, Rickover had been locking horns with officials in the Department of Defense over the construction of five missile frigates, which he believed were critical to the U.S. naval fleet. Rickover had argued that on a per-ship basis, taking into account the economies of scale, it was cheaper to build five frigates than the three ships that the Department of Defense had authorized. In the end the admiral's negotiating team prevailed, gaining a fixed-price contract for three ships with an option to build two more. The Pentagon chose to award the contract to the Newport News Shipyard.

Newport News, the giant shipbuilding company at the mouth of Chesapeake Bay, was one of the oldest shipyards in the country. It delivered the first of the frigates, christened *California,* in February 1974, almost eighteen months late. The second ship, *South Carolina,* wasn't completed for almost another year, nearly twenty months late. Rickover knew the delays were not only costing money but also hindering chances that the additional two ships would ever be built. He was furious, and well before delivery of the second ship he sent representatives to find out what the problems were at Newport News.

Freeman then contacted Tommy Corcoran, who arranged for a meeting between Freeman and the navy's top brass, including Elmo Zumwalt, the chief of naval operations. With Corcoran at his side, Freeman told Zumwalt that Rickover had "blackmailed" the shipyard by threatening to pull nuclear work if Newport News bid for a design of a non-nuclear ship. Freeman warned Zumwalt that unless Rickover was controlled, the shipyard might stop building ships for the navy altogether.

According to Zumwalt, Corcoran then pointed out that "there is nothing as dangerous as an old man with a dream," and that "Admiral Rickover is trying very hard to accomplish his vision for a nuclear-propelled Navy before he dies." Corcoran admonished Zumwalt that there were concerns on Capitol Hill for "the corners that Admiral Rickover is now cutting." As Zumwalt later recalled, he left the meeting with Freeman and Corcoran somewhat ambivalent that "we were about to kill the goose that laid the golden egg" — meaning that he was being asked to take on the most powerful man in the navy, who had done more than anyone to modernize the service.

According to Rickover's biographers Norman Polmar and Thomas B. Allen, Rickover had long held a deep antipathy to Corcoran. The dispute between the two men dated back to World War II, when Corcoran had represented the defense industry and Rickover was running the "BuShips" electrical station. The Bureau of Ships was one of the seven bureaus within the navy during the Second World War, and Rickover was in charge of one its most vital components. Supervising 350 employees at the electrical station, Rickover oversaw the modernization of electrical equipment used during peacetime so that it would hold up against the effects of explosions and waterborne shock waves during war. It was during this period, according to Polmar and Allen, that Rickover developed "his theory that all industry sought to make a profit at the expense of government. Contractors — or vendors — could not be believed; they had to be watched and harassed." While there is no evidence of any specific confrontation between Rickover and Corcoran, it is no surprise that the extraordinarily moralistic Rickover would have despised an industry lawyer such as Corcoran. For his part, Corcoran never maintained a grudge and seems actually to have thought highly of Rickover. In 1957 he sent his son Tim, then a student at Phillips Exeter Academy, a paper written by Rickover on the relationship between energy resources and political power. With evident admiration, Corcoran told his son, "I hope you find time to read this. . . . This is the kind of work you will be doing some day."

Rickover's dislike for Corcoran simmered for many years until it became public in 1977 when he told a congressional committee that "Corcoran lobbied extensively to prevent my reappointment." Rickover then claimed that Corcoran had, in his presence, telephoned the secretary of the navy and urged that the admiral "be assigned to duty somewhere — perhaps to Kamchatka," a Russian peninsula in the Bering Sea. For his part, Corcoran denied that he had tried to force Rickover to retire. According to Corcoran, "I said take him out of the construction business, but, please, promote him. Let him redo Annapolis. Let him be the teacher of the future Navy. But do you know what the boys said to that? They said, 'Jesus Christ, we'd sooner do without ships!'"

Presumably Corcoran's rejoinder only inflamed Rickover's hatred, and in early December 1979 the admiral stumbled upon the perfect way to punish the lawyer. Thumbing through the *Washington Post,* Rickover read an excerpt from a new book on the Supreme Court called *The Brethren.* The book's authors, Bob Woodward and Scott Armstrong, had interviewed numerous clerks on the Supreme Court and had learned that Corcoran had allegedly lobbied two justices about the *El Paso* case while it was pending before the Court. Rickover wrote to the District of Columbia Bar and asked for an investigation "to determine whether the behavior of Mr. Corcoran violates the legal profession's code of professional responsibility," and if so, whether "appropriate legal action" was warranted. To turn up the heat on Corcoran even higher, Rickover sent copies of the letter to key members of Congress and the press.

On December 21, 1979, the front page of the *Washington Post* carried the headline, ATTORNEY CORCORAN FACES ETHICS PROBE. *Post* reporter Morton Mintz reported that District bar president John H. Pickering had forwarded Rickover's complaint to the Board on Professional Responsibility of the District of Columbia Bar with a copy of a letter in which he told Rickover that private contacts with judges relating to pending cases are "generally condemned" by the code of conduct for the American Bar Association. Mintz noted that Corcoran might be subject to "Disciplinary rule 7-110," which read: "In an adversary proceeding, a lawyer shall not communicate . . . as to the merits of the case with a judge . . . before whom the proceeding is pending. . . ." According to Mintz, if the board found that Corcoran had violated the rule, he could be reprimanded, suspended, or even disbarred from the further practice of law in the District of Columbia.

Corcoran was angry at Rickover and irritated by the allegations. He privately complained to his young friend Tommy Boggs, "What's wrong with talking to a justice?" But Corcoran did not take the charges lightly, and he knew that the allegations, if proven, might jeopardize his nearly sixty years as a member of the bar. He moved quickly to assemble a defense team. He called upon the esteemed Washington criminal defense lawyer John Douglas. Next, Corcoran asked John Kelly, now a young associate in his firm, to help with his defense, and then he turned to another former protégé, up-and-coming criminal defense lawyer Robert Bennett.

Bennett, after finishing his year of study at Harvard Law School, had returned to Washington, where he interviewed with a number of the city's leading law firms. Corcoran actually offered him a job at a higher salary than anyone else, but Bennett remembered Corcoran telling him, "You're a trial lawyer. I just know you are." Corcoran told the young man that what he really should do was to get some real trial experience, and recommended that he spend a few years prosecuting. Bennett heeded the advice and went to work for the U.S. attorney's office in Washington, DC. He discovered quickly that Corcoran had been right. He loved trial work: "I was a fish in water."

Now it was Bennett's turn to help Corcoran. "It was my way of paying him back, even though it was just a drop in the bucket for everything he had done for me," Bennett later recalled. He continued, "I sized it up, and it was an easy case — there were only three people who knew what happened. Justice Black. He was dead. [Black died in September 1971.] Tommy Corcoran. He adamantly denied ever having lobbied the Supreme Court. That left Justice Brennan." Bennett wrote Justice Brennan and asked him about the allegation. Brennan was seventy-three years old in 1979 and had known Corcoran ever since Brennan's 1956 appointment to the Supreme Court. The justice wrote back to Bennett that he had "no independent recollection" of ever having been lobbied by Tommy Corcoran in the *El Paso* case. As Bennett put it, "Brennan couldn't remember, so [the board] dropped it." The ethics charges were dismissed.

Corcoran had escaped again. He denied having lobbied Justice

Brennan or Justice Black; perhaps in his own mind, he believed that he hadn't technically lobbied them. But the truth was that since Corcoran left government in 1940, he felt that somehow he had the right to speak to the members of the Supreme Court, most of whom he knew on a first-name basis, on any issue he pleased. It was an arrogance that he refused to recognize, much less overcome.

A Fire in His Heart

By the late 1970s, the vast majority of Tommy Corcoran's friends had retired from the government or from practicing law. Many of them from the New Deal years had died. Tommy's closest friend, Ben Cohen, had retired in 1952 after serving for six years on the American delegation to the United Nations. He lived alone in his apartment near Dupont Circle with his little dog. Cohen had numerous offers to practice law, including several from Corcoran, but he chose to spend his time reading, thinking, and talking with friends. He relaxed by playing tennis on the clay courts at St. Alban's School. He would tie his dog up to one of the net posts, and while the little animal slept in the sun, Cohen ran around the court swatting the ball inartfully in tennis shoes that one young friend later described as resembling "hospital shoes."

Corcoran, on the other hand, refused to retire. He continued to practice law and seemed to have recovered from the losses of his wife and daughter. He was active socially, alternately dating three women on a regular basis. He still squired Anna Chennault around town. They often appeared in Anna's chauffeur-driven Cadillac at social events. Tommy also escorted Lindy Boggs, the widow of former House leader Hale Boggs, who had died in an airplane crash in 1972. Lindy Boggs's son, Tommy, has said unconvincingly that the two were not romantically involved, but he acknowledged that his mother and Corcoran saw each other frequently, often gathering both families together for holidays and large dinners. Corcoran also dated Ceci Bauman, a very attractive woman thirty years his junior who worked on Capitol Hill.

Many years later Anna Chennault complained that Corcoran used her car and driver to take his girlfriends on dates around the city. The man who'd never had time for women when he was working in the New Deal had discovered that he not only enjoyed being in the company of the opposite sex, but could charm them as well. Carlisle Bolton-Smith remembered that the only time he got a little annoyed with Tommy was at a New Year's dance when Corcoran wouldn't stop dancing with Bolton-Smith's wife.

In his later years, Corcoran even contemplated marriage. Boggs, who became ambassador to the Vatican during the Clinton administration, only said that "Tommy was the most fun I ever had with anyone." She laughingly (and unconvincingly) claimed that she didn't remember if she and Corcoran ever discussed marriage. Anna claimed that Tommy wanted to marry her, but that she'd vowed never to marry again after General Chennault. Corcoran, however, told one friend that he would not marry Lindy or Anna, or anyone else for that matter, because "once you marry, they're not nice to you."

Corcoran had become something of an icon in Washington. Robert Strauss, who chaired the Democratic Party in the 1970s, remembered approaching him for a contribution to the party: "Tommy Corcoran was a very important man and I was just a pissant. But you could always count on that firm to contribute five thousand dollars."

With the election of Jimmy Carter in 1976, it seemed likely that Corcoran would become one of the grand old men of the Democratic Party. Just a few months after Carter's inauguration in January 1977, a New Dealers' Reunion Dinner was held at the Mayflower Hotel to commemorate the forty-fourth anniversary of Franklin Roosevelt's inauguration. Carter had campaigned for the presidency as a Washington "outsider," and no one from the newly installed administration attended the dinner. Arthur Schlesinger Jr. later wrote Vice President Walter Mondale asking, "How in the world do you suppose a Democratic President . . . could not manage a few words expressing his sense of the occasion?" Several weeks after the dinner, as the promise of the Carter presidency faded, Corcoran and Cohen were invited to the White House to meet over lunch with several of President Carter's chief advisers, including the chief of staff, Hamilton Jordan.

Over the course of the following three years, the nation settled uncomfortably into the "malaise" of the Carter presidency. Corcoran and Cohen were never invited back to the White House, but many in Washington and around the country began to look back to the New Deal for inspiration. Corcoran, who had largely avoided the press since leaving government thirty years earlier, became much more available for interviews.

On one occasion Corcoran was asked to appear on the NBC's *Today Show*. Interest rates were spiraling upward, double-digit inflation racked the economy, and long lines were forming at the gas pumps as the United States confronted an oil shortage. Ronald Reagan, running for president, declared in Jersey City that "a recession is when your neighbor loses his job. A depression is when you lose yours." The United States was facing its most critical economic challenge since the 1930s. When pressed by NBC news anchor Tom Brokaw, Corcoran, who didn't think too highly of President Carter, nevertheless pointed out that there was a big difference between standing in line for gasoline and wondering where your next meal would come from.

In the spring of 1979 Sandra McIlwaine, a reporter at the *Washington Star,* was asked by her editors to write a profile of the seventy-nine-year-old Corcoran. McIlwaine, only thirty years old, knew virtually nothing about him, but Corcoran patiently submitted to an interview. After her largely positive page-one story, Corcoran telephoned her and suggested that she write a profile on Anna Chennault. McIlwaine liked the idea, and Corcoran arranged for an interview.

Several months later McIlwaine returned home one Sunday evening from a weekend in the country to find five messages on her answering machine from Mrs. Chennault and three from Corcoran. The next day, Monday, the *Star* was scheduled to run McIlwaine's piece on Chennault, and to advertise it, the front page on Sunday had emblazoned across the top, TOMORROW, THE DRAGON LADY — ANNA CHENNAULT. McIlwaine called Chennault to apologize and to tell her that she had not written the headline. But Chennault would not be assuaged: "Tommy tells me you're a nice girl. I don't trust you." An exasperated McIlwaine then contacted Corcoran and explained that she had known nothing about the headline. Corcoran just laughed.

A few months later McIlwaine invited Corcoran to a dinner party. She told him that she was inviting all of the people she had profiled in major articles that year. Corcoran asked her advice on whom he should bring: He feared Chennault would not come, and he couldn't decide whether to invite Lindy Boggs or Ceci Bauman. McIlwaine was delighted to hear that a man in his seventies was facing such a dilemma.

On December 15, 1979, President Carter met with congressional leaders in the White House to tell them that in a few hours he would appear on national television to announce that the United States was establishing full diplomatic relations with the People's Republic of China. Even though the U.S. was effectively abrogating the twenty-three-year-old mutual defense pact with Taiwan, President Carter had not personally informed the Taiwanese ambassador, C. H. Shen.

The president hoped that the announcement would provide a shot of adrenaline to his anemic presidency. The change in foreign policy clearly had extraordinarily important economic, political, and strategic implications for China, the United States, and Taiwan. Just a few days after Carter made the announcement, Shen left for his country.

As one of the principal lawyers for Taiwan in the United States, Corcoran immediately recognized that the president's action had important consequences for the island nation's economic holdings in the United States, most particularly its embassy and the ambassador's residence, known as Twin Oaks, which taken together were worth millions of dollars. As the newly recognized representative of the Chinese people, the People's Republic was entitled to occupy the embassy then occupied by the Republic of China. However, before there was an official changing of the guard, Corcoran placed the real estate holdings of the Republic of China in a trust and sold them in a private transaction for twenty dollars to a nonprofit organization called Friends of Free China.

The government of the People's Republic of China was infuriated and demanded that the United States bring suit against the government of Taiwan. Zbigniew Brzezinski, the president's national security adviser, asked one of his top aides, David Aaron, to explore the legal options. At the State Department, Assistant Secretary Richard Holbrooke advised that the People's Republic of China should be allowed to bring a legal proceeding against Republic of China. And according to a State Department cable, Deputy Secretary of State Warren Christopher told Chinese president Chiang Ching Kuo and other government leaders that "he understood their concern over assets in the United States," and "promised painstaking study of this issue upon his return to Washington."

At the Department of Justice's Office of Foreign Litigation, Bruno Ristau, an experienced lawyer, closely examined the case law and concluded that there was nothing that could be done. "Corcoran and his colleagues had done a stupendous job," Ristau later remembered. "Corcoran had the deed recorded in just two days — ordinarily it takes three months." Ristau concluded that the United States had no standing to bring suit against the Republic of China. According to Ristau, President Carter should never have indicated that he was going to recognize the People's Republic in two weeks: "It should have been done overnight. You never give notice of future derecognition. He got poor advice."

Several months later, after the People's Republic was officially recognized, Corcoran arranged for the assets to be sold back to the government of the Republic of China. Although it not longer retained embassy status, Taiwan at least retained its Washington real estate.

"It was classic Corcoran," recalled his friend David Acheson, reminiscent of the tactic Corcoran had used to save Chiang Kai-shek's air force more than thirty years before. Anna Chennault suggested to the Taiwanese ambassador that a plaque should be erected in Corcoran's honor somewhere on the embassy grounds, but one never was.

Tommy Corcoran loved to help young people, particularly young lawyers. John Kelly, who worked in the firm for nine years beginning in 1971, claimed that "I was really like a surrogate son, and he was like my adopted father. We used to spend whole days together, evenings and weekends. I knew him better than any best friend even though I was in my twenties and he was in his seventies."

Corcoran liked to dispense advice to young lawyers such as Kelly, usually telling them that they should follow a career path much like his own. When Jonathan Cuneo — the twenty-one-year-old son of Tommy's law partner Ernest Cuneo — was on the verge of graduating from Columbia University, he confessed to Corcoran that he had no idea what he would do after graduation. Corcoran told him: "You're going to get a haircut. Then we'll get you into Harvard Law. After that you are going to clerk for a Supreme Court justice." Cuneo remembered, "I was just a kid, but he had it all planned out. By the time I was forty-one, he told me that I would be a judge. All I could say was, 'Thank you, Mr. Corcoran.'"

Ben Ivins, a summer clerk in the Corcoran office, had a similar experience. Ivins told Corcoran that after graduation from Georgetown Law he didn't have any real plans. "You are going to clerk for a judge, of course," Corcoran told him. Before he knew it, Corcoran had set up interviews with several of the judges in the District of Columbia federal court. "Tommy had had a hand in getting most of them appointed, and I had interviews with judges even before they had my résumé." In the end, Ivins clerked for Tommy's brother Howard. "It was a kind of pipeline," Ivins later recalled.

Corcoran did more than just give advice. His generosity among those who knew him was famous. When the fitness trainer at the University Club, a gentleman named Mr. Whip who had been Jack Dempsey's trainer, was asked to retire, no pension was provided. Corcoran, who worked out at the club almost every day, according to his son Tim, "sort of took him on as his personal trainer." When the *Washington Star* closed its doors and the young reporter who had profiled him, Sandra McIlwaine, found herself without a job, Corcoran telephoned her and said, "If you ever need anything, you call me."

Indeed, Tommy was constantly using the law firm to take care of people. When the barber on the first floor of his building needed a loan, Corcoran put him on the law firm's payroll. When Maureen Dowd, the young cousin of his late wife Peggy, needed a summer job, he put her to work on the firm's switchboard answering telephones. On one occasion he ran into an out-of-work lawyer named Dick Walsh at a cocktail party. Walsh, like Corcoran, had gone to Brown, and according to Bob Bennett, "Next thing you know, he's in the office and I wondered, 'Why the hell is he here?' It was just because he had gone to Brown and he needed a job."

Bennett also remembered delivering unmarked brown envelopes to a former high-ranking official at the Justice Department who had been a close friend of Tommy's during the Truman administration. "I used to go to the Pick, which was short for the Pickwick Hotel, and I'd knock on the door of his apartment. The door would be answered by this old, short Irishman with a four-day growth of a beard. He was clearly an alcoholic. He'd say to me, 'Oh you are from the Corcoran firm. I've been working with Tommy.' I'd hand him the envelope with the money. I knew Tommy was just taking care of him."

Just before Thanksgiving, 1981, Jonathan Cuneo, home from law school for the holidays, visited Corcoran in his law offices and was shocked to see how old the man seemed. After they chatted for several minutes, Tommy asked the young law student to escort him to his car. As they stepped into the elevator, Tommy placed a hand on Cuneo's shoulder and told him what a good thing it was that he was studying law because laws formed the bedrock of democracy. As if to make the connection for Cuneo, Corcoran began reciting ancient Greek. Cuneo thought to himself that Corcoran continued to be one of the most extraordinary men he had ever met.

Just after Thanksgiving Tommy entered the hospital to have his gall-bladder removed. Although he remained a strong man who regularly exercised, the operation greatly weakened him. Still, he was expected to make a full recovery.

A week later, on Saturday, December 5, Tim visited his father in the hospital. They had a long and pleasant talk. Tommy gleefully reminisced about some of the great jurists he had known: Brandeis, Frankfurter, and Holmes. Brandeis was brilliant, but he had betrayed Roosevelt. Corcoran described his relationship to Frankfurter by telling Tim that he and the justice had been a little like the father and son in the Irish play *Playboy of the Western World.* Holmes was the most wonderful man who had ever lived — even though he was cheap. Speaking of money, Tommy told his son — who managed the family finances — when he got out of the hospital he was going to make a lot more money. He had given most of it away, substantially to his children, but he could always make more — and maybe he wouldn't give that away. He and his son laughed together.

On Sunday night, December 6, Tommy Corcoran suffered an embolism and died. He was eighty years old. The hospital contacted Dr. David Corcoran, Tommy's second son, and David called Tim. Tim couldn't believe that the man who had been making plans only the day before was gone.

A strong, bitter wind forced the elegantly dressed mourners to pull their overcoats tightly against their bodies as they ascended the steps of Cathedral St. Matthew, the great redbrick Catholic church with its colorful green dome on Rhode Island Avenue. Inside, the gray stone offered little warmth to the several hundred people who had come to pay their last respects to Tommy Corcoran. Lindy Boggs was there. Stu Eizenstat, the domestic policy adviser for President Carter, was also there. So were John Connally, Clark Clifford, Senator Daniel Patrick Moynihan, and Katharine Graham. Senators Strom Thurmond of South Carolina and Orrin Hatch of Utah were honorary pallbearers because "the family gave in" to Anna Chennault, according to Jim Rowe. The crowd stood silently, some gazing at the translucent windows, while others studied the ornamented, vaulted ceiling that cast cold shadows over the stone floor.

Jim Rowe, Corcoran's good friend and law partner, gave one of the eulogies. The six-foot-one Rowe stood at the pulpit and began, "I thought

he would live forever." He went on to describe how Tommy had recently
gone to the doctor and complained that he didn't have as much energy as
he used to. When the doctor told him, "It goes with the territory,"
Tommy replied, "Not with my territory, it doesn't." Rowe described
Corcoran as "a great advocate at the bar . . . and a superb intellectual per-
suader of men." He went on to tell lighthearted stories about Tommy's
career and after a few minutes concluded with the words of both his and
Tommy's hero, Oliver Wendell Holmes: "When a great tree falls, we are
surprised to see how meager the landscape seems without it. So, with a
great man." Many of the older men in the audience, such as Ben Cohen,
were wiping their eyes when Rowe sat down. Jim Rowe, who would himself die four years later, had beautifully captured the energy, the kindness,
and the stature of his friend with sensitivity and humor.

Anna Chennault then strode to the podium. In her clipped accent, she
proclaimed, "Tommy Corcoran lived a full life, a rich life, a life full of
dreams and passions." Some in the audience, particularly those who had
never particularly cared for her, were not completely certain that she had
been asked to speak by anyone in the Corcoran family. "It seemed as
though she was trying to steal the show," recalled one person in attendance. She spoke for several minutes, concluding by observing that "he
always laughed. He always sang."

Corcoran made millions of dollars during his lifetime, but most of his
friends assumed that he died with very little money. He supported the
law firm, supported his friends, and gave a great deal away. In fact, he
died with a modest estate, but over the years he had transferred a substantial amount of his wealth — investments in companies that had greatly
appreciated — to his children.

In his will he left the house on Woodland Drive to Anna Chennault.
Anna, however, was content with her apartment and sensed that the children, particularly the younger ones, had a sentimental attachment to the
property. She requested that it be retained by the family.

In 1993 President Bill Clinton, newly elected, pledged to "uphold the highest ethical standards" and "guarantee that the members" of his administration would be "looking out for the American people and not for themselves." Only minutes after taking the oath of office he signed a tough

executive order requiring senior administration officials to wait five years after leaving government before lobbying any federal agency for which they had held "any responsibility." The new president also imposed a lifetime ban on representing a foreign government. But as his presidency wound down in the summer of 2000, it was reported that the White House was mulling "whether or not to soften those restrictions." The rationale for a possible review was that the lobbying ban made it difficult to recruit top-notch executives to the new administration and that there was nothing particularly sinister about representing a foreign government that was dealing with U.S. agencies.

With the election of George W. Bush as president in 2000, followed by Republican majorities in both the House and Senate in 2002, the separation between lobbyists and policy makers all but disappeared. In drafting the administration's energy policy, for example, lobbyists had a seat at the table alongside industry executives and members of the executive branch. The lobbying profession has ballooned to a $1.5 billion industry that employs hundreds upon hundreds of former government officials.

Lobbying at its most fundamental level is no more than art of communication to influence a particular government decision. One of the fundamental tenets of democratic government is that decisions should be made in full public view so that decision makers can be held accountable. Even though lobbyists often perform a valuable service to the political system by providing useful information and expertise, the effort to work behind the scenes to influence a decision is what has given the lobbying profession its often deserved reputation for corruption. The question today is the same as it was in Corcoran's era: What do lobbyists have to give in order to influence the process?

Tommy Corcoran was not a great statesman, although he did have a significant influence on the New Deal. After World War II Corcoran, who had been the first White House liaison to Congress, became one of the preeminent lobbyists in Washington. While he did not invent modern-day lobbying, he understood perhaps better than any of his contemporaries the nexus between government and the postwar economy, and he refined many of the techniques for making things happen behind the scenes, usually — though not always — without leaving any fingerprints. He came to symbolize the silent, but often critical, role that lobbyists play in shaping public policy.

During his lifetime, Corcoran witnessed, and ultimately profited from, some of the most important political trends of the twentieth century. After Roosevelt's presidency, a shift in power occurred between Pennsylvania Avenue and Capitol Hill, and Corcoran was there to take advantage of his knowledge and contacts. With the increasing use of electronic media, campaigns became much more expensive and politicians relied on raising money from Washington lobbyists. As LBJ's top aide, Bobby Baker, put it, "Tommy knew how to spread it around."

After he left government, Corcoran, it seemed, was constantly under investigation by the Congress, the Department of Justice, and even the legal profession itself. But unlike his contemporaries and competitors Clark Clifford and Abe Fortas, both of whom ultimately fell from grace as the result of apparent avarice — Fortas over an insurance scandal in the 1960s and Clifford from an international banking scandal in the 1990s — Corcoran was never proven to be corrupt.

Yet Tommy Corcoran was always working an angle. While in government he dispensed "pork," and in private practice he doled out campaign contributions. Both in public service and in private practice, his most valuable currency was himself. As John Lane, one of the many young lawyers who remained loyal to him over the decades, put it, "I think what people got in return from him was wit, clarity of thought, and sheer intelligence. He could figure out how to get to people intellectually." And another of his young protégés, John Kelly, described him as "the most decent, most moral, and most moralistic individual" he had ever known — hardly the epitaph for a mere "fixer."

Corcoran is remembered for his extraordinary ability to get things done. In an age where government is paralyzed by the twin pillars of ideology and bureaucracy, Corcoran scorned both. Although a Democrat, he was first a pragmatist who believed in a government marked by excellence — one in which the best young people in the country would be proud to serve.

In 2000 *Washington Post* columnist David Ignatius wrote, "One of the sidelights of the current political dynamic is the decline of the Washington lawyer as presidential counselor, power broker and all purpose political fixer. It is rare that an individual lawyer can get a bill passed or a political appointment scuttled or a secret deal negotiated." Ignatius asked, "How can you put in the fix with a Congress that doesn't pass any legislation?" And answering his own question, he opined, "The demise of the Washington lawyer is doubtless a healthy trend for the republic. A mandarin class of lawyers doesn't fit well with a democracy, but their decline coincides with a deeper Washington malaise: the eclipse of government. In the fixer's heyday, at least there was something to fix."

Washington lawyers for the twenty-first century are not really distinguishable from their brethren around the country. At one time, however, the best of them — men such as Edward Bennett Williams, Clark Clifford, and Abe Fortas — considered themselves legal statesmen after a fashion. They were wise men. But their seat at the table of power in Washington has been replaced by campaign strategists and wealthy campaign contributors. "Mostly it's the economics of specialization — the day of the generalists is over," explained Lloyd Cutler, one of the few lawyers from another era who continues to exercise influence in both political and legal circles. Bob Bennett attributed it to "conflict-of-interest rules, over-interpretation by the press, and a general 'antsy' state of concern." Part of what made the old model work was the illusion that a Washington lawyer could be above the fray.

Interestingly, Corcoran never cast himself in such a self-serving light. Corcoran didn't worry for a minute about being politically correct — not when he was in government, and certainly not after he left it. He clearly was blinded by his aversion to communism, which led him to actively support and assist the CIA coup in Guatemala in 1954, considered by most historians as a foreign policy disaster. And he may have been blinded by his affection for Anna Chennault, forgoing the opportunity to have exposed Richard Nixon's secret and probably illegal contacts with the South Vietnamese government in 1968. In lobbying, Corcoran exercised occasionally extremely poor judgment, as in his attempts to lobby members of the bench. According to Arthur Schlesinger, "He ultimately betrayed the ideals and standards of the New Deal." He was also described by all who knew him well as one of the most generous and decent people in Washington.

In an interview with Schlesinger in 1957, Tommy Corcoran, who had been out of government nearly two decades, described the awesome responsibility of the presidency and the necessary qualities needed to lead from that position. Corcoran said, "There isn't enough time to explain everything to everyone, to cajole everyone, to persuade everyone, to make everyone see why it has to be done one way rather than another. If a president tried to do this, he would have no time left for anything else. So he must deceive, misrepresent, leave false impressions — sometimes even lie — and trust to charm, loyalty and the result to make up for it. . . . A great man cannot be a good man."

Corcoran was probably referring to the man who had the most profound influence on his career: Franklin Roosevelt. Undoubtedly a great leader, FDR could be personally cold and calculating. It is significant that Corcoran claimed he was discussing only the presidency — after all, his greatest hero, Oliver Wendell Holmes, was both good and great.

Corcoran, however, may simply have been describing himself. Although not a great man, he exerted extraordinary influence in Washington, DC, for nearly half a century, beginning with the New Deal and extending through the presidency of Jimmy Carter. His "goodness" was more complicated. On a personal level he betrayed his wife and was too often an absent husband and father. On a professional level, too often his intense loyalty to his president, his faith, and his clients clouded his judgment. Too often, particularly as he grew older, he seemed to care less about explaining why something should be done a certain way, simply resorting to deception because he knew he could achieve the desired result. In short, too often his morality extended no farther than the ends justifying the means. If nothing else, however, Corcoran's famous words show how clearly he understood the exercise of political power in Washington.

A NOTE ON THE SOURCES

Introduction: An Irish Ballad

The opening scene is based on an interview I conducted with Harry McPherson in 1998. Information on the New Deal is from Graham and Wander's survey of the Roosevelt years, *Franklin D. Roosevelt: His Life and Times.* I also consulted Jordan Schwarz's *The New Dealers.* Background on the lobbying profession was gleaned from *Congress A to Z*, a publication of *Congressional Quarterly.* Kenneth Davis's characterization of Corcoran is on page 86 of his biography of President Franklin Roosevelt, *The New Deal Years.* The story of Corcoran and his younger law partner, Robert Perry, was told to me by Perry in 2000.

1. Most Likely to Succeed

The section on Corcoran's family history is based his unpublished memoir, documents from the Corcoran Papers, container 23, in the Library of Congress, Joseph Lash's *Dealers and Dreamers,* Louis Koenig's *The Invisible Presidency,* Ken Crawford's December 7, 1981, obituary of Corcoran in the *Washing Post*, and interviews with Tim Corcoran and Esther Corcoran. The information on Corcoran's years at Brown University and Harvard Law School is based largely on Koenig's *Invisible Presidency,* although I also consulted Lash's *Dealers and Dreamers* and Corcoran's unpublished memoir. Frankfurter's mentoring of Corcoran is discussed in *Dealers and Dreamers,* and the opportunity to spend an extra year at Harvard is recalled by Corcoran in Katie Louchheim's *The Making of the New Deal.* Corcoran's Harvard Law School article is cited on page 135, footnote 1, in Lash's *Diaries of Frankfurter.* The story of Corcoran's decision to forgo a job on Wall Street in favor of a clerkship with Oliver Wendell Holmes is based on Corcoran's unpublished memoir and his recollections in Louchheim's *The Making of the New Deal.* The reference to Oliver Wendell Homes is based on Liva Baker's biography of Holmes, *The Justice from Beacon Hill.*

2. A Wonderful Education

Corcoran's recalled his introduction to Justice and Mrs. Holmes in the Holmes chapter of his unpublished memoir, as well as in recollections contained in Katie Louchheim's *The Making of the New Deal*. Joseph Alsop's observation that "Holmes became Corcoran's substitute for a personal God" is contained in his book, *The Men Around the President*. The descriptions of Holmes's daily routine is from the recollections of Alger Hiss and Corcoran in *The Making of the New Deal*. Holmes's description of Corcoran as "quite noisy, quite adequate and noisy," is repeated in several sources, including Merle Miller's oral history of Lyndon Johnson, *Lyndon*. How Holmes related to his legal clerks is recalled by Donald and Alger Hiss and by Corcoran in *The Making of the New Deal*. The final section on the Sacco and Vanzetti case is based entirely on information contained in Baker's *The Justice from Beacon Hill*.

3. The Coming of the New Deal

The information on Corcoran's years on Wall Street with the law firm Cotton and Franklin is based largely on the chapter "The New York Connection" in his unpublished memoirs and on information contained in Louis Koenig's *The Invisible Presidency*. I also consulted Lash's *Dealers and Dreamers*, Robert Slayton's *Empire Statesman*, and Alva Johnson's profile of Corcoran in the *Saturday Evening Post*, "The Saga of Tommy the Cork," which appeared in October 1945.

Corcoran's letters to his family are from Lash's *Dealers and Dreamers*. The death of Fanny Holmes is recalled by Corcoran in Louchheim's *The Making of the New Deal*. Corcoran's decision to move back to Washington and work in government is discussed in *Dealers and Dreamers*, William Lasser's *Ben Cohen*, and by Corcoran in Katie Louchheim's *The Making of the New Deal*. I also referred to a 1963 *New York Times* article about Corcoran in which he reminisced about his early years.

The information on Ben Cohen and his relationship with Corcoran is from Louis Koenig's *The Invisible Presidency*, Joseph Alsop's *The Men Around the President*, and Alan Brinkley's *The End of Reform*. The description of Corcoran's early years at the RFC is based on his recollection contained in *The Making of the New Deal*, Arthur Schlesinger's *Coming of the New Deal*, Elliot Rosen's *Hoover, Roosevelt and the Brain Trust*, and Lash's *Dealers and*

Dreamers. I found Roosevelt's quote about Felix Frankfurter in Graham and Wander's survey of the Roosevelt years, *Franklin D. Roosevelt: His Life and Times.* For information on the collapse of the financial markets I referred to Ron Chernow's *House of Morgan* and Schlesinger's *The Coming of the New Deal.* Corcoran's decision to withdraw half his personal savings is from the 1963 *New York Times* article. The final quote on the virtuosity of Corcoran and Cohen is from Alan Brinkley's *The End of Reform.*

4. Battling Wall Street

The information on Justice Holmes is based on the recollection of Donald Hiss in Katie Louchheim's *The Making of the New Deal.* In describing the continuing weakness in the economy and Roosevelt's commitment to reform of the financial markets, I consulted Arthur Schlesinger's *Politics of Upheaval,* Donald Ritchie's *James M. Landis,* William Leuchtenburg's *Franklin D. Roosevelt and the New Deal,* and Ellis Hawley's *The New Deal and the Problem of Monopoly.* The information on Peggy Dowd is from an article written by her younger cousin, Maureen Dowd, "Capital Ghosts" in the *New York Times* on May 9, 1993.

The story of Corcoran's ride on the elevator with J. P. Morgan is told in Joseph Lash's *Dealers and Dreamers.* Frankfurter's testimony is recalled in Michael Parrish's *Felix Frankfurter and His Times.* The correspondence between Frankfurter, during the time he was on sabbatical in England, and Corcoran is mentioned in Bruce Allen Murphy, *The Brandies/Frankfurter Connection,* and in *Dealers and Dreamers.* Reference to the correspondence between Brandeis and Frankfurter is also based on *Dealers and Dreamers.*

Rayburn's admiration for Corcoran and Cohen is discussed in Hardeman and Bacon's *Rayburn,* and Rayburn's speech on the House floor is described in Ritchie's *James M. Landis.* Corcoran's disdain for John Foster Dulles is noted in chapter 4 of his unpublished memoir, while Frankfurter's recommedation of Cohen is contained in Joseph Alsop's *The Men Around the President.*

5. The Little Red Schoolhouse

The information on Jim Landis is from Donald Ritchie's excellent biography, *James M. Landis.* Ben Cohen's background is gleaned from Louis

Koenig's *The Invisible Presidency* and from Joseph Lash's *Dealers and Dreamers*. In 2003, however, William Lasser published a fine biography of Ben Cohen that is the best source for information on his life and career. The information on the house at 3238 R Street is based on several sources, including: the recollections of Frank Watson and Kenneth Crawford in Katie Louchheim's *The Making of the New Deal*, an interview with Carlisle Bolton Smith, and Joseph Alsop's *The Men Around the President*.

Corcoran's views on women during this period are noted in *The Invisible Presidency* and *Dealers and Dreamers*, as is Tommy's brief tenure at the Department of the Treasury. The biographical sketch of James Rowe is from his papers at the Roosevelt Library. Corcoran's return to the RFC is described by Max Freedman in *Roosevelt and Frankfurter*, and is mentioned in Koenig's *The Invisible Presidency*, Alsop's *The Men Around the President*, and Arthur Schlesinger's *Politics of Upheaval*.

The story of Corcoran playing the accordion for the president is from *Men Around the President*. Corcoran's ability to place capable young lawyers throughout the government is recalled by Thomas Emerson and Frank Watson in *The Making of the New Deal*, as well as in Jordan Schwarz's *The New Dealers* and Schlesinger's *The Politics of Upheaval*. The quote from Joe Rauh is from Alan Brinkley's *The End of Reform*.

6. Frankfurter's Hotdogs

The information on the economic situation in 1934 and Raymond Moley's decision to enlist Corcoran and Cohen in drafting further regulation of the financial markets is based on Kenneth Davis's *The New Deal Years*. The brief section on Peggy Corcoran is based on the recollection of Frank Watson in Louchheim's *The Making of the New Deal*. I consulted Alfred Steinberg's biography of Sam Rayburn on the drafting of the legislation and referred to Louis Koenig's *The Invisible Presidency* for Wall Street's reaction to the specter of regulation.

In writing about the attacks on Corcoran and his attempts to thwart Wall Street's lobbyists, I consulted Lasser's *Ben Cohen*, Ritchie's *James M. Landis*, Steinberg's *Sam Rayburn*, Lash's *Dealers and Dreamers*, and Koenig's *The Invisible Presidency*. Corcoran's unpublished memoir was also helpful. The section on Miton Katz is based on Katz's recollection contained in Louchheim's *The Making of the New Deal*. Corcoran's appearance before the House Commerce Committee is described in Koenig's *The Invisible Presidency*, and FDR's congratulatory phone call is mentioned in Patrick Anderson's *The President's Men*.

Information on the attacks on Corcoran and Cohen by Republican House members is found in Hardeman and Bacon's *Rayburn* and Ritchie's *James M. Landis*. The establishment of the Securities and Exchange Commission and the appointment of Joseph P. Kennedy as its first chairman is discussed in Ritchie's *James M. Landis*, Ron Chernow's *House of Morgan*, Ronald Kessler's *Sins of the Father*, David Koskoff's *Kennedy*, and Harold Ickes's *Diary*.

7. Battling Big Business

The information on the political situation in late 1934 and President Roosevelt's decision to confront the monopoly power of big business is largely based on Ellis Hawley's *The New Deal and the Problem of Monopoly*. I also consulted William Leuchtenburg's *FDR and the New Deal*, Kenneth Davis's *The New Deal Years*, Hardeman and Bacon's *Rayburn*, and William Lasser's *Ben Cohen*. The tactics of the utility companies were discussed in Louis Koenig's *The Invisible Presidency* and Robert Caro's *Path to Power*. Corcoran wrote about the death of Oliver Wendell Holmes in his unpublished memoir. The section on Senator Wheeler and his decision to schedule hearings is based on Wheeler's autobiography, *Yankee from the West*. I also consulted *The Invisible Presidency*. The attacks on Corcoran and Cohen are dicussed in Joseph Lash's *Dealers and Dreamers* and Hardeman and Bacon's *Rayburn*.

The story of Roosevelt's visit to Kennedy's Marwood estate is based on Ronald Kessler's *Sins of the Father* and Arthur Krock's *Memoirs*. Corcoran's confrontation with Senator Brewster is mentioned in numerous sources, including Hardeman and Bacon's *Rayburn*, Koenig's *Invisible Presidency*, Arthur Schlesinger's *The Politics of Upheaval*, and Ken Crawford's obituary of Corcoran on December 7, 1981, in the *Washington Post*. Information on the legal challenge to the Public Utility Holding Company Act is included in *Invisible Presidency* and Joseph Alsop's *The Men Around the President*. Information on the House and Senate investigation is based on *Politics of Upheaval*. Corcoran's quote is from Lash's *Dealers and Dreamers*.

8. Apex of Power

The background material on presidential staff is from Michael Medved's *The Shadow Presidents*. I also consulted Patrick Anderson's *The President's Men*. Corcoran's emergence in the press is highlighted by two articles in the *New York Times:* Delbert Clark, "The President's Advisers Come and Go," in the magazine section on August 4, 1935, and Arthur Krock, "Quoddy Project Charges Kindles Republican Hopes," on July 3, 1935. Joseph Alsop's memoir, *I've Seen the Best of It*, was also helpful.

Information on the death of Tommy's mother was supplied to me by Tim Corcoran. The section on the death of Oliver Wendell Holmes is based on material from Corcoran's unpublished memoir as well as Monica Niznik's dissertation. Raymond Moley's falling-out with President Roosevelt is described in Kenneth Davis, *The New Deal Years*. I also consulted the Corcoran Papers, as well as Harold Ickes's *Diary*, William Lasser's *Ben Cohen*, and Arthur Schlesinger's *Politics of Upheaval* on the emergence of Corcoran as a key figure in the White House. The description of how Corcoran physically entered the White House and gained access to the Oval Office is based on Lash's *Dealers and Dreamers* and Norman Littell's *My Roosevelt Years*.

Corcoran's accordion playing and the personal relationship that he formed with the President are described in Koenig's *Invisible Presidency* and Harold Ickes's *Diary*. The observation by several Washington insiders that Corcoran became one of the most influential White House advisers is based on several sources, including Schlesinger's *The Coming of the New Deal*, Davis's *The New Deal Years*, Elliott Roosevelt's *Rendezvous with Destiny*, Koenig's *The Invisible Presidency*, Schwarz's *The New Dealers*, and the recollection of Thomas Elliot found in Katie Louchheim's *The Making of the New Deal*. The section on Sam Rayburn is from Hardeman and Bacon's *Rayburn* and Caro's *Path to Power*.

I pieced together the story about Hall Roosevelt from information found in Doris Kearns Goodwin's *No Ordinary Time* and Jesse Jones's *Fifty Billion Dollars*. Elliott Roosevelt's observation that his mother did not "take to Tom" is from his memoir, *Rendezvous with Destiny*. For background on Eleanor Roosevelt's political activism and political views, including her opinion of the Catholic Church, I consulted Harold Ickes's *Diary*, John Cooney's *The American Pope*, and Arthur Schlesinger's *The Politics of Upheaval*. Joseph Kennedy's request to Corcoran that he find his son a job is from Niznik's dissertation. Corcoran's stature in 1936 as a member of Roosevelt's inner circle in described in Lash's *Dealers and Dreamers* and Schwarz's *The New Dealers*. The inscription on the photograph that Holmes gave to Corcoran was given to me by Tim Corcoran, who displays the photograph in his law office.

9. The Second New Deal

The information on Roosevelt's reelection in 1936 and the celebration at Hyde Park is found in Kenneth Davis, *The New Deal Years*, Nathan Miller's *F.D.R.*, Joseph Lash's *Eleanor and Franklin*, and Arthur Schlesinger's *The Politics of Upheaval*. Roosevelt's focus on the economy in 1937 is chronicled in Ron Chernow's *House of Morgan*, T. H. Watkins's *Righteous Pilgrim*, and Leuchtenburg's *FDR and the New Deal*. The split within the administration over how best to deal with the economy is described in Jim Farley's autobiography, *Jim Farley's Story*, Joseph Lash's *Diaries of Frankfurter*, Eric Goldman's *Rendezvous with Destiny*, and Harold Ickes's *Diary*. The quote of Bernard de Voto is from *FDR and the New Deal*.

10. Corcoran and Court Packing

The background on President Roosevelt's decision to reform the Supreme Court is discussed in several sources, including John Gunther's *Roosevelt in Retrospect*, Leonard Baker's *Brandeis and Frankfurter*, William Lasser's *Ben Cohen*, Burton Wheeler's autobiography, *Yankee from the West*, and Graham and Wander's survey of the Roosevelt years, *Franklin D. Roosevelt: His Life and Times*. The sources for the story of Corcoran's visit to Senator Wheeler are from Corcoran's unpublished memoir, T. H. Watkins's *Righteous Pilgrim*, and Wheeler's *Yankee from the West*. The president's and Corcoran's lobbying of congressional leaders is described in William Leuchtenberg's *FDR and the New Deal*, Bruce Allen Murphy's *The Brandeis/Frankfurter Connection*, Roger Newman's *Hugo Black*, Leonard Baker's *Brandeis and Frankfurter*, Louis Koenig's *The Invisible Presidency*, and Claude Pepper's autobiography, written with Hays Gorey, *Pepper*. I also used contemporaneous articles from the *Chicago Tribune*, the *Washington Post*, and a 1937 profile of Corcoran written by Alva Johnson for the *Saturday Evening Post*.

The information on Izzie Stone and William O. Douglas was discovered in the Roosevelt Library; that on Milton Katz is from Joseph Lash's *Dealers and Dreamers*. The quote from Jesse Jones is from his autobiography, *Fifty Billion Dollars*, and the description of Vice President Garner's opposition to Court reform is found in Robert Caro's *Path to Power*. The final section of this chapter dealing with Congressman Johnson's support for Roosevelt and his visit to the Oval Office is found in Merle Miller's *Lyndon*, Robert Mann's *Walls of Jericho*, Caro's *Path to Power* and *Means of Ascent*, Hardeman and Bacon's *Rayburn*, and Louis Koenig's *Invisible Presidency*.

11. The Price of Loyalty

In his 1945 profile of Tommy Corcoran in the *Saturday Evening Post*, "The Saga of Tommy the Cork," Alva Johnson claimed that Corcoran had been mentioned as a possible candidate for the Supreme Court. The description of the role Corcoran played in the selection of Supreme Court justice Hugo Black is based on Gerald T. Dunne's biography, *Hugo Black and the Judicial Revolution*, Jim Farley's *Jim Farley's Story*, and William O. Douglas's *Go East, Young Man*. Stanley Reed's elevation to the High Court is also discussed in *Go East*.

The story of Felix Frankfurter's nomination to the Court is based on Bruce Allen Murphy's *The Brandeis/Frankfurter Connection*, Tyler Abell's *The Drew Pearson Diaries*, Joseph Lash's *Diaries of Frankfurter*, Leonard Baker's *Brandeis and Frankfurter*, and Michael Parrish's *Felix Frankfurter and His Times*. William O. Douglas's nomination to the Court is recalled in his autobiography, *Go East*, as well as in Jordan Schwarz's *The New Dealers* and by Ed Prichard in Katie Louchheim's *The Making of the New Deal*. The story of Corcoran's role in the 1938 purge is based on Niznik's dissertation, Schwarz's *The New Dealers*, Culver and Hyde's biography of Henry Wallace, *American Dreamer*, Koenig's *The Invisible Presidency*, as well an article that appeared in the *New York Times* on September 15, 1938, "Corcoran Deaf and Dumb When Queried on Tydings."

Jim Farley wrote about his anger and dislike for Corcoran over the purge in *Jim Farley's Story*. The story about Lyndon Johnson is from Merle Miller's *Lyndon*. The discussion of Corcoran's restlessness in the Roosevelt administration is from Corcoran's unpublished memoir, Lash's

Dealers and Dreamers, as well as an interview with Lash that I came across at the Roosevelt Library. The information on the Catholic Church, Cardinal Mundelein, and Father Coughlin is from Robert Dallek's *Franklin Roosevelt and American Foreign Policy,* Pearson and Anderson's *The Case Against Congress,* Alan Brinkley's *Voices of Protest,* Burton Wheeler's autobiography, *Yankee from the West,* Harold Ickes's *Diary,* and Niznik's dissertation, as well as articles in the *New York Times.*

12. Time to Make a Million

The mounting disaffection with Corcoran at the White House and among the press is based on several secondary sources, including Louis Koenig's *Invisible Presidency,* Patrick Anderson's *The President's Men,* Jordan Schwarz's *The New Dealers,* Joseph Lash's *Dealers and Dreamers,* and Hardeman and Bacon's *Rayburn.* Likewise, the section of Harry Hopkins is derived from several sources: His background is gleaned from Henry Adams's biography, *Harry Hopkins.* The stories of Hopkins's visits to Corcoran's office are contained in T. H. Watkins's biography of Harold Ickes, *Righteous Pilgrim,* as well as in Corcoran's unpublished memoir. Hopkins's son was unaware of the story of his father's alleged affair with a woman in New York, but did confirm that his father had a brief flirtation with the idea of running for president. Other sources consulted on Hopkins included Rudy Abramson's *Spanning the Century,* Nathan Miller's *F.D.R.,* and Beatrice Berle's *Navigating the Rapids.*

The section on members of the administration whom Corcoran had antagonized is based on the first volume of David Lilienthal's *Journals;* Jim Farley's autobiography, *Jim Farley's Story;* Ed Flynn's autobiography, *You're the Boss;* Koenig's *Invisible Presidency;* and Watkins's *Righteous Pilgrim.* The description of Corcoran's dwindling support in the White House is from the recollection of James Rowe contained in Louchheim's *The Making of the New Deal,* Kessler's *Sins of the Father,* Littell's *My Roosevelt Years,* Koenig's *Invisible Presidency,* Baker's *Brandeis and Frankfurter,* Grace Tully's autobiograpy, *My Boss,* and Lash's *Dealers and Dreamers,* as well as Corcoran's unpublished memoir, particularly chapter ten. The letter that Corcoran wrote to his brother David about the cricitism directed at him is taken from Niznik's April 1983 dissertation. Other sources I consulted included William O. Douglas's *Go East, Young Man,* Berle's *Navigating the Rapids,*

Hardeman and Bacon's *Rayburn,* and Graham and Wander's marvelous survey of the Roosevelt years, *Franklin D. Roosevelt: His Life and Times.*

The quote from William Shannon is found on page 331 of his book, *The American Irish.* The section on Corcoran's role as a political liaison with the Catholic Church is based on Alan Brinkley's *Voices of Protest,* John Cooney's *The American Pope,* Lilienthal's *Journals,* Volume 1, and Niznik's dissertation. Corcoran's final ostracism from the inner circle of the White House is gleaned from Douglas's *Go East* and Lash's *Dealers and Dreamers.* Corcoran's role in organizing independent voters for Roosevelt is taken from articles in the *New York Times* during the fall of 1940, as well as Watkins's *Righteous Pilgrim* and Joseph Goulden's *The Superlawyers.* Corcoran's marriage to his secretary, Peggy Dowd, is based largely on chapter ten of his unpublished memoir, although the quote from Tommy's mother about Peggy is taken from Lash's *Dealers and Dreamers.* I also consulted newspaper accounts of the time.

13. A New Stage

The opening scene describing Tommy's late-night telephone call from his brother is described in his unpublished memoir. The infomation on David Corcoran is derived from a thirty-page tribute to him titled "DMC — The Sterling Years," published by Sterling Pharmaceutical at his retirement; it was given to me by John Kelly. The history of Sterling is found in Mann and Plummer's *The Aspirin Wars.*

President Roosevelt's views on foreign policy during this period are found in Robert Dallek's *Franklin Roosevelt and American Foreign Policy.* The letter from Frankfurter to Roosevelt expressing concern about Corcoran is from Max Freedman's *Roosevelt and Frankfurter.* The birth of Corcoran's first child was noted in a very short article in the *New York Times,* "Inaugural Baby Is Born," on January 20, 1941. The letter from President Roosevelt to Corcoran is found in the Corcoran Papers at the Roosevelt Library and is reprinted in Lash's *Dealers and Dreamers.* Corcoran's story about Roosevelt at Hyde Park is recalled in his unpublished memoir.

David Lilienthal's harsh appraisal of Corcoran is found in Volume 1 of his *Journals.* The description of the role Corcoran played in starting Civil Air Transport is contained in the Pacific War chapter of his unpublished memoir. The information on the situation in China and Corcoran's introduction to General Claire Chennault is from Dallek, *Roosevelt and Foreign Policy,* William Leary's *Perilous Missions,* Anna Chennault's memoir, *The Education of Anna,* and Corcoran's unpublished memoir.

14. Peddling Influence

Corcoran's nascent law practice is described by him in his unpublished memoir. His decision not to list himself in the telephone directory is noted by John H. Criden in an article in an article in the *New York Times* on December 12, 1944. The description of wartime Washington can be found in David Brinkley's *Washington Goes to War.* Corcoran's representation of Henry Kaiser is described by Joseph Goulden in *The Superlawyers;* I also used information about Kaiser that I found in Jesse Jones's autobiography, *Fifty Billion Dollars,* and John Morton Blum's *V Was for Victory.*

The information on Corcoran's other domestic clients and the attendant publicity is from newspaper articles in the *World Telegram,* the *New York Times,* and Scripps Howard. The information used to describe Corcoran's involvement with international interests, the Flying Tigers, and Sterling Pharmaceutical is contained in Robert Dallek's *Franklin Roosevelt and American Foreign Policy,* Lash's *Dealers and Dreamers,* Mann and Plummer's *Aspirin Wars,* and an article in the liberal journal *PM.*

The section on Corcoran's attempt to become solicitor general is based on many sources, including Corcoran's unpublished memoir, the recollections of Joe Rauh and Ed Prichard found in Katie Louchheim's *The Making of the New Deal,* Bruce Allen Murphy's *Brandeis/Frankurter Connection,* Leonard Baker's *Brandeis and Frankfurter,* and Louis Koenig's *The Invisible Presidency.* The letter from Jim Rowe to President Roosevelt is dated December 5, 1941, and is found in the Rowe Papers at the Roosevelt Library. The information on the consideration of Ben Cohen as solicitor general is found in Lash's *Dealers and Dreamers* and Schwarz's *The New Dealers.* The letter from Wendell Wilkie to President Roosevelt in support of Ben Cohen is dated November 14, 1941, and is found in the Cohen Papers in the Roosevelt Library. The poignant scene of Ben Cohen's departure for England is found in Koenig's *Invisible Presidency,* and in Murphy's *Brandeis/Frankfurter Connection.*

The information on Sterling Pharmaceutical is derived from Mann and Plummer's *Aspirin Wars,* and commentary on Corcoran by Thomas Stokes in the *World Telegram.* The section on Lyndon Johnson's unsuccessful run for the Senate and his subsequent purchase of a radio station is based on several biographies of Johnson, included Robert Caro's *Path to Power* and *Means of Ascent,* Merle Miller's *Lyndon,* and Ronnie Dugger's *The Politician.* Lash's *From the Diaries of Felix Frankfurter* was also consulted, and an article in *The American,* "Senator O'Daniel's New Deal Thorn," was helpful.

15. Under Investigation

Corcoran described in his unpublished memoir his conversation with T. V. Soong on December 7, 1941. On that same day, the *New York Times* reported that he would testify the following week before Senator Truman's defense investigation committee. Information on the Truman hearings is found in David McCullough's masterful biography, *Truman.* Corcoran is mentioned in several articles in the *New York Times* and the *World Telegram* between August and December 1941, in connection with his lobbying efforts on behalf of Todd Shipyard. Corcoran's appearance before the committee on December 16, 1941, is recounted in several sources, including Jules Abels's *The Truman Scandals,* Alva Johnson's 1945 profile in the *Saturday Evening Post,* and contemporaneous accounts in the *New York Times* and the *Washington Post.* President Roosevelt's concern about Corcoran's lobbying is found in Lasser's *Ben Cohen.*

The midchapter summary of Corcoran's international business dealings is derived from Mann and Plummer's *Aspirin Wars,* Ross Y. Koen's *The China Lobby,* and information from the Corcoran Papers in the Library of Congress. The events surrounding Corcoran's handling of the Savannah Shipyard case are based entirely on Norman Littell's *My Roosevelt Years,* which provides a diary of events with accompanying commentary. My description of Littell's subsequent dismissal from the Department of Justice and his attempt to discredit Attorney General Biddle, Jim Rowe, and, especially, Tommy Corcoran is based on several newspaper accounts in November and December 1944, found in a variety of newspapers, including the *New York Times,* the *Washington Post,* the *New York World Telegram,* and *PM.* Other sources consulted in this chapter include Merle Miller's *Lyndon* and Jordan Schwarz's *New Dealers.*

16. The Wiretap

The opening discussion of the 1944 election and Corcoran's desire to replace Vice President Henry Wallace with Justice William O. Douglas is based on several secondary sources, including Bruce Allen Murphy's *The Brandeis/Frankfurter Connection*, Izzie Stone's *The War Years*, Bruce Allen Murphy's *Wild Bill*, Leonard Baker's *Brandeis and Frankfurter*, and David Koskoff's *Kennedy*. John Lane confirmed the outlines of the story in an interview, and Michael Janeway provided supporting material from an unpublished manuscript.

The death of Roosevelt and Corcoran's views on the nascent Truman administration are found in his unpublished memoir. The background on FBI wiretapping and the decision to wiretap Corcoran is found in Theoharis and Cox, *The Boss*. Description of material gleaned from the wiretap is based on that volume as well as on Theoharis's *From the Secret Files of J. Edgar Hoover*. The description of the events known as the Amerasia case is based on the book by Klehr and Radosh, *Amerasia*, on *The Boss*, and on FBI transcripts. The final section of the chapter dealing with the kind of gossip picked up by he wiretap, Corcoran's knowledge of the wiretap, and Truman's decision to discontinue the wiretap is based on an article in the *Sacramento Bee* by Alexander Charns, Corcoran's unpublished memoir, and two books: Victor Lasky, *It Didn't Start with Watergate*, and Theoharis and Cox, *The Boss*.

17. The Key to Lobbying

The description of Alva Johnson's profile of Corcoran and the WMCA case is based on FBI transcripts of the Corcoran wiretap as well as Johnson's story, which appeared in the *Saturday Evening Post* in October 1945. The information on Elliott Roosevelt's interest in WMCA is from Ted Morgan's biography of Roosevelt. Corcoran's role as a lobbyist and as a fixer is based on the FBI transcripts, a marvelous article by Alan Lichtman that appeared in the *Washington Monthly*, and numerous books, including Bruce Allen Murphy's biography of Abe Fortas and Virginia Hamilton's biography of Lister Hill. The section on the Merchandise Mart draws from Ronald Kessler's biography of Joseph Kennedy, *Sins of the Father*, as well as interviews with John Lane and James Rowe Jr. The discussion of the wiretap on Corcoran and particularly his conversations concerning a replacement for Chief Justice Harlan Stone is based entirely on FBI transcripts located at the FBI, as well as those reprinted in Theoharis and Cox, *The Boss*.

18. The Truman Years

Corcoran's disdain for President Truman was described by Virginia Hamilton in her biography of Senator Lister Hill, *Hill*. It is also clear in several places in the FBI wiretap transcripts located at the FBI. Likewise, Truman's contempt for Corcoran was recorded by Drew Pearson in his *Diaries*. Clark Clifford's background and use of Jim Rowe's memorandum in the 1949 election has been taken verbatim from my biography of Clifford, *Friends in High Places*, coauthored by Douglas Frantz.

Lyndon Johnson's run for the Senate in 1948 and the legal battle that followed his election is based entirely on pages 310–45 in Robert Dallek's biography, *Lone Star Rising*. Information on Ed Prichard draws on Tracy Campbell's biography, *Short of the Glory*. The section on Duncan Lee and Elizabeth Bentley contains material from an interview with David Acheson, from the Corcoran Papers, and from two books: Theoharis and Cox, *The Boss*, and Weinstein and Vassiliev, *Haunted Wood*. Donald Ritchie's biography of Landis, *James M. Landis*, has been instrumental in my discussion of the man. The story of Justice Douglas's affair and Corcoran's representation of his wife is from Bruce Allen Murphy's recent biography, *Wild Bill*. Finally, the closing paragraph dealing with lobbying during that era is from Jeffery Birnbaum's *The Lobbyists*.

19. Foreign Policy by Other Means

My accounts of Corcoran's role in the creation of Civil Air Transport and the airline's connection to the Central Intelligence Agency are based entirely on William Leary's *Perilous Missions*. Material in Corcoran's unpublished memoir, though incomplete in this area, corroborates parts of Leary's account. The description of Corcoran's early involvement with Samuel Zemurray and the United Fruit Company is based largely on Thomas McCann's *An American Company*, and is supplemented by information from Cullather's *Operation PBSuccess*, an account of CIA involvement in the 1954 Guatemalan coup I obtained from the Central

Intelligence Agency under the Freedom of Information Act, and by Stephen Kinzer's and Stephen Schlesinger's authoritative account of the coup, *Bitter Fruit.*

20. Corcoran's Cold War

The information at the beginning of the chapter on events in China in 1949, and the reaction in the United States, is from *Across the Pacific* by Akira Iriye. The sections that follow describing how Civil Air Transport operated in China, why the CIA eventually decided to acquire the airline, and Civil Air's subsidiaries that were retained by Chennault and Corcoran are based on Leary's *Perilous Missions.* The contoversy and ensuing legal battle between Corcoran, Chennault, and the government of Hong Kong is detailed in a series of articles in the *New York Times* between February and May 1950.

The information on Joseph McCarthy was obtained from Richard Rovere's *Senator Joe McCarthy* as well as from Corcoran's unpublished memoir. The events leading up to the coup in Guatemala, and the coup itself, are based on Schlesinger and Kinzer's *Bitter Fruit,* Cullather's *Operation PBSuccess,* and McCann's *An American Company.* The disclosure in the press of Corcoran's representation of United Fruit is from a short article in the *New York Journal* of June 1954.

21. Family and Friends

My discussion of Tommy Corcoran's home life is based on interviews with Tim Corcoran, Esther Corcoran, Bob Perry, and John Lane. The information on the Corcorans' social life is from the diary of Claude Pepper located in the Claude Pepper Library, and from the diaries of Justice and Mrs. Hugo Black. Tim Corcoran told me in an interview of the stress he believed his mother, Peggy Corcoran, was under. I have founded my treatment of Kennedy's use of Corcoran as an intermediary between Rayburn and Johnson on Jeff Sheshol's *Mutual Contempt,* although the story is told in many places, including Corcoran's unpublished memoirs.

Drew Pearson's recollections are from his diaries. The section on Johnson's perception of Corcoran at that time, as well as his successful effort to bring Corcoran's partner Jim Rowe onto his Senate staff, is recalled by Rowland Evans Jr. and Robert Novak in their acclaimed biography of Lyndon Johnson, *The Exercise of Power.* Harry McPherson also contributed useful recollections to this section.

22. The Late 1950s

The story of the events surrounding Peggy Corcoran's death was told to me by Tim Corcoran and Robert Perry. In his unpublished memoir Corcoran wrote that Felix Frankfurter sent flowers in remembrance, while Margaret Dowd told me the story of the death mask. The descriptions of Tommy's efforts as a single father were gleaned from letters contained in the family files in the Corcoran Papers, as well as from interviews with Tim Corcoran, Jim Nathanson, Robert Perry, and John Lane. Margaret Corcoran's "debut" to Washington society is based on an article from the *Washington Star* of January 1959, as well as an interview with Tim Corcoran.

Tommy Corcoran wrote about the death of General Chennault in his memoirs. The ensuing description of Chennault's widow, Anna, is based on a profile in the *Washington Star* written by Sandra McIlwaine, as well as a footnote from Bill Bundy's *Tangled Web* and two interviews with Mrs. Chennault. The information on Henry Grunewald is based on a lengthy, humorous description written by Corcoran in his unpublished memoir. Additionally, there were numerous articles about Grunewald around the time of his indictment and, later, his death. He is also captured on several occasions on the FBI wiretap. Irwin Gellman's book *The Contender,* on the early years of Richard Nixon, tells how Grunewald laundered money for the Nixon campaign.

23. Using the Back Door

The information on the status Corcoran had achieved as a lobbyist by the late 1950s and early 1960s is taken from Joesph Goulden's *The Superlawyers* and Susan and Salvatore Trento's *The Power House.* The comparsion to Clark Clifford is from my book on Clark Clifford, coauthored by Douglas Frantz, *Friends in High Places,* as well as from Clifford's autobiography, *Counsel to the President.* Mason Drukman's biography of Wayne Morse provided some background on the extent to which there was abuse in the lobbying profession during this era. The settlement of the lawsuit between Corcoran, Chennault, and the government of Taiwan is based on information contained in Leary's *Perilous Missions,* as well as newspaper accounts, Corcoran's unpublished memoir, and an interview with Tim Corcoran during which he showed me a blown-up photograph of Corcoran, Chennault, and Donovan aboard the SS *Esperance.*

The information on the FPC investigation is based largely on a series of *New York Times* articles, many by Anthony Lewis, between March and December 1960. Additionally, John Lane provided critical information, such as his advice to Corcoran not to turn over any documents and his ability to influence the outcome of a congressional report. The editorial on the FPC case was taken from the *New York Herald Tribune.*

24. LBJ for the USA

The background on the 1960 election contained in the beginning of this chapter is based on articles in the *New York Times* during the spring of that year; specific references to Corcoran's assistance to Lyndon Johnson are from Theodore White's *The Making of the President 1960.* The events surrounding the nomination of Senator John F. Kennedy and his selection of Senator Johnson as his running mate are taken from many sources, including a lengthy *New York Times* article published by Arthur Krock in 1965, Corcoran's unpublished memoir, Sheshol's *Mutual Contempt,* McKean and Frantz's *Friends in High Places,* and Arthur Schlesinger's *A Thousand Days.*

The information on how Corcoran's friends fared in landing prominent positions in the Kennedy administration is based on an interview with Jim Rowe Jr. as well as Corcoran's unpublished memoir, Donald Ritchie's biography of James Landis, and Joseph Goulden's *The Superlawyers.* Corcoran's letters to Johnson, one on inauguration eve and the other several months later, were given to me by John Zentay and are contained in the Corcoran Papers in the Library of Congress. Corcoran's observation that Johnson was shut out from power during the Kennedy administration is contained in *Lyndon* by Merle Miller, as is the comment by Wilbur Mills.

The description of Corcoran's affair with Digna Gomez is based on two telephone interviews in August 2003 with Corcoran's daughter by Gomez,

Alice Howard. The material on the Baker scandal is based on interviews with Bobby Baker and with John Lane. The telephone conversation between Corcoran and Johnson at the 1964 convention was described to me by Robert Bennett. The background on the Jenkins affair is contained in McKean and Frantz, *Friends in High Places,* and Corcoran's conversations with Johnson about the scandal are from White House tapes, transcribed and contained in Michael Beschloss's *Reaching for Glory.*

Corcoran's letter to Jenkins is from the Corcoran Papers, as are his letters to Johnson in November 1964 and September 1966. The description of Corcoran's relations with the Johnson White House is based on interviews with John Lane and Tim Corcoran, Goulden's *The Superlawyers,* Lady Bird Johnson's *White House Diary,* Laura Kalman's *Abe Fortas,* and newspaper accounts from the era.

25. Lobbying the Court

The material in this chapter is based largely on Bob Woodward's and Scott Armstrong's book on the Supreme Court, *The Brethren. Mr. Justice and Mrs. Black: The Memoirs of Hugo L. Black and Elizabeth Black,* published seven years after *The Brethren,* provides useful corroborative information. Additionally, I relied on interviews with Tim Corcoran, Tommy Boggs, and John Lane. The comparison between Corcoran and Clifford derives from my biography of Clark Clifford, coauthored by Douglas Frantz, and the information on John Sonnett was gleaned from newspaper accounts.

26. Plenty of Action

The opening antedote on Corcoran's help for a tool-and-die company is from Joseph Goulden's *The Superlawyers.* The description of the Corcoran law firm is based on numerous interviews with associates and partners in the firm, including John Kelly, Ben Ivins, Robert Perry, and Jim Nathanson. John Lane, who was not a member of the firm, nevertheless knew it well and described it for me. In addition, Jon Cuneo and Jim Rowe Jr., the children of two of Corcoran's partners, provided useful information. Joseph Goulden's *Superlawyers* and Thomas Powers's *The Man Who Kept the Secrets* were also helpful sources.

The information on Corcoran's representation of aviation interests and connection to the U.S. intelligence establishment came from the Corcoran Papers in the Library of Congress and from documents obtained from the Central Intelligence Agency under the Freedom of Information Act. The information on Corcoran's representation of pharmaceutical interests and his relationship with Everett Dirksen is largely based on William MacNeil's biography of Dirksen, *Dirksen*. Bob Bennett told me the wonderful story of how Dirksen tried to disguise his voice when he telephoned Corcoran's law firm. Newspaper accounts from the era gave some flavor of the controversies that embroiled Corcoran.

27. Vietnam, Watergate, and Nixon

Corcoran's views on the Vietnam War are based on interviews with John Kelly, Tim Corcoran, and John Lane. The section on American involvement in Vietnam in 1968 is based on Lyndon Johnson's autobiography, *Vantage Point*, as well as William Bundy's *Tangled Web* and Anthony Summers's *Arrogance of Power*. The latter two works, in conjuction with Anna Chennault's memoir, *The Education of Anna*, formed the basis for the description of Chennault's interaction with the Nixon campaign during the 1968 presidential election. The section on Margaret Corcoran is based on interviews with contemporaries of hers at Harvard Law School, as well as her brother Tim and friends of her father's. Margaret's clerkship with Justice Hugo Black is recalled by Mrs. Black in *Mr. Justice and Mrs. Black*.

The description of Tommy's birthday party is based on interviews with Robert Perry, John Lane, and Tim Corcoran — all of whom attended the party — as well as selective descriptions in Joseph Goulden's *The Superlawyers* and Joseph Lash's *Dealers and Dreamers*. Tommy's attempt to adopt Maureen Dowd was related to me by Dowd, who, while I was interviewing her, telephoned her mother, Peggy; Peggy Dowd also recalled the scene at the Dowd house after the funeral of Michael Dowd. Finally, Corcoran's relationship with John Connally and the narrative of the Connally trial in 1975 are based on documents contained in the Corcoran Papers as well as well as James Reston's exhaustive biography, *Lone Star*.

28. The Admiral

The history of frigate construction at Newport News, as well as the characterizations of the intereaction among Corcoran, Zumwalt, and Rickover, are based entirely on Polmar and Allen's biography of Admiral Rickover, *Rickover*. The letter from Tommy Corcoran to his son Tim, then a student at Phillips Exeter Academy, is contained in the Corcoran family papers. The section detailing the ethics probe of Corcoran, and his eventual exoneration, is based on interviews with Tommy Boggs, Robert Bennett, and John Kelly, as well as newspaper accounts — notably Morton Mintz's "Corcoran to Face Ethics Probe," in the *Washington Post*, December 1979.

Conclusion: A Fire in His Heart

The description of Ben Cohen is from an interview on a street corner with Jonathan Cuneo. The section on Corcoran's later-life romances is based on interviews with Tommy Boggs; his mother, Ambassador Lindy Boggs; Tim Corcoran; Carlisle Bolton-Smith; Anna Chennault; and Sandra McIlwaine. Information on Corcoran's role as a senior statesman, including his relations with the Carter White House, is drawn from interviews with Arthur Schlesinger Jr. and Robert Strauss as well as newspaper accounts from the time. Bruno Ristau, a former State Department official, provided me with personal reminiscences, original documents, and newspaper clippings detailing events surrounding recognition of the People's Republic of China and the sale of the Tawianese embassy in December 1979.

I also consulted Lasky's *Jimmy Carter: The Man and the Myth*, and David Acheson, whom I interviewed in 2000, proved helpful as well. The description of how Corcoran helped young people, colleagues, and friends is based on several people who attested to his generosity, including Jon Cuneo, Ben Ivins, Tim Corcoran, Sandra McIlwaine, and John Lane. Corcorans's sudden illness and death was recalled by his son, Tim Corcoran. The funeral service was pieced together by reading letters from the Roosevelt Library that Jim Rowe wrote to friends in the weeks after Corcoran's death. I also referred to the obituary in the *Washington Post* written by Ken Crawford. The eulogies of Rowe and Chennault are contained in the Corcoran files at the Roosevelt Library. The information on

Corcoran's wealth and estate is based on an interview with Tim Corcoran. The references to modern-day lobbying in the Bush and Clinton administrations are from newspaper articles, including Charles Babington's "White House May Rethink Lobbying Ban," which appeared in the *Washington Post* on June 25, 2000. The appraisal of Corcoran's loyalty and integrity is based on interviews with Bobby Baker, John Lane, and John Kelly. On June 11, 2000, David Ignatius worote an opinion piece in the *Washington Post* entitled "So Long, Superlawyers," that mentioned Corcoran and provided an excellent analysis of how the legal profession has changed in Washington. The final quote from Corcoran is taken from Lash's *Dealers and Dreamers*.

REFERENCES

Abell, Tyler, editor. *Drew Pearson Diaries, 1949–1959*. Holt, Rinehart and Winston, 1974.

Abels, Jules, and Harry S. Truman. *The Truman Scandals*. Regnery, 1956.

Abramson, Rudy. *Spanning the Century: The Life of W. Averell Harriman, 1891–1986*. William Morrow, 1992.

Adams, Henry H. *Harry Hopkins*. Putnam, 1977.

Alsop, Joseph, and Robert Kintner. *Men Around the President*. Doubleday, Doran, 1939.

Alsop, Joseph W., with Adam Platt. *I've Seen the Best of It: Memoirs*. W. W. Norton, 1992.

Anderson, Patrick. *The President's Men*. Doubleday, 1968.

Baker, Bobby, with Larry L. King. *Wheeling and Dealing*. W. W. Norton, 1978.

Baker, Leonard. *Brandeis and Frankfurter: A Dual Biography*. New York University Press, 1986.

Baker, Liva. *The Justice from Beacon Hill*. HarperCollins, 1941.

Berle, Beatrice Bishop, and Travis Beal Jacobs. *Navigating the Rapids, 1918–1971: From the Papers of Adolf A. Berle*. Harcourt, Brace, Jovanovich, 1973.

Beschloss, Michael R., editor. *Reaching for Glory: Lyndon Johnson's Secret White House Tapes, 1964–1965*. Simon and Schuster, 2001.

Birnbaum, Jeffrey H. *The Lobbyists*. Times Books, 1992.

Bishop, Jim. *FDR's Last Year: April 1944–April 1945*. William Morrow, 1974.

Black, Elizabeth, and Hugo Lafayette Black. *Mr. Justice and Mrs. Black: The Memoirs of Hugo L. Black and Elizabeth Black*. Random House, 1986.

Blum, John Morton. *V Was for Victory: Politics and American Culture During World War II*. Harcourt, 1977.

Blum, John Morton, editor. *The Price of Vision: The Diary of Henry A. Wallace, 1942–1946*. Hougton Mifflin, 1973.

Brandeis, Louis B. *Other People's Money and How the Banks Use It*. Frederick A. Stokes Co., 1914.

Brinkley, Alan. *The End of Reform: New Deal Liberalism in Recession and War*. Alfred A. Knopf, 1995.

———. *Voices of Protest: Huey Long, Father Coughlin and the Great Depression*. Alfred A. Knopf, 1982.

Brinkley, David. *Washington Goes to War*. Alfred A. Knopf, 1988.

Bundy, William. *A Tangled Web: The Making of Foreign Policy in the Nixon Presidency*. Hill and Wang, 1998.

Campbell, Tracy. *Short of the Glory: The Fall and Redemption of Edward F. Prichard, Jr.* University of Kentucky Press, 1998.

Caro, Robert A. *The Years of Lyndon Johnson*. Volume I, *Means of Ascent*. Alfred A, Knopf, 1980.

——. *The Years of Lyndon Johnson.* Volume II, *The Path to Power.* Alfred A. Knopf, 1982.

——. *The Years of Lyndon Johnson.* Volume III, *Master of the Senate.* Alfred A. Knopf, 2002.

Charns, Alexander. *Cloak and Gavel.* University of Illinois Press, 1992.

Chennault, Anna. *The Education of Anna.* Times Books, 1979.

Chernow, Ron. *The House of Morgan.* Atlantic Monthly Press, 1990.

Clifford, Clark M., and Richard Holbrooke. *Counsel to the President.* Random House, 1991.

Congressional Quarterly. *Congress A to Z: A Ready Reference Encyclopedia,* 2nd edition. Congressional Quarterly Books, 1993.

Cooney, John. *The American Pope.* Times Books, 1984.

Cullather, Nicholas. *Operation PBSuccess: The United States and Guatemala, 1952–54.* Center for the Study of Intelligence, 1994.

Culver, John C., and John Hyde. *American Dreamer: The Life and Times of Henry A. Wallace.* W. W. Norton, 2000.

Dallek, Robert. *Franklin Roosevelt and American Foreign Policy, 1932–1945.* Oxford Univerity Press, 1979.

——. *Lone Star Rising: Lyndon Johnson and His Times.* Oxford University Press, 1991.

Daniels, Jonathan. *Washngton Quadrille.* Doubleday, 1968.

Davis, Kenneth S. *FDR: The New Deal Years, 1933–1937.* Random House, 1979.

Douglas, William O. *Go East Young Man.* Random House, 1974.

Drukman, Mason. *Wayne Morse: A Political Biography.* Oregon Historical Society, 1997.

Dugger, Ronnie. *The Politician: The Life and Times of Lyndon Johnson.* W. W. Norton, 1982.

Dunne, Gerald T. *Hugo Black and the Judicial Revolution.* Irvington, 1977.

Evans, Rowland, and Robert Novak. *Lyndon B. Johnson: The Exercise of Power.* New American Library, 1966.

Farley, James A. *Jim Farley's Story: The Roosevelt Years.* McGraw-Hill, 1948.

Flynn, Edward J. *You're the Boss.* Collier Books. 1962.

Frantz, Douglas, and David McKean. *Friends in High Places: The Rise and Fall of Clark Clifford.* Little, Brown, 1995.

Freedman, Max. *Roosevelt and Frankfurter: Their Correspondence 1928–1945.* Little, Brown, 1967.

Gellman, Irwin F. *The Contender: Richard Nixon, The Congress Years, 1946–1952.* The Free Press, 1999.

Goldman, Eric F. *Rendezvous with Destiny: A History of Modern American Reform.* Alfred A. Knopf, 1952.

Goodwin, Doris Kearns. *No Ordinary Time.* Simon and Shuster, 1994.

Goulden, Joseph C. *The Superlawyers.* Weybright and Talley, 1971.

Graham, Otis L. Jr., with Meghan Robinson Wander. *Franklin D. Roosevelt: His Life and Times: An Encyclopedic View.* G. K. Hall, 1985.

Gunther, John. *Roosevelt in Retrospect.* Harper and Brothers, 1950.

Halberstam, David. *The Fifties.* Villard Books, 1993.

Hamilton, Virginia Van der Veer. *Lister Hill: Statesman from the South*. University of North Carolina Press, 1987.

Hardeman, D. B., and Donald C. Bacon. *Rayburn*. Texas Monthly Press, 1987.

Hawley, Ellis W. *The New Deal and the Problem of Monopoly*. Princeton University Press, 1966.

Howard, J. Wofford. *Mr. Justice Murphy*. Princeton University Press, 1968.

Ickes, Harold L. *The Secret Diary of Harold L. Ickes: First Thousand Days, 1933–1936*. Simon and Schuster, 1953.

Iriye, Akira. *Across the Pacific*. Harcourt, 1967.

Irons, Peter H. *The New Deal Lawyers*. Princeton University Press, 1982.

Johnson, Lady Bird. *A White House Diary*. Holt, Rinehart and Winston, 1970.

Johnson, Lyndon Baines. *The Vantage Point: Perspectives of the Presidency, 1963–1969*. Henry Holt, 1971.

Johnson, Robert David. *Ernest Gruening and the American Dissenting Tradition*. Harvard University Press, 1998.

Jones, Jesse H., and Edward Angly. *Fifty Billion Dollars*. Macmillan, 1951.

Kalman, Laura. *Abe Fortas: A Biography*. Yale University Press, 1990.

Kessler, Ronald. *The Sins of the Father*. Warner Books, 1996.

Klehr, Harvey, and Ronald Radosh. *The Amerasia Spy Case: Prelude to McCarthyism*. University of North Carolina Press, 1996.

Koen, Ross Y. *The China Lobby in American Politics*. Octagon Books, 1974.

Koenig, Louis William. *The Invisible Presidency*. Holt, Rinehart and Winston, 1960.

Koskoff, David E. *Joseph P. Kennedy: A Life and Times*. Prentice Hall, 1974.

Krock, Arthur. *Memoirs: Intimate Recollections of Twelve American Presidents from Theodore Roosevelt to Richard Nixon*. Cassell, 1970.

——. *Memoirs: Sixty Years on the Firing Line*. Funk and Wagnalls, 1968.

Lash, Joseph P. *Dealers and Dreamers*. Doubleday, 1988.

——. *Eleanor and Franklin*. W. W. Norton, 1971.

——. *From the Diaries of Felix Frankfurter*. W. W. Norton, 1974.

Lasky, Victor. *It Didn't Start with Watergate*. E. P. Dutton, 1977.

——. *Jimmy Carter: The Man and the Myth*. Putnam, 1979.

Lasser, William. *Benjamin V. Cohen: Architect of the New Deal*. Yale University Press, 2002.

Leary, William M. *Perilous Missions: Civil Air Transport and CIA Covert Operations in Asia*. University of Alabama Press, 1984.

Leuchtenburg, William E. *In the Shadow of FDR*. Cornell University Press, 1983.

——. *Franklin D. Roosevelt and the New Deal*. Harper and Row, 1963.

Lilienthal, David E. *The Journals of David E. Lilienthal*. Volume I, *The TVA Years, 1939–45*. HarperCollins, 1967.

Littell, Norman M. *My Roosevelt Years*. University of Washington Press, 1987.

Louchheim, Katie, editor. *The Making of the New Deal: The Insiders Speak*. Harvard University Press, 1983.

MacNeil, Neil. *Dirksen: Portrait of a Public Man*. World Publishing, 1971.

Mann, Charles C., and Mark L. Plummer. *The Aspirin Wars: Money, Medicine and 100 Years of Rampant Competition*. Alfred A. Knopf, 1991.

Mann, Robert. *The Walls of Jericho: Lyndon Johnson, Hubert Humphrey, Richard Russell and the Struggle for Civil Rights.* Harcourt, Brace, 1996.

Markowitz, Norman D. *The Rise and Fall of the People's Century: Henry A. Wallace and American Liberalism, 1941–1948.* The Free Press, 1973.

McCann, Thomas. *An American Company: The Tragedy of United Fruit.* Crown Publishers, 1976.

McClellan, David S., and David C. Acheson. *Among Friends: Personal Letters of Dean Acheson.* Dodd, Mead, 1980.

McCullough, David. *Truman.* Simon and Schuster, 1992.

McPherson, Harry. *A Political Education.* Little, Brown, 1972.

Medved, Michael. *The Shadow Presidents.* Times Books, 1979.

Miller, Merle. *Lyndon: An Oral Biography.* G. P. Putnam's Sons, 1980.

Miller, Nathan. *F.D.R., An Intimate History.* Doubleday, 1983.

Moley, Raymond. *After Seven Years.* Harper and Brothers, 1939.

———. *27 Masters of Politics.* Funk and Wagnalls Company, 1949.

Morgan, Ted. *FDR: A Biography.* Simon and Schuster, 1985.

Murphy, Bruce Allen. *The Brandeis/Frankfurter Connection.* Oxford University Press, 1972.

———. *Fortas: The Rise and Ruin of a Supreme Court Justice.* William Morrow, 1978.

———. *Wild Bill: The Legend and Life of William O. Douglas.* Random House, 2003.

Neal, Steven. *Dark Horse: A Biography of Wendell Willkie.* University of Kansas Press, 1984.

Neuse, Steven M. *David E. Lilienthal: The Journey of an American Liberal.* University of Tennessee Press, 1996.

Newman, Roger K. *Hugo Black.* Pantheon Books, 1994.

Niznik, Monica Lynn. "Thomas G. Corcoran: The Public Service of Franklin Roosevelt's 'Tommy the Cork.'" Dissertation, Department of History, University of Notre Dame, April 1983.

Novick, Sheldon M. *Honorable Justice: The Life of Oliver Wendell Holmes.* Little, Brown, 1989.

Parrish, Michael. *Felix Frankfurter and His Times: The Reform Years.* The Free Press, 1982.

Pearson, Drew, and Jack Anderson *The Case Against Congress.* Simon and Schuster, 1968.

Pepper, Claude Denson, and Hays Gorey. *Pepper: Eyewitness to a Century.* Harcourt, 1987.

Polmar, Norman, and Thomas B. Allen. *Rickover: Controversy and Genius.* Simon and Schuster, 1982.

Powers, Thomas. *The Man Who Kept the Secrets: Richard Helms and the CIA.* Random House, 1979.

Reston, James Jr. *The Lone Star: The Life of John Connally.* Harper and Row, 1989.

Ritchie, Donald. A. *James M. Landis: Dean of the Regulators.* Harvard University Press, 1980.

Roosevelt, Elliott. *A Rendezvous with Destiny: The Roosevelts of the White House.* Putnam, 1975.

Roosevelt, Elliott, editor. *FDR, His Personal Letters, 1928–1945.* Duell, Sloan and Pearce, 1950.

Rosen, Elliot A. *Hoover, Roosevelt and the Brain Trust.* Columbia University Press, 1977.

Rovere, Richard H. *Senator Joe McCarthy.* 1959. Reprint, University of California Press, 1996.

Schlesinger, Arthur M. *A Thousand Days: John F. Kennedy in the White House.* Random House, 1988.

——. *The Age of Roosevelt.* Volume I, *The Crisis of the Old Order, 1919–1933.* Houghton Mifflin, 1957.

——. *The Age of Roosevelt.* Volume II, *The Coming of the New Deal, 1933–1935.* Houghton Mifflin, 1958.

——. *The Age of Roosevelt.* Volume III, *The Politics of Upheaval, 1935–1936.* Houghton Mifflin, 1960.

Schlesinger, Stephen, and Stephen Kinzer. *Bitter Fruit.* Doubleday, 1982.

Schwarz, Jordan A. *The New Dealers.* Alfred A. Knopf, 1993.

——. *Adolf A. Berle and the Vision of an American Era.* The Free Press, 1987.

Shannon, William V., and Edward M. Kennedy. *The American Irish: A Political and Social Portrait,* 2nd edition. University of Massachusetts Press, 1990.

Shesol, Jeff. *Mutual Contempt.* W. W. Norton, 1997.

Slayton, Robert A. *Empire Statesman: The Rise and Redemption of Al Smith.* The Free Press, 2001.

Steinberg, Alfred. *Sam Rayburn: A Biography.* Hawthorn Books, 1972.

Sternsher, Bernard. *Rexford Tugwell and the New Deal.* Rutgers University Press, 1964.

Stone, I. F. *The War Years, 1939–1945: A Nonconformist History of Our Times.* Little, Brown, 1990.

Summers, Anthony, and Robbyn Swan. *The Arrogance of Power: The Secret World of Richard Nixon.* Viking, 2000.

Swanberg, W. A. *Luce and His Empire.* Charles Scribner and Sons, 1972.

Theoharis, Athan G., and John Stuart Cox. *The Boss.* Temple University Press, 1988.

Theoharis, Athan G., editor. *From the Secret Files of J. Edgar Hoover.* Ivan R. Dee, 1991.

Trento, Susan B., and Salvatore M. Trento. *The Power House: Robert Keith Gray and the Selling of Access and Influence in Washington.* St. Martin's Press, 1992.

Tugwell, Rexford G. *In Search of Roosevelt.* Harvard University Press, 1972.

Tully, Grace. *FDR, My Boss.* Charles Scribner's Sons, 1949.

Watkins, T. H. *Righteous Pilgrim: The Life and Times of Harold L. Ickes, 1874–1952.* Henry Holt, 1990.

Weinstein, Allen, and Alexander Vassiliev. *The Haunted Wood: Soviet Espionage in America — The Stalin Era.* Diane Publishing, 1999,

Wheeler, Burton K., with Paul F. Healy. *Yankee from the West.* Doubleday, 1962.

White, Theodore. *The Making of the President, 1960.* Atheneum Publishing, 1961.

Winter-Berger, Robert N. *The Washington Pay-Off.* Lyle Stuart, 1972.

Woodward, Bob, and Scott Armstrong. *The Brethren: Inside the Supreme Court.* Simon and Schuster, 1979.

Wyden, Peter. *The Passionate War.* Simon and Schuster, 1983.

Interviews

David Acheson: November 18, 1999

Jack Anderson: November 16, 1999

Bobby Baker: March 25, 1999

Howard Baker: February 23, 2000

Robert Bennett: November 12, 1998

Jack Blum: February 22, 2000

Tommy Boggs: December 2, 1999

Lindy Boggs: August 3, 2003

Carlisle Bolton-Smith: July 9, 1999

William Bundy: November 29, 1998

Anna Chennault: January 5, 1999; November 27, 2000

Esther Corcoran: January 18, 2000

Thomas Corcoran Jr.: February 15, 1999; January 26, 2001; July 29, 2001; December 14, 2002

Jonathan Cuneo: May 23, 2000

Lloyd Cutler: April 10, 2000

Margaret Dowd: February 6, 2003

Maureen Dowd: February 6, 2003

Rowland Evans Jr.: January 12, 2000

Harry Gasset: April 26, 1980

David Ginsburg: June 15, 1998

Richard Helms: January 2000

Townsend Hoopes: January 1999

Harry Hopkins Jr.: March 17, 2000

Alice Howard: August 3, 2003; August 13, 2003

Ben Ivins: June 10, 1999

Michael Janeway: July 18, 1999

John Kelly: April 8, 1999

John Lane: November 24, 1998; March 12, 1999; July 6, 2000; July 28, 2000; October 21, 2000; October 23, 2000; May 9, 2001

Sandra McIlvaine: February 9, 2000

Harry McPherson: June 1998

Charles Moneypenny: February 10, 2002

Jim Nathanson: November 17, 1998

Robert Perry: June 1, 2000

Bruno Ristau: July 2002

Jim Rowe Jr.: October 2000; November 23, 1999

Arthur Schlesinger: August 2001

Hugh Sidey: July 9, 1999
Jake Stein: July 8, 1999
Robert Strauss: December 2001
John Sununu: December 22, 2003
Jack Vardaman: July 19, 1999
William Vanden Heuval: March 22, 1999
John Zentay: March 2001

INDEX

Numbers in italics refer to the photo section.